THE ROYAL NAVY AND FISHERY PROTECTION

For my granddaughter Sidney and in loving memory of my parents Bill and Dorine

'I said that in default of a special agreement, we had never admitted the right of any country to interfere with a British ship beyond the 3-mile limit. This was the standpoint we were taking with regard to Russia at the present time, and we could not contend for less with Norway. It was a principle on which we might be prepared to go to war with the strongest power in the world.'

Sir Edward Grey, Foreign Secretary, 26 June 1911, relating to the arrest of the trawler Lord Roberts.

The
ROYAL NAVY
and
FISHERY PROTECTION

From the Fourteenth Century to the Present

Jon Wise

First published in Great Britain in 2023 by
Seaforth Publishing
An imprint of Pen & Sword Books Limited
Yorkshire – Philadelphia

www.seaforthpublishing.com

Copyright © Jon Wise 2023

ISBN 978-1-39904-170-6 (Hardback)
ISBN 978-1-39904-172-0 (ePub)
ISBN 978-1-39904-173-7 (Kindle)

The right of Jon Wise to be identified as
Author of this Work has been asserted by him in accordance
with the Copyright, Designs and Patents Act 1988.

A CIP catalogue record for this book is
available from the British Library

All rights reserved. No part of this book may be reproduced or
transmitted in any form or by any means, electronic or mechanical
including photocopying, recording or by any information storage and
retrieval system, without permission from the Publisher in writing.

Typeset in 10.5/14pt Sabon by Mac Style
Printed in the UK by CPI Group (UK) Ltd, Croydon, CR0 4YY.

Pen & Sword Books Limited incorporates the imprints of After the
Battle, Atlas, Archaeology, Aviation, Discovery, Family History,
Fiction, History, Maritime, Military, Military Classics, Politics,
Select, Transport, True Crime, Air World, Frontline Publishing, Leo
Cooper, Remember When, Seaforth Publishing, The Praetorian Press,
Wharncliffe Local History, Wharncliffe Transport, Wharncliffe True
Crime and White Owl.

For a complete list of Pen & Sword titles please contact

PEN & SWORD BOOKS LIMITED
47 Church Street, Barnsley, South Yorkshire, S70 2AS, England
E-mail: enquiries@pen-and-sword.co.uk
Website: www.pen-and-sword.co.uk
or
PEN AND SWORD BOOKS
1950 Lawrence Rd, Havertown, PA 19083, USA
E-mail: Uspen-and-sword@casematepublishers.com
Website: www.penandswordbooks.com

Contents

Foreword		vii
List of Photographs, Maps and Diagrams		ix
Introduction		xii
Chapter One	A Nursery for Seamen 1379–1815	1
Chapter Two	Seeds of Dispute and Conflict Amidst Conventions & Accords 1815–1905	29
Chapter Three	'To Foster a Bond of Mutual Sympathy and Respect' 1905–58	54
Chapter Four	How the Protected Became Protectors 1914–45	75
Chapter Five	Gunfire off the Murman Coast 1917–30	99
Chapter Six	Norway's Red Line 1882–1951	125
Chapter Seven	In Home Waters 1815–2005	139
Chapter Eight	A Settlement and a Gathering Storm 1930–58	165
Chapter Nine	A War of Nerves – of Sorts 1958–70	189
Chapter Ten	The Last Gasp of *Mare Liberum* 1971–76	213
Chapter Eleven	The Offshore Tapestry 1976–99	248
Chapter Twelve	What's in a Name? 2000–22	273

Appendix One	Royal Navy Fishery Protection Ships 1896–2022: A Statistical Comparison	288
Appendix Two	The Icelandic Coastguard Vessel Fleet	290
Appendix Three	'Voices'	292

Acknowledgements	294
Glossary	296
Notes	298
Bibliography	329
Index	335

Foreword
Rear Admiral John Lippiett CB CBE DL

EARLY IN 1976, at the age of twenty-six, I took command of the 'Ton'-class minesweeper HMS *Shavington* serving in the Fishery Protection Squadron (FPS). Thus I entered an entirely new world of naval operations, equipped after a short course with a basic knowledge of the newly changed laws of our UK waters regarding licences and inshore fisheries limits. Now, nearly fifty years later, it is ironic to note our exit from the European Union has renewed fresh disputes about fishing licences. In that same timescale, regrettably, the size of the UK fishing fleet has shrunk spectacularly, with the Scottish fisheries representing some 70 per cent of the entire UK output. The Royal Navy has a role today, as it did fifty years ago, in policing our waters. Indeed, the official RN website currently points out that our Exclusive Economic Zone is the fifth-largest in the world, and that fishing rights have always been an emotive and politically sensitive issue, and in the wake of Brexit, fishery protection will be more important than ever.

Incidents at sea can create tensions between nationalities and can flare up into a major dispute, even sometimes with shots being fired, ships rammed and boarded, and hostages taken. The Royal Navy has been seen by UK fishermen as the guardian of 'their' waters – that is, until they are apprehended for infringements that put themselves on the wrong side of the law. However, at times when fishing vessels face a crisis on board such as a fire, flood, medical emergency, or whatever, their radio call for help might well be answered by an FPS vessel.

Importantly, the interactions between the FPS ships and the fishermen around our coastline have created a mutual understanding and respect for each other's professionalism, and recognition of the hardships each bear. Small ships, both warships and fishing vessels, are hard hit by foul weather as they continue their tasks in conditions in which most would run for shelter. This relationship has, over the centuries, further strengthened our national maritime capabilities and standing.

Dr Jon Wise names his first chapter 'A Nursery for Seamen 1379–1815', looking at the early history of fishery protection. From those earliest days the fishing fleets produced hardy seamen who, in times of war, might help man the warships required for fighting. More importantly, perhaps, for centuries fish provided the meal for three days of the week at sea in warships, so the fishing fleets were vital for victualling the Navy. That the fishing fleets were active in Tudor days right across the North Atlantic has recently been proven by the DNA of a codfish found in a barrel on board the *Mary Rose* (which sank in 1545), showing that it came from Newfoundland waters.

Jumping to the 1970s, the FPS still held a role as a nursery for seamen. I, for one, learned a huge amount during my eighteen months in command. We faced the challenges of operating in a small ship the year round, in gales, snowstorms (with an open bridge!) or thick fog, in tricky navigational waters, and in even trickier diplomatic incidents. Lessons were learnt and self-confidence built up. Yes, mistakes were made, but usually small ones. Ship handling in tiny ports could be interesting, to say the least, and leadership of a small ship's company in sometimes challenging situations was, to me, the most demanding, yet satisfying and interesting aspect of being in command. I count my time in the FPS to be a significant stepping stone in my career, and to be one of my most rewarding and enjoyable appointments.

The Royal Navy and Fishery Protection: from the Fourteenth Century to the Present gives the reader a fully comprehensive insight into the long history, spanning over 600 years, of the Navy protecting our fishermen and our waters, a story well worth recording. I have found Jon Wise's work to be a well-researched and very thorough study, telling us so much about the work of the Royal Navy in a rarely sung role.

List of Photographs, Maps and Diagrams

Photographs, between pages 142 and 143 and pages 270 and 271
1. HMS *Godetia*: *Arabis*-class 'fleet sweeping vessel' or sloop, photographed in 1924. (World Ship Society Photographic Library)
2. HMS *Doon*: *Mersey*-class trawler. (Abrahams, Devonport)
3. HMS *Hastings*: 1930s sloop used extensively in the fishery protection role. (Author's Collection)
4. HMS *Mariner*: despatched to the Murman coast during a tense post-Second World War stand-off with the Soviet Union. (World Ship Society Photographic Library)
5. HMS *Hound*: the last Second World War vintage FPS vessel in active service. (World Ship Society Photographic Library)
6. The Fishery Protection Squadron base at Port Edgar in 1960. HMS *Russell* and probably HMS *Wotton* can be seen. (UK MoD)
7. & 8. Checking nets aboard a French trawler on the Dogger Bank. (Courtesy of Adrian Wilkinson)
9. The Fishery Protection Squadron operations room at Port Edgar in the late 1960s. (MoD)
10. HMS *Wotton*: originally a member of the FPS 'Home Division', this 'Fish Ton' had been fitted with an enclosed bridge by the time the photo was taken in 1983. (Author's Collection)
11. HMS *Lincoln* with prominent wooden protection in the bow area, which was fitted too late to see action during the last Cod War. (UK MoD Crown Copyright, 1976)
12. HMS *Palliser*: the Type 14 played a central role in the *Milwood* incident in 1963. (Author's Collection)
13. HMS *Leopard*: the ageing Type 41 frigate was involved in the Second and Third Cod Wars and placed on the disposal list soon afterwards. (Author's Collection)

14. ICGV *Baldur* sheers away from HMS *Mermaid* after colliding on 6 May 1976. (UK MoD Crown Copyright, 1976)
15. ICGV *Óðinn* just prior to a collision with the *Leander*-class HMS *Galatea*. (UK MoD Crown Copyright, 1976)
16. The RN's first purpose-built offshore patrol/fishery protection vessel, HMS *Jersey*, in the Bruges Canal in 1988. (Courtesy of Mike Louagie, Ostend)
17. RFAs *Wave Ruler* and *Wave Baron* were criticised for their poor performance and design in a Report of Proceedings during the First Cod War. (UK MoD)
18. ICGV *Óðinn* cuts across the bows of the trawler *Arctic Corsair* on 1 May 1976. (UK MoD Crown Copyright, 1976)
19. 'Dutch herring busses on the fishing ground' by W V Velde. (National Maritime Museum PAH 1711)
20. HMS *Champion*: HM sloop on the North America & Newfoundland Station in the late 1820s. (National Maritime Museum)
21. 'Fleeting': the face of fishing's increasing industrialisation in the 1870s. (North East Lincolnshire Museums Service)
22. HMS *Hearty*: fishery protection vessel in the 1890s. (Author's Collection)
23. HMS *Halcyon*: torpedo gunboat and senior naval officer command North Sea Fisheries, in 1905. (Author's Collection)
24. HMS *Harebell*: *Anchusa*-class sloop, which undertook extensive service on the Murman coast in the 1920s. (Abrahams, Devonport)
25. S/T *Lucida*: HMS *Doon*'s adversary during the Skipper Jinks 'saga'. (Author's Collection)
26. The reactivated Batch 1 'River'-class HMS *Tyne* at Falmouth in January 2019. (Author's Collection)
27. The infamous trawl cutter gifted by the Icelanders to the Maritime Museum at Hull. (Courtesy of Maritime Museum: Hull Museums)
28. & 29. Neither the 'River'-class MSF HMS *Blackwater* nor the 'Bird'-class HMS *Kingfisher* proved adequate for fishery protection work. (Author's Collection)
30. The innovative 'Castle'-class OPV HMS *Leeds Castle* entering Portsmouth Harbour. (Courtesy of John Jordan)
31. A brand-new Batch 2 'River'-class HMS *Medway* photographed in 2019 with HM Naval Base, Portsmouth, in the background. (Courtesy of Stephen Dent)

Maps

Map 1:	Distant water fishing grounds. (Stephen Dent)	30
Map 2:	The British Isles, showing the principal fishing ports. (Stephen Dent)	55
Map 3:	North Norway and the Barents Sea. (Stephen Dent)	100
Map 4:	Iceland. (Stephen Dent)	190
Map 5:	Nova Scotia and Newfoundland, and the much-contested fishing grounds, are pictured in this late nineteenth-century print. (Author's Collection)	Plates

Diagrams

Figure 1:	HM *Mersey*-class Admiralty trawler, general arrangement, 1917. (John Lambert Collection)	77
Figure 2:	Types of trawler fishing. (Stephen Dent)	140

Introduction

ON 3 FEBRUARY 2020, Prime Minister Boris Johnson, having helped to secure the public vote to leave the European Union, stood in the Painted Hall at Greenwich beneath Sir James Thornhill's paintings of some of the nation's most glorious naval interludes and declared with unmistakeable symbolism, 'This is the newly forged United Kingdom on the slipway.'

Ironically, aside from the seemingly intractable problem of what became known as the Northern Ireland Protocol, the only other shackles that threatened to restrain the Brexit 'ship' from executing an untrammelled launch – was fishing. Fishing was an issue that, according to one writer, had become 'totemic among Brexiters', despite accounting for just 0.03 per cent of the total UK economic output and involving a workforce of 11,000 people.[1]

It remained a contentious issue in the aftermath of Britain leaving the EU. For example, in May 2021, a dispute over the issuing of fishing licences brought urgent calls for the Royal Navy to intervene as French boats threatened to block the entrance to the port of St Helier. The Royal Navy's Fishery Protection Squadron (FPS), which the Navy claims as its oldest front-line squadron, became directly involved.

Yet ironically, despite an ancient lineage, fishery protection is not part of the warp and weft of mainstream British naval folklore. Nor indeed does the subject merit more than a passing reference or footnote in some of the more authoritative and academic works on the subject. Nevertheless, the protection of the country's fisheries remained a vexed matter right to the end and beyond the signing of the exit agreement. Why was this the case?

Before answering that question one has to ask if the United Kingdom is still a maritime nation, one that cares about the sovereignty of the waters surrounding it, the fishers who work in its much-diminished industry, its seaborne trade routes and its Navy – the ultimate provider of protection along its extensive coastline. The answer is probably no. Unless, of course, the matter becomes newsworthy through any threat to daily life, for instance a disruption to the smooth passage of the 95 per cent of the country's trade that arrives or leaves by sea each year.

If the country can no longer be considered 'maritime-oriented', there is enough evidence to show a fondness for being by the sea and, by default, for sea-fishing. One can point to the popularity of both documentary and dramatised televised depictions of fishing communities and their work. Sadly, such is the aspirational draw of owning a second home in a picture-postcard fishing village that many of the indigenous population have been simply priced out of the market. By the same token though, there is lasting admiration for those who work in one of the riskiest and yet most unregulated of occupations.

It can be plausibly argued that the Brexiters capitalised on the UK's dispute with the EU over fishing because of what might called the natural insularity of British people. Jan Rüger, describing the increasing fervour in 1905 that led to the Anglo-German naval rivalry prior to the Great War, writes, 'The "island nation" was a powerful trope in Victorian and Edwardian Britain. Evoked in cultural as much as in political discourses, it served as an important *Leitmotiv* in British identity politics.'[2] Winston Churchill, of course, used a similar 'trope' in 1940 by helping to engender the 'Dunkirk spirit'. In reality, Johnson's 'Brexit launch' too played on the nostalgic assumption that, although this was a new beginning, our history told us we had been 'great' as an independent nation in the past. By contrast, Edward Heath's 'new greatness', when celebrating Britain's successful joining of the EU in 1971, meant just that – a true step into the unknown.[3]

One comes back to the question of how much is known about or matters to the populace that Britain, Northern Island Protocol apart, is an island nation, 'compass'd by the inviolate sea'.[4] Certainly, the country is no longer educated about the Navy. Big ships are often referred to in the media as 'battleships', while small ones are 'gunboats'. Navy Days at Portsmouth, Devonport and other naval bases have been quietly dropped from the annual calendar, while probably the last of the fifty-four Royal Fleet Reviews, dating back to 1346, was held in 2005. Significantly, at that event, a *Daily Telegraph* reporter remarked, '… spectators on the beaches and seafront (facing the Solent) enjoying the largest international review of its kind, admitted that they were embarrassed about their knowledge of the naval battles that shaped the modern world ... At times it seemed that the spectacle unfolding before them was a source of curiosity rather than national pride.'[5] No warship was present in the Thames near Tower Bridge or elsewhere to fire a valedictory salute at the passing of Queen Elizabeth II and there was no fleet review to mark the ascendancy to the throne and Coronation of King Charles III – in spite of all his personal and family associations with the Senior Service.

This then is the background to a book about what can be very loosely termed the 'fishery protection squadron', which first came into being well before the Royal Navy even existed, was only officially called a 'squadron' fairly recently and has since been subsumed within the obscurely named Royal Navy Overseas Patrol Squadron. Yet to marginalise the existence of this branch of the service is to ignore an aspect of the Royal Navy's history that exactly mirrors the nation's rising and declining naval fortunes and likewise its status as a world power. Moreover, the Royal Navy, on its website, reiterates its age-old remit to keep guard over home and international waters in order to protect citizens and allies alike and to ensure that trade can flow freely. Fishery protection forms part of this tasking. Fishery protection forms part of this tasking.

This book mostly follows a chronological pattern, although several chapters overlap in time. Chapters Three, Four and Seven deviate more extensively for reasons that will become obvious. Chapter One covers a long period, starting in 1379 and concluding with the end of the Anglo-French Wars in 1815. The earliest requests for fishery protection to be provided were born of necessity, '... the sea was widely perceived as a lawless realm beyond the frontiers of all nations, where neither law nor truce nor treaty ran'.[6] Thus, command of the sea surrounding the British Isles was very soon perceived as a prerequisite if the country was to prosper. 'Cheryshe marchandyse, kepe thamyralte/That we bee maysteres of the narowe see ...'.[7] The recognition of the importance of fish as an economic asset, the need for its safe conveyance and the significance of territorial waters all served to highlight the philosophical question of who, if anyone, 'owns' the seas. The eighteenth century introduced a further dimension. The fishermen themselves were increasingly recognised and cherished as providing a 'nursery of seamen' for the Royal Navy.

Britain enjoyed unrivalled economic hegemony for at least the sixty-year-period 1815–75 and, as Chapter Two relates, its all-powerful navy could rightly claim 'command of the sea'. There was still no organised system of fishery protection in the modern sense, although the Coastguard provided a form of monitoring and regulating service and responded to need when required. Later in the century, the introduction of steam power revolutionised fishing. The agreements emanating from the North Sea Fisheries Convention of 1882 was the most significant event with regard to international consensus on the increasingly contentious matter of the right to exploit what many regarded still as an endless bounty.

Chapter Three presents an overview of the Royal Navy's fishery protection responsibilities from the beginning of the twentieth century until the first of the three major disputes with Iceland in 1958. The function and very need for the Navy's participation was debated against a backdrop of international upheaval. Successive governments continued to respond to the need to support one of its key industries. In complete contrast, Chapter Four describes a reversal in role when the fishermen and particularly their trawlers and drifters played a key part in both world wars. The usefulness and durability of the fishing boats, together with the experience and hardiness of their crews, proved invaluable particularly in combating mines and enemy submarines.

International disputes over territorial delimitation in more distant waters, particularly with the Soviet Union and Norway, are related in Chapters Five and Six. Britain's position as the premier naval power was starting to be challenged at the same time as there was growing opposition to the historic adherence to the 3-mile territorial limit. British fishermen fiercely supported this delimitation, true to their doggedly, independent spirit.

Chapter Seven, 'In Home Waters', is intended to give a flavour of some of the squadron's activities in the UK's coastal waters covering the whole of the twentieth century. There are a variety of headings, including a historic overview of the provision for Scotland, which was slightly different from that pertaining to the rest of the United Kingdom. The settlement to the long-running dispute with the Soviet Union and the origins of the looming crisis of relations with Iceland are described in Chapter Eight, while the three so-called Cod Wars are related in Chapters Nine and Ten.

The Fishery Protection Squadron, as it was at last officially called, had a much altered and enlarged set of responsibilities after 1976 and these are the subject of the chapter entitled 'The Offshore Tapestry', which covers the last quarter of the twentieth century. Although coastal tasking remained largely unaltered, the squadron now also policed the 200-mile extended fisheries zone (EFZ), including a growing number of oil and gas fields, particularly in the North Sea. At last, the FPS was equipped with vessels that were designed and built for the purpose. The century ended with a fresh round of calls for protection duties to be privatised.

Chapter Twelve brings the story of fishery protection to the present day. The Royal Navy now works in partnership with the Marine Management Organisation (MMO) and has a contractual arrangement to provide a fixed number of days of fishery protection per year. Currently, just three vessels are tasked with these duties in addition to a range of other offshore patrol undertakings.

The statistics provided in the last chapter starkly demonstrate the decline in the fishing industry in the period since the Second World War. The UK has been a net importer of fish over the last four decades, while Scotland currently accounts for just under 70 per cent of the total UK output covering fishing, aquaculture (fish farming) and fish processing. An overall decline had been evident for many years though. In an article written in 1969, E.E.D. Day showed that, in the 1960s, although the British Sea Fishing Industry was at time the fourth largest in Western Europe after Norway, Spain and Denmark, production had fallen from 1,098,149 metric tons in 1938 to an average landing of 883,316 metric tons in the period 1962–66.[8]

Certainly fish is no longer an essential part of the British diet as it was in past times. Rough comparisons in price per kilo show that meat is now cheaper to buy than fish: a kilo of cod or hake costs about the same in a supermarket as beef steak, while other meat products such as mince or chicken are considerably cheaper. Recently, the cost of living crisis has resulted in fish and chip outlets fearing for their futures as in some areas of the country prices have risen to £12 per portion, making this traditional 'takeaway' meal simply unaffordable.

Therefore, fish is now something of a luxury food, mostly consigned to a filleted state in a plastic package on a supermarket shelf. Where it came from and how it arrived at the table are matters that have largely dropped from the public consciousness. Likewise, words such as dredgerman (who fished for oysters), condor or balker (whose job it was to look for shoals of fish from a high vantage point ashore), and kedger (an ordinary crew member), have dropped almost entirely from common knowledge and usage.[9]

Traditionally, fishing was a family business, sometimes involving more than one generation. The derogatory term 'fish wife', and its associations with coarseness and swearing, can be explained by the fact that their wares were highly perishable and so lost value if not sold quickly. This narrative deliberately uses the gender neutral word 'fisher' in the last chapter only because prior to the millennium sea fishing was almost entirely a male occupation.[10] Even in 2022, women made up only 23 per cent of Europe's entire aquaculture workforce.

This book limits its scope to describing fishery protection in the waters around the British Isles, the North Atlantic and the Arctic. It does not cover the whale fishing industry nor the administration of close inshore or riverine fishing. The Royal Navy employed a wide variety and number of ships for this role. These have only been purpose-built comparatively recently; in the past they were drawn from other duties, often for very short periods of time. Therefore, the listings are necessarily illustrative rather than comprehensive.

This is not a narrative filled with the exploits of inspired individuals or feats of outstanding bravery. However, a few persons have influenced the tide of events in quite different ways. A Dutchman, Hugo Grotius, influenced how the British regarded freedom of the seas for over three hundred years. Admiral Peter Warren, in the mid-eighteenth century, used striking strategic and political intelligence to grasp the importance of and link between sea power and fishery protection. Captain G.C. Dickens, in the 1920s, very cogently and perhaps uniquely, articulated the nature and innate value of his service's role in protecting the nation's fishery. Finally, David K. Brown, of the Royal Corps of Naval Constructors (RCNC), was responsible, during the 1980s, for the design of only the second class of the Royal Navy purpose-built fishery protection vessels. The unusual and unique profile of the 'Castle' class is testament to the attention Brown paid, for the very first time, to the requirements of the very demanding tasks undertaken by these ships.

Chapter One

A Nursery For Seamen
1379–1815

THERE IS EVIDENCE that the East Anglian port of Great Yarmouth used guard-ships in 1379 to defend its fishing fleet. It is likely that the town paid for this service, as had been the case the previous year when Scarborough was raided by the French for the same reason. Yarmouth's prosperity had benefitted greatly from the traditional annual harvesting of herring on its southerly, autumn migration. Although King John had granted this increasingly prosperous town its Charter and the right to self-govern in 1208, the prerogative was later disputed and not settled again in the town's favour until the reign of Edward III. This occurrence is often cited as the first example of a call to a central authority for protection to be provided for an English fishery, a request that was to be repeated many times over the centuries.

The seas surrounding the British Isles in the late fourteenth and early fifteenth century were widely regarded, 'as lying beyond laws, treaties and truces ...'.[1] The east coast fishing ports were isolated and therefore vulnerable to raids by the French and the Scots, and there was no assurance that outside assistance would be forthcoming. Indeed, Parliament had decreed some years earlier that the cost of such a service would have to be borne by the owners of the fishing and trading vessels themselves.

Sea fishing, and its development as a commercial enterprise, grew in importance from this time onwards and the need to protect this 'asset' evolved commensurately, though not evenly. This chapter shows how a range of factors have contributed to the claim that the 'Fishery Protection Squadron' is the Royal Navy's oldest unit, with a lineage that can be traced back to 1379. The starting point of this narrative pre-dates the establishment of the Royal Navy (RN) itself. However, evidence of its earliest interventions is fragmentary and, as such, is a subject that merits further investigation.

The sixteenth and seventeenth centuries were to witness the ascendancy of an efficiently organised Navy adopting a central role in relation to Britain's rise as a commercial power, a trading nation and later a colonialiser. The four, so-called Dutch Wars spanned the seventeenth and eighteenth centuries and included a battle over the rights to harvest herring in the North Sea. The vexed question of the 'freedom of the seas' and territorial rights to the waters adjacent to a nation's shores grew in importance as commerce became more sophisticated and regulated.

The eighteenth century, in particular, found Britain at war or in confrontation for long periods of time with its European neighbours, culminating in the protracted conflict with France that began in 1793 and lasted well into the next century. The chapter concludes with an account of the colonial wars on the north-eastern American seaboard and the climax of the French wars during the second decade of the nineteenth century, by which time fishery protection and its safe convoying as part of the nation's trade had become an essential part of the Royal Navy's remit. Alongside that, the security of the workforce, ensuring a ready supply for the RN to draw upon in time of war, was an oft-repeated maxim at the time and later, ' … a glorious nursery for seamen upon whom the security and prosperity of Great Britain does very much depend'.[2]

Something of a luxury

The geographical location of the British Isles on the North West European continental shelf provides immediate access to one of the largest areas of shallow seas in the world. The combination of water depth, climate, currents and supplies of essential nutrients help to create an abundance of fish.[3] In medieval times, seafood of various kinds formed a major part of the diet for those living adjacent to the shore or to lakes and rivers. Shellfish bred prolifically on some parts of the coast and could be gathered easily in shallow waters.

Thus, there was a wealth of fresh and sea water fish in rivers that could be caught using unsophisticated techniques mostly bereft of technology – by hand, in weirs and traps or by hook and line. Similarly, open fishing boats were basic affairs propelled either by oar or by rudimentary sails.[4] Many commentators have noted that sea fishing is a unique pursuit, a final iteration of the 'hunter-gatherer' of ancient times, that it, 'defies many conventional land-based classifications of economic activity'. It is not agriculture or transport, nor is it a typical 'industry' in the strict sense of the word, yet it shares many characteristics of all three pursuits.[5]

However, throughout the more than four centuries covered in this section of the book, transportation presented a major obstacle that prevented fresh fish from being available to poorer people inland. This product remained a luxury for most until the coming of the railways in the second half of the nineteenth century.

An insight into the central importance of fish in the diet of a prosperous settlement in the Middle Ages is accessible in the Durham Priory accounts for the year 1333–34. Fish accounted for around one third of the Priory's annual expenditure on food and drink. The variety of species consumed seems truly expansive, with two thirds comprising demersal fish such as cod, conger, plaice, skate and turbot, while herring and mackerel represented the principal pelagic fish purchased.[6]

By contrast, the only option for the less well-off was cured or salted fish. In the fourteenth and fifteenth centuries, with farming existing at a subsistence level, there was a general scarcity of meat. Most cattle had to be slaughtered and salted at the onset of winter; there were insufficient supplies to feed the growing urban populations. However, crucially and quite fortuitously, the last of the winter weeks did coincide with the six-week Christian observance of Lent when the Catholic Church decreed that there should be abstinence from consuming flesh on Fridays. Pragmatically, this could be considered as an economic necessity: at such times of the year the country simply could not have fed itself on a meat diet anyway.[7]

The fourteenth and fifteenth centuries

There was already an awareness of the importance of the sea and of shipping to the prosperity of the country well before 1379, as witnessed in this 1344 edict during the reign of Edward III:

> We order that you choose four of the most intelligent men of your town [in this instance Great Yarmouth but over 40 other coastal towns as well], best informed about the state of the shipping of our kingdom of England, and send them to London to arrive without fail on the Monday after next Quadragesima Sunday; in order that we the Council may be informed about maritime affairs.[8]

However, the idea that such a meeting led seamlessly to the birth of what we now call the Royal Navy is misleading. At the time, there was no concept, let alone organisation, of a fighting service in England. For example, when the word 'Navy' was used in the House of Commons in 1415 as being, 'the chief support and prosperity of the kingdom' it described the merchant fleet as a whole and not an organised, standing military force prepared to come to the aid of besieged coastal towns or vulnerable fishing boats.[9]

Despite the general lawlessness on the high seas to which the Crown actually contributed by encouraging privateering and maintaining a dubious relationship with those who practised outright piracy, there was nevertheless an acknowledgement of the commercial value of the fishing industry. This is illustrated in the willingness to intervene in matters of domestic dispute, such as the one between Yarmouth and the Cinque Ports. The Crown was also inclined to adjudicate on matters of the supply, quality and price of fish. Interestingly, the necessity to conserve fish stocks was recognised: fine-mesh nets being discouraged or banned.[10]

When Henry V came to the throne in 1413, the country he inherited was not renowned for its exploitation of sea power. There was limited usage made to resupply besieged castles on the Welsh coast during the Owain Glyndŵr rebellion, for instance, and the continuation of a proxy war with the French involved privateering rather than an outright conflict between nations.[11] The ships actually owned by the Crown were never numerous during the time of Henry V's father, Henry IV. The royal fleet numbered three when he ascended to the throne in 1399 and had declined to just two by 1409. When his son became king there were four vessels but two were non-operational. Ian Friel notes, 'The king's ships were not a state navy in the modern sense. They were, quite literally, the personal possessions of the sovereign. This meant that while fighting was part of their "remit", they were used for all sorts of other purposes.'[12]

When larger numbers of vessels were required for particular operations, such as the transportation of troops, the ships and crews were hired from private contractors. But these requirements were, by nature, impermanent. 'The navy that came into being was initially a very *ad hoc* affair, men and ships called to serve at their king's command from fishing and trading resources and dissolved and dispensed with by similar caprice.'[13] Nevertheless, it seems that between 1413 and 1416 there were a number of trading voyages that involved the king's ships. It is thought these vessels were used principally to escort convoys and also to undertake 'war operations'. Nevertheless, what was described as a fishery protection cruise did take place in 1413. England was still in the middle of the Hundred Years' War with France and fishing fleets were encouraged to sail in convoys, copying the practice adopted by the wool and wine trades.[14]

It is possible that the 1413 cruise included some form of war-like action against raiders, probably of a defensive nature. Administrative accounts show a considerable expenditure of weaponry on that occasion. Two balingers, *Peter* and *Paul*, were included in this fleet, which numbered eight ships. Balingers were extremely versatile vessels and fishery protection is listed as one of the minor functions they were called upon to perform.

They could move under sail as well as oars, they were of relatively low tonnage, and they were fast and manoeuvrable when compared with vessels driven only by sail. As oared ships, they needed to be long, narrow, low-built and light, to accommodate a rowing crew, to enable the oars to reach the water and to make the most of the power developed by the rowers.[15]

These vessels, and their equivalents, varied considerably in size. The number of rowers could be altered according to the nature of the undertaking. When functioning as convoy escorts they carried a double crew, the additional members often comprising troops. The balingers *Peter* and *Paul* were listed as being of '24 tons burthen or burden' – the old measurement of displacement used to calculate the amount of tax to be levied on the hire of ships. They shipped one mast and could carry a maximum of twenty-one and twenty oars respectively. Crew size varied between twenty-four on *Peter* and twenty-four to thirty-four on *Paul*.[16]

John Bohun is an example of a private ship-owner contracted to undertake protection duties on behalf of the Crown. He was commissioned to escort a shipment of wool to Calais in 1413 and later to ensure the safety of English fishermen and other subjects at sea. In September 1413, three royal balingers, *Gabriel*, *Paul* and *Peter*, undertook a month-long deployment in the North Sea, the aim being to deter aggressors rather than to fight them. Apart from the 1413 operation and a small sea-keeping patrol in 1418, however, Henry did little to 'police' the North Sea, and it does not seem to have been high on his list of priorities. However, towards the end of Richard III's reign an actual fishery protection squadron was formed with the specific purpose of guarding North Sea fishermen against Scottish attacks, which were becoming ever more frequent.[17]

These few early examples show that fish was sometimes considered to be an important enough commodity to warrant expenditure by the Crown in the form of armed escorts for convoys, or for groups of fishermen, in order to deter aggression. But there was the lack of a consistent policy. The seas were still open to all; the concept of territorial waters did not exist at the time. Thus, around the British Isles, fishermen from France, the Low Countries, the Iberian Peninsula and England were all engaged in working the same waters in competition with one another.

It was only in the 1480s, following years of *ad hoc* and private arrangements, that a more regular form of protection was introduced and paid for by the Crown. There were calls for a permanent or standing naval force a few years before that, in a document called The Governance of England, written around 1470. 'And though we have not always war upon the sea, yet it shall be necessary that the King have always some fleet upon the sea, for the repressing of rovers, saving our merchandise, our fishers, and the dwellers upon our coasts ...'[18] The use of convoys remained the best form of deterrence for fishing fleets or for the conveyance of fish. In fact, convoys in England had been in use from the reign of Henry II in the twelfth century.

In the fifteenth century, the country was not an exporter of fish. Its chief exports at the time were wool, cloth, tin and grain. Instead, it imported fish from Iceland, Ireland and from Scandinavia.[19] Fishermen had exploited Icelandic waters for several centuries and, during the reign of Richard III (1452–85), convoys were instituted in order to protect the Iceland trade.

It is at this period that the English language developed its first words relating to convoy: to 'waft' and a 'wafter'. The 1484 Iceland fleet was informed that William Combershall, captain of the *Elizabeth*, was appointed 'your conveyer and wafter to such place or places as he shall think convenient', and that they were, 'to be ordered and guided by him and in no wise to depart from him unto such time as the whole fleet of you shall come together and meet with other of our army now being upon the sea'.[20]

The Icelandic convoys of the 1480s were thought to be among the first occasions in which oceanic voyages were undertaken accompanied by English warships. Why the cargo carried warranted properly administered convoying was due to the fact that by then cod constituted a staple part of the country's diet. The technique of drying what was often called stockfish in the sun and wind and then salting or smoking it, meant that the fish could withstand being transported overseas and kept in a preserved state for later consumption.[21]

Disputes with England had begun to emerge when Norwegian merchants started to import dried fish from Iceland to Bergen. English merchants sought to copy the practice and shortly after 1400 began sailing to Iceland themselves both to catch fish and to buy it from local fishermen. The Danish crown repeatedly tried to stop this trade and ill-feeling was exacerbated in 1467 when the Danish Icelandic governor was killed while trying to enforce regulations. But generally, what was then called the Kalmar Union simply lacked the means with which to defend this resource from being exploited.[22]

The need to provide escorts for the Icelandic convoys continued into the next century. For example, records show that a small force of warships was despatched in 1557 to meet a home-bound Icelandic fishing fleet off Orkney.[23] The commander, Sir John Clere, unwisely decided to land on the island, where he was repelled and later drowned while attempting to escape along with three of his captains. The Scots had been a 'thorn in the flesh' during the previous half century, dominating the North Sea to the detriment of the east coast English fisheries. At the same time, the prosperity of the herring trade was diminishing at the hands of the Dutch.[24]

The naval legacy of King Henry VIII

One has to be careful not to assume that the English Navy that existed by the late fifteenth and early sixteenth centuries resembled its contemporary equivalent. 'The basic confusion arises from a refusal to acknowledge that navies, in our modern sense of the word, are a modern creation, a product of the early modern and modern state. Naval warfare existed long before navies, but it took other institutional forms.'[25]

Henry VIII was the first king to organise the Navy as a permanent force, with an administrative and logistical structure, funded by tax revenue and supervised by a newly created Navy Board. As a result of the war with France, it was decided to keep the thirty ships active during peacetime and by 1540 the Navy consisted of forty-five ships. Alongside the establishment of a standing naval fleet, a number of shore facilities in the form of storehouses were also commissioned. Although historians argue that Henry lacked strategic nous with regard to the actual execution of sea power, they do agree that the legacy he left of an administrative and logistical structure ensured that the Navy would not be allowed to wither through neglect, as had happened in the time of several of his predecessors. Nothing like it existed anywhere else outside the Mediterranean, with the possible exception of Portugal, and the resulting naval infrastructure established could be regarded as the single most important achievement of the English sixteenth century with regard to the development of sea power.[26]

Following John Cabot's 1497 voyage to the coast of North America under the commission of Henry VII of England, fishing fleets from France, Portugal and Spain began to work the grounds off Newfoundland and Nova Scotia. Cod was brought ashore to be cured before being despatched to Europe. Although the English had voyaged to Iceland for centuries, they were slower to make use of North American waters than their continental counterparts. But, by the second half of the sixteenth century, West Country fishermen in particular started to exploit the Newfoundland area as the Portuguese and Spanish presence declined. In its place, Anglo-French rivalry began to fester towards the end of the 1700s, which would develop into outright conflict during the next century.[27]

Territorial waters

John Grainger describes Francis Drake's circumnavigation of the globe between 1577 and 1580 as constituting, 'the first seaman-like view of the Pacific and Indian Oceans by an English captain'.[28] Logically, and perhaps inevitably, exploitation followed on from exploration and the possibilities of access to untold amounts of wealth from the navigational possibilities that these early adventurers uncovered with their voyages into the unknown, led in time to the creation of the vast British Empire. The English global explorers found that the Portuguese and Dutch had preceded them in the Indian and Pacific Oceans and, as with the French and later the Americans on the north-eastern seaboard, settlement and with it the matter of offshore territorial rights, assumed the kind of importance that has profoundly affected sea fishery and its protection ever since.

The notion of the significance of a ship entering territorial waters was introduced during the reign of James I when the English tried to define what they termed *the narrow seas*. These were the two areas of water that lay between England and France (the English Channel) and England and the Netherlands (the southern North Sea). The Scots had preceded them by declaring sovereignty over the waters adjacent to their shorelines. Other European nations also developed similar systems. The Scots, for several centuries, charged foreign fishermen for the rights to work in coastal and inland waters; boats had to carry licences if they fished within a 'land-kenning' of the shore. Later, this crude measurement of distance was replaced by the distance a cannon could be fired, before that too became an obsolescent form of calculation.

James's initial concern during a period of neutrality was to safeguard the country's coastal integrity. The waters were defined as, 'the "King's Chambers", within which the belligerents (of other nations) were not to supposed to fight'. All foreign ships entering these narrow seas were expected to salute, by lowering topsails and striking their flag, if they encountered an English warship.[29] An admiral of the narrow seas was appointed, whose duties included patrolling the fisheries and enforcing the salute. This claim of English sovereignty was maintained until the official adoption of a 3-mile delimitation in 1822 by several European nations including Britain.

Piracy and Privateering

Piracy had been a menace on the high seas for several centuries and was not recognised as a crime in English courts until 1536. The Cinque Ports were prominent among the offenders. Internecine rivalry among the various 'Portsmen' erupted intermittently and the port of Yarmouth, mentioned above, which had several enemies in other ports, was undoubtedly the worst culprit.[30]

Piracy and privateering continued to threaten commercial trade during the seventeenth century; its effect was also felt on fishing and consequently on the livelihoods and indeed the very lives of the fishermen themselves. What are somewhat erroneously referred to as Barbary pirates, during the early years of the century, constituted a particular danger to West Country fishermen on the East American seaboard. In 1611 they lost no fewer than twenty boats either in the Atlantic, as the North Africans ventured as far west as Nova Scotia and Newfoundland, or in the Mediterranean, where the fishermen brought their fish to sell. The crews, sold on as slaves, constituted the key targets rather than their cargoes. Even coastal towns and villages in the West Country were not safe from attacks by the Barbary pirates; in 1625 Plymouth lost a thousand seamen and the tiny village of East Looe in Cornwall a further eighty in 1628 and sixty-nine a decade later.[31]

Closer to home, the tolerance, indeed encouragement of privateering, was exploited when the country was torn apart in the 1640s by the English Civil War. As noted earlier, Great Yarmouth's prosperity had grown in part due to the herring fishery, which had contributed greatly since the town's foundation. The valuable catch also spawned shoreside industries including craftspeople who refitted and equipped the fleet and provided smokehouses, casks and salt to pickle the town's most popular product – the red herring. However, as had occurred two centuries earlier, due to its geographical location, Yarmouth was vulnerable to threats from the sea.

The Navy had declared for Parliament at the onset of the Civil War but the security of the North Sea was not an issue until the Royalists began to contract privateers. They were based in English, Welsh and Channel Islands ports, while Ostend was used as a marketplace to sell the vessels that had been captured. Consequently, by 1643–45, the Royalist fleet numbered some 250 vessels, dominating the North Sea and posing an immediate problem for Parliamentarian Great Yarmouth.[32]

In 1644 Thomas Allin, a Royalist privateer and merchant from nearby rival town Lowestoft, instigated a 'confederacy against Yarmouth, to retaliate the injuries they had received from that town [this included a personal grudge as his boat had been confiscated and later sold by the Great Yarmouth Assembly after a previous abortive uprising in Lowestoft] ... with the design of fitting out vessels to distress the trade at Yarmouth'. This 'distress' consisted of harassing and attacking the Yarmouth herring fleet at the vulnerable points of their annual fishing expeditions. Allin, in 1644, managed to seize twenty out of the twenty-three Great Yarmouth boats travelling to Iceland, This had an immediate, adverse effect on the price of fish and the town's herring trade was practically wiped out in 1643–44.

The town's Assembly, in desperation, appealed to Parliament for guard-ships. After protracted negotiations and further heavy losses during the winter of 1644, five vessels were secured with additional protection afforded by its own warship, the *Adventure*, a former merchantman captured while transporting troops and equipment to England. *Adventure* was initially outfitted for, 'the takeing (sic) of such prize Shippes (sic) vessels [and] goods as belong to persons or places that are in hostility against the Parliament'.[33]

The near destruction of Yarmouth's herring fleet had the effect of distancing the town's authorities from its fishing community. The mood of discontent continued until the end of the Civil War and despite Great Yarmouth, at Parliament's persuasion, paying compensation for those most afflicted, there was an uprising by disgruntled fishermen in 1648.

Freedom of the seas

Thomas Mun was one of the first 'mercantilists'. These economic theorists broke away from medieval thinking on economic matters and presented, 'a composite rather than an integrated body of ideas, with variations from country to country, from time to time'. However, with respect to those countries that bordered the sea, they were united by a profound concern for the fishing industry.[34] Mun believed that a nation's holdings of gold were the main measure of its wealth and that governments needed to regulate trade in order to produce an excess of exports over imports to gain more gold for the country. He came into public prominence during the economic depression of 1620. Many people had blamed the East India Company for the country's economic downturn because it financed its trade by exporting £30,000 in bullion on each voyage. Mun argued more broadly that governments should regulate trade in order to produce an excess of exports over imports and thus provide an economic balance.

He singled out the Dutch Republic to illustrate his argument:

> The fishing in his Majesties sea of England, Scotland and Ireland is our natural wealth, and would cost nothing but labour, which the Dutch bestow willingly, and thereby draw yearly a very great profit for themselves by serving many places in Christendom with our Fish, for which they return and supply their wants both of forraign (sic) wares and Mony (sic), beside the multitude of Mariners and Shipping which hereby are maintained ...[35]

He concluded his diatribe with a particularly pointed attack at the United Provinces, which included an accusation that the Dutch were planning to seize the island of Lewis in the Hebrides.

Mun's original thesis, which was possibly added to in the interim, was still being quoted some forty years later, during the debate about the exploitation by the Dutch of the North Sea herring fishery. Willem Beukelesz had discovered in the late fourteenth century that herrings could be preserved by pickling them. Earlier, herring trades had used a lot of salt in the process, but the industry benefitted from a vital innovation. 'Instead of gutting and salting the herring, the Dutch realised that gibbing (gutting the herring, leaving the liver and the pancreas in the fish), allowed preservation with much less salt.'[36] This method turned a perishable foodstuff into a commercial commodity that was to assume huge national importance in the United Provinces. The yearly arrival of the season's herring catch was cause for celebration, a tradition that lasts to this day in the Netherlands. 'The first herring of the year, or new herring, was the focal point of widespread festivities in the fishing villages and, indeed, throughout the country, and it was accorded near mythical status.'[37]

The management of the Dutch fishing fleet in the seventeenth century was one of the most tightly organised in Europe. The boats were only allowed to sail to strictly specified areas off the Scottish and English coastlines on certain dates during the summer and autumn of the year, thereby tracing the southerly migration of the herring. All operations were brought to a halt on 31 January. The catches were forbidden to be sold abroad and were brought back to Dutch ports in 'busses' for pickling, which was managed under strict guidelines in order to maintain the quality of the product.

The introduction of the Dutch herring busses marked an important technological advance in fishing boat design. These decked vessels were much larger than the English open boats of the period and provided a greater sailing range. They could also carry a number of smaller boats that could be lowered into the water, which helped to increase the catch at certain times. Comparisons have been made with twentieth-century fishing 'mother' ships. Approximately one thousand busses were used in what was popularly known as 'the Great Fishery' and it has been reckoned that half a million people, not much short of a fifth of the country's total population, was involved in the industry at the time.[38]

The concern about the scale of this operation, which had been articulated earlier by Mun, and later by other commentators, was the subject of Anglo-Dutch diplomatic discussions for many years, after a proclamation was issued in 1609 stating that any person wanting to fish off the English coast would require a licence. The problem extended beyond political and economic issues and embraced the matter of legal right concerning the freedom of the seas.

In the same year as the English Proclamation about fishing licences, a book on international law titled *Mare Liberum* was published in Latin, the work of the Dutch jurist and philosopher Hugo Grotius. In *The Free Sea*, Grotius declared a new principle whereby the sea should be considered international territory and all nations should be free to use it for seafaring trade. It was intended as a riposte to the Portuguese claim of monopoly on their East Indian trade, which was an example of the policy of *mare clausum*, the closed sea, meaning a body of water under the control of a state that is closed or not accessible to other nations.

The Dutch adopted Grotius's theory as they had traditionally supported the argument that the seas should be open to all. This was backed by the mercantilist contention that a successful nation grew rich and thus powerful through the development of productive resources. This development could be fed by achieving the maximum access possible to natural resources, such as fish, which Grotius inaccurately described as 'an endless resource'. This helps to explain why the Dutch Republic held such a tight rein over the organisation of its fisheries.

Thomas Mun's interpretation of the mercantilist's path to economic prosperity was different. In his book *England's Treasure by Forraign Trade* (1664), he contended that productive resources consisted of two elements: natural and artificial wealth. Well-organised food production benefitted and grew the population, which led on to prosperity and with it power, and hence, the creation of artificial wealth. Successful exploitation of a natural resource such as fish could only be achieved if the English fishermen could undertake their work while undisturbed by foreign boats. This brought about the annexation of sea areas under sovereign authority.

Another effort was made by the English king in 1616 to enforce the issuing of licences after an unsuccessful attempt to do the same seven years earlier. This time it drew an aggressive response from the Dutch ships being used to protect the busses. The matter was then not revisited until 1635 when the Dutch ambassador to England was notified that King Charles was, 'preparing a fleet, "to preserve and maintain his sovereignty and hereditary rights over the sea, and for the preservation and protection of commerce. ... No one henceforth was to be allowed to fish in the King's Seas without express licence and suitable acknowledgment."'[39]

This time the threat to take action was backed by the weight of intellectual argument in the form of a treatise on the nature of maritime sovereignty. John Selden's Mare *Clausum Seu Maris* (Of the Dominium or Ownership of the Sea), effectively supported the king's right to exclusive sovereignty over the waters surrounding the British Isles. Ironically, as will be demonstrated on numerous occasions, Britain normally vigorously defended the principles of *mare liberum*. But this time, however, it suited it to adopt the exactly opposite stance. Claims of historical precedence, that traditionally there existed a belt of waters of unspecified width around the country's coastline (in 1618 it was stated as being 14 miles), were largely unsubstantiated. Barback remarks, 'English monarchs from James I attempted, in a switch from Elizabeth's policy, to reassert what was held to be an ancient right to sovereignty over the whole of the sea area around the British Isles. Foreigners might fish in this vaguely defined sovereign area, though sometimes it was attempted with varying degrees of success to make them buy a licence to do so, and in return they would receive protection by the English navy.'[40]

However, what gave Charles I the 'clout' to enforce his claim was the introduction of 'Ship Money', which enabled him to raise a quite formidable fleet to be used to collect this levy. This scheme had been employed at various times in the past, including demanding payment for protecting coastal towns, as in the case of Great Yarmouth. A properly argued scheme, supported by historical research into the matter, was introduced in 1634 whereby firstly counties with maritime borders, and later inland ones, were required to pay an annual stipend to pay for naval defence. The principle of levying Ship Money was neatly justified in Selden's treatise, in order to counter, 'the many depredations, violence, and hostile acts committed daily on the Narrow Seas, and even within his Majesty's ports – to the dishonour of his Majesty's sovereignty in those seas ... amid the infinite disturbance and prejudice of trade'.[41]

'Ship Money Fleets' were adopted as a means of drawing the correct measure of obeisance from neighbouring states in the form of saluting the English flag. Most countries complied in the interests of diplomatic nicety. But when Charles tried to exercise his powers to extract further revenue by issuing fishing licences to foreigners, he was met with stiff opposition from the Dutch Republic, as had happened in his father's time.

A fleet of twelve English ships sailed in July 1634 under Vice-Admiral Pennington to enforce the new ruling and levy the toll. Despite Dutch protests, this move was repeated in October, this time led by the Duke of Northumberland. The Dutch retaliated by despatching thirteen ships to provide defence for their busses: the threat of open warfare now appeared imminent. Wilson states that it was only extreme caution, exercised by both the Duke of Northumberland and his counterpart Admiral van Dorp, which prevented an already tense situation from escalating.[42]

Two years later, the reticence of Philips van Dorp to demonstrate the right degree of aggressive intent was to cost him his job. The English fleet arrived late in the 1636 herring season and only managed to issue approximately 200 licences. The Dutch, however, were much unsettled on both a political and economic level by this existential threat to their precious herring trade. The following year their fishing fleets were provided with much stronger escorts under a new command.

The commercial tensions between England and the Netherlands were brought to crisis point when Parliament approved the First Navigation Act in 1651. This meant that imported merchandise had to be brought directly in English ships or those of the exporting country. This Act had the effect of subordinating Dutch trade to the advantage of the British and is perceived as a major cause of the First Anglo-Dutch War, 1652–54.

The old claims about recognising sovereignty in the narrow seas and fishing levies surfaced once again. The navies of both nations were activated under their respective commanders, Admirals Robert Blake and Maarten Tromp. The Dutch fleet was handed a dual trade protection role both in home waters and to ensure the safe arrival of ships returning from the East Indies. The remaining naval ships were ordered to protect, 'the great fishery, which is of so great importance to the State'.[43]

Unsurprisingly, the English orders for battle largely echoed their opponent's strategy. In addition to harassing the Dutch East Indies convoys, Admiral Blake was required to, 'arrange that "the Dutch fishery upon the coast of Scotland and England, and in those seas, may be interrupted and disturbed and their busses and other ships attending thereupon taken and secured ..."'.[44] Although the plans fell short of open warfare with the Netherlands Navy, the intention was plain: to bring about the downfall of the Dutch economy.

Blake successfully attacked the Dutch in Scottish waters in the summer of 1652, scattering their busses and sinking or capturing the accompanying warships. Meanwhile, Maarten Tromp had sailed north and on 4 August was in sight of the English ships. That night a tremendous storm put paid to the chances of battle and in the midst of the resulting confusion a Dutch East Indies convoy arrived in the locality, which instantly took precedence. Although Blake had succeeded in one respect by disrupting the fishing fleet, he failed in relation to the greater prize, the capture of the lucrative convoy from the Far East. There were further clashes at sea during the rest of the war, which was ended on 15 April 1654 with the signing of the Treaty of Westminster.

There were numerous attempts, during the Stuart period and again in the middle of the eighteenth century, to reinforce the *mare clausum* theory through the formation of large-scale fishing companies with the immediate aim of countering the Dutch busses and helping to train Yarmouth citizens to pickle their own herring catch. These companies were bestowed royal patronage: the Corporation of the Royal Fishery was created in 1664 following the failure of earlier private enterprises. The company boasted the services of the Duke of York and his thirty-two assistants included some well-known members of the Court, the Navy and the City of London. Among them was Samuel Pepys, who was said to be 'flattered by the honour', especially perhaps as he benefitted personally from the promise of an annual stipend. Unfortunately, Pepys's fears that the enterprise would 'come to little' were realised when he found that, in its first year, the sole power the company had acquired were licensing lotteries and the services of a certain Captain Poyntz, a gaming house proprietor, presumably in the capacity of technical adviser. Subsequently the Corporation's accounts descended into chaos and, 'it disappeared in ignominy like its predecessors, a byword for corruption and incompetence ...'.[45]

Battle for dominance on the East Atlantic Littoral

The last section of this chapter covers the eighteenth and early nineteenth centuries and includes colonial wars on the east coast of what became Canada and the United States of America. Protection of the British migratory fishing community, principally off Newfoundland and Nova Scotia, formed an important part of the Royal Navy's responsibilities. Inevitably, the sheer distances involved in safely transporting the fish 'harvest' to Europe and at the same time protecting the fishing grounds themselves, coupled with the competing demands of what was becoming a near-global conflict with France in particular, meant that the Navy easily became, in modern parlance, overstretched.

This may well account for this example, much closer to home, in 1747. J. Collier of Hastings wrote first on 21 April to Andrew Stone, Under Secretary of State to the Duke of Newcastle, Secretary of State for the Southern Department of the Admiralty. The mackerel season was about to commence and as the Hastings fishery usually engaged a number of boats in this task, he was applying for protection in the form of a 20-gun ship, 'or one of the sloops of war'.

Just over three weeks later, Collier wrote again. This time, his tone was much more urgent:

> We are in a bad situation. Two or three small Boulogne, Dieppe or Dunkirk privateers keep lurking on our coast. We have upwards of sixty boats employed in the mackerel fishery, and the prime of the season commencing, on sight of one of these pickaroons [scoundrel or in this case pirate/privateer] they durst not stir out, which is some hundreds of pounds sterling loss to the fishery. In Queen Anne's wars, when greater complaints were made against the conduct of the Lords Commissioners of the Admiralty, we never failed having one or two men-of-war to protect our fishery, and now we only request a 20-gun ship or sloop of war.[46]

The British were late to respond to the possibilities afforded by the migratory habits of white fish along the North-East Atlantic coastline of America, particularly in the sea areas around Newfoundland, Labrador and Nova Scotia. Migratory European fishermen led by France, the Netherlands, Portugal and Spain had exploited the region in the sixteenth century, with France assuming a dominance during the 1700s as its European neighbours' involvement declined. Britain only started to outstrip France in the middle of the eighteenth century.[47]

The particular prize was cod. Atlantic cod prey on smaller fish, which in turn feed off the plankton that blooms in the cold, nutrient-rich coastal waters. Such conditions are to be found where the Labrador Current flows across the ragged eastern Newfoundland coastline with its promontories, inlets and small islands. The best of the catch is to be sourced closer inshore; the fish caught off the Grand Banks further out are generally of an inferior quality.

The early European exploitation of the fishery was by custom a migratory operation rather than one undertaken by settlers. They fished in small sloops and other open boats. A larger vessel brought the men and equipment across the Atlantic for the start of the summer season. A base, or 'fishing room', was established on shore where the daily catch would be cured on wooden drying platforms. The workforce returned to Europe each autumn with their cargoes in what were called 'sack ships' bound for the continental markets.

Archaeological evidence points to the fact that fishermen from specific towns returned year on year to the same location on the North American littoral and one can appreciate that they derived comfort from mixing with their own townsfolk while working in such an unknown and potentially hostile environment. A custom of 'first come, first served' developed. In the words of the Western Charter of 1634, which regulated the fishery on Newfoundland's English Shore, 'according to the ancient custom every ship or fisher enters a harbour in behalf of a ship, [will] be Admiral of the said harbour, wherein for the time being he shall reserve only so much beach and flakes or both as needful for the number of boats that he shall use …'.[48] Unfortunately, this otherwise pacific arrangement could not last and the demarcation of the Newfoundland coastline into the 'English Shore' and the 'French Shore' contributed to the open warfare that later took place between the British and French.

The migratory population was gradually eclipsed by permanent settlers but, although collapsing as a system in the 1790s, it did not disappear altogether until the nineteenth century. Both the periodic Anglo-French Wars and the American Revolutionary War (1775–83) contributed to general depressions in the fishing industry in the second half of the eighteenth century. A combination of enemy naval and privateering activity, the closure of markets and the depletion of the labour force owing to the demands of war, made the transatlantic trade both dangerous and costly.

The link between fishery and sea power has already been discussed in relation to the mercantilist theories of the previous century. A further factor in this equation relates to the traditional valuing of the workforce itself to the ongoing prosperity of the Navy, especially at time of war. 'From the days of Elizabeth (First) British statesmen saw in the fisheries a national incubator for seamen, "a feeder of the fleet as unrivalled for the excellence of its material as it was inexhaustible in its resources".'[49]

This 'feeder' was never 'inexhaustible', of course, but was a key factor with respect to the long series of Anglo-French conflicts on the North

American coast during the eighteenth century. What became popularly termed 'the nursery for seamen' drew the fishermen away from their work in time of war. Thus, control of the seas around Newfoundland came at a price as the requirement for naval protection fed directly into the health of the nation's fishing trade.

In terms of the peace treaties that routinely ended these conflicts, specific articles were invariably included that addressed the Newfoundland fisheries themselves. The Peace of Utrecht in 1713, for example, which concluded the War of Spanish Succession, handed Britain sovereignty over Newfoundland but allowed France to retain fishing rights. The emergence of the United States of America, following the American Revolutionary War, resulted in three countries gaining access to the Newfoundland Fisheries in accordance with the terms of the Treaty of Paris in 1783. As a consequence, none of the diplomatic changes emanating from the peace treaties actually served to resolve the Anglo-French impasse.

Three examples follow, each of which show the importance of sea control of the American littoral in this period in relation to the all-important fishery. Naval strategists generally acknowledge that true 'command of the sea' is rare and that, 'the uncommanded sea is the norm'. Neither Britain nor France, and certainly not the nascent United States, was able to claim command of those waters in the years between 1740 and 1790. The goal for the two European nations was a limited form of sea control, defined as, 'freedom of action to use the sea for one's own purposes in specified areas and for specified periods of time and, where necessary, to deny its use to the enemy'.[50] The USA employed what would now be called a form of asymmetric warfare in an attempt to achieve its particular objective.

Firstly, King George's War (1744–48) saw an inconclusive series of engagements between Britain and France for supremacy on the east coast of the continent. It formed part of the greater 'War of the Austrian Succession' (1740–48). During the conflict, an important victory was achieved through the capture of the French fortress at Louisbourg, Cape Breton Island. This gave the Royal Navy some measure of control over the Acadia (Nova Scotia) fisheries and a wider, strategic advantage at the entrance to the Gulf of St Lawrence.

Secondly, the French raid on the Newfoundland Fishery in 1762 witnessed an attempt by the French to achieve a better bargaining position for peace towards the end of what had been a series of chastening defeats during the Seven Years' War (1756–63). The campaign served to underline the maxim that true control of the sea could only be achieved through control of sea communications.

Lastly, during the Revolutionary War (1775–83), the Americans realised that the Newfoundland fishery was vulnerable as it lay at the end of a long sea communication route. The British might be persuaded to abandon its attempts to crush the rebellion if its precious fishing fleet was attacked and harassed. Like the French, the revolutionaries' aim was to disrupt the Royal Navy's maritime superiority on the littoral rather than openly to contest sea control.

Captain, and later Admiral, Peter Warren played a key role both before and during the war of 1744–48. He had commanded the 24-gun sixth rate HMS *Squirrel* between 1736 and 1742, operating out of Boston, Massachusetts. *Squirrel* was by then quite an old warship, having been launched in 1707 and rebuilt in 1727. During that time Warren had gained a good knowledge of the French fishery on Cape Breton Island at the north eastern end of Nova Scotia. He wrote a long report to the Admiralty in London in June 1739, for example, giving a detailed description of the fishery and of the strength of the French garrison. He included outline plans for the reinforcement of the British settlement at Canso, further south on the Nova Scotia mainland, showing an acute awareness of the strategic advantages accruing from a future challenge to French domination of the region.[51]

Four years later, with war looming, he was directed by the Admiralty Board, 'to consider maturely and let them know your opinion and judgment how the French may be annoyed in their fisheries and settlements to the northward of Boston, and what strength would be proper to carry out any attempts you may think advisable'.

A year later, Warren wrote to the Admiralty Secretary from HMS *Launceston* (this time his command was a new 44-gun fifth-rate ship) with bold and expansive proposals for seizing control of the Cape Breton peninsula. 'To be sure nothing could be a greater acquisition to Great Britain and its dominions, than the dispossessing the French of Cape Breton, by which the whole fur and fish trade would be in our hands.'[52]

The actual impetus for mounting an assault on the key fortress of Louisbourg came from the General Assembly of Massachusetts. Although the Massachusetts militia could raise the manpower, the assault required the Royal Navy to provide transport. Commodore Peter Warren responded immediately by despatching four warships from his base in the Leeward Islands. The Governor of Massachusetts, William Shirley, was of like mind to Warren concerning the importance of Cape Breton and Louisbourg. He wrote in a letter to him in January 1745, 'I need not observe to you that the consequences of succeeding in the expedition (the seizure of Louisbourg) would be the preservation of Nova Scotia and gaining Canada as well as Cape Breton, which would secure his Majesty, the whole northern continent, gaining the whole fishery exclusive of the French, increasing greatly the nursery of seamen for the Royal Navy ...'.[53]

The same month, Warren was appointed C-in-C North America (to the north of Carolina) in the rank of rear admiral. Britain was then at war with the French again, who had invaded Nova Scotia, captured the fortress at Canso and would have taken Annapolis Royal in New England had not the weather intervened. It was fully expected that they would try again in the spring, 'the reducing of which will bring the whole province under their subjection, which cannot be prevented but by employing a superior strength of ships in those seas'. Again, the letter written to Warren on behalf of the Admiralty Board stressed that wresting control of the seas was the only way to save the settlements and the fishery in the province.

The Board ordered Warren north from the Leeward Islands to reinforce the area with ships and guns and urgently to gather intelligence on his arrival. Troops were landed near Louisbourg on 30 April and the fortress surrendered on 17 June 1745. But Admiral Warren was not satisfied with securing the town alone. Even before the assault began he was writing to the Admiralty arguing that the retaking of Canso and the establishment there of a properly organised, civil government would ensure the future of the fishery and serve to encourage permanent settlers. He wrote again in June, requesting four or five more ships that, 'could destroy the French fishery in the summer'.[54]

Clearly, Admiral Warren could see that the future security of Nova Scotia and its fishery depended on creating a lasting infrastructure. He realised that maintaining a permanent military garrison at Louisbourg would be enormously expensive, money much better being spent on encouraging a permanent settlement supported by a local militia, as was the case in other colonies. However, he did not neglect the advantages derived from the strategic position of Louisbourg. In October the same year he wrote again to Corbett proposing, 'a cruise on the enemy about the entrance of the gulf of St. Lawrence and Newfoundland to distress the French in their fishery'.

General plans to harass the French trade route and specifically to attack their fishery on the north-east side of Newfoundland were expressed in another of his communications with the Admiralty, this time in May the following year. Warren suggested, 'taking their ships and burning or otherwise their boats, flakes and salt, great quantities of which I am told they always have in store there. This, if it can be done, will make us sole masters of the cod fishery.'[55]

Peter Warren's efforts and successes off the eastern American coast were rewarded later with a seat on the Admiralty Board. Julian Gwynn sums up nearly a decade of his achievements between 1739 and 1748 thus:

> At the outset he was just one of many undistinguished officers, yet by 1748 he was, with Anson and Hawke, one of the most successful, most honoured and richest naval figures to emerge from ten years of campaigning. His war experience fell into two phases, the first from 1739 to 1745 when he developed his fighting skills and advanced his fortune on a modest scale as a prize hunter, and secondly from 1745 to 1748 when he achieved recognition from the Admiralty, was given high command and acquired great wealth.[56]

To which one might add that throughout Warren showed an ability to look beyond the immediate gains of a particular campaign to the strategic advantages that might accrue in the long term. Moreover, during King George's War he fully recognised the pivotal importance of the maintenance of the fishery, underpinned by a permanent, civilian-led leadership and population.

Étienne François, duc de Choiseul, was French Minister of Marine, of War and of Foreign Affairs during the Seven Years' War. His country, by 1761, was trying to reach agreement to end the war. Both countries regarded migratory fishery as an economic resource of primary importance and that the whole issue was not simply *sine qua non* but was also non-negotiable.

The French Minister's plan therefore was to pressurise its enemy by conducting a trade war in the North Atlantic, preceded by the destruction of the British Newfoundland fishery. Accordingly, a squadron of four French warships commanded by Charles-Henri-Louis d'Arsac, chevalier de Ternay, left Brest on 8 May 1762. On board were

560 troops. Initially, Choiseul's plan was not confined to Newfoundland but embraced the squadron making raids on both the African and South American coasts. However, in reality, France at the time simply lacked the naval resources to challenge its rival on this grand scale. In the end, the attack on Newfoundland presented the best option if an end to the conflict was to be achieved.

The object of the mission, according to Ternay's instructions, was 'to ravage and destroy, as much as he could, the commerce of the fishery at the island and on the banks of Newfoundland'. Ternay was to attempt to capture St John's, which served the fishery at Newfoundland as a rendezvous (by virtue of its defences and administrative centre). He was to proceed with the destruction of that fishery, using St John's as a base. These operations were to occupy Ternay for no more than a month.

A *temporary* occupation of St John's was key to Choiseul's strategy. He reasoned that if Ternay did little more than harass the enemy by striking at the vulnerable and commercially vital Newfoundland fishery before moving on to a fresh target, the British would be unlikely to despatch its overwhelming naval forces, especially over such a great distance.[57]

Choiseul's plan, in modern parlance, could be described as an example of 'Manoeuvre Warfare' undertaken, in this case, by an inferior power. 'Theoretically Manoeuvre Warfare offers the possibility of results disproportionately greater than the resources applied, and thus the chance of success for the weaker side. ... It can also fail completely if disruption does not occur as predicted.'[58]

In the event, the garrison at St John's was seized with little resistance. The defences there had been weakened through neglect and the Royal Navy, which provided a small squadron for the defence of the Newfoundland fishery, only operated on a seasonal basis. It consisted of just two twenty-gun frigates when Ternay arrived off the coast.

Instead of undertaking a time-limited occupation, the French commander stayed on at St John's and immersed himself in fortifying the settlement, in contradiction to Choiseul's overall strategy, which was based on the realisation that France did not have the naval resources to support a permanent occupation. More importantly, he failed to carry out the most important parts of his instructions – the total destruction of the fishery and the disruption of British commerce in the North Atlantic. Meanwhile, however, Ternay's victory at St John's was celebrated in France and drew a muted response from Choiseul for his deviation from the overall strategy for the deployment. This can probably be explained by the fact that peace negotiations had resumed and by the summer of 1762 they had reached a critical phase.[59]

The British were slow to realise what was happening in the colony and that the French manoeuvres during the summer of 1762 were more than an isolated raid on the fishery. As the year wore on, Ternay became ever more convinced that a co-ordinated response by the enemy to the occupation of St John's would not be made until the following year. He was mistaken and was forced to flee, abandoning St John's and his troops to their fate.

Subsequently, Ternay claimed that his campaign had been a success, calculating that the cost to the British economy of the disruption to the cod fishery alone had been in the region of £1 million. 'The physical damage to the boats and facilities there would take time and money to repair. The effect on trade, which had already suffered a setback when Spain entered the war and closed that country as a market for British fish, was equally serious.' Crucially however, the shore-side infrastructure of the industry had escaped largely unharmed. In the earlier years of migratory fishing there were few permanent shore-side facilities. This had changed by 1762 and there were now a number of expensive establishments on Newfoundland upon which the future prosperity of the fishery depended.

The initial success of the American warships and their privateers during the American War of Independence (1775–83) stemmed partly from the fact that the Royal Navy was unable to muster enough strength to defend the entire North American littoral. The scenario during this war was not dissimilar to the Seven Years' War the previous decade. The Americans could not hope to compete with the Royal Navy on the high seas but considered that a campaign of harassment and damage to the infrastructure would have an influence on the British Government's efforts to crush the rebellion.

What assisted the Patriots was the fact that the RN had been denuded in strength in the years following the Seven Years' War owing to stringent cutbacks required in order to reduce the national debt. The Newfoundland Fishery once again found itself vulnerable after years of poor funding and neglect and by 1775 the Navy's fishery protection force had been reduced to HMS *Romney* (50 guns), *Surprize* (28 guns), two sloops and assorted brigs and schooners. Instead of being able to cruise the fishing grounds, this depleted squadron was restricted to defending the main towns.[60]

Competing demands from other naval stations meant that the situation did not immediately improve in spite of the successes, particularly of the privateers. At first, they concentrated on attacking the fishing boats operating on the Grand Banks but in 1778 also focused on the inshore fishery. Vice-Admiral Montagu, who commanded the station between 1776–78, was forced to adopt a defensive posture, concentrating on guarding the fishermen at sea, keeping a watch on the trade routes and protecting the major fish-processing centres. Even that limited strategy proved too much for his meagre forces. In 1778, realising that the greatest threat from the privateers was coming from the harassment of the fishermen operating on the Banks, he decided to concentrate his forces in that area, which unfortunately left the coast of Labrador totally exposed. 'The American privateer *Minerva* (24 guns) chose that year to cruise and destroy the fishery of Labrador.'[61]

The intervention of France in the war, following the Treaty of Alliance in 1778, proved to be a turning point. It did allow the beleaguered naval station to be reinforced by the British and, in the long run, contributed to the establishment of Newfoundland as a permanent colony rather than as a temporary haven used by migratory fishermen. However, there was a downside. Reinforcement on the western side of the Atlantic Ocean served to weaken the RN nearer to home and privateers operating out of French ports began to prey in the Western Approaches on British incoming trade (including from Newfoundland).

Captain Horatio Nelson had a passing involvement in fishery protection during the American War of Independence, although more in an offensive capacity. He set sail with a Quebec-bound convoy from Cork Harbour on 26 April 1782, in command of HMS *Albemarle*, a 28-gun, sixth-rate frigate. He paused briefly on the way at St John's, which he described as 'disagreeable', and deposited the convoy halfway up the St Lawrence before reporting to the C-in-C North America Station.

He was then ordered to cruise against enemy shipping off the New England littoral. There was promise of prize money. He had some success against the local fishing boats, although some proved to be surprisingly elusive. However, he did manage to trap an American fishing schooner named *Harmony* in Boston Bay. He took it in tow and then 'used her for a month, with the co-operation of her master, Nathaniel Carver'.[62]

During that time, HMS *Albemarle*, when in company with the schooner, had a very narrow escape from a squadron of French warships. Carver's knowledge of the very shallow St George's Banks, south-east of Cape Cod, which were rich fishing grounds, helped Nelson to keep just ahead of the pursuing enemy, despite the *Albemarle*'s weak sailing qualities. Afterwards, Nelson restored *Harmony* to its owner together with a certificate permitting Carver to continue fishing without interference.[63]

The great British victory at the Battle of Trafalgar did not hand the RN immediate command of the sea. The transatlantic trade route remained vulnerable and the problem of ensuring the safe arrival of convoys was exacerbated during the Anglo-American War of 1812–15 with the successful deployment of American warships and privateers. Britain found that it was impossible to reinforce its fleet on the North American Station because of the shortages of seamen owing to the demands of the Continental war.[64]

The stakes were high. Newfoundland exported goods to the value of £1.2 million in 1815. This included codfish, salmon, cod oil and seal skins. Half the cod went to northern Europe markets, the other half to southern Europe and the Mediterranean.[65] To underscore the importance the Government placed on this matter, the 1803 Convoy Act stipulated that all ships engaged in foreign trade had to sail in convoy and ships' masters ran the risk of punishment if they sailed alone.[66]

Privateers presented a particular threat during the American war. A request for more protection made by British merchants in 1813 led Admiral Thornborough to write frustratingly to the Admiralty about the overstretch of resources, 'I have not sufficient ships in the squadron even to furnish the convoys required, much less to protect the homeward-bound trade and coast of this Kingdom from the American privateers.' The capture of eight British whaling ships, the same year, must have been particularly galling, as three of the number were later repurposed as privateers and crewed by the former whalers.[67]

Conclusion

The early examples of protection being requested by those involved with sea fishing perhaps inevitably involved remuneration. But by the end of the period covered in this chapter, Britain's fishery had assumed such importance that its health and prosperity, and particularly its workforce, was considered to be of primary importance to the nation.

It has been shown that the fisherman was essentially vulnerable not only to the elements but also from individual or organised attack.

Likewise, in the early years particularly, isolated fishing towns along the exposed east coast of England had to find the means to defend themselves from Scottish raiders or others from the near continent. The wafting, or convoying, of fishing boats became a requirement from the fifteenth century onwards because the safe passage of cargoes of preserved fish was needed in order to supplement the diet of the masses, particularly in winter.

Very gradually, the state assumed responsibility for supporting and protecting its developing fishing industry as what we now call the Royal Navy gradually assumed an organised and consistent shape. However, the financial burden was ever present; the 'ship money' method of taxation did provide a measure of cost-sharing. When this was extended to the issuing of fishing licences, the nation fell into conflict with the Dutch Republic on the other side of the North Sea.

This brought to the fore what was to become a key and a lasting conundrum. Who, if anybody, owns the sea, particularly the area adjacent to the landmass that was also most likely to be where the richest fishing grounds were located? The opposing philosophies of *mare liberum* and *mare clausum* were adopted by the Dutch Republic and Great Britain respectively and became one of the areas of contention during the Anglo-Dutch Wars and a repeated basis of international dispute over fishing rights thereafter.

Britain envied the organised and tightly regulated Dutch herring fleets and sought to disrupt the work of the large and technologically advanced busses in the North Sea and beyond. Who should or could claim jurisdiction over the waters through which herring migrated southwards each year was basically the same issue that had been raised three centuries earlier when the Danish Government tried to stop the English fishing boats and traders exploiting the waters off Iceland.

Britain's adoption of the closed sea philosophy, which suited its needs at the time, is ironic in view of its long-term championing of freedom of the seas, the stance it adopted and persisted with well into the latter half of the twentieth century. The related matter of what constituted a country's territorial waters was also contentious in the sixteenth and seventeenth centuries but, in the absence of consensus on any precise form of measurement, the matter was left in abeyance for quite some time.

The possession of a powerful Navy to support and protect trade and of an expanding worldwide empire, together with the ability to provide a fleet capable of deterring or matching rivals in time of war, was considered all important during the eighteenth century, when Britain seemed constantly 'at loggerheads' with rival Western European colonial powers. The examples given above show the logistical problem of providing the resources to protect the fishery infrastructure and the west–east trade route from the American coastline and at the same time ensuring the prosperity of the fishermen themselves who provided vital, experienced manpower when the fleet had to be expanded in time of war. This was a 'double-edged sword' as although they constituted a much better alternative to draw upon than the cruder forms of impressment, removing them from the workforce inevitably led to a depression in the fishing industry.

The reason why the phrase 'a nursery of seamen' occurs so frequently in documents in the eighteenth century can be traced, at least in part, to the fact that naval ships were largely demobilised in peacetime. 'The major navies were standing forces in that they possessed a permanent administration, a substantial infrastructure and a fleet of ships, but in time of peace few of the ships, and very few ships of the line, would be in commission.' This did not wholly apply to Britain, which retained small warships, for example maintaining a presence in the West Indies in the 1720s and in the case of Nelson in the Boreas in 1786. Commissioned officers could be retained on half pay and were free to pursue other occupations provided they did not leave the country. But the government was unable to afford to retain and pay the ordinary seaman. The demands for seafarers during the Seven Years' War and the American War of Independence were simply colossal, calculated at 130,000 and 150,000 respectively. It is small wonder, therefore, that the skilled fisherman became such a prized asset.[68]

Lastly, several of the issues, which later were to be the causes of serious international disputes during the twentieth and twenty-first centuries, can be detected as being present during the early centuries covered in this narrative. As far as the Royal Navy's role in being the primary provider of fishery protection, in terms of allocating materiel and manpower and determining its priority alongside the more eye-catching tasks undertaken by the Navy, this has proved to be an almost impossible balance to strike.

Chapter Two

Seeds of Dispute and Conflict Amidst Conventions and Accords
1815–1905

FOLLOWING THE FINAL defeat of Napoleon at the Battle of Waterloo, Britain emerged in 1815 from what historians often refer to as the 'Long Eighteenth Century' into an era of peace and prosperity both on land and at sea.¹ This was a period lasting approximately sixty years, during which the phrase *Pax Britannica* could be accurately applied – when Britain was the undisputed mistress of the oceans.² Writing at the end of the century, Admiral Vesey Hamilton described the Royal Navy as, 'that maritime arm which safeguards the kingdom from invasion, protects its food supplies and its commerce, and, as a defensive force, binds the Empire itself together'. The accent on 'defence' and 'commerce' are telling: little wonder that Hamilton emphasised maintaining the *status quo* in view of the wealth that had been accrued by the nation hitherto during the long reign of Queen Victoria.³

The country had been the first in the world to undergo an industrial revolution and was to build on that inevitable lead by adopting a policy of free trade and successfully persuading many other countries to follow suit. Linked to that was still the notion of the freedom of the seas. The repeal of the historic Navigation Acts in 1849 was a key marker, making a central part of British import strategy the lowering of the price of food through cheap foreign imports and in that way reducing the cost of maintaining labour power.

These three factors had a bearing on issues relating to fishery protection in the nineteenth century. There were a number of international agreements reached and treaties signed by the most advanced and increasingly industrialised western nations that served to advance the growth of the fishing industry. From Britain's point of view, reaching international accord helped in turn to foster free trade. Underpinning that notion, 'nineteenth-century Britain asserted a view of international law in which territorial fishery limits were confined within three miles of national shorelines'. Thus, the undisputed hegemony exercised by the Royal Navy over most of the period between the Congress of Vienna and the outbreak of the First World War meant that Britain's interpretation of the law of the sea became the accepted norm.[4]

The fact that the notion that territorial waters only applied to a narrow coastal band was left largely unchallenged was due in part to the past sufficiency of fish stocks to meet local needs. But during the course of the nineteenth century there were signs that this situation was changing, that Hugo Grotius was wrong, that fish were not a limitless resource.

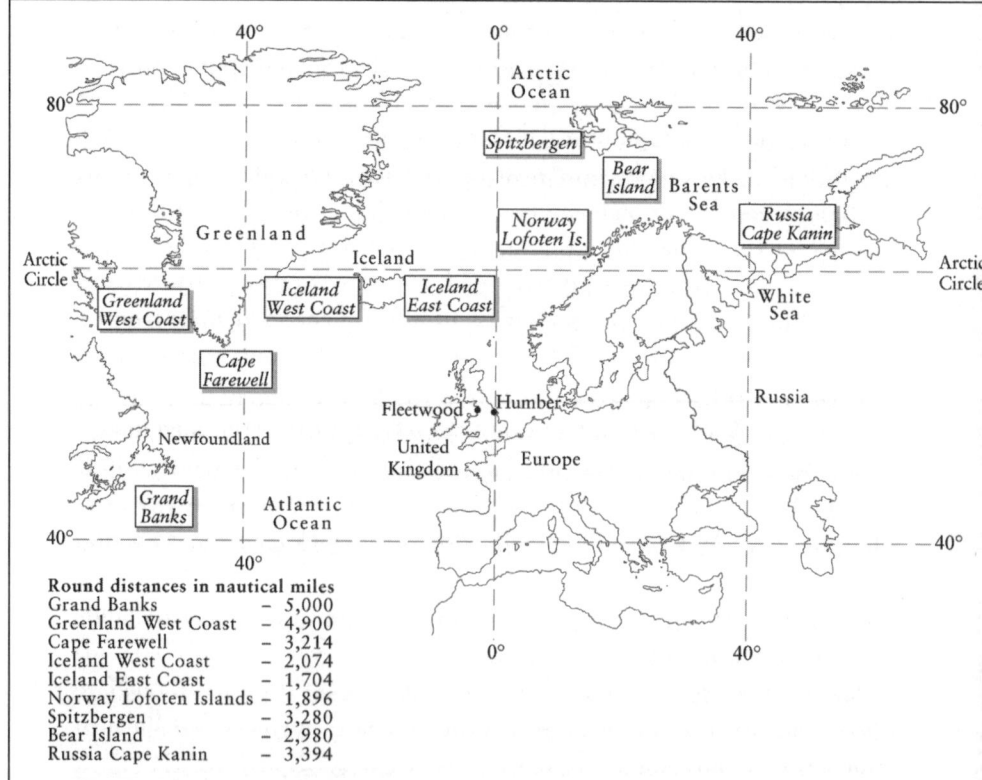

Map 1: Distant water fishing grounds. (Stephen Dent)

This chapter describes the work undertaken by what were referred to at that time as fishery protection 'cruisers' both in inshore and in distant waters – particularly on the east coast of North America. The North Sea Fisheries Convention, signed on 6 May 1882, constituted the most significant international milestone on policing a key part of the North West European continental shelf, one of the world's largest areas of shallow seas with an abundance of fish stocks.

In the meantime, and in different ways, the widening range of the railway network in Britain and the invention of the steam trawler revolutionised the country's fishing industry. 'Railways smashed the transportation bottleneck, which had long constrained the fish trade. For the first time there was a relatively cheap, as well as fast, means of conveying fresh fish from the coast to the burgeoning inland towns and cities.'[5] Similarly, admittedly late in the day, the adoption of the triple-expansion steam engine by the country's marine sector constituted a highly significant breakthrough. Steam swiftly replaced sail in trawlers; one marine scientist at the time estimated that a steam trawler was four times as efficient as a sailing smack. Additionally, these new boats carried a far greater range.[6]

However promising agreements might appear on paper or during conferences, they were not the ultimate panacea for a range of different peoples living in the northern Atlantic with contrasting traditions and practices with respect to the use of the sea. Likewise, the measures agreed by industrially advanced states did not necessarily apply to countries at very different stages of development. Nor did they automatically accommodate the attitudes of independently minded and often tight-knit fishing communities for whom, traditionally, freedom of the seas meant just that.

Therefore, especially towards the end of the period covered by this chapter, disputes and clashes began to occur. Worries about over-fishing, incursions by increasingly large and sophisticated foreign trawlers, and differing views on the delimitation of territorial waters were problems that began to be aired. These were to be the self-same issues behind the major international fishery disputes of the twentieth century, which will be described subsequently.

Administration and organisation

Before 1857, the protection of fisheries in home waters had been part of the work of H.M. Coastguard. The Coastguard had been officially formed in 1822 but by 1831 the Admiralty had been given the right to appoint officers and select boatmen from paid-off naval crews – in other words to make use of the service as a naval reserve and as a recruiting agency. The 1856 Coast Guard Agency Act removed responsibility from H.M. Customs' Controller-General and handed it to the Royal Navy. In 1874, command of the Coastguard itself passed to the Admiral Superintendent of Naval Reserves, who was to retain the commission under the auspices of the office of the Second Sea Lord until the First World War.

The duties of 'an Inspecting Commander of the Coastguard Service' had included the jurisdiction, 'to go on board any British vessel employed in fishing and examine the certificate of Registry, and the Nets, Instruments and Implements of Fishery belonging to or used with such vessel, and whether the Regulations of the Said Act have been complied with ...'.[7]

The Navy's desire to exercise control over the cohort of coastguard service men carried a different agenda than simply the need to run an efficient customs and excise operation. As in previous centuries, the Admiralty's primary aim was to maintain a reserve of experienced seamen in the event of war. Vesey Hamilton is critical of the level of efficiency of the Coastguard personnel when it was under Board of Customs control, 'The difficulty of getting good men at the time of the Russian War [Crimean War 1853–56] made the defects of this system apparent.' He adds, however, '... after the transfer to the Admiralty, the Coastguardsmen becoming a reserve of seamen of the Navy, their quality was gradually improved'.[8]

In contrast to its importance, the actual status of fishery protection in the eyes of the Navy remained fairly insignificant, as evidenced here:

> This outline of the Admiral Superintendent's instructions will show that – while exercising, in peace time, a high function of the Navy in keeping the peace and preserving the safety of the seas, in ministering to the welfare of the fisheries and the mercantile marine, and in protecting the Customs revenue of the country – he pursues the great work of preserving efficient the Naval reserves in readiness for the war needs of the State.[9]

The above assessment stands in marked contrast to the economic importance to the country of the fisheries industry, which in 1883 was estimated to be worth no less than £10 million annually. There were some influential Parliamentarians at the time who were calling for a more structured and cohesive approach to the organisation of the industry, arguing for the introduction of a centralised England and Wales Fishery Board as had been adopted by the United States, several European countries as well as by Ireland and Scotland. In a speech to the House of Commons in March 1886, Sir Edward Birkbeck identified no fewer than seven government offices connected with or responsible for the fisheries. The Admiralty, 'to which fishermen looked for protection and assistance on the sea', was mentioned as well as the Naval Reserves Office, 'which was also connected with the protection of the fisheries'. Although the official Admiralty instructions for the supervision of the North Sea Fisheries that followed on from the 1883 North Sea Fisheries Act was to bring some clarity and rationalisation to the Navy's overall role in fishery protection, it was not until after the end of the First World War that a comprehensive brief was agreed.[10]

Responding where necessary

The analogy of the policeman on the beat has remained apposite to vessels assigned to fishery protection tasks down the centuries. They patrol at sea to act as a reassuring presence, try to ensure adherence to the law and respond to crises when they occur. A typical example of the time is to be found in a Parliamentary Select Committee Report into the then current state of the British Channel Fisheries, and the Laws affecting the Fishing Trade of England, published in 1833.[11]

The Report observed that, 'a large proportion of the British Channel Fisheries, and the various interests with which they are connected' had been in decline over the previous twenty years, a decline that had accelerated in the previous decade, causing both boys and men to abandon their jobs with the result that families previously connected with the industry had become 'dependent upon the Poor-rates for support'.[12]

A major cause of the decline was stated as being, 'the extensive interference and aggressions of the French Fishermen on the coasts of Kent and Sussex; the large quantity of Foreign-caught fish illegally imported and sold in the London Market; and the great decrease and comparative scarcity of Fish in the Channel'. It was noted that, for many years, large fishing fleets from Calais, Boulogne, Dieppe and other French ports had been accustomed to working close to the English coastline, 'frequently within half a league of the Shore, and occasionally much nearer'. These fleets, now estimated to number between 200–300 boats from Boulogne alone, were both greater in tonnage and carried larger and heavier nets and gear than their English equivalents. Constant competition, especially during the busy herring and mackerel seasons, was causing damage and consequent loss of livelihood. The relevant part of the Parliamentary Report concluded that the RN protection cruisers should be instructed to deter foreign fishing boats from encroaching too close to the shoreline and to deter any aggression shown towards British fishermen.[13]

Three years later, a Bill was introduced to Parliament calling for better protection for the fisheries in England and Wales. Captain Pechell reminded the House of Commons that, some eighteen years previously, a Bill had been brought in that warned about the decrease in fish in the English Channel. This had been 'lost' at the third reading and when it was renewed in 1822 it had passed through the Commons but was rejected in the House of Lords.

Ever since, Pechell claims, there had been constant aggression from the French boats, who were in the habit of taking young fish that by French laws would have been banned from catching in their own waters, 'great destruction of the brood and spawn takes place by trawl and ground nets during the breeding season'. He hoped that the recommendations of the Parliamentary Committee of 1833, referred to above, would be heeded. Regarding the provision of naval protection for the English fishermen, Pechell commented, 'although it had been refused by one Board of Admiralty, had, he rejoiced to say, been granted by another …'.[14]

It is clear from the above that there was no organised or pre-arranged system of protection at the time. The Navy, and in this case Customs and Excise, had to be called upon to intervene. Moreover, there appeared still to be uncertainty about what constituted territorial waters. There is a telling footnote in the Report that points to a lack of clarity and knowledge about the law and the absence of international agreement, 'The Committee understand that one league from the shore out to sea is considered to be the territory of the adjoining country, which seems to be asserted by the French and the Dutch, and is acted upon by our Custom-house in their grant of Licenses to go within that distance of foreign coasts.'

It was to take a very long time for any form of international settlement to be agreed. A bilateral agreement regarding the regulation of fisheries in the Channel seemed to have been reached with the French some thirty-four years later. The 1867 Anglo-French Convention informed part of the British Sea Fisheries Act the following year. It included a section relating to a reciprocal arrangement concerning the boarding of vessels either by French or English fishery officers. Unfortunately, corresponding legislation was not passed in France and the Act proved, a 'dead letter' as far as fishermen and French fishing boats were concerned.[15] It was to take a further fourteen years for a workable international agreement to be reached.

The coming of steam power

George Stephenson opened the first public inter-city railway in Britain in 1830, the Liverpool and Manchester Railway, using a steam locomotive to haul carriages with passengers on a public railway. The railways then expanded exponentially during the 1840s. When the decade began, lines in Britain were few and scattered but, within ten years, virtually a complete network had been laid down connecting the vast majority of towns and villages.

The first railway link with Grimsby, for example, was achieved in 1848 and less than a decade later the Manchester, Sheffield and Lincolnshire Railway financed the construction of the first fish dock and later actively encouraged a new influx of fishing smack owners by building twenty-five new houses especially for fishermen. Further improvements made to the dock area helped to increase productivity and brought about the development of ancillary businesses such as specialised ship brokers, marine insurance agents and exchanges for the hiring and selling of ships.[16]

The 1851 Census showed for the first time that the urban population of Britain had outstripped the rural one. This shift in the demographic meant that the cities and towns required substantial amounts of inexpensive and nutritional food. Fish was sufficient to provide this commodity and could be sourced straight and quickly from the quayside via the newly established rail network. Getting the fish to market in as fresh a condition as possible was key. The concept of 'fleeting', with fishing smacks working together, supported by fast cutters used to collect the catch and ferry it ashore, had been in use for some time. In the 1870s, 'box-fleeting' was introduced in Hull, which meant that individual fishing boats sorted their catches into personalised boxes on board and these were then transported to market, enabling the ensuing revenue to be credited to the correct owner.[17] This provided a further incentive that helped to grow the industry, although the practice of fleeting in the winter months was abhorred by the fishermen.

Steam also revolutionised the fishing boat. During the 1840s, the majority of white fish was caught off the British coasts using the baited hook and line method. By the 1870s most were being brought ashore by trawlers.[18] Initially, these were wooden-hulled sailing boats but, by the early 1880s, they were being rapidly replaced by steel-hulled vessels fitted with triple-expansion steam engines.[19]

The output from the triple-expansion engines was also harnessed to operate powerful deck winches and wire rather than rope warps was used to haul the trawl. By the following decade the more efficient and manoeuvrable 'otter trawl' was being widely deployed.

The wide mouth of one of these nets was kept open by a pair of otter boards – otherwise known as kites – which stretched it apart when dragged through the water. This system not only made the trawl a far more efficient fish-catching contraption, it also offered many possibilities for adaptation and development that were to prove useful in sectors outside fishing.[20]

An abundance of cheap coal meant that steam trawlers were economic to run and also had a longer range. However, the growth in the numbers of fishing boats working the North Sea had a negative impact on fish stocks and these two factors led to British trawlers venturing further afield. In 1889, British fishermen, 'first experimented with a beam trawl in Icelandic waters. Although British, Dutch and French had fished in those distant waters a long time before, this particular departure was to have long-lasting consequences.'[21]

The North Sea Fisheries Convention 1882

An historic landmark was established in the early 1880s when an agreement was reached about the policing of international waters by the countries surrounding the North Sea. The treaty titled 'The International Convention for regulating the Police of the North Sea Fisheries Outside Territorial Waters' was signed May 1882. The conference that preceded it was aimed at agreeing a set of regulations that would govern the conduct of the North Sea fisheries. The signatories included Great Britain, Germany, Denmark, Netherlands, Belgium and France, which entered the convention for an initial period of five years.

Before that, pressure to reach an international agreement had been growing for some time. The Board of Trade (BoT) had been lobbying the Foreign Office with accounts of clashes that had taken place in the North Sea between British and French, Dutch and Belgian fishing boats. Calls were made for the Royal Navy to be directly involved, not for the first time, 'the Board of Trade have suggested to the Lords Commissioners of the Admiralty the expediency of occasionally sending a cruizer (sic) from time to time to the spots where fishing is being carried on by foreign as well as British Fishermen with a view to the preservation of order'.[22]

Some incidents involved the loss of valuable gear, others included the use of threatening and dangerous behaviour shown by the fishermen. One such example began with what appeared to be an accidental tangling of nets between the Grimsby smack *Henry & Lydia* on 3 September 1879 and a Dutch boat (later identified as the *Anna Margaretha*). The skipper of the smack, Joseph Spooner, alleged that he had tried to avoid a collision by keeping his vessel 'sheared off'. His account continued, 'The Dutchman however, hauled in his gear until he could reach the warp of our vessel, when he could do so, he dropped a grappling under the warp, which became fast, and then he hauled our warp to his (the Dutchman's) rail, and cut it in two with an adze.' Spooner claimed that all his boat's gear had been lost, together with 25 fathoms of warp that he valued at £40 – plus the loss of eight days' work. When the two boats had disentangled, the *Henry & Lydia*'s skipper sailed round the Dutch vessel to try to ascertain its name, number and homeport. This provoked the Dutch skipper to pick up a gun and point it at Spooner in a threatening manner.[23]

Another account passed on to BoT by the Lowestoft Collector of Customs the same autumn described a far more dangerous occurrence. The Lowestoft herring drift trawler *Jessamine* had been working at night when he alleged he had been 'trawled into' by the Boulogne boat 'Alance Lorraine' (later identified as *Alsace Lorraine*)', which had 'H.O.7' marked on its starboard bow but no identifiable name or number. The *Jessamine*'s skipper had fired a flare to illuminate the *Alsace Lorraine*. This move prompted the incident to turn ugly, 'the stranger cut from trawl directly, fired a double volley, wounding three of the "Jessamine's" crew, Gorad (sic) Thacker and Simon Kirk, both conveyed to Lowestoft Infirmary, the former said to be very badly wounded, the shots in question also striking James Flint, another of

Jessamine's crew, lodging one shot in his right shoulder, and another in his left.'

Later the same year, reports of a net-cutting tool, appropriately nicknamed 'The Devil' by the British fishing boat crews, prompted calls for the protection vessels to have the right to board foreign boats suspected of carrying the implement. It led to a petition to the BoT by the Lowestoft owners, which included some testimonies from skippers purporting to have seen the 'Devil'. The instrument, purportedly used by Dutch and Belgian fishermen, consisted of a metal object that was hung at the bows of the trawler, and was used to cut through the drift net of British trawlers, which subsequently lost their equipment.

Some of the eyewitness reports were dramatically recounted, such as the account of the master of the lugger *Alliance* when he was invited on board an Ostend trawler in the company of another Lowestoft fisherman:

> That on going below I saw lying on the cabin seat a peculiar bright instrument but at the time did not know what it was, but almost immediately afterwards one of the crew came into the cabin and said something to the Master in their language which I did not understand, and at once covered the said instrument with an oily cloth. That when we left the said smack my companion asked me if I noticed the 'thing' they covered up and whether I knew what it was, when I replied I did but did not know what it was he then told me it was a 'Devil', he having seen one before.[24]

Accusations from both sides of the North Sea continued to be made during 1880 and 1881, leading to various exchanges of notes between the Foreign Ministers of the respective governments. Each of the claims seemed to have been followed up faithfully by legal departments but it was clear that action was needed.

Eventually, the North Sea Fisheries Convention of 1882 was to confront the matter of policing of the North Sea both inside and outside territorial waters. The wording of the Convention document was to stipulate that inside territorial waters the fishermen of the respective countries had exclusive rights to fish from the low-water mark to 3 miles across their entire coastline. In the case of bays and other inlets, the 3-mile boundary would be measured from a straight line drawn across the bay, in the part nearest the entrance, at the first point where the width did not exceed 10 miles. Freedom of navigation and anchorage within those territorial waters was to be granted to any of the signatories provided they adhered to local regulations. Significantly, not every European country on the western fringes of continental Europe automatically agreed to the 3-mile territorial delimitation. Sweden and Norway adhered to a Scandinavian tradition of 4 miles.[25]

The Admiralty produced a set of instructions for the supervision and protection of fishing fleets in the North Sea following on from the 1882 Convention and the 1883 Sea Fisheries Act. The 'gunboats and cruisers', selected by the Admiral Superintendent of Naval Reserves, would be under the command of a senior officer in charge of all matters concerning fishery duties:

> The Senior Officer in Charge will exercise a careful supervision over the cruisers, and distribute the vessels placed at his disposal in the manner best adapted to ensure the efficient protection of the Fisheries and Revenue. He will also himself cruise in the ship he Commands wherever it may appear to him that her presence will be most helpful, keeping the Admiral Superintendent informed by every opportunity of his proposed movements.[26]

The Senior Officer (SO) was also charged with liaising with local Fishery Associations and fishermen. A steam vessel would be provided in order to maintain communication with the mainland. The SO would also arrange for the cruisers under his command to be afforded regular relief in recognition of the arduous nature of the duty. The Scottish Fishery Board would be subject to different arrangements.

The Convention had fixed the geographical limits of the North Sea area. The entire UK coastline was divided into 'districts', with a 'District Captain' placed in charge for dealing with local arrangements and byelaws. All fishery cruisers were to be issued with copies of the 1884 edition of the Sea Fisheries Manual. The unique nature of the herring fishery, with its seasonal migratory pattern, was given special note; it was recognised that additional protection vessels would be required in order to supervise the large number of fishing boats attracted by the abundant shoals of herring in the area during the season.[27]

This set of regulations can be seen as a blueprint for the way in which fishery protection was to be organised and administered over the next century. The major difference would come with the extension of the coverage to include middle- and distant-water trawling as fishing vessels became larger with commensurately greater endurance.

The tone of the instructions is worthy of note. The accent is on harmonious co-operation with European neighbours rather than confrontation. Commanding officers were reminded that they were to exercise caution at all times when dealing with foreign fishing vessels, 'so as to avoid any appearance of harshness in their manner of enforcing due observance of the Sea Fisheries Acts and Conventions'. For example, foreign fishing vessels boarded were only expected to produce evidence of their nationality.[28]

Inevitably though, there were contraventions of the Act, some intentional and of serious note, others perhaps excusable. For example, the fishing vessel *Brilliant* was caught not exhibiting its lights off Yarmouth in October 1891. The skipper wrote in explanation:

> Sir, In answer to the above I beg to state that at the time mentioned the wind coming on bad we were busy reefing as soon as we got everything all snug we got our lights up as soon as possible.
> I am Sir, Your obedient Servant, William Fish.[29]

Others carried more serious consequences for the smooth running of the 1882 international accord. An announcement in the *London Gazette* in October 1892 provided a reminder of the expected conduct of British fishing vessels while in Belgian territorial waters. The national flag had to be flown and all fishing gear and implements stowed inboard. Belgian rules regarding lights, signals, marks, navigation and anchorage had to be observed. There were to be no obstructions to navigation at the entrances of harbours. Finally, Belgian regulations on the sizes of fish caught had to be followed.[30]

Damage to fishing gear, with the related replacement costs, was inevitably considered a serious matter, especially in cases where foreign vessels were involved. On 31 December 1890 a claim was made on behalf of the Emden Herring Fishery that the nets of two German fishing vessels had been damaged on 19 October of that year. It was alleged that a large English trawling fleet had 'worked over the grounds' near Silver Pits (an area of the North Sea adjacent to the Dogger Bank) where the German boats had set their nets. Losses of equipment were estimated at 17,610 German marks or £880. Further damage to two German drifters on 24–25 October was made at the same time but, on that occasion, there was no firm evidence of British nationality.[31]

Subsequently, a claim was received on 19 January 1892 by a Dutch solicitor regarding damage sustained by seven Dutch fishing vessels, again by British trawlers, that had occurred on the night of 17 October the previous year. There was an obvious link. In the case of the German allegation, however, there was no substantial evidence other than a claim that the offending boats were recognised as English 'from their rig and build'.[32]

The Dutch claim, on the other hand, was much stronger. Remnants of nets were picked up that helped the British Inspector of Fisheries to identify four trawlers that were in the vicinity at the time. They belonged to the Short Blue Fleet of Messrs Hewett of Yarmouth. Subsequently some thirty witnesses representing eighteen vessels were examined. The investigations were exhaustive and scrupulous. Possible evidence of criminality was only established in the case of one trawler, the *Mary Gowland*. Its skipper admitted passing through some nets but stated that there was no evidence as to whom they belonged. He could not identify any of the fishing smacks nearby, owing to, 'the thickness of the night'.

Solicitors acting for the Board of Trade and the Sea Fishery Officers concluded that, on the night in question, some Short Blue Fleet trawlers had passed through the nets of some of the Dutch fleet. The night had been dark and stormy; only the *Mary Gowland* could be positively identified. They judged that unless the Dutch and German lawyers could produce further information, there was insufficient evidence to proceed with compensation claims.[33]

There were claims made against the behaviour of foreign fishing boats on both sides of the North Sea. In the course of, to modern minds, a rather histrionically titled debate in the House of Commons in August 1887 titled 'Outrages by Belgian on English Fishing Vessels', Sir Edward Birkbeck asked the Secretary of the Board of Trade to comment on whether the Fisheries Department had managed to bring any pressure on the Admiralty, 'to establish a much more efficient system of protection than had been the case in the past for English drift-net fishing vessels within the limits of the North Sea Fisheries Convention, and also for the protection of English trawling fleets within the same area, with a view of guarding against a repetition of last season's losses and cases similar to the capture of the Grimsby smack *Lady Godiva* off the German coast'.[34]

Five years later, the same Member of Parliament raised the matter of the, 'destruction of nets belonging to the Lowestoft fishing vessel

Afghan on the 13th (March 1892) by an Ostend trawler, entailing a loss of £40 to the owner besides the loss of the night's fishing'. He then asked the Admiralty's representative whether he would, 'give orders that the cruisers on fishery protection duty be instructed to keep more on the fishing grounds for the future, and where depredations are likely to take place'. The First Lord of the Admiralty replied that, 'Two cruisers were on the fishing grounds at the time, and a constant and vigilant watch is kept; but with every precaution it is not possible to prevent an occasional act of depredation over such a large area as the North Sea.'[35]

Incidents like those described above often highlighted the difficulties faced by the authorities in prosecuting transgressors. They also rarely occurred in bright daylight conditions with pin-sharp visibility. Were the fishery protection cruisers dilatory in their duties? The Admiralty investigated the Dutch 1891–92 claim on behalf of the Board of Trade. Commander Russell of HMS *Hearty* informed the Admiral Naval Reserve that the cruisers that had been with the trawl fleets during the summer had been withdrawn around 15 September from the Dogger Bank, Botney Gat and Silver Pits area. This had been customary practice. As the First Lord of the Admiralty pointed out, it was the age-old problem of it being impossible to ensure that the protection vessels would always be in the right place at the right time.[36]

Latent suasion[37] *off the east coast of America*

By the late 1820s the rich fishing grounds off the east coast of America and Canada were not the 'battlegrounds' described in the previous chapter. However, the so-called 'War of 1812,' which had seen the nascent United States invade Canada and attack British ships, was still rich in the memory. The 1820s was a period of relative harmony between the two countries, due indirectly to the effects of the Monroe Doctrine of 1823. Andrew Lambert takes the 'long view', '… its outcome (the war of 1812) was decided by the failure of the American army to conquer Canada, the defeat of American attacks on British merchant shipping and a devastating British economic blockade that left America bankrupt and insolvent'. It is little wonder therefore that Lambert refers to the nineteenth century as a period when America showed repeated antagonism towards Britain.[38]

The instructions handed to the commanding officer of HM Sloop *Champion* in 1829 by the C-in-C North America and Newfoundland

Stations provides a perfect example at the time of Britain's unrivalled naval supremacy in action:

> You are required and directed to proceed to the coast of Newfoundland, where you are to cruize (sic) for the protection of the fisheries, and the prevention of illicit trade, attending to my instruction in the executions of their services. In your way, you will shew [sic] yourself off the Mingan Islands [an archipelago east of Quebec consisting of about 40 islands] and then make Cape Ray [a headland at the south west extremity of Newfoundland] calling at some of the harbours as you pafs (sic) along the coast as far as St. John's, where you will place yourself under the orders of Sir Richard Grant.[39]

These orders, for HMS *Champion* to provide fishery protection for the forthcoming season, are composed with the confidence of a nation with total command of the sea, even in the febrile atmosphere of the North American coast at the time. The instructions to 'shew yourself' on the Canadian shoreline at the Mingan Islands and Cape Ray, would have been to provide assurances for the understandably nervous local population, while the calls at harbours 'as you pafs along the coast' fulfilled both a 'showing the flag' function and an opportunity to gather naval intelligence. Although the sloop's primary purpose was to support the fishermen and to counter illicit trade, *Champion* was also to be made available for other work, such as hydrography, under the instructions of the local commander. Thus the ship undertook a multirole function of which fishery protection formed just a part.

This perception of a generally relaxed yet busy fishery on the North American shoreline, under the benign guardianship of the Royal Navy, does not reconcile with that of William Speiden aboard USS *Mississippi*. On 31 August 1852 his frigate met with what he describes in his journal as a 'delapidated (sic)' English fishing vessel. The encounter, he relates, 'convinces me what a small interest the English take in the fisheries on the North Eastern coast of America'. Speiden further complains that the English had jurisdiction over the fishing grounds but were unwilling to share. He ends, 'Our fishermen who are industrious and enterprising, thinking that that was not the right way to act, intruded on their grounds ... were captured and sold and thus created the fishing difficulties now so much talked of.'[40]

Two factors determined that relationships with the United States had deteriorated by the late 1860s. Firstly, during the American Civil War, 1861–65, the Confederacy had tried desperately to persuade both Britain and France to recognise it as a sovereign state. Britain maintained a neutral stance, however, despite various incidents to do with enforcement that caused great friction both during and in the aftermath of the conflict.[41] The other factor was the economy. Britain had, by the middle of the century, adopted a policy of free trade, as noted earlier, while the US, whose economy, like Germany's, was rapidly catching up and would overtake Britain's in the late nineteenth century, relied heavily on high tariff barriers. This did not please the British Government.

These matters informed the background to instructions given for H.M. vessels employed on protection duties in the North American fisheries in the period 1866–69. Despite the tensions, the fishery protection (FP) vessels were instructed to carry out their duties, 'in a spirit of conciliation'. The commanders were further informed that they were to, 'use the utmost temper and forbearance compatible with the duty entrusted to you'. United States fishing vessels were to be given one warning if they transgressed.[42]

Since the abrogation of a Reciprocity Treaty with the United States, a system of granting fishing licences on payment of a small fee had prevailed. The instruction to approach duties in a tactful and accommodating manner no doubt stemmed from the delicate diplomatic situation that existed at the time. Faced with the ending of the British Corn Laws, tariffs on food imported to Britain were repealed in 1846. There was lobbying from Canadian businessmen to annex Upper Canada to the United States – unless Britain negotiated a free trade deal. They achieved what they wanted in 1854 with the Elgin-Macey Treaty. In return, the Americans were granted fishing rights off the east coast in payment.

The instructions for the protection vessels did emphasise the need to learn about and track the movements of the American fishing boats. Otherwise they were directed to acquaint themselves with the local fishermen, to gather intelligence and to gain knowledge of the geography of the region. Interestingly, there was a call to cruise as much as possible under sail, although fires were to be kept banked in order to respond to an emergency by steam power.[43]

Relationships with the US improved towards the end of the century. Three ships were employed on FP duties in 1881, and the relevant documents of the period, together with enclosures describing their cruises, were sent to the C-in-C American Station. The Senior Officer afloat, Captain Kennedy in HMS *Druid*, reported on the fishing season April–October 1881. His notes include the places he visited on his cruise, the types of fish that were being caught – principally cod, herring, caplin and salmon – and the size of the catches. His remarks also referred to comments about the villages and towns that the *Druid* visited. In the eighteenth century fishing in the region had been carried out largely by migratory fishermen, as described in the previous chapter. In contrast, in the nineteenth century, the area was peopled by settlers whose existence was never guaranteed in a harsh and sometimes dangerous environment. Thus, Kennedy found the community in Fortune Bay, Newfoundland, in a pitiful state, 'The people at Harbour Briton have had a poor winter's fishing, and are very poor, many families receiving Government relief. No American vessels have arrived as yet for [fish] bait.' In contrast, however, Belloram was, 'a snug little place and a thriving settlement ... no Americans here, all quiet, no complaints'.[44]

In June the following year, it was found that a forest fire had devastated the Hall's Bay community, prompting Captain Kennedy to remark, 'several poor families were left homeless, and utterly destitute. Our arrival was a god-send.' HMS *Druid*, in naval time-honoured fashion, set about a programme of disaster relief.

Captain Kennedy's general summary of the fishing season concluded that the catches had varied in quantity, with plenty of cod and caplin but herring and salmon had been scarce. On the other hand, the cod fishery had been above average except on Labrador, where it was down in size by about a third. The weather generally had been cold, wet and stormy.

Reports by the other two vessels assigned to the duties varied; HMS *Fantome*'s, for example, consisted principally of a hydrography report, which reflects the additional undertakings expected of these vessels.

By 1886 the desired state of peaceful co-existence on the American seaboard seemed to have been achieved. The report by Captain John Masterman of HMS *Bullfrog* highlights the good relationship that had been forged with the French. Again there are comments about the size of the catches around Newfoundland – cod, herring, caplin and salmon again providing the main headings. However, the 1886 had been, 'almost as bad a season for the fishing on the North west coast of Newfoundland as the last'. Conversely, it had been 'fairly good' off Labrador. Caplin and salmon had been scarce but the three lobster factories had prospered. In contrast to a thriving home market that treasured the fish, 'Herring have been plentiful at many places towards the latter end of the season but there is no market for them and the trades refuse to take them so they have not been much fished except for bait.'[45]

A long shadow

Although the signing of the North Sea Fisheries Convention might have held the prospect of a new era of international harmony in local waters, this was not to be the case across the wider north-east Atlantic region. In the less developed countries on the periphery of the continent, such as Norway and the remoter reaches of northern Russia, there still existed quite primitive communities. Likewise, on island groups further west such as the Faroe Islands and Iceland, there was the absence of a developed fishing industry, and yet a dependence on the sea and fishing as a traditional and vital source of protein.

Iceland had become involved in dried cod exports as early as the late thirteenth century, with Norway facilitating the trade though Bergen (as was shown in Chapter One). After fluctuations in the fishing industry, particularly in the eighteenth century, the fisheries enjoyed a revival and expansion in the later part of the nineteenth century. Fishing was still undertaken in open boats for much of the century, although decked sailing boats were gradually introduced together with the deployment of longlines rather than handlines. However, despite the resurgence, it could not hope to match the technologically more capable steam trawlers that started to appear off the coasts of the island in the last decades of the nineteenth century.[46]

There were historic, cultural differences that existed between the Icelandic fishermen and the increasingly sophisticated industrial nations that had recently signed the North Seas Convention, 'Icelandic fishermen were often part-time subsistence farmers. Their market was small and mainly domestic. ... For Icelanders, the fishing grounds off the coast were an extension of the land, over which they had an exclusive right of ownership, while for distant-water fishermen the same fishing grounds were part of the free seas, which could be utilized by anybody.'[47]

When the union between Denmark and Norway was abrogated as a result of the Treaty of Kiel in 1814, Denmark had retained possession of the Faroe Islands, along with Greenland and Iceland. Despite both being signatories to the Convention, friction between Britain and Denmark over their colonies had been growing for some considerable time.

In 1870, the British Foreign Office had received a complaint from the Danish Government via their minister in London that, 'crews of certain fishing vessels' had plundered a French vessel that had been wrecked on the Icelandic coast. The official note also called on the British Government, less specifically, to investigate the 'Faroe Island Fishery question'. In response, the Admiralty despatched HMS *Valorous* two years later to cruise around both Iceland and the Faroes. Captain Thrupp's subsequent Report of Proceedings concluded that the complaints did not appear to be well-founded.[48]

Another complaint from the Danish Government was received five years later. It seemed that fishing boats had landed in Icelandic ports and their skippers had not immediately reported their arrival to the civic authorities. The ship's articles needed to be endorsed and a harbour tonnage fee paid. On this occasion, the BoT placed a note in Lloyd's List reminding skippers of the regulations governing their conduct within foreign territorial waters.[49] Although the matters described above might appear to be minor, they demonstrate a determination on the part of the Danish Government not to be subjected to the will of the most powerful nation in the world.

The imminent introduction of the steam trawler only served to exacerbate the problem. It encouraged Hull and Grimsby owners in particular to look to exploit fishing opportunities further afield in the North Atlantic as their vessels gained capability in terms of size and power and were thus more suited to longer journeys. The Faroe Islands and Iceland were considered particularly attractive regions for exploitation.

In the 1890s, the Danish government claimed a fishing limit of 13 miles around the shores of the islands. Denmark had been a signatory of the North Sea Fisheries Convention in 1882, which had agreed on a 3-mile fishing delimitation although the agreement only was intended to last five years. But this was not the North Sea. Unsurprisingly, the trawlermen refused to recognise this new limit, continued to fish and were consequently intercepted by Danish gunboats. Their boats were escorted to Icelandic ports, the catch often confiscated and the skippers fined. There were periodic calls for the Royal Navy to intervene but despite a show of force in 1896 and again the following year, no consistent presence in the area was maintained.

Several incidents occurred in 1899 that threatened to fuel an atmosphere of bitterness and resentment between the fishermen, the Danish authorities and the British Government in particular, which was perceived as having neglected the interests of the long-distance trawlermen. That relationships at a governmental level remained cordial was due to the fact that these were near neighbours with practically no history of animosity or rivalry.

Nevertheless, it was reported in the House of Commons on 20 April that the Hull trawler S/T *Iolanthe* had been fishing in company with two others off the south coast of Iceland on 27 March 1899 when the boat was arrested, taken into the capital Reykjavik, and the skipper charged with encroaching to within 2¾ miles from the nearest point of land. He protested that he was a long way outside the limit and received the backing of the other trawlers that had accompanied him. Nevertheless he was fined, his gear confiscated and his catch destroyed. He was required to sign a paper admitting his guilt otherwise his vessel would be detained. All this had taken place on board the Danish gunboat, not in a court of law ashore.

A second incident had occurred on 10 April the same year when the Grimsby-based S/T *Corvos* was apprehended while navigating a fjord in the Faroe Islands and escorted into the port of Tórshavn. Again a charge of illegal fishing was laid but this time it appeared that the evidence had been brought by, 'some shore men who were in a small boat', not the gunboat commander, who had not sighted the *Corvos*.[50] According to the trawler skipper, he was advised to plead guilty otherwise the fine imposed would be increased heavily and if he did not pay his boat would be sold.

The most serious incident occurred in the same month when the Grimsby trawler S/T *Caspian* was fishing, again off the Faroe Islands, and a Danish gunboat attempted to arrest it for working within the declared limit. According to one version of events, the *Caspian* refused to stop when ordered to and blank shots were then fired by the gunboat followed by live shells. A pursuit followed of the kind that was to become all too familiar during the twentieth century. Twice the trawler tried to cut across the bows of the gunboat before eventually stopping. But before going aboard the Danish ship, the trawler's skipper Johnson called to his brother, the second hand, to 'make a dash for it'. Another chase ensued, more shots were fired but this time the gunboat could not match the speed of the trawler, which eventually limped back to Grimsby riddled with holes.

Meanwhile, aboard the gunboat, it was alleged that the Danish crew thought that Johnson was about to assault their captain and, as a safety measure, lashed the trawler skipper to the mast! A court at Tórshavn, the capital of the Faroe Islands, convicted Johnson on several counts including illegal fishing and attempted assault. He was sentenced to thirty days imprisonment and a strict, bread and water diet was imposed. The same account stated that, 'a colleague visited him in jail and reported that his condition as being reduced almost to a skeleton'.[51]

The other version of the *Caspian* incident, reported in the House of Commons, is broadly similar but differs in some details and takes a very different stance with respect to the response of the government of the day. The Under Secretary of State for Foreign Affairs St John Brodrick, stated that Skipper Johnson, 'whether within territorial waters or not, was seriously to blame'. Brodrick asserted that Johnson, when ordered to stop, had sailed on at full speed, and had twice threatened to ram the gunboat by turning towards its beam in order to make it slacken its speed. He had then given the order to his brother to make his escape. The Under Secretary of State concluded that while everything possible had been done for Johnson in court in mitigation, 'unless some facts transpire which are not at present known, it does not appear a case for the intervention of Her Majesty's Government'.[52]

Eventually, pressure to take action was brought on the Admiralty by the Foreign Office (FO) to despatch a protection vessel to the region. The Sea Fisheries Protection Agency had lobbied the FO, claiming that Danish gunboats had harassed British trawlers, 'near their imaginary limits'. The Foreign Office, writing to the Secretary of the Admiralty, claimed that some fifty or more trawlers had been seized and fined. The Secretary of State had concluded that it was a matter of urgency for the RN to despatch one or more warships to Icelandic and Faroese waters in order to safeguard the interests of the fishermen and to arbitrate in matters of dispute.[53]

The Admiralty, rather inexplicably, seemed reluctant to acquiesce, requesting that the Navy should be 'energetically seconded' by the FO. Nevertheless, HMS *Galatea* was sent to the region with orders to render support and advice to the fishermen, to remind them of their obligations to observe national territorial limits and to monitor any arrests and seizures of equipment.[54]

The ship's commander, Captain Cross, wrote a very detailed account of his voyage on his return. He reported that British fishermen had only begun to work in Faroese waters in any numbers the previous year. There were no fish close inshore so the islanders tended to work 6 to 10 miles offshore. They used traditional longlines. Tensions had occurred when these had become tangled with the British trawlers' gear. In contrast to the 'flashpoint' that had occurred during the S/T *Caspian* incident described above, Captain Cross found, during a series of discussions with Captain Brastrup, commander of the Danish cruiser KDM *Heimdal*, and authorities ashore, an acceptance that problems would occur when fishermen were working the same waters. The Faroese buoys, used to mark their lines, would not be visible in poor weather or at night. However, Cross reported that the recent Danish ruling that prevented the British trawlermen from taking shelter inshore during bad weather except in a real emergency was a genuine source of discontent – with which the captain was in agreement.

HMS *Galatea*'s CO found the atmosphere in Iceland much improved from the tensions that had prompted the show of force by the RN in 1896 and 1897, as mentioned above. He also discussed with Captain Brastrup another recent controversial incident, the pursuit and arrest of the trawler *Fulmar*. Captain Cross concluded his report, 'I would state that in my opinion the owners and skippers of English steam trawlers have no just cause for complaint against the local or Danish naval authorities.'[55]

HMS *Galatea* was succeeded on station by HMS *Blonde*. Commander Dare's report of his deployment seems to draw similar conclusions as Captain Cross had made regarding the situation in the local area as opposed to what had been reported at home in the press and in Parliament. He remarked that, 'The poaching by our trawlers is carried on in the most barefaced and determined manner, and the Heimdal is unable to cope with them as she is watched round the coast, and the trawlers close in behind her.'

Dare also reported that the Icelandic Parliament had recently passed a law, expected to be ratified by Denmark, banning Icelandic fishermen from trafficking with foreign trawlers. He gave an example of a local farmer who had allegedly made over £1,000 the previous year by obtaining cod from the fishermen. 'This farmer ... owns a smack and he frequently boards our trawlers and shews the masters where to fish inside the limit, taking the catch of cod as payment and giving them Spirits and Tobacco.' He continued ' ... often large quantities of these cod fish are thrown overboard, as the masters of the trawlers will not give them stowage room, their aim being to load with flat fish, this will now be more frequently the case and a large amount of food will be lost to the poor Icelanders who have a hard struggle to make both ends meet'.[56]

For its part, the Danish Government felt its actions in arresting and fining British vessels had been misrepresented. When the FO investigated the matter, the Minister for Foreign Affairs told a representative of the British Legation in Copenhagen he agreed and that the British public were being misled with tales of arrest and condemnation of fishermen being carried out by the Danes.[57]

The century ended with the Royal Navy withdrawing its ships from Icelandic waters for the winter. Indeed, HMS *Blonde* had had to be replaced anyway in September because of a defective boiler that had prevented it from catching up and identifying one or more of the recalcitrant British poachers. The Foreign Office turned down a request from the Hull fishing vessel owners for the Navy to remain on station over winter with the promise that they might return in spring 1900.

Similar, fairly basic living conditions to those on Iceland and the Faroes existed on the fringes of the Barents Sea in the far north-west of the Russian Empire. The harsh weather of the Kola Peninsula and its surrounds precluded extensive agriculture, with a growing season limited to around three months. The indigenous Sámi population of the province numbered just 2,070, according to the all-Russia general census of 1907, and traditionally it had looked to the sea for sustenance. However, the coastal fisheries were backward in method. Rowing boats and sailing vessels were still in use as they had been for centuries.

Two factors were at play that were to become the cause of unrest on the Murmansk coast during the 1860s. Firstly, there had been a number of incidents of Norwegian fishermen being mistreated while seeking shelter on the Russian shore. In 1866 the Governor of the Archangel region instructed his fishing inspectors to ban Norwegian fishermen from working 'close to the Russian coast'. The Norwegians ignored the instruction and the following year the Russians commissioned a patrol boat to enforce a 3-mile exclusion zone.[58]

The second, linked issue concerned the lack of clarity over what the Russians considered to be their territorial waters. The country's Rules on Prize Law of 1869 stated that they governed, 'waters within cannon shot of shore batteries or extending from shore to a distance of three nautical miles'. However, the separate Statutes on Maritime Prizes of

1898 and 1914 omitted references to territorial waters, leaving an exact definition open to debate. The repercussions of this matter, and a further unilateral declaration of a 12-mile delimitation in 1909, were to lead to the seizure of the British trawler *Onward Ho* by a Russian cruiser the following year.[59] Friction between the British and the Russians over the fisheries was to worsen considerably during the first half of the next century.

Conclusion

Britain was the leading industrialised nation through much of the nineteenth century with a vast empire and a Navy powerful enough in 1889 to be able to adopt a two-power standard as part of the Naval Defence Act.[60] Sea fishing became more industrialised and sophisticated: the introduction of 'fleeting' and the expansion of the railways brought goods to the market both quickly and efficiently, while the introduction of the steam trawler was nothing short of revolutionary. Fish consumption rose among most sectors of the population, accompanied by the introduction of the highly popular fried fish and chip trade.[61]

Britain's distant-water fishing interests off the eastern coast of Canada enjoyed a century of comparative harmony that can be perceived as a model example of total 'command of the sea' in action. The Royal Navy also progressively assumed full responsibility for fishery protection in home waters, a task previously shared with the Coastguard. The signing of the international North Sea Fisheries Convention in 1882 was a key milestone as that in turn led to a more cohesive and regulated approach to the task in home waters not dissimilar to the model adopted ever since.

The 1882 Convention, as with other accords of its kind, did not magically bring international disputes in the North Sea to an end. The independent spirit of sea fisherman, the competitive nature of his occupation, the vagaries of the weather and the fact that controversial incidents often happened at night, all added to the complications of policing those highly productive areas of the continental shelf. The RN tended to respond to 'crises' as they occurred, apparently having neither the resources nor the willingness to establish a 'standing force'.

There were signs, as mentioned above, of disquiet beyond the confines of the North Sea that were to become the major sources of acrimonious dispute during the twentieth century. For instance, Sweden and Norway did not recognise the 3-mile territorial delimitation, nor did Tsarist Russia. Moreover, the differences between the developed industrialised nations with their sophisticated long-distance trawlers and the traditional methods employed by island fishermen became more pronounced. As has been shown, British fishermen far from home were prepared to break local laws or even indulge in black market practices in order to prosper in their gruelling and downright dangerous profession.

There was, finally, rising concern among many nations about the depletion of fish stocks. This can be seen as one of the origins of the move towards a system of *mare clausum* where individual countries would claim control of the waters including the seabed adjacent to or surrounding their land beyond the traditional 3-mile delimitation – a move Britain was to resist in increasing isolation during the next century. Prince Charles of Denmark summarised the dilemma succinctly when asked to comment on the fairness or otherwise of penalising the transgressing fishermen, 'And as for the confiscation of the catch of fish, which was the worst part of the penalty, it was to be remembered that the fish belonged to the Icelanders, from whom it had been taken and to whom it was returned.'[62]

Chapter Three

'To Foster a Bond of Mutual Sympathy and Respect'
1905–58

AN ARTICLE ENTITLED 'Fishery Protection' in a 1953 edition of *The Naval Review* begins:

> It may be of interest to the readers of THE NAVAL REVIEW to hear something more of the duties and organisation of a little-known branch of the service, the Fishery Protection Squadron. That their Lordships are eager that knowledge of it should be disseminated, is evident from the fact that officers attending the Senior Officers' Technical Course are now treated to a lecture on the work of the Squadron by one of the Commanding Officers, and from the steps taken to provide the Press with more information about it.[1]

What is surprising is that, despite being acknowledged as the oldest squadron in the Royal Navy, it required an awareness-raising campaign to be launched to inform a readership comprised of its own serving officers.

This chapter gives an overview of what was then called the Fishery Protection Flotilla essentially from the start of the twentieth century until the late 1950s. It describes the structural organisation of the flotilla and the inevitable challenges it faced during a period when fishing in distant waters particularly began to assume ever greater importance in the face of increasing demands for bigger catches of fish to be landed. It coincided with a period of intense debate and controversy about the dimensions of territorial waters. At the same time, there were repeated calls from those associated with the UK fishing industry, as well as from within the Royal Navy itself, for the latter to relinquish its historic

Map 2: The British Isles, showing the principal fishing ports. (Stephen Dent)

fishery protection task in favour of a non-military organisation or a contracted private company.

According to 'Albacore', the anonymous contributor to *The Naval Review*, Lieutenant Commander Rooke was appointed the first Senior Naval Officer, North Sea Fisheries in 1905 and, 'duties began to approximate to those of today'. This was not strictly accurate, of course, as the previous chapter shows: the organisational structure for fishery protection in the North Sea had been in place for twenty years, following on from the North Sea Convention of 1882.[2]

Lieutenant Commander Rooke initially took command of the torpedo gunboat HMS *Halcyon* in 1905, as Senior Officer. *Halcyon* was one of five *Dryad*-class torpedo gunboats, first commissioned in 1895. It displaced 1,070 tons, was armed with two 4.7in quick-firing guns and was equipped with five 18in torpedo tubes. The *Dryad* class had an unusual profile with the two funnels set wide apart. *Halcyon* shared the inherent weakness of the previous *Alarm* class, being fitted with unreliable and troublesome locomotive boilers that may well account for the fact that it was allocated to the FP task where the radius of operation was limited to the parameters of the North Sea.

The torpedo gunboats, sometimes called 'catchers' in reference to their role as counters to the numerous torpedo boats of the French and Russian navies, were not a great success as a generic design. As mentioned above, they suffered from very bad boiler trouble and so were unable to keep the sea even in favourable weather conditions such as during summer manoeuvres. This general shortcoming, to be allocated ships that had proved inadequate in other roles or were otherwise surplus to requirements, was to adversely affect the work of the squadron at various intervals throughout the period under question.[3]

Pre-First World War, the squadron also included HMS *Skipjack* and *Spanker* of the thirteen-strong *Sharpshooter* class. These torpedo gunboats were smaller than the *Dryads*, displacing 735 tons, and had a marginally faster maximum speed. HMS *Leda*, of the above-mentioned *Alarm* class, was also assigned and, in 1913 HMS *Wear* was commissioned into the North Sea Fishery Protection Flotilla as a temporary replacement for *Leda*, which had paid off for refit. *Wear*, as a 'River'-class destroyer, differed from the other early members of the squadron. The destroyers, which were replacing the torpedo gunboats, at over 25 knots enjoyed a considerably faster maximum speed. The sturdiness of this Admiralty design allowed the ships to maintain this speed in most sea conditions, making them appear, at least on paper, quite suitable for the protection task. The ageing HMS *Ringdove*, of the *Redbreast* class of composite gunboats, was assigned to the Fishery Board of Scotland.[4]

Records show that this assorted collection of ships undertook both fishery protection and coastguard duties at various times and for differing lengths of time during the decade prior to the Great War. The Admiralty, in addition to the regular, RN-manned fishery protection vessels, also employed five coastguard cruisers: *Squirrel*, *Thrush*, *Argon*, *Julia* and *Watchful*. These ships were manned by executive officers and ratings of the Permanent Cruiser Service. The executive personnel holding special qualifications were recruited from leading seamen of the fleet. Promotion was made by selection through all grades up to Chief Officer in Command, who officially ranked with, but after, lieutenant RN.[5]

The Board of Agriculture and Fisheries (the forerunner of the Ministry) had general superintendence of fisheries in England and Wales and liaised directly with the industry. Its duties included making suggestions about regulations and improvements and carrying out research for promoting the industry, together with the maintenance of relevant statistics. It had no vessels operating directly under its jurisdiction other than a few small craft used to enforce local bye-laws. These bye-laws were made by local committees and related to the territorial waters in their respective districts. The Fishery Board for Scotland (later the Scottish Fishery Protection Agency) was tasked with the supervision of fisheries in their waters and with the maintenance of its own bye-laws. In addition to the attached RN naval vessel (see above) the Board also operated four or five civilian manned fishery cruisers and one research vessel in the period up to and including the 1920s.[6]

Name changes

The half century covered in this chapter is noted for frequent and sometimes confusing changes in nomenclature to identify the ships involved in fishery protection. Therefore, 'fishery protection' needs to be regarded as a generic term because it was not applied consistently, if only because it was not an accurate representation of the range of tasks these ships were expected to undertake. This was particularly the case in the immediate aftermath of the First World War. Lieutenant Commander Rooke was given the very specific title of Senior Officer North Sea Fisheries in 1905 but by the First World War the ships had been grouped together under the catch-all Auxiliary Patrols.

Thus, in December 1919, Captain L G Preston was appointed Senior Officer of the Patrol, Minesweeping and Fishery Protection Squadron under the jurisdiction of the Captain Auxiliary Patrols (or Captain A.P.) His senior officer's ship was the *Anchusa*-class 'convoy sloop' HMS *Windflower* and he had under his command the *Arabis*-class 'fleet sweeping sloop' HMS *Lupin* and five minesweeping trawlers. The composition of this squadron emphasised the enormous minesweeping clearance operation left over from the First World War, which became a necessary part of the Auxiliary Patrol's remit at the time.[7] Further vessels could be drawn from what was described as a fifty-two-strong Central Reserve should any be required as replacements. Minesweeping duties were to remain appended to the tasks undertaken by the ships assigned to fishery protection for most of the rest of the twentieth century.

Captain Preston was instructed to be guided by the duties laid down in the 1914 Fishery Manual and by further regulations compiled pre-war. A separate undertaking was made by the Admiralty with respect to Scotland: one vessel, no smaller than a sloop, would be allocated to fishing duties in Scottish waters. At the time, Preston was charged to correspond directly with the Admiralty unless matters came under the direct control of individual Commanders-in-Chief (C-in-C). For example, correspondence relating to fishery protection in Irish waters was within the remit of the C-in-C Western Approaches. In addition to fishery protection, all vessels under Captain Preston's command would be available for minesweeping and anti-submarine tasks together with additional training duties.[8]

This arrangement remained in place until 1928, when an Admiralty internal memo decreed that the title Auxiliary Patrol had become misleading. Its wartime use to group together local defence, patrol, minesweeping, escort, submarine hunting, boom defence and local transport services (excepting craft built as men-of-war and armed merchant cruisers), was too generalised. The memo states that in future Auxiliary Anti-Submarine Flotillas and Auxiliary Minesweeping Flotillas would be included under the general classification Auxiliary Flotillas.[9]

It is pertinent to ask why fishery protection was not specifically listed among the various auxiliary duties. It was in fact grouped with minesweeping with the FP arm to be commanded by a 'Captain Fishery Protection and Minesweeping' or 'Captain F.M.S.'. Inevitably, this classification was to prove both confusing and unworkable, particularly with regard to the chain of command, and in 1932 the whole matter was revisited.

Was fishery protection and minesweeping to be administered under Home Fleet command or should it report directly to the Admiralty, as had been decreed in 1919? A Fleet Order of the time stipulated that:

the Captain A/P is to be regarded for general purposes as under the orders of the C-in-C Atlantic Fleet. He is, however, authorised to communicate direct with the Admiralty upon questions related to Fishery Protection and Minesweeping, keeping the C-in-C Atlantic Fleet informed of important matters and also keeping the Commanders-in-Chief of the Home Ports duly acquainted with all matters affecting their commands. As a result of the confusion caused by Captain F.M.S. not being properly informed it was suggested that, in view of the scattered nature of his flotilla, the F.M.S. command should be regarded as an independent command under the direct orders of the Admiralty.[10]

The prospect of a fresh mountain of paperwork and bureaucracy resulting from these directives must have caused the staffs of those commands to quail in anticipation!

Unfortunately, it did not end there. In November 1932, the Captain F.M.S., Captain K Macpherson wrote to the Secretary of the Admiralty:

Be pleased to inform the Board that I find there is a general misconception throughout the Service that the title 'FMS Flotilla' represents 'Fleet minesweeping Flotilla' and not 'Fishery Protection and Minesweeping Flotilla'. It is therefore submitted for consideration that the present full titles of 'Captain, Fishery Protection and Minesweeping' and 'Fishery Protection and Minesweeping Flotilla' should stand but, in order to obviate misunderstanding in the future, that the respective short titles should be amended to 'Captain FP and M' and 'FP and M Flotilla.[11]

The twin purpose of the FP & M Flotilla saw a further adjustment made in 1936 in which all available minesweepers were allocated to two flotillas: the First and the Sixth. This resulted in the *Mersey*-class trawlers, which composed the backbone of the FP Flotilla at the time, being distributed two each between the major fishing ports of Grimsby, Lowestoft, Milford Haven and the Channel.[12]

A post-war reassessment

The ending of the First World War brought about a comprehensive review of the provisions made for the protection of British fisheries and of the Navy's future role in providing that service. In fact this was unfinished business. Responsibility for fishery protection had been the subject of a Government Interdepartmental Conference in 1907. The Navy had wanted that conference to be wide ranging and to include the views of as many departments as possible. At the Conference it argued that the vessels currently used for FP were rapidly becoming obsolescent and unfit for 'war purposes'. Although it conceded that the terms of the 1882 North Sea Fisheries Convention might require it to undertake certain specialist duties, the main thrust of its argument turned inevitably to the matter of finance, questioning whether the Navy should continue to undertake full responsibility for fishery protection and thus be charged on the Navy Vote.[13]

In the aftermath of the Conference, the Treasury constituted the stumbling block in what appeared to be the Navy's plan to rid itself of fishery protection. The Admiralty claimed the Treasury had 'misunderstood ... the recommendations of the Conference'. The Treasury refuted the suggestion and the matter lay unresolved until it was resurrected in 1919.[14]

A report entitled 'Admiralty Responsibility for Protection of Fisheries' was commissioned by the Admiralty and written by a senior naval officer, Captain Dugmore, on the basis of the conclusions reached by a sub-committee that had previously investigated the matter. Among other issues, the report examined the existing structure of the service, questioned the Royal Navy's continuing participation, the types and numbers of vessels required and the sea areas under its jurisdiction.

Captain Dugmore was very thorough in his task and many of his observations and recommendations were subsequently adopted. He was particularly critical with respect to the complexity of the organisation. He pressed instead for a central department or Ministry with oversight for the whole of the UK, which is what happened subsequently with decreasing amounts of responsibility being devolved to local areas.[15]

Dugmore then turned his attention to the thorny issue of the Admiralty's own involvement and although his report is suitably without bias, his personal opinions and perhaps those of his colleagues on the sub-committee, particularly with regard to finance, are pretty clear. He underlines this argument by stating that the maintenance of the pre-war torpedo gunboats then in use was unnecessarily expensive: the annual cost of HM ships *Halcyon*, *Skipjack*, *Spanker* and *Leda* for 1913 amounted to £53,701 out of a total of £102,249 allocated to fishery protection in 1913. He does admit that if fishery protection was undertaken by another department, it would need to have the powers to exercise the same authority to deal with foreign vessels outside territorial waters as currently possessed by ships flying the White Ensign, which included being armed.

A former Senior Officer of Fisheries had been consulted by the sub-committee. Commodore Ellison had remarked that the act of showing the White Ensign in various ports, both at home and abroad and among the fishing fleets, was a sound one. Captain Dugmore added, in relation to 'showing the flag', that it 'certainly exercises a more effective influence on the fishing population than any other service would be likely to exercise'.[16]

This section of the report concludes, 'Taking all the circumstances into account it would appear desirable that the Sub-Committee should recommend the continuance of Fishery Protection by the Admiralty, but not to a greater extent than before the war.' Dugmore then returns once more to the question of cost, which he argued should be shared by other Government departments including the Board of Trade and H.M. Customs. In effect, one detects in all of this a feeling shared perhaps by many in the Navy at the time: that fishery protection was an unnecessary burden, and that H.M. ships should not be called upon to undertake that kind of constabulary-type duty. As will be shown later, this matter did not end with Dugmore's report.[17]

The third section considers the numbers and types of vessels most suitable for the task. In general, the sub-committee considered they should be not too distinctive in appearance, have sufficient speed and be capable of keeping the sea in bad weather. The pre-war torpedo gunboats failed these criteria, being found impossible to navigate around the islands and headlands encountered in the Shetlands, for example, which in turn inhibited them from apprehending trawlers that were breaking the law. Moreover, their distinctive appearance was visible miles away on shore, where there were reported to be 'spies' on watch to observe and report the movement of the protection vessels.

Indeed 'appearance' seems to have been an important factor in determining suitability. The report suggested employing the very convoy sloops of the 'Flower' class that were found woefully lacking when used in the Barents Sea some three years later (see Chapter Five). The 'Flower' class was recommended as they resembled tramp steamers and therefore would be less obvious as being RN manned. Commodore Ellison was again consulted and he recommended, 'a specially built trawler, considerably larger than ordinary fishing trawlers, with decent accommodation for officers and men; a vessel that would keep the sea in all weathers and would be more or less comfortable'.[18] Ellison's words in 1919 seem prophetic, particularly in the light of the problems of finding the right vessels to support distant-water trawling, notably in the next decade.

The use of force

Ultimately, the relationship between the fishermen and the Navy, which carried responsibility for upholding the law offshore, was the key factor dictating the successful prosecution of the fishery protection task both in this period and beyond. It became a focus for debate both before and after the Great War, particularly with respect to the ultimate use of force. If the law was deemed to have been broken in the eyes of the fishery protection CO, what measures could be taken lawfully to apprehend the offender, particularly if arrest was avoided simply by sailing away to avoid capture?

There was a test case, debated by the Treasury's legal department in 1912, involving a Belgian trawler that had fled after being discovered fishing illegally inside British territorial waters. HMS *Spanker* had apprehended the Ostend-based sailing trawler, identified as '*0.100*', off Southwold in Suffolk and had sent across the ship's boat with the intention of putting an officer on board. There was no compliance from the Belgian skipper, who immediately hauled his nets and then fled, nearly swamping *Spanker*'s boat in the process. The torpedo gunboat set off in pursuit, closed the *0.100*, ordered it to lower its sails and came alongside. The trawler then 'drifted' on to *Spanker*, its mizzen boom was allowed to catch in the after back-stay of the gunboat's fore topmast, which then carried away both the topmast and the trawler's mizzen-mast. The trawler then escaped again.

HMS *Spanker*'s CO concluded that, as he had enough evidence to identify the fishing boat, he did not need to pursue. He also resisted the temptation to open fire in order to comply with Admiralty instructions about only using force in self-defence. It was concluded that the trawler skipper was guilty not only of fishing inside territorial waters but also of resisting the lawful orders of the fishery officer. The matter was referred to the Belgian Government. But there was no subsequent prosecution as the incident had occurred inside British territorial waters. If it had been outside, it would have contravened the rules of the North Sea Fisheries Convention.

The question was raised as to whether *Spanker*'s CO would have had powers to arrest the trawler with the use of force if the incident took place outside territorial waters. The Treasury Solicitor concluded that if force was used that resulted in death, the commanding officer would have been be liable for a conviction for manslaughter.

A reassessment of the HMS *Spanker* incident, made in 1926, reached a similar conclusion, which reopened the debate about how best to apprehend a fishing vessel thought to be transgressing while in territorial waters but refusing to comply with instructions issued by the FP vessel. Should a boarding party be used to 'arrest' the offending vessel? Was some form of force permissible such as the firing of blanks or live rounds aimed 'off-target'? Could aircraft be employed to identify and track offenders? Should a 'softly, softly' approach be adopted whereby the alleged culprit was followed to his homeport where an arrest could be made? Overall, how exactly should one define the role of the fishery protection vessel in relation to its 'charges' – the fishing vessels?

The 1926 legality debate within the Admiralty included the recent case of the Scottish Fishery Board Protection ship *Vigilant*, which had encountered a Fleetwood trawler that had subsequently refused to stop. The Scottish Fishery Board wanted to know of any 'armament or device' that could be used in the circumstances. Responses from various Admiralty departments ranged from the passive 'following the offender into port', through the use of a chemical dye to spray the offender in order to make identification easier, to the firing of tear gas cartridges. The employment of long-range photography was also suggested, either from the air or from aboard the FP vessel. Some accusations were levelled at 'weak' RN officers for failing to take decisive action.

There was a negative response to those ideas from two quarters. Firstly, the Scottish Office considered it impractical to follow trawlers into port, particularly across national borders, and that photography was not always an option because of the weather and the ability of the offending vessel to disguise its profile or its equipment. The Naval Air Arm considered aircraft not to be the solution because of the vagaries of the weather. However, this conclusion was reached before two sets of experiments were conducted using aircraft operated by the RAF in 1928–29 and again in 1933, which are described in Chapter Seven.[19]

The matter of the exact legality of the use of force in such instances was revisited. The 1914 edition of the Sea Fisheries manual was quoted as stating that force should never be used, 'unless this should prove imperatively necessary or their part of self-defence or to prevent the escape of foreign fishing vessels found fishing within British territorial waters'. This latter point was different from the advice given by the lawyers in the 1912 *Spanker* case. This time, the recommendation in the Manual added that if the protection vessel fired only with intent to disable the offender and that death was caused inadvertently as a result, it was *very unlikely* that a British coroner's court jury would bring in a verdict of manslaughter in the case of the death of one of the crew of a foreign fishing vessel found poaching in British territorial waters.[20]

It was concluded that extreme force (in other words the firing of a weapon) should only be used when it could be carried out without endangering life, e.g. by firing at short range. The same applied in the case of a pursuit that took place outside territorial waters, usually involving a foreign fishing vessel. If the vessel could be identified there was no requirement for the use of force.

Captain G C Dickens, Captain Auxiliary Patrols at the time, addressed the whole matter in a paper entitled *Use of Force by Fishery Protection Vessels* dated 31 December 1925. He agreed that FP vessels should have the right to use force in apprehending an offender. 'I am of the opinion ... that a shot across the bows of a fishing boat refusing to stop when ordered and – in serious cases – a shot fired over her, are measures that should be permitted.'

Importantly, he elaborated more widely on the nature of the ideal relationship between the Navy and the fisherman. He considered that a firm, friendly approach should be adopted that he likened to that of the Metropolitan Police. It was important that the Navy should be liked both by national and by foreign fishermen in the interests of foreign relations. He saw a responsibility with the home fishing industry, 'to foster a bond of mutual sympathy and respect'.

Dickens concluded his paper:

Fishing people need never know to what extreme commanding officers of cruisers are likely to go under varying circumstances and I am convinced that, under practically all conditions, a naval officer showing energy and determination can make his orders obeyed without having recourse to too drastic action.

But there is almost inevitably a gulf between theory and practice. This was illustrated clearly seven years after Captain Dickens wrote these words in the case of S/T *Lucida*, whose skipper, Bert Jinks, persistently refused to obey orders and was subsequently involved in an extraordinary and prolonged 'hot pursuit' by a RN protection vessel. This is described in Chapter Seven.

The post-war 'revival'

Shortly after VE-Day there was a firm commitment made by the Admiralty to reorganise its fishery protection fleet now hostilities had ceased, as had happened after the end of the Great War. A memo noted briefly that, during the Second World War, RN ships allocated to FP were withdrawn for other duties and protection of fishing was carried out by what was termed 'other agencies' such as patrol vessels with local naval officers in command. There was a general call for reorganisation in anticipation of, 'a rush back to the fishing grounds'. This move was later officially referred to as the 'post-war revival'.[21]

However, even before the war's end, the debate over who should have responsibility for fishery protection was revived. A memo by Captain Mark Pizey, Director Operations Division (DoD), suggested, 'a separate coastguard service under Admiralty (supervision), and run somewhat on the American lines'.[22]

Details of the composition of the fishery protection arm of what was still referred to as the Fishery Protection and Minesweeping Flotilla were issued on 9 November 1945. The flotilla was to consist of the *Grimsby*-class sloop HMS *Fleetwood* (Senior Officer command), two 'Castle'-class corvettes, *Allington Castle* and *Bamborough Castle*, two trawlers and three HDMLs.[23] HMS *Fleetwood* was almost immediately replaced by another sloop, HMS *Stork*, which had become famous as the early wartime command of the anti-U-boat 'ace' Captain F J Walker.[24] Requirements had changed by July 1947 with the additional commitments of the Murman Coast Patrol and the Andanaer Patrol (Iceland). *Stork* was selected because its endurance made it suitable for the type of long-range patrols required. The flotilla was distributed across three sea areas: the North Sea, the Channel and the Irish Sea, with HMS *Stork* based at Lowestoft.

The altered priorities prompted the DoD to outline the need for an additional vessel to be allocated. At the time, aside from the senior officer's frigate, there were three *Algerine*-class ocean minesweepers assigned to the North Sea, three to the south and west coast of England, one to Scotland plus two motor fishing vessels (MFV) to cover the English Channel.[25] Interestingly, the DoD fell short of demanding an additional *Algerine*, stating that he did not consider that, 'this ship should be provided at the expense of maintaining our fleets up to strength and in view of the present manpower situation which has necessitated placing some of our latest destroyers in reserve', and that he did not therefore feel justified in pressing now for an increase in the existing FP flotilla.[26]

The DoD did concede that in future the Senior Officer would need to review the situation in the light of the experience of having to cope with the additional requirements for patrols off the Murman Coast and off Iceland using his existing eleven-strong flotilla. This included the two MFVs, which were not suitable for long-range overseas deployments. His cautious response illustrates the wider problems faced by the Royal Navy in the immediate post-war era. The responsibilities inherent in coping with Britain's widespread empire, together with the imminent challenges of the Cold War, had to be undertaken in the face of economic austerity at home. This in turn impacted on the problems the Royal Navy faced with manpower shortages and the need to maintain front-line fleet strength.

Nevertheless, the Admiralty's commitment to reshape the provisions for fishery protection was carried further in a widespread review of its work and organisation carried out in liaison with the Chief Inspector of Fisheries in autumn 1947. As a result it was recommended that the shore headquarters of the Senior Officer should be relocated from Lowestoft to Hull. The reasoning was that the Humber River ports were the epicentre of British fishing, being responsible for over 40 per cent of the entire annual catch. Additionally, its geographical position was closer to what was described as the 'long-range side of the industry', of which HMS *Stork* was a key component.[27] If based at Hull, the SO would have local contact with the owners and skippers of the trawlers that worked the Murman Coast and off Iceland. Moreover, *Stork* was considered too large to support the local herring fishing fleet and also had difficulty entering Lowestoft Port itself in bad weather owing to its size.[28]

Prior to the Second World War, the headquarters had been located in HM Naval Base Portland, because of the priority accorded to the minesweeping component of its duties. However, since the war, minesweeping was no longer considered a significant part of the flotilla's remit, although that situation was soon to change yet again. The proposed move to Hull opened the possibility of appointing a Local Fishing Naval Officer (LFNO), North Sea, based at Lowestoft, as had been the practice in the pre-war years. This was subsequently approved and the LFNO took command of the *Algerine*-class minesweeper HMS *Wave*.

In a sign of the times, the increased decentralisation of the organisation allowed the SO to play the role of arbiter with regard to policy, in the manner of a company chairman. Thus, at a conference held aboard HMS *Stork* at Chatham that same autumn, the LFNOs, the Chief Inspector of Fisheries, with Captain Mackay in the chair, were able to agree on the overall fishery protection priorities, which, in descending order, were:

- Support of the deep sea fleets, more particularly those fishing on the borders of foreign territorial waters, where incidents are likely to arise;
- Enforcements of the various international conventions to which Great Britain is a party;
- Protection of British territorial waters against foreign poachers;
- Assistance to Local Sea Fisheries Committees when practicable, and only on the request of the District Inspector.[29]

It was also noted at the Conference that the position of Northern Ireland, the Isle of Man and the Channel Islands remained a 'grey area' with regard to jurisdiction. It appeared to have been accepted by the Admiralty that the enforcement of local fishery bye-laws with respect to the first two did not exist and in the case of the Channel Islands was simply not known!

In a move to integrate the roles of the interested parties, both service and civilian, it was agreed that the Inspector of Fisheries and the District Inspectors should be regarded as the equivalents of the Director of Naval Intelligence and his staff officers. In future, the fisheries inspectorate would assume responsibility for all aspects of fishery intelligence and for integrating information and suggestions from commanding officers within the flotilla and elsewhere. Furthermore, the line of communication between the Senior Officer FP and the Inspector of Fisheries on major issues of policy was placed on a formal footing as opposed to functioning informally as it had done in the past.

The reclassification of the flotilla as a 'reserve' minesweeping flotilla had meant that armament and minesweeping gear had been progressively landed. In a sign of the times, however, this process was stopped and what were described as 'minimum standards of equipment' were issued. All ships were instructed to carry out a full week's practice once in every four-monthly cruise period. Such practices were to include individual minesweeping in the case of the *Algerines* and anti-air warfare HA/LA drills in HMS *Stork*.[30]

The following year a lengthy memorandum was issued by the Senior Officer FP to the commanding officers of his flotilla ships and the respective Fishery Officers around the country including Scotland. It covered organisational matters and gave a detailed analysis of the required strength of the flotilla if it was to maintain the level of support for the fishing fleets in the future. Perhaps the most interesting section dealt with tactics. For the purposes of the report, three broad classifications of fishing areas were determined: distant, intermediate and local. Although the relative importance of the three areas, in terms of annual landings of fish, were of a descending order: 7 to 3 to 1, the report states that, 'the vocal strength of the British fishermen working in the area appears to be more like 1 to 3 and 7'.

The tactics to adopt in each classification were enunciated. The raising of morale among the fishermen, 'showing the flag' in foreign ports and reassurance that support from the Navy would always be on hand provided trawler skippers worked within international law, were to be emphasised. The 'village policeman' metaphor was used to describe the tactics to be employed in the intermediate areas of the North Sea and around the UK coast. It was felt that from a morale point of view these areas needed less frequent visits than distant waters, the exception being during the autumn herring season when the concentration of boats, both British and foreign, was greater.

The report admitted that the work of the flotilla in local areas was 'perhaps the least agreeable duty, consisting as it does almost entirely of police work'. Poaching by foreign fishing boats was the greatest problem and, without large numbers of protection vessels to hand, the chances of making arrests were slim. However, visits to nearby foreign ports and the displaying of the distinctive flotilla pennant together with the White Ensign had proved to be a deterrent. A less prominent, but probably a more effective measure, was to liaise with foreign fishery inspectors.[31]

New challenges

By the middle of the next decade, seven years after the deliberations aboard HMS *Stork* in late 1947, circumstances had changed yet again and warranted a fresh review. A memo sent to Captain, Fifth Fishery Protection and Minesweeping Squadron, detailed the main events that had occurred in the interim that, it was claimed, 'radically change the whole emphasis of Fishery Protection work, and considerably complicate the operation of the Fishery Protection Squadron'.[32]

The memo referred back to the 1947 reorganisation measures, noting somewhat inaccurately, that at the time, 'there were no international matters of note affecting exclusive fishery limits' – although as successive chapters will show, there were ongoing disputes with Norway and the Soviet Union and an emerging one with Iceland in particular. The memo added that in 1947, 'the Fishery Protection Squadron appeared set to re-establish a routine similar to that pursued prior to 1939'.[33]

The events that had 'radically changed' the role of the flotilla were listed as:

- The extension of the Norwegian fishery limits by the Hague Court decision of 1951.
- The extension of Icelandic fishery limits, which are still a matter of bitter dispute.
- The bringing into force in 1954 of the Overfishery Convention, as a result of which fishery protection vessels are invited to measure the sizes of nets of British vessels at sea.
- The establishment of the Fifth Fishery Protection and Minesweeping Squadron under the Commander-in-Chief, Home (Designate), available for Home Defence or allocation to NATO tasks.

What were described as other 'looming' tasks, which would have a bearing on operations, included increased fishing off Greenland, the presence of Soviet and Polish trawlers in the North Sea and off Bear Island, the proposals to change fishing limits around the Faroe Islands and the possibility of an international agreement on mesh regulations that would mean foreign fishing vessels around home waters would need to be intercepted and their nets measured.[34]

In 1953 it was calculated that the total value of British catches was worth £30.3 million against that of imported fish, which cost £13 million. Further analysis underlined the importance of deep sea catches off North Norway and Iceland, which accounted for 70 per cent of that total. Thus, the new set of priorities for the deployment of the FP flotilla was listed as:

- Maintaining a patrol in Icelandic waters;
- one in the Barents Sea, Bear Island and North Norway areas;
- one in the North Sea, particularly at the height of the herring season from October to December;
- occasional visits to the other less important areas on the south and west coasts and the Faroe Islands.
- Two 75ft MFVs to be employed on a year-round basis in the Channel area with seasonal deployments made to the North Sea during the herring season.

Additionally, as usual, one ship would operate in the Scottish Fishery areas, including the Hebrides and Shetland.

In a further sign of changing times, in order to maintain a proper degree of operational efficiency, the Fifth Fishery Protection and Minesweeping Squadron would be withdrawn entirely from fishery patrols three times a year for a three-week period, twice to take part in NATO minesweeping exercises and once for a squadron exercise. The SO, as a senior captain, would be regularly selected to command the international exercise. The squadron exercises would also provide the opportunity to train RNR and RNVR personnel.[35] During that time the Icelandic patrol would be maintained by a vessel on loan from the 4th Minesweeping Squadron.

Why had the FP ships reverted to being a part-time minesweeping squadron? By 1949–50, NATO planners were placing mines at the top of the list of threats to be countered – even above submarines. Given the Soviet Union's lack of experience in oceanic submarine warfare, mining perhaps provided the easiest anti-shipping target going in and out of home ports. Based on that prognosis, it was estimated that in the event of war the Soviet Union could lay 4,500–6,000 per month in British waters. It was calculated that it took twenty-five to thirty mines to be laid in order to sink one merchant ship. This meant restricting the number of mines to approximately 1,500–2,000 if subsequent losses were to be tolerated. It is small wonder, therefore, that minesweeping duties were reactivated and given such priority above other tasks.[36] It is also of note that Iceland was considered at the time to be of such importance that the 'Arctic Patrol' was exempt from the thrice-yearly exodus for minesweeping exercises. The first of the Cod Wars was just five years away.

Perhaps the most interesting section of this long report comes towards the end, when it moved on from the practical and organisational and reflected on the value accruing from maintaining the flotilla. The report states that deep-sea trawlers operating, for example, in the remotest parts of the Arctic Ocean had grown accustomed to the 'psychological support' provided by the Royal Navy's presence, 'and that any abandonment of Fishery Protection would cause great harm and dismay'.

The report then argues the intrinsic value of this work to the Royal Navy itself. The benefits included lengthy spells of sea time, experience of harsh conditions in the Arctic and elsewhere, the first-hand knowledge gained of strategically important sea areas and the great variety of navigational and ship-handling problems faced. It ends on a somewhat defensive note, which emphasises the still marginalised status of fishery protection within the Fleet:

> Any idea that the Squadron is a 'private navy' whose value is doubtful is mistaken. The need for fishery protection ships is greater today than ever. The work these ships do is entirely appropriate to the Royal Navy, and brings a variety of direct benefits to H.M. Service by affording splendid seagoing training and experience, as well as keeping in touch with a section of our seafaring community whose service in war have been and are likely to continue to be, invaluable.[37]

This defence of and justification for the maintenance of the fishery protection force should be viewed firstly within the context of the 1950s, a decade when the Royal Navy found itself having to argue its ongoing relevance in the nuclear age as a central tenet of the country's defence. Secondly, the country's dogged determination to adhere to the principles of *mare liberum*, in the face of widespread opposition, which is discussed widely in other chapters, had brought the issue of fishing to the fore of the national agenda once again in the years since the war.

Changes made on the brink of 'war'

A final, important step was taken towards presenting a coherent approach in this matter with the allocation of 'Ton'-class coastal minesweepers for FP in inshore waters and the use of Type 14 frigates for distant waters support. This decision was made shortly before the start of the First Cod War.[38] Although none of the ships was actually purpose-built for the task, all were modern, having been constructed in the last decade. This contrasted sharply with previous practice when availability rather than suitability had been the watchword. However, although this decision looked positive on paper, the reality was not entirely satisfactory.[39]

When the 1957 White Paper *Defence: Outline of Future Policy* was published it was noted that the post-war coastal and inshore minesweeper programme, as mentioned above, was almost complete. In point of fact, the Admiralty was embarrassed by the numbers that had been constructed and it is little wonder, in order to cover up what might have been construed as a gross over-estimation, it was stressed in the Paper that these vessels had an important additional role as 'patrol vessels'. The FPS became the beneficiary with a virtual plethora of new ships. Thus the composition of the FPS in December 1959 was four Type 14 frigates, HMS *Duncan, Malcolm, Palliser* and *Russell,* four Coniston- (or 'Ton')-class minesweepers, *Belton, Soberton, Wasperton* and *Wotton,* and two 'Ley'-class inshore sweepers, HMS *Squirrel* (ex-*Burley*) and *Watchful* (ex-*Squirrel*).[40]

The Type 14 or *Blackwood* class design was conceived as a 'second-rate' frigate, a successor to the 'Flower'- and 'Castle'-class corvettes of the Second World War, and relatively cheap and quick to build. In point of fact, the actual complexities of the resulting design meant that it took on average three years to construct each ship, while the overall aim of increasing numbers of hulls at no extra cost resulted in a very austere ship not best suited to a peacetime navy. The Type 14's high prow enabled the ships to ride up and over a wave without it going over the forecastle. Structurally, however, the hull proved to be frail and subsequently needed considerable strengthening for fishery protection duties in stormy northern waters. Moreover, accommodation was rather sparse and 50 per cent 'hard-lying' money had to be paid to the crews while they were assigned to the FPS.[41]

Charles Wylie recalls a potentially disastrous incident that took place in the notorious Pentland Firth as HMS *Russell* returned to Port Edgar after a period on patrol off Iceland. He was the Navigating Officer. There was a following sea with strong winds, which built large waves made larger by the shallowing waters of the Firth:

Steering was tricky as the ship veered, and the quartermaster on the wheel used a little too much to correct a lurch to starboard. As a result the ship swung to port as a big wave caught the stern and lifted it to starboard, causing a broach which rolled us over so far that the bridge guardrails were submerged. Everyone on the bridge was flung into a heap of arms and legs on one side. When I scrambled back to the pelorus I found that we had been swung about 120 degrees off course and were heading towards the rocks. Although the broach had reduced our speed from 24 knots to 18 we still had full power accelerating the ship. The QM (quartermaster), who could not see out, was correctly turning his wheel to starboard to regain the ordered course, but that would have driven us ashore. Training kicked in. I ordered, 'Midships. Hard a-port.' With full power, the rudder was highly effective, so we swung away from the rocks into clear water. It cost us quite a lot of broken crockery.[42]

Nonetheless, as far as the squadron was concerned, the Type 14s were available in the right numbers and they were new ships, even allowing for the distinct question marks regarding their suitability in the stormy northern waters.

Conclusion

The Royal Navy's fishery protection branch emerged from this period as a larger force and in a more coherent state than when it started in 1905. By the end of the 1950s it was equipped with modern ships that were generally suited to the task at hand. Commonality of type, in any naval scenario, holds considerable advantages in terms of interoperability and maintenance; some of the assortment of vessels available to the Senior Officer in pre-Second World War days, for example, were simply not suitable, for instance for deployment in the High Arctic and off Iceland and Greenland. The FPS headquarters was now more conveniently and centrally sited at Port Edgar on the shore of the Firth of Forth. The distribution of the ships of the squadron among the principal fishing towns, under the local control of an LFNO, appeared to be working efficiently on an organisational level. The chain of command, with the Senior Officer reporting directly to the Admiralty, had been thrashed out after much tinkering.

The concept of the role as being akin to a policeman on the beat, enunciated back in the 1920s by Captain Dickens, was sound and still pertinent – to encourage and to support but at the same time to uphold the law among a fishery community often prepared to bend the rules because the rewards were high. But the imminent Cod Wars were to constitute a highly unusual and at the same time a considerable challenge for the Royal Navy over the next eighteen years and the resources it demanded in terms of ships and logistics were to extend far beyond the capabilities of the FP squadron alone.

More broadly, the fifty-three-year period covered in this chapter witnessed what Hannes Jónsson describes as the 'decline of the 3-mile limit', the historic acceptance of a fixed delimitation of territorial waters. He cites the French extension to 6 miles in 1907, followed by Italy, again to 6 miles, and Uruguay to 5 in 1914 and the Soviet Union to 12 miles in its European waters in 1921, as indications of a trend that was to gather pace over the next forty or more years. The League of Nations Codification Conference held in The Hague in 1930 had demonstrated the widely differing views held by participating countries and provided clear evidence that there were no agreed principles then in existence with which to establish an internationally agreed ruling on the matter.[43]

The Second World War accentuated the global importance of oil and as a consequence the continental shelf and the seabed itself became vital additional resources for countries with coastlines. Likewise, the conservation of fish stocks, not a new concern by any means, assumed major importance. The 1945 Truman Declarations on coastal jurisdiction, described elsewhere, established an unstoppable trend that has since brought an end to the age-old concept of the freedom of the seas in coastal regions.

Chapter Four

How the Protected Became Protectors 1914–45

THE TWO WORLD WARS of the twentieth century severely disrupted the UK fishing industry and threatened the lives and livelihoods of the thousands involved. The sheer numbers of fishermen involved should not be under-estimated, particularly in comparison with the equivalent statistics for the industry one hundred years later (see Chapter Twelve).[1] On the eve of the First World War, there were 45,382 British fishermen in work aboard some 7,200 craft, which included 1,657 trawlers and 1,555 drifters. Approximately a further 100,000 were directly involved in some aspect of the industry.

In previous centuries, as Chapter One in particular has shown, those who had experience of working at sea were regarded as a precious commodity by the Royal Navy. By the time of the two great wars of the twentieth century, it was recognised that the fishing boats themselves, particularly the trawlers and drifters together with some of their equipment, were also of huge value in tackling two enemies – particularly the mine and later the submarine. The naval historian Julian Corbett, understanding the irony of the situation as Britain prepared for the Great War wrote, 'In all tradition it had been a constant duty of the Grand Fleet to protect our fishing fleets; now it was the fishing fleets who must protect our Grand Fleet.'[2]

This chapter describes the immense but often overlooked contributions made by fishermen and their boats during the war years before the fleets could be returned to their peacetime work. However, accounts and analyses of individual actions are largely beyond the scope of this book. Therefore, particular stories of the heroism, resilience and courage of the men who fought, together with their families and the wider fishing communities who endured ten long years of war, are only acknowledged *in passim*.

An asset recognised

The sea mine became a particularly potent threat during the Russo-Japanese War (1904–05) when it was realised that these comparatively cheap and unsophisticated weapons could inflict substantial damage on naval fleets.[3] A total of three battleships, five cruisers and three destroyers were lost to mining during that war together with the lives of thousands of sailors.

Admiral Charles Beresford had the foresight and purpose to seek answers to neutralising this problem and, following a visit to Grimsby, saw the potential of employing trawlers with their wire ropes and steam-driven winches as minesweepers. Trials were carried out off Portland in 1908 using two modern Grimsby trawlers, the *Andes* and *Algoma*. The methods used were to prove simple yet effective during the coming war.

The otter boards used on a conventional trawl were replaced with prismatic kites and a single wire warp was towed between two trawlers, its depth regulated by the kites. The experiments showed that by spreading the sweep over two cables in width the trawlers could maintain a seagoing sweep of between 5 and 6 knots, dependent on the weather.[4]

It was realised during the experiments, no doubt to the chagrin of some in the Royal Navy, that the trawlermen possessed superior skills in the business of sweeping mines to those of the professional servicemen.

The Royal Naval Reserve (Trawler Section) was created in 1910 specifically to crew a calculated 100 minesweeping trawlers in time of war. Thus, the RNR(T) was established with some 142 skippers and 1,136 men at the outbreak of war on 4 August 1914.[5] On the evening of that day, the small German excursion steamer *Königen Luise* steamed at full speed across the southern North Sea and laid the first minefield of the First World War off the northern bank of the Thames Estuary. It was clear that the Germans were going to adopt both a defensive and an aggressive minelaying policy.[6]

By 1 September, no fewer than 250 trawlers and drifters had been requisitioned. The trawler owners and skippers showed much willingness to co-operate and not just for patriotic reasons. An immediate cessation of fishing in the North Sea had been ordered at the commencement of hostilities and although that was relaxed shortly it could only be performed under a complex set of Admiralty rules and regulations. Consequently, fewer fishing boats were required and with the prospect

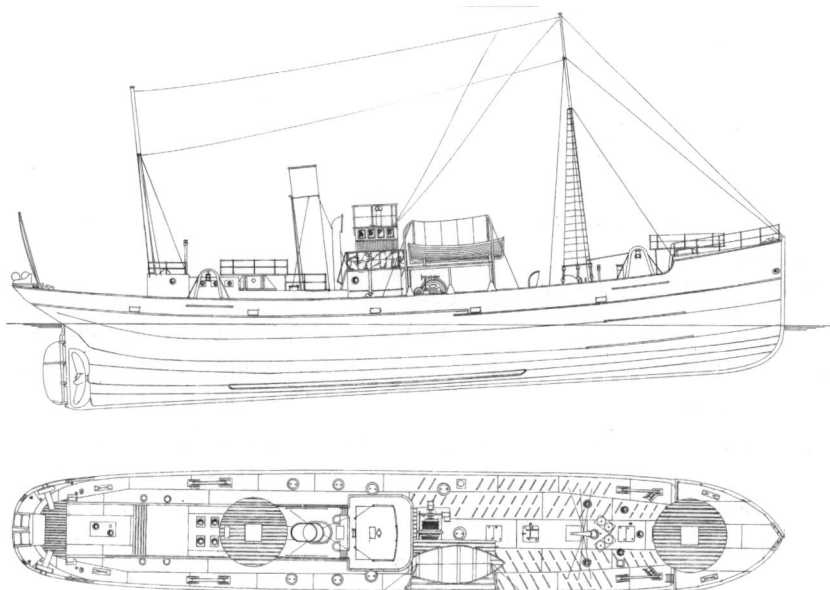

Figure 1: HM *Mersey*-class Admiralty trawler, general arrangement, 1917. (John Lambert Collection)

of unemployment looming, war service in the RNR(T) became an attractive alternative for some.[7]

The early months of the war proved to be a great challenge to this new division of the Royal Navy. A number of the trawlers were sunk during efforts to clear entire minefields. It was decided instead to concentrate on creating swept channels through the fields together with prominently placed marker buoys. Further experiments using drifters were tried in order to speed up the process but those were later abandoned after determining that the techniques were too complicated and dangerous.

An Admiral Minesweeping Services, Rear Admiral Charlton, was appointed in the light of the growing importance of the role of the RNR(T). The stark reality of the cost in human and materiel terms of the minefield menace had become all too apparent:

> By the time he [Admiral Charlton] assumed command, an average of one ship had been destroyed for every two mines sunk and the carnage they could create amongst those vessels tasked with their removal was already apparent: a member of a crew of minesweepers was said to have been lost for every mine destroyed.

The deadliness of this seaborne device was all too evident, as was the inexperience of officers and crew.[8]

Despite a brief lull in the German minelaying offensive later in 1914, the threat was immediately magnified with the loss of *King George V*-class battleship HMS *Audacious* to a mine in October 1914. This meant that elements of the Grand Fleet had to retreat to Lough Swilly in Ireland while the search went on for the exact location of the minefield off the North Scottish coast that had accounted for the super-dreadnought.

The bombardment of the seaside town of Scarborough by two German battlecruisers in December 1916 is remembered both for its audacity and the fear it engendered among the British population at large that the war was being brought to their doorsteps. However, while the attack was taking place a light cruiser, SMS *Kolberg*, was also laying a minefield south of Scarborough. Shipping losses were immediate and included two trawlers and four minesweepers. It took until April of the following year for the field to be swept in its entirety, although a narrow passage had been cleared and 'buoyed' before the end of the year.

By this time, the minesweeping forces had grown from an initial ninety-four vessels to over 200; the trawlers had been supplemented by paddle steamers, which provided exceptional manoeuvrability and shallow draughts at the expense of range and sea-keeping capabilities. The cost in terms of lives lost by the fishermen who volunteered continued to be considerable, however, and never more keenly felt than in the close-knit communities in traditional fishing towns such as Grimsby. The local paper, the *Grimsby Daily Mail*, published the grim statistics on 15 December 1915, stating that no fewer than fifty-five of the town's vessels had been lost through various causes during the year with an overall death toll of 269.[9]

Another role

The sinking of the cruisers HMS *Cressy*, *Hogue* and *Aboukir* in the southern North Sea off the Netherlands in late September 1914 awakened the Royal Navy to the submarine menace. Despite the fact that these cruisers were regarded as obsolescent, *U-9*'s success sent shock waves that were felt not only by the RN but internationally, inasmuch as the most powerful navy in the world could be dealt such a grievous blow – apparently with comparative ease. Other sinkings followed with increasing intensity: the cruiser HMS *Hawke*, the aircraft ferry *Hermes* and the first of many merchant vessels, SS *Glitra*, off the coast of Norway on 20 October.

There was no regular anti-submarine capability available, initially only a set of recommended Admiralty precautions in the event of an attack. Nets were favoured by the Admiralty in the early part of the war and were used in large quantities across harbour entrances and on coastal routes. Ingenious, yet totally ineffective devices, were thought up such as the 'lance bomb' (a 7lb charge of amatol on the end of a wooden pole), which was to be hurled at the surfaced submarine from the deck of the attacking vessel.[10]

Trawlers were investigated for their possible usage in deterring, damaging or even destroying enemy submarines.

Trawl gear was developed in order to indicate the presence of a submarine, snare it or even damage or destroy it while submerged. Fishing drifters were also brought into naval service, their long surface-suspended nets, used to catch pelagic species of fish, were modified to restrict the movement of submarines and force them to the surface, where they could be engaged by guns that had been fitted to the fishing boats' decks.[11]

If these tactics sound rudimentary they were but this was the early days of submarine warfare when the German U-boats fired their torpedoes or guns while on the surface and took their opponents captive rather than abandon them to the elements. Unrestricted submarine warfare was fully implemented by the Germans in 1917, although instances of unprovoked attacks on fishing boat crew occurred earlier than that, as evidenced below. Nevertheless, by the end of the war, RN trawlers and drifters were to prove to be the most successful anti-submarine weapon, accounting for thirty-seven of the 112 U-boats sunk during the conflict.[12]

In 1915, the Germans added a further hazard in the form of minelaying submarines. Although these lacked the capacity of surface vessels, they could carry out more operations and were much harder to detect. During the first phase of a coastal offensive, the Germans claimed to have laid 648 mines between Dover and Grimsby. These accounted for 104 vessels sunk, of which nine were Admiralty trawlers and drifters. The following year, the operational area had increased to encompass most of the British Isles. Inventions such as serrated wire sweeps were introduced, which made it easier to cut through mine cables and, because they were lighter, could be operated by drifters as well as the more powerful trawlers.[13]

Nevertheless, as is apparent from an internal memorandum, 'Remarks on Submarine Patrols', dated 28 June 1915, the problem of how to counter the anti-shipping offensive by a handful of German submarines became deeply concerning. Having waded through and eliminated 'the enormous number' of false reports of submarines being sighted, no doubt many emanating from an increasingly jittery populace, it was reckoned that between six and eight submarines were at sea at any one time during that month, operating against commercial traffic. It was deduced that the U-boats circuited both ways round the north of Scotland. They picked up vessels on the west coasts of Scotland and Ireland on their way, especially off the Flannan Islands, the neighbourhood of Achill Head and the south-west of Ireland. It was estimated that an average patrol circuit lasted about a week, with an additional four or five days spent loitering in the vicinity of the English and Irish Channels. A crumb of comfort was derived from the fact that although submarines had been frequently reported in the English Channel, no ship had been sunk there since 15 April. This was attributed to them avoiding the mine and net barrage that had been laid.[14]

The report shows that it had been possible to track the movements of one submarine, believed to be *U-34*.[15] On the evening of 1 June, it had sunk the trawler *Victoria* by gunfire 145 miles west by south of St Ann's Head in the Western Approaches. The following day *U-34* had disposed of another trawler, *Hirose*, 130 miles west by south of Lundy Island. No action had been possible because the news only reached the naval base at Pembroke Dock on the evening of 3 June. The same day the Belgian trawler *Delta B* was sunk in the same area, followed by two other ships over the next couple of days.

A further two victims were added to the tally on the 6th and 7th of the month but thereafter there was some uncertainty as to whether the sinkings were attributable to *U-34* or *U-35*. The latter boat then proceeded to dispose of a further seven ships, including Russian, French and Norwegian vessels, on a patrol undertaken during the second week in June.[16]

What is immediately clear from the report is the quality of the intelligence at the disposal of the Admiralty. This was the work of Room 40, which, by the start of 1915, was providing signal-derived intelligence (SIGINT) beyond major fleet movements in the North Sea:

The most significant contribution, ever more important as the war progressed, was knowledge of U-boat operations. By January [1915], Room 40 was well informed on the strength and location of the U-boat fleet in home waters and the Western Approaches, and initiated daily returns to Churchill, Fisher, Oliver [Chief of War Staff] and Wilson [Admiral of the Fleet], giving the last-known position of each U-boat gleaned from decrypts. Traffic to and from U-boats was extensive out to a range of 300 miles, and relevant signals were intercepted from FdU [Senior Officer U-Boats], fleet broadcasts and coastal stations.[17]

The tactic formulated by the RN to counter the U-boats was to try to 'swamp' the area with as large a number of vessels as available. For example, the Southern Patrol Force Operations Orders recommended, 'As many Units as can be spared from other necessary duties should be pushed out 30 or 40 miles from Scilly, Milford and Queenstown respectively.' As soon as reports were received that a vessel had been attacked, provided that it was within twenty-four hours, all the vessels were to endeavour to close within 20 to 30 miles of the adversary and attempt to surround it, 'keeping on their own sides of the position where the vessel was attacked in the first place, and afterwards on their own sides of any position in which the submarine is subsequently seen, being careful not to be led away by any false reports'.[18]

These instructions, although logical on paper, seem inordinately prescriptive and difficult to carry out effectively with an immature communications network in other than serene sea conditions. Few trawlers were equipped with wireless; the Admiralty long remained reticent to grant requests from Auxiliary Patrol commanders for wireless sets to be fitted, partly because it was feared that the increased traffic would interfere with more important naval communications. The use of Morse code, semaphore or coastal signal stations were poor substitutes, meaning vital intelligence often took far too long to reach the right destination.[19]

Douglas d'Enno describes the June U-boat offensive as 'the Summer Onslaught' and catalogues many instances of quite small fishing smacks being targeted within a comparatively short space of time: a total of 249 boats sunk and fifty-three lives lost. Perhaps the most infamous episode involved the Milford Haven trawler S/T *Victoria*, mentioned above. According to *U-34*'s log, the *Victoria* was acting as a 'guard vessel', therefore, supposedly, a legitimate target for an otherwise unprovoked attack.[20] The incident underlines the fact that the seas around the British coast had become very much a part of the front line.

Improving countermeasures

By the last year of the war, the rapid expansion of what had become known since the end of 1914 as the Auxiliary Patrol resulted in the creation of twenty-one operational zones that covered every part of the British Isles. Each area came under the command of an SNO and varied in size depending on the nature of the coastline.

In addition to a comprehensive organisational structure, two important anti-submarine countermeasures had been developed, namely the hydrophone and the depth charge, which improved the chances of damaging or destroying what had been virtually an undetectable underwater foe. Also, the introduction later in the war of the paravane, a construction comprising cables, cutting gear and kites fitted and towed from the bows of a ship, proved to be an effective counter to laid mines. Finally, by early 1918, Auxiliary Patrol vessels were better armed, many having been received 12pdr guns, a move initiated by Admiral Jellicoe following the loss of three Peterhead trawlers, which in surface engagements had been outgunned by U-boats in July 1916.[21]

Originally, hydrophones had only been able to detect the presence of a submarine in the general vicinity but later sets could give an indication of direction as well, although the technology was still in its infancy and the sets were not very efficient. Nevertheless, by 1917, many of the new Admiralty trawlers coming into service were equipped with these devices as built. There were drawbacks, of course, including the need to stop engines when the hydrophone was in use, which added to the vulnerability of the hunting vessel.[22] The depth charge also proved an increasingly effective weapon and A/S trawlers were equipped with them from 1916 onwards. When a 'thrower' was added in the latter half of 1917, the potency of the weapon increased as it became possible to project a heavier charge out to a distance of some 40ft.

By the last months of the war it is evident that, with experience and technologically advanced countermeasures, a much more sophisticated response could be made to the submarine threat in comparison with what might be described as the 'corralling' manoeuvres of 1915 described earlier in this chapter. The Southern Patrol Operations Orders describe tactics not vastly dissimilar from those adopted by Escort Groups during the Battle of the Atlantic nearly a quarter of a century later.

The flotilla of trawlers in the Southern Patrol Force area was divided into twenty divisions each comprising three trawlers. In daylight hours and during good weather, on the signal 'take up patrol formation', the three vessels would adopt a line-abreast formation, a mile apart. One paravane (fish) would be deployed unless the Senior Officer judged that a submarine was likely to be in the vicinity, in which case more sets would be employed. While in patrol formation the vessels would stop at twenty-minute intervals to enable the hydrophones to be operated. Separate orders covering night-time patrols were also issued.[23]

When hunting by day, the 'No. 1' or 'supporting' ship, usually that of the Senior Officer, would undertake the key role, conducting the search, working out the plot and bombarding when considered advisable. The supporting ship would also initiate the course of the accompanying trawlers, designated 'No. 2' and 'No. 3' respectively, endeavouring to obtain good cross bearings. Signal flags were used to pass orders. Exact instructions were given about the role of the hydrophone officer and the intervals at which the vessels should stop in order to use their underwater detection system. These included when to open fire on the opponent:

> The Senior Officer has to bear in mind the possibility of opening fire with Bomb Throwers or Howitzers when the plot shows him to be within the range of these weapons. The morale of a submarine's crew might well be shaken by the explosion of a few bombs even though she is not within their danger radius.

Depth charges were used, particularly if it was thought that the submarine was sitting on the sea floor.[24]

The requirement for Auxiliary Patrol trawler minesweepers was not confined to home waters. They were despatched to the eastern Mediterranean in preparation for the naval assault on the Dardanelles and also in the aftermath of the failed campaign during the evacuations at Suvla and Anzac. In September 1915, sixty drifters were despatched from the UK to lay a net barrage across the Straits of Otranto before being diverted to evacuate what was left of the Serbian army, which was retreating into Albania. The barrage was fought over for the next two years, causing a number of drifters to be lost in action in addition to the trawlers that had been sunk through a number of causes during the Dardanelles Campaign.[25]

Trawlers were also involved in the White Sea, where the Germans laid a number of mines in an attempt to disrupt Allied supplies reaching Russia. This was a particularly harsh environment in which to operate, lacking the engineering infrastructure available in home waters.

Counting the cost

There are many factors involved in coming to a value judgement on the contribution made by the Auxiliary Patrol ships measured against the cost in terms of lives lost, the disruption it caused to the fishing industry and the impact on the everyday lives of the UK population. The losses were painful and considerable. A total of 1,456 fishing vessels were requisitioned and operated during the conflict, of which 266 were sunk. At the same time, 25 per cent of the fishing fleet was not taken up for war work and continued to fish under Royal Navy direction regarding the areas in which they could operate – in theory at least.[26]

Robb Robinson's statistical analysis shows that an average of 735,000 tons of catch had been landed in England and Wales during the period 1909–13. This had fallen to 240,000 tons between 1915 and 1918. There was a similar trend for Scotland. However, the value of the catch almost doubled and, perhaps surprisingly, fish was never rationed.[27] Douglas d'Enno notes that the price of food in general increased by 81 per cent in large towns and 74 per cent in smaller ones during the first two years of the war but the price of fish was practically double that percentage rise.[28]

In an effort to present a balanced picture in his history of fishermen in the Great War, d'Enno also describes some of the misdemeanours, which ranged from rule breaking to desertion and general non-conformity.[29] Of course, there is enough evidence in this book to suggest that following the rule book did not come as second nature to the independently minded fisherman.

Interwar planning and shortcomings

The International Mine Clearance Committee was established following the end of the Great War to deal with the immense, unwanted legacy of the recent conflict. The remuneration was attractive and a number of fishermen were prepared to volunteer. In the meantime, the RNR(T) was decommissioned in 1920, to be replaced by the Royal Naval Reserve Patrol Service (RNPS).

The combination of the disarmament lobbies, the world financial crises and the reluctance of the Royal Navy to move forward tactically from the rigidity of the battleship era have all been cited as reasons why the service was ill-prepared in many ways for the next conflict. The threat from the mine and the submarine, which had been so pertinent during the 1914–18 war, appeared to have been largely overlooked. The first post-war purpose-built minesweepers, the *Halcyon* class, did not enter service until the mid-1930s, although the slightly earlier *Bridgewater*-class sloops of the 1927 building programme were designed with a minesweeping capability.[30]

The first mention of a 'convoy sloop' appeared in the 1933 building programme, which can be interpreted as a vague acknowledgement of the submarine threat, although Stephen Roskill adds, somewhat caustically, 'But as sloops of two other types were included in the same programme it is fairly plain that no one was very clear regarding their function.'[31] The same author, otherwise notable for his reticent, prosaic style, employs italics in the first volume of his authoritative work on the interwar Navy to drive home the point, '*But no one exercise in the protection of a slow mercantile convoy against submarine or air attack took place between 1919 and 1939.*'[32]

Although the National Socialist Workers (Nazi) Party would not achieve full power in Germany for another three years, the Admiralty's Trade Division proposed as early as 1930 that on the outbreak of any future war the Royal Navy should assume immediate control of the entire fishing fleet. Each major fishing port would have its own senior naval officer in charge and each fishing fleet would be assigned to a squadron, one in four of which would be armed with a 12pdr gun. Twelve hundred fishing vessels would continue to work around the coast, 'working under the control scheme in order to provide a degree of fisheries protection'.[33] The MAF drew up plans to earmark a group of experienced fishermen to work with the Navy in wartime and not be drafted into either the Army or the Air Force. Fundamentally, as will be shown, these plans were sound and practical but, in the outcome, other issues received priority.

Obviously, the planning departments had the comparatively recent experience of the First World War on which to draw. There was trepidation in the minds of some within the Navy at the prospect of working closely with fishermen again. Memories of the wartime difficulties were still fresh involving efforts to impose service discipline on recruits from the fishing industry. There was to be considerable opposition when it was suggested that the acute manning problem then affecting fishery protection and minesweeping could be eased by recruiting unemployed fishermen. That proposal was subsequently scrapped.

By the middle years of the decade the prospect of future conflict involving Germany became more and more likely. Indeed, the impact of this is reflected in the Senior Officer Fishery Protection Quarterly Reports of the time, which include sections on intelligence gathering undertaken during visits to northern European ports where German merchantmen flying the swastika were frequently present. In one report there is even an eyewitness assessment of the physical appearance and demeanour of the German leader Hermann Goering.[34]

Nevertheless, one can still detect an air of complacency, for example with respect to the estimates for the minesweeping requirements for a future war in a report written by the Admiralty Director of Plans (DoP) in 1936 – ironic in the light of the subsequent magnitude of the Second World War mine threat at sea. The DoP considered that the 'essential needs' for minesweepers could be met if twenty-one minesweeping sloops and twenty-seven trawlers and motor minesweepers were available, with a further twenty-seven held in reserve at Malta, Trincomalee and Singapore. Meanwhile, the then current Captain Fishery Protection and Minesweeping, Captain V Crutchley, reported that his 1st M/S Flotilla consisted of seven new minesweeping sloops, three 'old trawlers' and five Fishery Protection 'gunboats' (trawlers) fitted as auxiliary minesweepers – a similarly modest force.[35]

However, the 1936 Admiralty report did fully appreciate the importance of the fishing industry both to the economy and to the well-being of the population. It was noted that in peacetime the vast majority of the annual catch was consumed by the home market. If the Admiralty requisitioned large numbers of trawlers there would be less fish for public consumption. By the same token, 80 per cent of the drift net catch (predominantly herring) was exported, bringing significant revenue in foreign earnings. In time of war, on the other hand, it was emphasised again that there would have to be immediate control of fisheries. This would include direct supervision of the Chief Inspector of Fisheries and the MAF staff, with similar jurisdiction exercised over the administration of the Scottish fisheries. Other measures would include the requisitioning of fishing boats for fleet purposes; military control and protection of vessels while fishing – even technical control of the marketing of fish. It was realised that such a large undertaking, in addition to minesweeping, might require the recreation of the post of Admiral of Patrols, used during the Great War.[36]

In the meantime the fishing industry had been undergoing a serious crisis. The herring fisheries had suffered a sequence of setbacks, including aggressive foreign competition, and would never fully recover. Following the end of the Great War, the trawling sector had boomed, with the annual catch reaching over a million tons. Fishing boats were larger, more powerful, but also more costly to run. Over-fishing and decreased stocks had resulted. Therefore vessels were voluntarily laid up by their owners in an attempt to counter a general spiral of decline. This led to unemployment during some of the worst years of the Great Depression. Many fishermen left the industry altogether as a consequence. Although the Admiralty expressed sympathy for the plight of an industry it continued to recognise as a vital resource both in wartime and peace, it did not and probably could not offer any sort of subsidy from the Navy Vote.[37]

In December 1938, with war less than twelve months away, an Admiralty Committee charged with planning the organisation of fishing in wartime produced a report that at last reflected both a new-found urgency and the sheer scale of the task ahead. The requisitioning of fishing boats could not be undertaken all at once and needed to be staged. This would require prior warnings being issued in secret to fishing boat owners; this task would be entrusted to MAF. Distant-water trawlers would have to keep in regular touch with base via W/T or R/T to be kept up to date. Inevitably peacetime fishing routines would be disrupted and, after the actual outbreak of hostilities, the Admiralty would assume full and direct control. This would be exercised through individual port Fishery Committees working under the leadership of naval officers in charge. The requisitioned fishing vessels would be chartered by the Admiralty at a nominal rate of hire. The crews would be enrolled into a Fishery Reserve Force and come under routine naval discipline. All subsequent movements would be directed by the naval officer in charge and the vessels would be assigned to groups of between twelve and twenty.[38]

The report recognised the unrealistic presumptions made in earlier plans. Owing to the expected volume of work, it was anticipated that there would be delays in converting fishing boats for their new roles. The conversion of an anti-submarine escort trawler took between three and ten weeks to complete, once an available shipyard had been identified. Typically the work included extensive internal and external structural reorganisation together with the fitting of the necessary military equipment to enable the vessel to undertake a war role.[39]

Appropriate armament and communications equipment were key components in the preparation of fishing boats for their wartime duties. The recommended best weapon was a 12pdr (3in) HA/LA gun. Training, especially for gunners, was an added requirement. It was realised that there were no suitable guns available at the time – which seems a glaring omission for a country on the brink of war. The position regarding communications was better. There were 391 trawlers fitted with W/T sets suitable for working with naval on-shore stations; of these 198 would be requisitioned for the anti-submarine and minesweeping services, leaving 193 W/T-equipped boats to continue their peacetime fishing role.[40]

Trials were carried out in June 1939 after three trawlers had been fitted with Type 123 asdic sets. A memo by Captain Anti-Submarine Warfare warned that congestion in the shipyards would be caused while the necessary conversion work was carried out on the first 100 vessels already earmarked. There was debate about what work was absolutely necessary in the time available – in other words, which shortcuts might be acceptable. What would be the impact on the trawler owners of the necessary structural work needed to be undertaken? The major item in conversion was the gutting of the fish hold and the subsequent fitting of accommodation, magazines and stiffening needed for the extra weight imposed by adding a gun – all within the confines of one compartment.[41]

By the following month, with the prospect of war ever closer, immediate action was required. Although clearly not ideal, it was decided that some fifty trawlers would be deployed with only minesweeping gear fitted; weaponry and other conversion work would have to be added later. It was also decided to approach individual owners and/or the British Trawlers Federation (BTF) to invite them to meet the cost of structural modifications of their boats prior to the fitting of asdic domes and 4in guns in order to circumvent the anticipated bottlenecks in the shipyards.[42]

War

Despite the preparations, when war was declared in September 1939, the Royal Navy had just ninety-four trawlers and drifters at its disposal, as opposed to the approximately 3,000 available towards the end of the First World War.[43] Given the scale and the complexity of the operation, it was almost inevitable that there would be further problems once war was declared and the requisitioned fishing boats began to appear at their new destinations. Several ports, including Newhaven, reported that no trawlers had arrived by the middle of the September, while the Director of Local Defence Division stated that at least six had already left their requisitioning ports with no W/T and V/S (visual signals) ratings aboard. At Sheerness, the Captain Extended Defences commented, 'these trawlers have not been fitted for W/T communication and as they have to lie at buoys at Sheerness, where there is no wharfage, it is essential that they should be able to receive visual signals'.[44]

The misgivings among professional naval officers regarding manning, expressed pre-war, surfaced again as the country stood on the brink of war. Captain A/S HMS *Osprey*, Portland, observed, 'It is desired, however, that the lessons learned during the Abyssinian Crisis should be taken into account, and that any large scale "dilution" by fishermen should not be lightly undertaken.'[45]

The impact on the fishing industry was felt immediately. Ernest Bevin, in his capacity as General Secretary of the Transport and General Workers Union (TGWU), wrote to Winston Churchill, First Lord of the Admiralty, on 10 October 1939. Bevin was greatly concerned about the effect of the requisitioning of trawlers on the men he represented and the likely increase in unemployment in the fishing towns caused by the disruption to livelihoods. He drew Churchill's attention to the impact on distant-water fishing and the need for an overall strategy to oversee a regular reintegration of the fishing fleet once the current emergency was over. Moreover, he felt that an advisory council needed to have the authority to fix prices and to develop a marketing and distribution strategy.

The First Lord responded promptly and a meeting was initiated, convened by MAF. In the meantime, Churchill organised his own to work out a plan, 'the object of which is the Utmost Fish [his emphasis] subject to naval necessity'. In outline, he considered that industry losses should be shared among ports and that priority be given by shipyards to trawlers that could be constructed quickly. He emphasised that it was vital for the fishing industry to keep working.⁴⁶

The MAF-led initiative prompted a conference involving many of the interested parties: MAF itself, the TGWU, the assistant Chief of Naval Staff (ACNS), the Ministries of Labour and of Food and the Scottish Home Department. It was chaired by the Parliamentary and Financial Secretary to the Admiralty, Geoffrey Shakespeare MP. Several matters were settled at the meeting, which was intended to allay the worst fears of the owners and the union in particular. Details were given of the trawlers that would be returned in the near future to Hull, the worst-affected port. In future it would be the policy for trawlers to be purchased rather than requisitioned. When the existing, requisitioned fleet became surplus to requirements, they would not be 'thrown' on the open market without prior consultation with the owners. Other assurances included the immediate return of around twenty minesweeping vessels. Consideration would be given to the immediate building of some sixty new and standard-sized trawlers and the formation of a new, advisory standing committee that would meet monthly.⁴⁷

In the meantime, events took an unexpected turn in the midst of the 'phoney war' period. In December 1939, the magnetic mine crisis was considered serious enough for the ACNS to announce a 'modification in promises made', with the likely outcome being further calls on the resources of the fishing fleet. His statement that 80 per cent of the trawler fleet had been taken up during the previous war, in comparison with 50 per cent of the current number, seems, at this distance anyway, a slightly desperate attempt to 'sugar the pill'.⁴⁸

A 'raw deal'

Barely a month after war started, two of the leading fishing ports, Hull and Grimsby, through their respective MPs, made formal advances to the Admiralty about the impact the requisitioning of boats and compulsory purchase had already made on their towns and the livelihoods of the inhabitants. Hull claimed in peacetime to land the greatest weight of fish of any port in the UK. It had been practically dispossessed of all its working boats and fishing had been brought, more or less, to a standstill. It had the most up-to-date fleet, which it recognised would make it a target for appropriation, but there had been scant evidence of equity in comparison with other ports. Furthermore, the wider impact had been felt in terms of local unemployment, ancillary industries, investment in the infrastructure, even the lack of affordable fish for the working-class parts of town.

The statistics seemed to support Hull's claim. On 1 July 1939 the city had 210 boats, a number already depleted as twenty-three had been sold to the Admiralty since the beginning of the year. Since the war started 124 fishing boats had been requisitioned, with a further twenty-one scheduled to be taken, leaving only nineteen of the smallest craft – just 6.6 per cent of Hull's peacetime gross tonnage. The two MPs' conclusion simply highlighted an unfortunate conundrum, 'It is submitted that this is a "raw deal"; no port should be penalised in this way simply because it happens to have the up-to-date type of boats required by the nation in time of war.'[49]

The Mayor of Grimsby submitted a separate plea, stating in a letter that 116 boats had been requisitioned thus far and nearly all of them had belonged to the distant-water fleet (Grimsby also operated smaller North Sea fishing smacks). In August 1939 the approximate weekly landings amounted to 4,500 tons; by the end of September it was down to 1,650 tons. Likewise, five of the borough's fish meal factories had been in operation six weeks previously; in early October only one was left working just a three-day week. Earlier, the Bishop of Lincoln had written to Churchill about the plight of the town, underlining the importance of the industry to the life and prosperity of Grimsby. At the other end of the scale, two Cardiff skippers also contacted the First Lord on behalf of the 168 men of the city's deep-sea fishing fleet who were all now unemployed because the entire fleet had been requisitioned. The letter ended poignantly, 'Some of these men, including ourselves, gave our services during the last war and are now over the age of service. We are, nevertheless, still fit and deplore the fact of our inactivity.'[50]

In June 1940 a further deputation by the Hull fishing boat owners was taken to the Admiralty and this reiterated many of the points that had been made the previous year.

A breed apart

Paul Lund and Harry Ludlam's classic book *Trawlers at War* focusses frequently on the characteristics of the men who skippered and crewed the requisitioned or purchased boats that bore the brunt of the escort, anti-submarine and minesweeping tasks, particularly in the early years of the war before their ranks were 'diluted' by hostilities-only ratings who did not necessarily have a seagoing background. Lund and Ludlam pepper their narrative with anecdotes that typify the fishermen as being tough, independent, often cussed – sometimes contemptuous of authority. It is a description that no doubt resonated with its audience, particularly when the book was first published in 1971. For many, at the time, the experiences of thirty years earlier were still fresh in the memory. 'These Patrol Service fishermen were tough men. Out trawling they thought nothing of working sixty to seventy hours on deck without sleep; they would carry on gutting and washing fish automatically, and fall asleep while on the job.'[51]

According to the writers, most skippers were, 'uncommonly stubborn, many thoroughly harsh men', while the mates were required to 'command absolute authority over their crew, even fighting them if necessary'. The discrepancy in class, upbringing and education between the typical skipper and his Royal Navy commanding officer equivalent are often highlighted in the book, as in this example:

> We were working with a convoy in the North Sea in horrible weather when the destroyer in charge of the escort called us up by lamp, but as the skipper couldn't read the signals he called me up top ... The destroyer was ordering us: 'Proceed with consort to search area – suspected U-Boat in the vicinity.' The skipper said to me: 'What the hell does he mean – what's a consort?'[52]

The trawlers and their crews soon became embroiled in some of the larger actions as the Allies retreated westwards across Europe. In April 1940 some thirty trawlers were despatched to Norway in support of the British Expeditionary Force sent to try to stem the German advance across the country. Fourteen boats were lost during the campaign, all of them falling victim to enemy aircraft – a deadly new threat that would not have been encountered by their forebears during the First World War. The next month, May, a number of herring drifters, in particular, were involved in the evacuation of British and French troops from Dunkirk. A further evacuation, involving trawlers on that occasion, took place two weeks later further south from the port of St Nazaire.

Away from the more eye-catching major events of the early months and years of the Second World War, the trawlers were utilised for mundane, but nevertheless vital, tasks. The Northern Patrol was devised to try to prevent German surface raiders from reaching the Atlantic via the straits between the Faroe Islands and Iceland. At first armed merchant cruisers were used, followed by cruisers; eventually this mostly monotonous task fell to coal-burning trawlers that were found to be ideal for the job owing to their endurance, which was superior to that of destroyers. The Northern Patrol trawlers were based at Kirkwall in the Orkneys and typically spent eight to ten days patrolling their sectors at 6 knots, 'in some of the roughest seas imaginable'.[53]

In fact, the trawlers fared better than many of the regular Navy ships on Atlantic convoys. Lieutenant Colin Warwick, posted aboard *St Loman*, claimed that his vessel and other trawlers, 'made light of the worst of the North Atlantic weather despite their low freeboard amidships. The fleet destroyers with their shallow draught and knife-like bows made heavy going in the usual rough weather, severely reducing their cruising speed to avoid taking heavy seas forward.'[54]

Looking forward to peace

Essentially, one could ask, what had changed with respect to the two main wartime tasks of A/S and minesweeping in the intervening interwar years? The German U-boat arm had grown exponentially: its boats were larger, had far greater range, were more sophisticated technologically and could operate alone or in 'packs'. The trawlers had benefitted from some of the developments in tracking/detecting and in weaponry. Some, but not all, were fitted with asdic, which was effective at speeds below 18 knots when ship-generated noise came into play; performance was also adversely affected in bad weather. The Type 271 surface search radar proved to be effective at detecting a U-boat's periscope at comparatively short range. The trawler's slow speed was partially offset by the fact that its single screw was identical to the sound made by a merchant ship and the submarine might be too late in detecting the threat bearing down on it.[55] The depth charge remained the principal A/S weapon against the submerged U-boat; tactics for its use grew more sophisticated but a good deal depended on the efficiency of the crew in discharging the explosives.

It was expected that despite countering the contact, the moored mine would constitute the principal task for the minesweeping trawlers and drifters. A lighter-weight, single-wire Oropesa sweep had been developed that was suitable for fitting in these vessels. What had not been anticipated was the magnetic mine, the impact of which was mentioned earlier in this chapter. This was followed by the acoustic and later still pressure mines, all of which required a variety of countermeasures.

By the mid-point in the war, although the outcome was far from certain, the Navy was beginning to review the future for the fishing industry in the light of the ongoing requirement for its vessels and personnel. In March 1942 an assessment by the Head of Military Branch of the lessons that had been learned since the start of the conflict reached some interesting and often surprising conclusions. Although pre-war there were conceptions that fishing boats and their skilled and experienced crews would prove a useful resource in war, the Admiralty had since recognised that the seamen themselves were of even greater value than their vessels. By the same token, drifters had been thought to be of marginal use, whereas two and a half years' experience of war had proved that those craft had diverse and vital applications.

On the latter point, an undated memo titled 'Herring Industry: post-war condition' pointed to the value to the Navy of 'a large and flourishing herring industry'. It listed the 'valuable reservoir of personnel', and the large number of craft, not designed for naval purposes but currently providing an important service. On the downside, there was the problem of finding suitable shipbuilding firms with the skills to cope with the need for new craft. The Admiralty building programme was producing either small craft or large minesweepers, and both types would be unsuitable for later conversion back to fishing vessels.

It was predicted that mine clearance and wreck removal would delay the eventual return of vessels and men to the industry, as had been the case following the First World War. Magnetic mines, for example, were dangerous and difficult to sweep, so clearance would take a long time. Therefore, in relation to herring drifters, in service as auxiliary minesweepers, it was impossible to forecast an early release of vessels or of men.

Looking ahead, the Director of Mine Services' (DMS) sober forecast echoed many of the above points. Particularly, he considered it unlikely that modern minesweepers could be designed that might have a future use, for example in the fishing industry:

> It is unfortunately true that the requirements of modern minesweeping have been found to clash in almost every particular. We have got a long way to go before we can say that the war has been won, or even enemy minelaying controlled, and for this reason DMS can make no helpful suggestions towards building warships which can be converted to industry.[56]

Later in 1942, some measures were drawn up to alleviate the prospect of a winter shortage of fish for the home market due to the demands of naval requisitioning. The problem had been exacerbated in recent times by another heavy demand for even more fishing vessels to be requisitioned. Therefore, as a concession, the east coast fishing grounds would be extended, fishing boats would be equipped with larger-calibre guns for defensive purposes and one third of boats newly arrived in the UK from Allied countries would be allocated to the fishing industry.[57]

The urgency to bolster the fishing fleet continued unabated into the following year. A letter from the Minister of Food to the First Lord in July 1943 almost pleaded, 'After nearly four years, some of your trawlers may be in such a condition that they could be of more value to me than they are to you.' A V Alexander replied levelly that surplus craft were immediately returned to their owners as a matter of course. He added that arrangements had been made for requisitioned boats to be converted, twelve were under way at present with a further twenty-five scheduled to be returned by the end of the year, to include a number of steam drifters.[58]

Meanwhile, afloat it was generally accepted that the Arctic convoys constituted the worst assignment of all. Up to four trawlers at a time were employed as convoy escorts and rescue ships, sailing north and then east from Hvalfjord in Iceland with the convoys. They hugged the limits of the polar icefield in order to keep as far as possible from the enemy aircraft based in north Norway. Lund and Ludlam describe the experience in graphic terms:

> There was a special horror about working up there on the icy roof of the world which struck at a man's heart. It was an emotion compounded of the sick fear of those dark, desolate waters which froze a man as he fell into them; fear of the treacherous weathers; fear of the enemy sea and air raiders; and last but not least, a nagging distrust of the almost unknown Russians themselves.
>
> In particular, there was the ever-present danger of capsizing under the weight of quick-frozen ice.[59]

The plight of Hull came to the fore again in autumn 1944. The city's fishing industry was a victim of its own success. The distant-water fishing fleet of specialised trawlers was large enough to deal with the most rigorous of environments and carried the most modern and specialised equipment. Therefore, they were simply the best suited for naval service. The other major fishing ports, Grimsby, Aberdeen, Milford Haven and Fleetwood, had considerable numbers of smaller and middle-waters trawlers and older vessels, and therefore were less attractive targets for requisitioning. The submarine threat coupled with the shortage of minesweepers meant that every fishing boat over 130ft in length was required, which deprived Hull of its remaining forty trawlers. Unfortunately, of those forty only three had thus far been released back by the Navy.[60]

The view that the city had suffered the most was endorsed by a long letter from a Mr A Dobson at the Ministry of Agriculture and Fisheries to the Admiralty Head of Military Branch on the same subject. He referred to the city of Hull as being normally very independent in outlook but now felt unfairly neglected by the government. Its crews were highly proficient at deep-sea fishing and had been responsible, for example, for landing huge quantities of very marketable cod during pre-war. Although Dobson considered it proper to deal with all fishing ports evenly, he thought that Hull deserved special consideration.

MAF had received a deputation from the city headed by one of the local MPs, representatives of the trawlers' owners and Hull's economic advisor. There were also concerns about the way in which the trawlers had been maintained while in Navy hands. Could this work not be undertaken by trawler experts? Would it not be possible for the trawlers to combine 'warship' duties with fishing? Additionally, there was a historic claim that Winston Churchill, while First Lord, had promised to leave Hull with its forty trawlers prior to the June 1940 'cull'. However, there appeared to be no written evidence of such an undertaking. A similar deputation from Grimsby was also received.[61]

As the war in Europe drew to a close, statistics showed that in the period 1 January 1944 to 8 June 1945, 382 trawlers had been released back into service and that in June 1945 a workforce of 6,000 was engaged in the task of reconversion. At the same time there were calculated to be 324 trawlers working around the coasts of England and Wales; no figures for drifters were available. Scotland had 125 trawlers and 111 drifters at work.

Churchill was in the vanguard of this drive towards returning to peacetime normality, eager in particular to see distant-water fishing resume as soon as possible. Nevertheless, there was some resistance from the workforce, 'There is, as I understand, an element of uneasiness in the yards that the work should be taken on at all – it is palpably not military in purpose and in the eyes of some workers is simply intended to put money into the trawler owners' pockets.'

There was a constant battle fought at the time between military and non-military tasks. The war against Japan was still in progress and the build-up of forces for the anticipated future invasion of the Japanese mainland in the shape of troopships, assault ships, the Fleet Train, hospital ships etc. constituted a rival demand.[62]

Conclusion

The value and inherent adaptability of the fishing vessel was recognised 'just in time' for it to be utilised during the First World War to counter the twin threats posed, firstly from the sea mine and secondly from the submarine. Admiralty documents of the 1914–18 period show the way in which the Navy sought to integrate the Auxiliary Patrol and the strategies and tactics it adopted to counter the two potent, yet still technologically immature, threats.

It can be argued that the Navy, with the already established Royal Naval Patrol Service, as it was then called, was generally better prepared for the 1939–45 war in organisational terms at least, ready to commandeer large numbers of civilian vessels for its purposes from the beginning of 1939 onwards. Nevertheless, the sheer numbers of vessels required for the task was underestimated, which resulted in conversion 'bottlenecks' in shipyards across the country. Likewise, the unexpectedly potent aerial threat made the small fishing vessels extremely vulnerable, while the scarcity and sometimes complete absence of suitable armament was an embarrassing example of poor planning.

Such was the vital requirement for trawlers and drifters and experienced fishermen that unexpected crises such as the appearance of the new magnetic mine in the early months of the war and the national emergency in June 1940 just added to the impact of war on the fishing towns and cities. Both the Admiralty and the Department of Agriculture and Fisheries bore the brunt of protests from the likes of Hull and Grimsby and the smaller fishing ports, all faced with a rapid diminution of the very industry they depended upon. Much time and effort had to be directed to reassuring and placating the representatives who lobbied both the Navy and MAF.

It has been calculated that approximately 500 trawlers were lost during the two conflicts, which constituted one in six of the total number. Nearly half were victims of enemy mines. Fifty-five drifters were sunk by mines during the Second World War; the extent of the magnetic mine threat accounting for no fewer than thirty-nine of that number during 1940–41 alone.[63] Whereas air power made little impact on the Great War at sea, seventy-one trawlers were destroyed by enemy air attack in the 1939–45 period. While the submarine had proved a growing menace, particularly to merchant shipping, during 1914–18, in the second war forty-eight trawlers were accounted for by German and Italian submarines.[64]

Finally, referring just to the Second World War, Lund and Ludlam place this selection of statistics in quite startling perspective, 'They were losses far in excess of those of any other branch of the Royal Navy, and were actually more than the combined losses of destroyers, sloops, corvettes, frigates, fleet sweepers, motor torpedo boats and motor gunboats.'[65]

Chapter Five

Gunfire off the Murman Coast
1917–30

O N 28 APRIL 1923 the Grimsby trawler *Jeria* was steaming at full speed on a course north-west by west from Sem Island towards the Norwegian coast. It was snowing, with a 'smart breeze' and a swell from the north-east, when the skipper spotted what he described in his log as, 'a Russian man-o'-war' a quarter mile distant on his starboard bow:

> He came straight towards us but I ignored him. Just as he got past us he gave a signal on his whistle and manned his guns. I stopped and being too rough to launch his boat, he came alongside and spoke to me but I couldn't understand. He tried to make me understand by steaming towards the land and waving me to follow.

The Russian gunboat tried five times but on each occasion the *Jeria*'s skipper refused to comply. Gradually, over the next two and a half hours, he edged towards the known position of the nearby fishery protection vessel. He fired five red distress rockets. Finally, HMS *Godetia* answered the call and *Jeria* turned towards her. The CO advised the *Jeria* to proceed while he dealt with the Russian gunboat.[1]

A range of circumstances had led to this 'flashpoint' on a remote stretch of coastline on the Murman coast east of North Cape. Natural geographic and climatic conditions, social and economic control introduced by a nascent Soviet Union, the disputed declaration of a 12-mile territorial limit, the construction of a railway line linking St Petersburg to Romanov-on-Murman (later Murmansk) and the diminishing fish stocks around the British Isles all contributed to the Grimsby trawler's presence on that April day.

This, in summation, was the basis of an eight-year long dispute during the 1920s between Britain and the Soviet Union over fishing rights on the Murman coast. It neatly delineated into two phases. The first, 1921–23, ended when the British trawlers temporarily withdrew from the area, only to resume five years later in 1928–30 ahead of a *modus vivendi* the following year pending the conclusion of a formal convention.[2]

An unexploited and backward region

The waters bordering the Kola Peninsula are infiltrated by the last northeastward reaches of the Gulf Stream. The Murman and Spitzbergen currents, two branches of the North Atlantic Drift, carry warm tropical water into the Barents Sea. The combination of warmth and turbulence associated with the two flows, together with the influence of the continental shelf, help to keep most of the southern stretches of the Barents Sea ice free throughout the year and also encourage the growth of plankton and other fish nutrients. This results in favourable breeding grounds for cod, sea perch and other demersal fish.[3]

Essentially, living conditions in this remote corner of European Russia had not changed for centuries by the time of the November Revolution in 1917. By that year, steam trawlers, for example, were still a rarity.[4] A single powered vessel had been introduced in 1906 but had met with little success, so by 1913 only four were in operation in the Barents Sea, working out of Archangel, with an annual catch amounting to a paltry 512 tons. Meanwhile, highly efficient and modernised neighbours Norway provided stiff local market competition.[5]

Map 3: North Norway and the Barents Sea. (Stephen Dent)

The First World War, however, resulted in the construction of a railway linking St Petersburg with the Murman coast. Russia's southern and western ports had been blocked by Turkey and Germany, effectively severing links with the country's allies and the ice-free Kola Bay. The first 300km stretch to Petrozavodsk on the shores of Lake Onega, financed by French credit, took a year to construct (1914–15), while the more ambitious second 1,044km project joining Petrozavodsk with Murmansk was completed in a remarkable year and a half and put into operation on 3 November 1916. The rate of construction, across extremely demanding terrain, is considered 'an outstanding event in the history of railway construction'.[6] That stretch was paid for through state finances.

The economic development of the entire Barents Sea region took on an entirely different perspective following the October Revolution. The Bolshevik Party determined that its primary responsibility was to strengthen the national economy, thereby raising the standard of living of the populace and improving military security. Organised state activity in the area began in earnest in 1920 following the withdrawal of the White Russians from Murmansk and Archangel and the assumption of power by the communists.[7] The stability brought about by the New Economic Policy (1923–28), which permitted small trade and a moneyed economy to flourish, allowed a modest growth in the annual trawler catch. For example, the Barents Sea catch of slated fish amounted to 3,650 tons in 1922; by 1929 it had reached 21,100 tons. But it was not until the 1930s that construction began on the first of twenty-eight Soviet-built trawlers.[8]

As far as the future of the fishing industry was concerned, there were immediate benefits. Nationalisation brought into government hands twelve small minesweepers already rigged for trawling by their White Russian owners. They were initially based at Archangel, the traditional leading port in the area. However, Archangel was ice-blocked for half the year, during which time the new fleet sat idle. Sense prevailed in 1924 when the headquarters of the northern fishing industry was transferred to the year round ice-free Murmansk, which boasted not only a deep and well-protected anchorage but was also sited at the head of the newly completed railway line to St Petersburg.[9]

Tensions were evident during the early 1920s related to the question of the USSR's recognition of the Svalbard (or Spitzbergen) Treaty, which is discussed in Chapter Six. Norway's expanding fishing industry became an important factor as before the granting of Norwegian sovereignty the archipelago had been open to all countries to exploit its natural resources. Consequently, the Soviet Union pressed for Norway's *de jure* recognition as a sovereign state in order not only to secure an important ally 'next door' but also to win support in any future request for fishing rights. After some hesitancy, Norway recognised its neighbour in 1924. Thus, it remained an onlooker during the events described in this chapter but Norway's permission for the Royal Navy to use Kirkenes in the far north for replenishment and anchorage presented a difficult and delicate diplomatic challenge.

The British fishing fleet and the 12-mile limit

As long ago as 1837, Tsarist Russia had explicitly rejected the concept of a 3-mile offshore limit as a being an accepted rule of international law, although, paradoxically, it was later incorporated into the Russian Code of Prize Law (1869) and the Customs Code (1892). In the 1860s, the archaic 'Bynkershoek' (cannon shot rule), which was defined as 'waters within cannon shot or extending from shore to a distance of three nautical miles', was still in use, although it was acknowledged that, owing to technological changes that increased ranges, there was an in-built flexibility.[10]

During the same decade the activities of neighbouring Norway's fishermen resulted in a number of incidents. Despite warnings, incursions close to the coast persisted and by the 1880s a Russian fishery protection cruiser was being used to patrol the area. Only Britain and Japan entered formal protests but to no avail.[11]

Various Russian Government commissions looked into the matter over the next twenty years and proposed territorial sea limits of 6, 10 or more miles. Indeed, in 1906, an ambitious proposal for a 20-mile limit to be established with parts of the White and Kara Seas being closed to international shipping was announced but this was subsequently rejected. Three years later a dedicated 'maritime customs belt' received international approval. This decreed that every vessel must be supervised while sailing within a 12-mile limit. In 1911 this was incorporated into the rules regulating foreign vessels fishing in the so-called Maritime Province.

However, the overall lack of clarity and international acceptance with respect to the new laws was highlighted in July 1910 when the British trawler *Onward Ho* was arrested by a Russian cruiser. The boat had been trawling between 3 and 12 miles outside a line connecting Capes Sviatoi Nos and Kanin Nos between the Barents and White Seas. *Onward Ho* was subsequently released because it was evident that the vessel was operating outside the declared territorial limit. The resulting claim for compensation underlined the need for a precise delimitation of coastal authority in the area. Meanwhile, the same problem of measuring territorial waters with the necessary exactness lay at the heart of the dispute between Britain and Norway.[12]

When the Soviet Government took power they were still confronted with the problem that the laws were open to interpretation. They assumed the Tsarist stance that there was no internationally adhered to regulations with respect to the breadth of territorial waters. For example, how exactly did one interpret such terms as 'coastal waters', 'shore waters' or 'sea water belt'? Unfortunately, instead of simplifying the matter, Soviet jurists concluded that owing to the terminological variations, the USSR, 'did not have territorial waters fully subordinate to its sovereignty, but rather special zones in which certain rights are exercised'. To make matters ever more complicated:

> a 1924 instruction regulating the navigation of vessels in coastal waters with zones of firing from shore batteries in peacetime applied the cannon shot rule; the 1927 statute on the state boundary established a twelve mile limit but did not specify that a belt of territorial waters had been delimited.[13]

It is small wonder, therefore, that British trawler skippers ignored the above and continued to work to their country's long-held adherence to the 3-mile territorial zone.

The same problems regarding acceptance of the 12-mile limit were still prevalent in May 1921 when foreign fishing vessels began to appear off the now Soviet coastline, at a time when severe famine was plaguing the country and the need for greater protection of local marine resources was urgently required. This was recognised by the Soviet leader Lenin, who initiated reforms that led to the expansion of the Murmansk-based trawling fleet. Lenin was influenced by research conducted by the internationally renowned ichthyologist N M Knipovich, whose work highlighted the need for a science-led, industrialised approach to fishing.[14]

The same month, the Soviets revived the faulty Tsarist proposal and excluded foreigners from fishing in the White Sea south of a straight line drawn from Sviatoi Nos to Kanin Nos and within 12 miles of the coast from the Finnish border in the west to the northernmost tip of the island of Novaia Zemlia in the east. Germany, Norway, Britain and Japan protested the decree, with Britain objecting to any extension beyond 3 miles.

While efforts were made to resolve the dispute, British trawlers continued to operate up to the 3-mile limit. As a consequence, on 31 January 1922, the *Magneta* was seized by a Russian gunboat about 9 miles off the Murman coast. Subsequently, while under Soviet detention, the vessel was wrecked during a storm with some loss of life. A month later the trawler *St Hubert*, allegedly working outside the 12-mile zone, also had its catch confiscated by a Soviet court.[15]

British demands for compensation over the *Magneta* were rejected by the Soviets amid claim and counter-claim. The British Government warned that 'warships' were being sent to the area to prevent any harassment of British trawlers. The first patrol was instituted in April 1922. Alarmed at this reaction, the Soviets threatened that such action would jeopardise British–Soviet relations and would result in their navy vessels reinforcing the border patrols. A second patrol began in the middle of October 1922 before being withdrawn at the end of December.

On 31 March 1923 the trawler *James Johnson* was seized, again off Murmansk, its catch confiscated and its skipper sentenced to hard labour. This arrest precipitated a concession by the Soviets in the face of a more hard-line approach by the British Government. The Royal Navy was able to withdraw its patrol on 18 June on the undertaking that the Soviet Union would not interfere with British fishing vessels outside the 3-mile limit.

These incidents had coincided with political changes in Britain. A general election was held in November 1922. It was won by the Conservatives led by Andrew Bonar Law, who gained an overall majority over Labour and a divided Liberal Party. Unlike the previous administration under Lloyd George, who favoured rapprochement with the Soviet Union ahead of full recognition, Bonar Law made no attempt to constrain his Foreign Secretary Lord Curzon's bellicose attitude towards the communist regime. The 'Curzon Note' was delivered to Moscow on 8 May 1923: a catalogue of grievances clearly intended to pave the way for a breach with the Soviet government. Among other matters, it listed the recent arrests of British trawlers. It was followed two days later by the despatch of a RN fishery protection vessel to the

Murman coast with the express instructions 'to prevent interference with British fishing vessels outside the 3-mile limit, using force if necessary'.[16] A change of government occurred in 1924 and Britain's first Labour Government took important steps to recognise the Soviet Union, a move that was followed by Norway. It also paved the way for a formal treaty to be signed on 8 August 1924 that confirmed the temporary 'exchange of notes' the previous year.

The realities of providing support

The above account of Britain's attempts to support its fishermen off the Murman coast appears to show that the Royal Navy had matters under control, that the pre-eminent world naval force could do the job and let the politicians resolve the problems with the upstart, largely unrecognised, Bolshevik regime. From an RN perspective, however, the reality was quite different.

In March 1922, in response to the arrests of *Magneta* and *St Hubert*, HMS *Harebell* (Captain H E F Aylmer, Captain Auxiliary Patrols) and *Godetia* were reported as being readied for deployment to the Barents Sea. Both were considered to be better seaboats with a greater radius than the twin-screw minesweepers they replaced – *Sherborne* and *Newark*. HMS *Godetia* was described in *Jane's Fighting Ships* at the time as a 'fleet sweeping vessel' or 'sloop' of a generic 'Flower' class comprising five separate 'Types'. *Godetia* belonged to the ten-strong *Arabis* class, while HMS *Harebell* was of the *Anchusa* class.[17]

Soon after the outbreak of the First World War the Admiralty had recognised the requirement for auxiliary-type vessels capable of undertaking a variety of duties including minesweeping, towing and the transport of servicemen and stores. A design produced by the Director of Naval Construction (DNC), based on mercantile scantlings, was aimed at being simple, robust and capable of being built in non-specialist yards. The coal-burning, single-screw ships had a displacement of between 1,200 and 1,250 tons, depending on the individual class, and carried one or two single 4in guns. Being single-screw ships meant that they had large turning circles and so required a 'steadying sail' to assist in keeping the head to the wind. Euphemistically described as 'very lively ships', *Godetia* and *Harebell* could hardly be described as being 'fit for purpose'.[18]

Captain Aylmer was not reticent in voicing his opinion in advance of the deployment. He felt that, on balance, the extra expense in terms of the allocation of coal was not justified in view of the numbers of trawlers currently fishing in the region and the market value of the prospective catch. On the other hand, he did concede that the power of parliamentary criticism and public opinion was considerable, arguing that the trawlermen were not being currently supported. Indeed, Leo Amery had been forced to admit in the House of Commons the same month, 'No Fishery Protection vessel has visited Russian waters since the war,' although he added that one was in readiness to depart.[19]

Meanwhile, Captain Aylmer pressed for a meeting between the Admiralty, the Foreign Office and the Ministry of Agriculture and Fisheries (MAF) to agree a common approach, otherwise he felt if the Navy was not present and supported by good authority, the independently minded fishermen would simply defy orders, go there anyway and get arrested.

His experiences during the deployment itself only served to reinforce his views. In a despatch on 3 June 1922 he reported that S/T *Lord Reading* had been 'harassed' by a Russian gunboat – but this incident had taken place before the authorised date for the commencement of fishing. Aylmer considered the behaviour of the trawler skipper to be 'improper'. By 8 June, fishing in the area had been deemed a complete failure and the trawlers had scattered. HMS *Harebell*, his command, had followed H48 *Marconi* along the Russian coast. When he had used the sloop's siren he had been ignored and the following day the same trawler had taken advantage of early morning mist to disappear. Later, as ten Russian trawlers and six British had gathered again, the *Marconi* attempted to slip away once more, prompting Aylmer to comment, 'It would appear that I have had to guard her against her will.'

He concluded disgruntledly:

British fishermen will only obey orders, whether given him by his owners or by a fishery protection cruiser, in so far as they may suit him. Consequently it is quite impracticable to keep the trawlers more or less concentrated unless they are all attracted to one particular area by the excellence of the fishing.[20]

A meeting with the Hull trawler owners was convened in early August. They argued that north Russia was currently the only profitable distant-water area for fishing. In addition, the owners stated that they could not afford to equip their ships with W/T as the Navy had suggested. The

Admiralty representatives concluded gloomily that for the protection vessels to try to impose any kind of order, such as the trawlers regularly reporting their movements and positions, was impracticable as, 'skippers would make no attempt to comply with any orders which did not suit them'.

A second meeting took place on 14 August, this time involving Grimsby fishermen as well. The tone was more conciliatory; this time the owners expressed their satisfaction with the support afforded by the Navy during the 1922 season and wanted it repeated in 1923. However, the Deputy Chief of Naval Staff (DCNS), in addition to citing Captain Aylmer's examples of 'wilful disobedience', said that to repeat the 1922 level of support would require three or four FP vessels and would subject the crews to 'arduous and unpleasant' service equivalent to that of wartime.[21]

The Admiralty already faced a crewing problem as part of the post-war austerity measures. In order to arrive at the right level of support on the Murman coast it would require four trawlers of the 'Axe' class to be withdrawn from the flotilla in order to man a single sloop. The Navy also stipulated that all the trawlers required W/T equipment and that sailing, arrival and departure times from the fishing grounds needed to be reported to the Admiralty via MAF. A long, internal discussion ensued within the Admiralty about the viability of commissioning another 'Flower'-class sloop, HMS *Lupin*, currently held in reserve at Rosyth. The debate went on for over two months and in the end the plan was abandoned.

HMS *Harebell* and *Godetia* did return to north Russian waters in 1923, having been withdrawn at the end of the previous year for what were described as 'technical difficulties'. One would assume that this referred to problems with the design of the sloops, as mentioned above, but this explanation was only partly true. Captain Aylmer subsequently reported to the Admiralty on a visit he had made to HMS *Godetia* at Sheerness following its patrol in late 1922. The commanding officer had found his ship's company 'thoroughly discontented', although nothing had occurred on which to base disciplinary actions. Aylmer's subsequent investigation discovered that the basis of the grievances centred on the 'harsh and uncomfortable conditions' experienced during such deployments, the absence of any hard-lying money that the crew felt they were owed and an unofficial report that had been circulated that stated the ship was unfit for service in Arctic waters and that the chances of *Godetia* making a safe return were poor.[22]

The Captain A/P carried out further enquiries. The report had originated from one of the trawlers with whom *Godetia*'s crew had fraternised at the port of Honningsvåg in Norway. Captain Aylmer deduced that what he described as the 'nervous condition' of the ship's company had originated mainly from their experiences during the return voyage to the UK. They had sailed through the Inner Lead off Norway in darkness and driving snow and *Godetia*'s CO had admitted that he had 'nearly lost his ship' on three occasions despite the presence of two Norwegian pilots on board. Furthermore, Aylmer discovered from talking to a trawler owner in Hull that all the skippers who had observed the sloops during the winter months considered them to be most unsuitable for the work owing to their light draught and high upperworks. The discontent among the crew appeared to emanate from the petty officers and the Captain A/P had already taken steps to have the men relieved. He ended by stating that with fresh personnel being drafted to the ship and approval given for hard-lying money he felt sure the discontent would disappear.[23]

A Treasury paper of the time suggested that a purpose-built replacement was urgently required with an estimated cost of £60,000. Who would pay? The Navy was reeling from the cutbacks imposed by what is commonly referred to as the 'Geddes Axe', the 'peace dividend' resulting from the Treaty of Versailles. It was suggested that an existing vessel suitable for conversion should be purchased at a cost of around £35,000. Not for the last time in the twentieth century, fulfilling fishery protection duties were met with twin problems: the lack of purpose-built vessels and the problem of who should finance them.[24]

In the meantime, the Minister for Agriculture and Fisheries, Sir Robert Sanders, reporting to the Cabinet in early 1923, made a strong case in support of the Navy continuing to provide the necessary protection in the face of Soviet interference in the disputed region. He stated that, in the period 1907–14, 227,000 cwt of fish had been landed from there per year; post-war that figure had dropped alarmingly to 143,000 cwt in 1921–22 as a direct result, he asserted, of the arrest of the trawlers *Magneta* and *St Hubert* resulting from the imposition of the 12-mile limit. He added that the setback had been temporarily ameliorated by the presence of RN fishery protection vessels in April/May 1922 and again in October of that year. However, during the first three months of

1923, forty-five trawlers had been operating off the Murman coast but that number would have been greater if it had not been for the absence of the Navy, which had withdrawn its protection vessels in December 1922. He warned that if there was further serious intervention by Russian gunboats it would result in the British fishermen permanently leaving the area with consequent job losses. He mentioned there would be a significant reduction in the vital supply of plaice, part of the staple diet in the UK, which was very difficult to obtain elsewhere. Sanders concluded that he understood there was no suitable RN ship available with the capability to provide year-round support and insufficient funds for a replacement in the Navy Vote. He argued for Government money to be found for a new construction that might have further uses in other disputed waters such as off the coast of Greenland.[25]

The Foreign Office supported the views of MAF, adding that if the situation was allowed to continue the Government would be faced with a number of 'troublesome claims' for compensation following the arrest of trawlers. It was further asserted that, 'HM Government will find themselves in the humiliating position of diplomatic protests, which experience proves to be futile, to a government they do not officially recognise.' The fact that Moscow had been informed the previous year that HMG was going to protect its fishing vessels meant that, 'if it failed to do so in 1923, it would be perceived as a tacit recognition of the territorial claim or "impotence" at the inability to protect its rights'.[26]

By July 1923 no further action had been taken to provide support during the worst of the weather between October and May. The FO could not recommend further expenditure from its budget. The Admiralty reaffirmed that again it would not be able to provide protection during the coming winter months.

Aggressive action by the Soviets

While the British Government had been debating what to do about protecting its fishing fleet, the Soviets had been displaying more aggressive behaviour towards the British trawlers in the disputed region. This was matched by a generally cautious approach by the fishery protection vessels *Godetia* and *Harebell*, with advice given to the trawlers not to encroach within the 12-mile limit.

HMS *Godetia* made two sightings of Soviet gunboats close to Sem Island in the vicinity of the trawler fleet. One was described as an 'armed yacht', thought to be the *Yaroslavna* (see below); the other a trawler, *T-23*, armed with a single 12pdr gun on its forecastle. Described as being 'exactly similar' to a British 'Axe'-class trawler, on closer examination *T-23* was also seen to be carrying two 10in projectors and wireless telegraphy equipment. Three days later, there was another brief encounter when the gunboats approached *Godetia* making 'unintelligible flag signals'.[27]

Godetia was ordered to leave the area on 3 May. Predicting trouble, its CO warned all the trawlers in the region, 'to keep well clear and outside the twelve mile limit as the Soviet armed vessels were very active'. Sure enough, while the RN sloop was visiting Hammerfest in Finmark, Norway, on 7 May, it was learned that the trawler *Lord Astor* had been arrested while fishing 10 miles off Cape Teriberski and had been taken into Murmansk. The exact details of the arrest were ascertained following a statement made by the skipper of another trawler, the *Guy Thorne*, which, with a third trawler S/T *Rudyard Kipling*, was working close by.

A Soviet gunboat had approached the group, prompting the trio to depart at full speed. The *Rudyard Kipling* and *Guy Thorne* hauled their trawls, while the *Lord Astor* was thought to have 'chopped' its nets. The Soviet vessel did not immediately set off in pursuit but was observed to pause, presumably to check its distance from the shore. It became clear that the *Lord Astor* and *Guy Thorne* were being singled out for capture. After steaming for approximately an hour and a half, the Soviet gunboat closed steadily before firing two rounds. One was a blank but the second was 'shotted', passing over the *Guy Thorne*. At this point the *Guy Thorne* drew away from the *Lord Astor* as the gunboat closed and captured her. The two other trawlers escaped.[28]

Agent X and Curry's 'trap'

HMS *Harebell* arrived at Hammerfest on 15 May 1923 to take on coal and provisions in preparation for replacing HMS *Godetia*. While in port, the CO, Lieutenant Commander Curry, stated in his subsequent Letter of Proceedings that he devised, 'a reliable system of communication' between his ship, 'and a person (hereafter referred to as "X") who was in a position to keep me informed as to the movements of the Russian Soviet War Vessels in North Russia'.[29]

Curry then enlisted the help of one of his officers, who had previous experience in intelligence work, to keep Agent X under close but not obvious scrutiny in case, presumably, he was a 'double agent'. The

Harebell departed Hammerfest two days later in order to rendezvous with the homeward-bound HMS *Godetia* at Honningsvåg for the official handing over of duties. Meanwhile, he had time to examine X's passport, papers etc. and having ascertained details of his previous career as a commercial traveller, concluded that he was 'eminently capable of carrying out the purport of his proposed plan' and that there was no doubting his integrity. What Curry does not explain is how he actually came to meet X in Hammerfest.

On arrival in Honningsvåg, having failed to receive a reply to a cypher signal to the Admiralty requesting financial support, Curry had prepared a formal contract and advanced his agent £25 in English money and 300 Norwegian Kroners for working expenses paid out of his own pocket.

Lieutenant Commander Curry explained his motives for taking this independent and quite radical action:

> An important reason, which influenced me in coming to immediate terms with 'X', was the possibility of a definite break with Russia, observing that at the time of contract, the result of the British Government's [Curzon] Note appeared ominous, and the use of 'X' as an Agent under more serious circumstances might be invaluable.

Before he disembarked, X was furnished with a code to use when communicating with HMS *Harebell*. He was bound for Vardø, the most easterly town in Norway, where he would be in a good position to observe the movements of the Soviet vessels. Curry commented that his agent left the ship, 'in a well acted display of extreme inebriation – the culmination of a condition he had been working up to throughout his stay on board'.

But *Harebell*'s CO was not finished yet with his plans for this deployment. On passage from the UK he had concocted a device for fitting some form of wireless telephone (W/T) installation in one of the trawlers. He singled out S/T *Lord Halifax* as the most likely candidate for what he told the Hull skipper Andersen was an experiment. While convoying *Lord Halifax* and two other trawlers to the fishing grounds, he trialled the extemporary set while out of hearing of the Soviet coastal W/T stations. A radius test was conducted and a range of 50 miles was obtained.

Satisfactory protection of the trawlers was then maintained between 18 and 23 May before at midnight on the 23rd, 'a Cypher signal was received, via Ingøy W/T station [a village on the northern coast of the island of Ingøya], from "X" at Vardo, – "ships going out" –. Time of transmission 11.30pm.'[30] This real-time intelligence seemed to prove the worth of Agent X. Curry then saw the opportunity to lay a trap for the gunboats:

> As it was necessary to escort the S/T 'Lord Ernle' at 0700 the following morning from Sem Islands past Kola Inlet (in accordance with orders from the Senior Officer, Barents Sea Patrol), I foresaw the possibility of combining this duty, and at the same time bringing off a 'Coup', should the Soviet gunboats molest the Fishing Fleet in my protection. Accordingly, I arranged a short emergency code and placed Lieutenant T. Ellis [the officer with previous experience of intelligence work] and a telegraphist rating, with a Boat's Signal Book and a camera on board S/T 'Lord Halifax', having previously given Lieutenant Ellis written instructions and verbally explained the following plan of operations. In short:-
>
> (a) HMS 'Harebell', on completion of her escort duty, would return by a wide sweep to seaward and take up a position 30 miles North by West from Kharlov Light, Sem Islands ... Position A. This placed 'Harebell' in a favourable position, well out of sight of land, and only 23 miles from Bolshoi Oleni (a Soviet Base to which S/T Magneta was taken under arrest on 31st Jany. 1922, and subsequently wrecked in a gale); the position being such that she could intercept any Russian Gunboats returning Westwards after committing a piratical capture or other breach of International Law.
> (b) Wireless silence was to be maintained by 'Lord Halifax', though 'Harebell' would call her up at intervals in order that she could keep her receiving instruments tuned.
> (c) Trawler was to report by Emergency Code, Cypher, or Boat's Signal Book, anything of an urgent nature, and if in any way molested, was to proceed immediately at Full Speed along the line of bearing N. by W. from Kharlov Light.

Curry then used some deceptions intended to test the Soviets' system. He communicated *en clair* (plain language) via the Ingoy

W/T station with the harbour master at Honningsvåg, giving instructions to, 'forward Harebell's mails to Kirkenes'. This would have been interpreted as routine practice for a ship due for relief from patrol. He then transmitted another *en clair* signal to *Godetia* that he was returning to base in order to coal, but this was sent on reduced power so that the latter would not receive it. He explained in his letter that Agent X had assured him that all movements and signals made by HM ships both at sea or in harbour were at once passed on to Murmansk and Archangel. Sure enough, the Sem Island W/T station duly passed a cypher signal to Archangel within a short period of his departure from Honningsvåg together with *Harebell*'s later messages.

Lieutenant Commander Curry's elaborate plan to entice the Soviet gunboats into taking offensive action did not produce results on that occasion. But important lessons were drawn from the experiment. The communications system between the trawler S/T *Lord Halifax*, Agent X ashore and HMS *Harebell* seemed to be in good working order on the morning of 27 May when the 'enemy', consisting of the *Yaroslavna* and two armed trawlers, was sighted at 0815. After an hour it was reported that the force was retiring westward. *Harebell* set off in pursuit but with the Soviet vessels appearing to be retiring to the Kola Inlet, the sloop returned to the fishing fleet. It was concluded that at least one of the *Harebell*'s transmissions had been intercepted, 'Bolshies last seen 1200 going west "all out". Presume Yacht smelt a rat after first "0" signal.'[31] Another British trawler was encountered later that day, which signalled by semaphore that the three enemy vessels had passed inshore but had also proceeded westward without interfering with them.

Curry drew three important conclusions from his recent experience:

After due consideration of the report from Lieut. Ellis (aboard Lord Halifax) and his movements while the Russian Vessels were in sight, it would appear that the Soviet Gunboats are indubitably chary of commiting [sic] any act of Piracy, if there is a likelihood of any British Man-o'-War being in the vicinity.

He then emphasised the point that the crew of *Lord Halifax* had witnessed at first hand the advantages of the W/T installation aboard their vessel. Curry felt sure that this would lead to more trawlers acquiring some form of communications equipment, an issue that had been raised by the Captain Auxiliary Patrols at the recent Conference of Trawler Owners in Hull. Finally, in a linked point, Lieutenant Commander Curry asserted that in future the Soviets would be:

> incapable of continuing aggressive operations (previously conducted with impunity, owing to the accuracy of their system of espionage), without due regard to the possibilities and dangers entailed in molesting a British Trawling Fleet, fitted with some form of Wireless Telegraphy.

Curry admitted that his bold and inventive action could be judged as being 'over rash' but it had been based on the frustration he had felt the previous year when he had been powerless to stop the Soviets from interfering with the work of the British trawlers. He quoted the Governor General of nearby Tromsø as describing the dilemma of any commanding officer of a fishery protection vessel on service off the Murman coast thus, 'The watchdog is not allowed to bark, till he sees the fox has the chicken in its mouth.'[32]

Communication and intelligence

Lieutenant Commander Curry's final contribution to a very busy deployment in the Barents Sea was to interview the skipper of the S/T *Lord Astor*, Samuel Greaves, aboard HMS *Harebell*, who was able to provide very recent intelligence on the situation in Murmansk and particularly the state of the 'naval enemy forces' ranged against them. The term 'naval forces', in this context, is something of a misnomer. By the summer of 1923, the Union of Soviet Socialist Republics was barely six months old. As Przemyslaw Budzbon points out, 'The Soviets had been left without a single vessel in the Black Sea, the Arctic or the Far East'; only a small Baltic Fleet remained from pre-revolutionary days. The former Arctic Fleet, named the Naval Forces of the North Sea, had been officially disbanded in January 1923 following the creation of the USSR.[33] Although the Tenth Party Congress in 1921 resolved to rebuild the Navy, retrenchment in the period 1922–23 saw 75 per cent of the Red Navy's total tonnage either retired or sold to German shipbreakers.[34]

What Greaves probably encountered in Murmansk was little more than a semi-autonomous armed militia. He stated that the officers and crew of the gunboats carried no formal disciplinary positions, that the communist commissary was in charge, no discipline or standard naval routines were evident and only the captain and mate wore uniforms.[35] Ashore, no one including the Red Guards wore uniforms but everyone carried a rifle.[36]

After being escorted into Murmansk, the catch of S/T *Lord Astor*, worth an estimated £2,000 to £3,000, was removed from the boat. During his arrest, Greaves spent a good deal of time with the mate of the *Yaroslavna*. He divulged that the CO of the yacht was Senior Officer of the Fishery Protection vessels at Murmansk but, being from an old aristocratic family, he did not enjoy good relations with the Bolsheviks. Importantly, the mate explained that when *Lord Astor* was arrested the Soviet controller had given the order that live shells should always be used when apprehending trawlers. However, his captain had refused to comply, had used a practice shell first and only fired a live one 'in the vicinity' of *Lord Astor* when it was clear that the trawler was fleeing.

Contrary to expectations, the dummy W/T equipment fitted in the trawlers *Guy Thorne* and *Rudyard Kipling* had hoodwinked the Soviets into believing it was genuine. This may well have accounted for the fact that the latter was able to escape when S/T *Lord Astor* was arrested.

Skipper Greaves was questioned as to the identity and appearance of the *Yaroslavna*. Various aspects of its construction were compared with an account given by Engineer Lieutenant Hearn when he was aboard *Harebell* during a visit to Murmansk in 1919. *Yaroslavna* was named *Setteles* at that stage and it was known that it was an ex-American vessel of around 1,300 tons with a speed of 15 knots. It was now armed with two 12pdr guns, one forward, one aft.[37]

Thus the interview with Greaves provided valuable and up-to-date intelligence from the description of the ad hoc naval force trying to uphold an internationally unrecognised 12-mile limit to the reticence shown by the gunboats when they believed that the trawlers were in contact with the RN fishery protection vessels.

But Curry's actions during the deployment of HMS *Harebell* drew an equivocal response from the Director of Naval Intelligence (DNI), Rear Admiral Maurice Fitzmaurice. While agreeing with others that the intelligence gained was of value and that the installation of W/T in trawlers might have a 'hastening effect' (whatever that meant), he drew attention to the 'grave risks run whenever officers become involved in "secret service operations"'. He further warned:

The employment of 'X' in a direct manner by an officer and with the evidence of a receipt for money passed, might have resulted in an awkward diplomatic situation at least, and the transposed cypher employed is thoroughly unsafe in every respect.

The admiral considered it fortunate that no incident resulted from Lieutenant Commander Curry's actions. He agreed that the officer should be compensated and generally praised his actions but added, 'it is thought that they (naval officers) should refrain from the employment of any agent in future without sanction'.[38]

Rear Admiral Fitzmaurice's comments can be construed as being very much 'old-school' and illustrative of what Andrew Gordon writes in his seminal work, *The Rules of the Game*, concerning the hidebound behaviour of officers that cost the Royal Navy dear during the First World War. The inference that his actions required 'sanction' ran counter to Lieutenant Commander Curry's approach, which was to take risks and to use independent judgement. In this particular case it produced valuable intelligence and proof that modern communication facilities were required if British trawlers were to operate in future in distant waters.[39] Admiral Fitzmaurice inherited the post as DNI from the renowned Reginald 'Blinker' Hall, who was instrumental in revolutionising intelligence-gathering during the First World War. Curry exemplified the philosophy extolled by Hall, an inveterate risk taker himself, who once said, 'Mistakes can be forgiven, but even God himself cannot forgive the hanger-back.'[40]

Return of the trawlers

The RN fishery patrol was withdrawn in 1924 after the formal agreement with the Soviets to the effect that British trawlers would not be 'molested' in the 3- to 12-mile zone off the Murman coast. At the same time, the Government decided that, in order to avoid further incidents following a worsening of relations with what was now the Union of Soviet Socialist Republics (USSR), the trawlermen would be dissuaded from fishing in the region. Subsequently there was compliance in the years between 1924 and 1927.[41]

Ironically, in 1927, the Icelandic catch more than compensated for the loss of the Murman one. However, the same year it was revealed that the Germans, having been granted permission by the USSR to use the disputed area, had profited hugely from a successful season, selling their catch at high prices and moreover being allowed to operate their own fishery protection vessel.[42] A cleverly worded response to the Cabinet debate by the Minister of Agriculture and Fisheries, Walter Guinness, argued for the return of the trawlers to the Murman coast because:

> it was an undoubted advantage to have two alternative regions from which supplies may be drawn, particularly in the winter months. There are times when, owing to weather conditions, there is a partial failure of supplies from Iceland and at those time catches from the Murman coast are a valuable addition to the markets and command very high prices.

Guinness went on to describe the German access to the waters as 'a grave injustice' from which the British people were being precluded.[43] Underneath the rhetoric one detects the assumption that Britain was still the most powerful nation in the world and certainly 'mistress of the seas', not to be outmanoeuvred by a recently defeated nation.

It is also important to note Guinness's choice of words in the above quotation. The Icelandic and Murman coast catches were 'valuable additions to the market', not the essential part of the nation's diet. Presumably he had in mind what might be considered 'luxury' fish such as plaice. The UK fishing industry he was referring to was, at the time, operating from a position of strength as far as home waters were concerned. Statistics show that the landings of the home fishing fleet reached its high point in 1913 when 1.2 million tons were brought ashore. This declined radically during the war years (for reasons related in the previous chapter) before recovering rapidly in the next decade with some peak years exceeding a million tons. It was only in the late 1960s that the landings began the inexorable decline to their present levels.[44] The First Lord of the Admiralty, William Bridgeman, added his own thoughts in another memorandum. He ended by stressing the importance of trawlers carrying wireless sets, which echoed the pioneering work of Lieutenant Commander Curry during the 1923 season.[45]

In the meantime, the signing of the Treaty of Rapallo in April 1922 had contributed to a warming of relationships between the Soviet and the German governments, with several industrial and particularly military collaborative projects getting under way during the decade. Thus the political climate was conducive to the granting of preferential treatment to the German fishermen. On the other hand, as Siegfried Breyer contends, as far as the Soviets' first Naval Construction Programme (1926–31) was concerned, 'It had been suggested that there might be some co-operation with Germany, but it would appear that this did not come about.'[46]

Eventually, the British Government bowed to pressure and a decision was taken at Cabinet level in the summer of 1928 to provide naval protection once again for the trawlers in the Barents Sea. HMS *Godetia* and *Harebell* were again on fishery protection duties but this time, in a show of 'muscle', the Admiralty resolved to place the *Caroline*-class cruiser HMS *Comus* on immediate standby to deploy as well. Plans advanced rapidly and by October the ship signalled that it was at short notice to steam.[47] It was reasoned that, 'a cruiser should be stationed off the northern part of Norway for the first few weeks of the patrol, during which the attitude of the Soviet Republics should become apparent'.[48]

Concern was expressed in some quarters. The FO was sensitive to the fact that co-operation was required to be shown by the British trawlers and respect for the Norwegian 4-mile fishing limit in view of the fact that the RN ships needed to use their ports for coaling and other facilities. There was also worry about the communist element in the Storting (the Norwegian Parliament), who would inevitably object to the presence of RN ships using Norwegian ports.[49] In 1922, a report by the Captain Auxiliary Patrols during a deployment in HMS *Harebell* had stated that his reception in Kirkenes was 'not altogether friendly'. Having been obliged to divulge his future movements to the harbour master, he was convinced that the information was being passed on to the Soviet authorities. This contrasted with the attitude found closer to the border in Hammerfest, where the people were more pro-British.[50] Elsewhere, the Danish Government agreed to keep a watch on Soviet naval movements out of the Baltic. The Russian Baltic Fleet was the only one to have survived the First World War and the upheavals caused by the Revolution in any significant numbers.

Harebell and *Godetia* sailed north on 17 October. Many of the trawlers had now been equipped with shortwave W/T equipment and the British Government informed the USSR that it would not comply with its ban on the use of W/T within 10 miles of its coast. With no immediate adverse reaction shown by the Soviets or their naval vessels to the reappearance of the British, HMS *Comus* was stood down in

December but ordered to remain at readiness should its services be required during the rest of the winter.

A meeting was convened in April 1929 between the Admiralty, the Captain Auxiliary Patrols and representatives of the fishing industry to review the experiences of the previous six months. In the event, winter 1928–29 had passed peacefully with few instances of attempted interference, especially while the protection vessels were in the vicinity. However, in his Report of Proceedings, HMS *Godetia*'s CO noted that on arrival at the fishing grounds east of Sem Island on 1 January he had been met by S/T *Girard*, which reported being fired on by a Russian gunboat on 29 December despite the presence of a number of German fishing boats in the same area.[51]

Later in January, HMS *Doon* reported an incident that had taken place on the 19th that illustrated the wariness being shown by the Soviet gunboats when in the presence of the RN. *Doon* was engaged in escorting a small group of British trawlers when 'a strange vessel', showing only its navigation lights, appeared through the snow and mist:

> It then rapidly approached 'Doon' and followed her for some minutes, ranging up close on the starboard side. On 'Doon' turning 10 inch searchlight on 'Doon's' (her) own Ensign and Gun the stranger sheared off at once. Two red rockets were fired as another strange vessel had been seen to the S.E. (not again seen) to tell trawlers to haul nets.
>
> ... the first stranger which had the appearance of a large trawler, then passed through the fishing fleet and disappeared to the S.E. apparently putting out all lights. She did not answer further attempts to communicate by flashing lamp and Aldis.

Other than describing the 'stranger' as a 'large trawler', no firm identification was possible owing to the very poor visibility at the time.[52]

A 'changing of the guard' had occurred first on 21 November when HMS *Rosemary* (*Arabis* class) relieved sister ship *Harebell* in the role of Senior Officer of the Murman patrol and was joined by HMS *Colne* and HMS *Doon*. *Colne* and *Doon* were *Mersey*-class minesweeping trawlers both completed towards the end of the First World War.

It is clear from the reports from the fishery protection commanding officers that were considered by the small committee in April 1929 that the bigger enemy was the atrocious winter weather:

With a rapidly dropping barometer and increasing wind, a heavy south westerly gale was blowing by 1900 and ship had to practically remain hove to during the night.

And:

The wind continued at gale force all though the night, with frequent snow showers during which visibility was nil; ... only making good 3 knots although revolutions for 10.[53]

A decision was taken in April, with the agreement of the Trawlers' Federation, to withdraw the FP vessels as it appeared at the time there was no further prospect of profitable fishing in the area at the time. It was almost immediately rescinded following a report of interference by a Soviet naval vessel reaching London on 4 May 1929. The Hull trawler S/T *Cape Spartel* had been fishing 3½ miles from shore when it had been forcibly compelled by a Russian gunboat to stop and to leave the area. Ironically, the event coincided with the arrival in the region of large shoals of plaice at a distance of 3 to 15 miles from the coast, which had been discovered by German vessels and had been subsequently landed in British ports and sold at high prices. As a consequence, the British had hurried back and more than twenty trawlers began working in the area. It was anticipated that this opportunity would last for approximately four to five weeks. HMS *Godetia*, *Colne* and *Doon* were ordered to resume FP duties off the Murman coast on 11 May.

Poaching

By July 1929, though, a modified, intermittent patrol was being proposed as again only a very small number of British trawlers were working in the area. This suggestion was made by what was now called Captain Fisheries and Minesweeping Flotillas (FMS), Captain M E Goldsmith. An extract from his report was received by the Secretary of the Admiralty. The rather disjointed account, composed while on board HMS *Harebell* on its deployment off the Murman coast in the summer of that year, makes interesting reading and stands in contrast with the usual factually dense reports of this kind. It includes an anecdotally based insight into the behaviour and attitude of the British skippers involved in fishing international waters.

He wrote:

I believe the Skipper of the 'Cambri' – an exceptionally fine type of man – rarely fishes outside the Iceland three mile limit; this being so I suppose the Russians are sure to arrest one of our trawlers some day who is brazenly poaching within a mile of the shore. The Skipper will of course boldly swear that he was outside the three mile limit and the word of the Russian 'Officer' will most surely be doubted in England. In any case the absence of an English Patrol Gunboat will be commented on, and if the patrol is withdrawn the whole question of its re-establishment will crop up.

He further comments that, as it was summer, the fish were at the time well away from the coast but would move inshore as winter drew on. 'Poaching will start immediately the nights are dark and probably before,' adding, 'So renowned are the English as poachers that the ignorant Norwegian fishermen are quite sure that the patrol is established to protect our trawlers while poaching.' Goldsmith concludes this theme with a further anecdote:

At Hull the other day a Skipper told me what fine fishing he was in the habit of getting in one of the fjords near the Nord Cap (North Cape, Norway). But, said he 'It was becoming more and more risky – but with your protection it will be better'. His owner, who was by this time displaying an uneasy mind, hastily hurried this embarrassing employee away.[54]

This frank account ends with Captain Goldsmith's recommendation that during the winter months, when 'it is pitch dark by 12.30 every day', that it was 'essential' that a FP vessel should be on near continuous patrol.

A temporary truce

Clashes between the British trawlers and Soviet gunboats petered out during the winter months of 1929–30 ahead of the signing of the Anglo-Soviet Temporary Fisheries Agreement (1930), which granted British fishermen permission to fish up to 3 nautical miles off the coast of North Russia. The Soviet Government believed at the time that a resolution, albeit a temporary one, would be advantageous because it was seeking to expand its trade with Britain.[55] This legislation was to remain in place for twenty-three years.

Only isolated incidents occurred. S/T *Surfflower*, while on passage with its gear stowed, was fired on by a Russian gunboat on 15 December 1929 off Cape Nymetski. Skipper Norton's account accentuates the rather confusing but potentially dangerous relationship between the Russian gunboats and the British trawlermen ahead of the signing of the agreement the following year. Having been approached by the gunboat, Norton relates:

> As soon as I make him out I stand on my course and still maintain full speed; also I put all my lights out. The Gun Boat altered his course and followed us, blowing on his whistle one long, two short, one long blasts several times. I blew down to our Chief Engineer and gave him instructions to give the best possible speed. After following in our wake about four or five ship's lengths away and for about twenty minutes, he fired on us. The flash of his gun appeared to be right over our foremast. The man at the wheel and the men on deck reported that the shell fell close on our port beam … This vessel that I sighted Morsed to me, but I cannot make anything of his signal. I then fire my distress rockets. Then this vessel called me up and asked in English if I were alright; also for us to show our lights [Norton had previously ordered all lights to be extinguished] and he would come alongside and talk.

A second Russian gunboat appeared but Norton decided to ignore both and with the first vessel still trying to communicate through Morse he proceeded to a new position off Vardoe Lights, where he started fishing.[56] HMS *Boyne* reported another minor encounter with a gunboat the following February near the Ribachi Peninsula. There was an exchange of names and both vessels raked one another with their searchlights before departing.

Meanwhile, the Norwegian pro-communist lobby was still active in Kirkenes, mirroring what was evident earlier in the decade. Captain Goldsmith, aboard HMS *Harebell*, reported the Norwegian town's communist newspaper, citing controversy, 'which served to show what the communists would say were the patrol to cease using Kirkenes as an anchorage'.[57]

However, by April 1930, Goldsmith was able to make a more optimistic assessment of the situation. He praised the less-offensive behaviour of the trawlers, a state of affairs for which the fishery protection vessels, in his words, 'should have a share of honour ... because they have done their best to prevent trawlers from trespassing at the risk of confiscation'. He added that co-operation between the British and Norwegian guardships operating in the waters had been good.[58]

Conclusion

The embryonic Fishery Protection Flotilla was able, just, to provide enough support for the British trawler fleet to work off the Murman coast during the 1920s. But the coverage it afforded was not always on a year-round basis during the two phases when the trawlers were actually operating: 1921–23 and 1928–30. Moreover, the Navy had to conduct operations with a makeshift squadron, principally HMS *Godetia* and *Harebell*, which were clearly unsuited to the task. Their withdrawal during the winter season 1922–23 for 'technical reasons' suggests a lack of suitability for the role, although there is no definitive confirmation that they were actually unseaworthy for the north Russian winter months. Calls for the construction of a dedicated fishery 'cruiser' appear ignored or disregarded. MAF and the FO, the other ministries with a vested interest in this respect, did not appear to carry enough 'clout' in this matter to influence governmental decisions.

It was fortunate that there were no reported injuries or loss of life as a consequence of the interference by the Soviet naval vessels. Although there were successful 'captures' made in the early days, together with confiscation of valuable catches and the imprisonment of some skippers, these were comparatively rare. When the RN protection vessels were present, the Russians became increasingly reluctant to persist with their harassment tactics.

Gudni Johannessón claims that 'the Bolshevik government intended to enforce the Tsarist twelve mile limit in the Barents Sea and only backed down because British warships were sent to the scene'. He quotes from James Cable's seminal study, *Gunboat Diplomacy*, to make his point that this policy was used in the Barents Sea, 'to realise Britain's will in maritime matters'. However, this calls to question the role the Royal Navy was undertaking in support of its fishing fleet in the 3- to 12-mile zone, which was at the time, by international agreement, international waters. It should be noted at this point that the advice given to the fishermen was to work outside the 12-mile limit if the Navy was not present. The deployment of the 6in gun cruiser HMS *Comus* to the area, as related above, would have been a different matter. The presence of this vastly more powerful warship would have been an overtly provocative way of 'raising the temperature' and a flagrant use of gunboat diplomacy by what was still the world's most powerful navy.[59]

It was demonstrated that modern W/T communications were employed successfully by both sides. The Soviets were able to use both shore stations and ship-to-shore communications to track the whereabouts of the trawlers and the RN. Information was also being passed from sympathisers on the Norwegian side of the border to the Soviets. Communication on the British side between the trawlermen and their Navy guardians, on the other hand, was initially more primitive. Lieutenant Commander Curry's 'experiments' and his innovative use of 'Agent X' in the early summer of 1923 exposed the existing inadequacies of ship-to-ship communications and up-to-date intelligence. During the first phase of the confrontation, communication between warship and trawler was executed by signal lamp, semaphore, flags, distress flares or even coming alongside and shouting! Knowledge of the whereabouts of the gunboats relied on visual sightings. When the trawlers returned to the area in 1928, W/T equipment was expected to be carried aboard.

Despite the growth in size of the flotilla, the Murman coast experience did not substantially change operational methods or the attitude of the Navy towards this small branch of its service. And, as will be shown, the trawlermen continued to go about their business and to push the boundaries as far as international law was concerned. However, as domestic stocks continued to decline, they, like other nations' fishermen, were forced to go further afield in search of their catches.

Chapter Six

Norway's Red Line
1882–1951

GUDNI JÓHANNESSON, who became the long-standing President of Iceland, claimed that the international fishing disputes that affected the United Kingdom during three quarters of the twentieth century can be traced to the previous century when British steam trawlers began to fish the waters around Iceland, the Faroe Islands, north Norway and the Kola Peninsula off Russia.[1]

This chapter examines the case of Britain's dispute with Norway, a near neighbour and erstwhile close ally across the North Sea. In 1920 it was Norway's most important trading partner: about one third of its trade was with Britain alone.[2] This was hugely significant in terms of Norway's gross domestic product as about 30 per cent of it relied on exports. Nevertheless, the problem with the 4-mile delimitation that the Scandinavian country claimed, founded on a succession of historical decrees, 'rumbled on' through two world wars with arrests, confiscation of catches, anger and bitterness on both sides and endless searches for solutions in a scenario made infinitely more complicated by Norway's unusual topography. It was not until December 1951 that the International Court of Justice (ICJ), in a historic judgement, decreed that Norway's claims to the disputed waters were consistent with international laws concerning the ownership of local sea space. For Britain, struggling in the post-war world to hang on to its great power status, this was a crucial setback in its efforts to influence international acceptance of the 3-mile territorial delimitation.

At the start of this period, many local fishermen, both in Norway and in the other countries mentioned above, were still using traditional small fishing boats with line and nets. They resented the competition from increasingly sophisticated British trawlers fitted with triple-expansion steam engines and powerful, steam-driven deck winches attached to wire rather than rope warps to haul 'otter trawls'. The wide mouths of these nets were kept open by a pair of 'otter boards' or 'kites' that stretched apart when dragged through the water. The nets tapering towards the other end, 'the cod end', were both efficient and adaptable.[3]

A long, drawn-out disagreement

The dissolution of the union between Norway and Sweden took place in 1905. It was caused, at least in part, by a growing sense of Norwegian national identity exacerbated by the fact that the country was not permitted to administer its own foreign service missions and was still subordinate to Sweden in all matters relating to foreign policy. This gave Norway a clear sense of inferiority in the union.

Undoubtedly though, the new-found freedom after 1905 contributed to the insistence shown in its claims for territorial jurisdiction over a belt of 4 miles of sea from the low-water mark. In terms of historical precedence, the Norwegians had enforced this independent delimited zone as long ago as June 1745.[4] This claim was much complicated by the intricate configuration of the Norwegian mainland caused by the deep indentations formed by many fjords and the presence off shore of a large number of islands and 'skerries'. In 1882, Norway had refused to be party to the North Sea Convention.

Tensions grew between Norway and Britain prior to the First World War, with the former accusing British trawlers of poaching within the disputed 4-mile zone. A notable case occurred in March 1911 when the 293-ton S/T *Lord Roberts* was arrested in Varanger Fjord by HNoMS *Heimdal*, the erstwhile Norwegian Royal Yacht, which had been requisitioned to serve as Norway's first fishery protection vessel.[5] The crew of the trawler were arrested, fined, detained for six days and their catch was confiscated. The case drew questions about compensation in the House of Commons. Subsequently a legal claim by the trawler owners was brought before the Supreme Court of Norway just as war was about to break out. The case was dropped before a settlement could be reached at the insistence of the Foreign Office in order to preserve a sense of unity with an otherwise friendly neutral country at a time of war.

Norway's foreign policy was to remain non-aligned during the First World War but it continued trading with both Britain and Germany under the rules of contraband of war. The Scandinavian countries profited during 1914–15 on the back of an economic boom caused by the demands by Germany and the Triple Alliance for raw materials. Norwegian 'real-money' exports in the period 1913–16 grew by an unbelievable 84 per cent. Nevertheless, the true extent of its political, economic and strategic reliance on Britain was underlined and Norway entered the post-war period with a substantial national debt caused, at least in part, by the factors listed here.[6]

Norwegian fishermen had benefitted particularly in spring and summer 1915 when the Germans bought large amounts of fish, causing prices to rise. This had an unfortunate knock-on effect on the domestic market with the result that fish, a staple diet, became a comparative rarity in Norwegian households. A more complex chain of events followed when it was realised that fish, destined for German consumption, was being imported from Iceland aboard Norwegian-crewed ships and using Lerwick in the Shetland Islands to refuel. To add insult to injury, the vessels were fuelled by British coal. A crisis was averted when Norway sought and gained an agreement with Britain that the latter would purchase the entirety of the Norwegian catch starting in early 1916. After a false start, which resulted in unwanted fish being left to rot on British quaysides, the 'Fish Agreement' was signed in August 1916, which gave Norway the right to export 15 per cent of its catch, with Britain obligated to purchase the balance of the annual landings after deducting what was required for Norwegian domestic consumption.[7]

During the Versailles peace negotiations in 1920, the Spitzbergen (later Svalbard) Treaty was signed, becoming effective in 1925. It handed sovereignty to Norway over the archipelago. This had a direct bearing on Britain's fishing dispute with the Soviet Union in the 1920s, as discussed in Chapter Five. The Spitzbergen Archipelago is approximately 650 miles from the North Pole, north of continental Norway. Prior to 1920, Spitzbergen had been regarded internationally as *terra nullius*, in other words open to all countries that wanted to take advantage of its rich resources. After gaining its independence, Norway set out to establish international rules for the archipelago and the Versailles-enacted treaty was seen to be in partial recognition and appreciation of Norway's merchant fleet's losses during the recent war as well as the country's new, relatively weak and small state status.[8]

What might be described as an accommodating stance during the war on the part of the British did not serve to soften attitudes to the fishing limit dispute in the immediate post-war years. In August 1921, the Norwegian Government signalled its intention to empower its customs officials to search vessels outside the 4-mile limit if they were suspected of liquor smuggling. The implications for trawlers suspected of 'poaching' in the disputed zone were obvious. In an effort to be conciliatory, when HMS *Harebell* arrived at Kirkenes en route for the Murman coast and fishery protection duties, the captain was instructed, in the event of a British trawler being arrested by the Norwegians outside the 3-mile limit and inside the 4-mile limit or within Varanger Fjord, merely to make a formal protest and to report the matter. British trawling organisations were warned that their vessels should not fish in waters claimed by Norway. The fact that the RN was permitted to use Kirkenes for replenishment played a significant part in the decision to accommodate the Norwegians.[9]

The advice given to the trawler skippers was ignored in some quarters and several boats were arrested during 1923. However, early the next year there were positive signs that an agreement might be reached. British delegates arrived in Oslo in March 1924 with a proposal that the two countries should enter into a bilateral Convention, or Agreement, which would provide protection for legitimate Norwegian fishing interests and regulate the operations of the vessels of the two countries. The 'bottom line', however, was that the Norwegians, as a condition of the Convention, would withdraw its claim to territorial jurisdiction beyond the 3-mile limit.

To embrace one of the most contentious issues, the Norwegians were invited to indicate on charts the seasonal concentrations of line fishing vessels with a view to excluding from those zones steam trawlers whose presence would necessarily cause damage to the Norwegian fleet. Crucially, they were also asked to mark out the territorial claims, particularly the base lines, from which the coastal belts would be measured. This proved problematic. The Norwegian delegates declared that these base lines could not be charted authoritatively because they were regulated by Royal Decrees and those decrees did not cover the entire coastline. It was then decided that the exercise would be undertaken provisionally. The Chief Inspector of Fisheries, in a fine example of understatement, commented, 'Without going into details, it will be sufficient to say here that the terms proposed did not find acceptance in this country.'[10]

A year later, talks resumed in London and, although some progress was made, the proposals were subsequently rejected in the Storting, the

Norwegian Parliament. There followed a four-year stasis during which the trawlermen were advised by HM Government to stay outside the 4-mile limit. But at the end of 1929, familiar complaints were received about incursions, particularly off the Finnmark coast in the far north. There were strong left-wing sympathies in this area in step with the nascent Soviet Republic next door, as has been shown in Chapter Five. Anti-British sentiments were rife and were fuelled by the local press and supported in the Storting by members of the small Communist Party of Norway, led by Adam Egede-Nissen.[11]

Consequently, an increasingly violent press campaign was conducted, aimed at the British trawlers and at the rather timid behaviour being shown by the Norwegian Fishery Protection Service. It continued into the next year. As a result of the pressure exerted, three trawlers were arrested in 1930 for trawling within the limits claimed by Norway. Arrests of British and German trawlers continued, with six British vessels apprehended in 1933 and five in 1934. Reports reached London in April 1933 that Varanger Fjord was being closed. Meanwhile, the trawler owners became insistent that their ships, 'should receive protection against the continued interference while fishing on "the high seas"'. Allegedly, action was also being taken by Norwegian line fishermen who, demonstrating their hatred for all trawlers, were laying their unlighted lines very close to the trawlers' dan buoys and then raising indignant claims when they were being fouled.[12]

There was continuing confusion over the exact delimitation of the Norwegian claims and a crisis meeting was convened in May 1933, attended by representatives of the trawler owners, the Ministry of Agriculture and Fisheries, the FO and Captain FMS. It was decided to press the Norwegians to state exactly what they did claim as their territorial waters. This action was prompted by the arrest the previous February of S/T *Crestflower* and *Loch Torridon*. Both vessels claimed to be working 2 miles outside the territorial limits declared by Norway in 1925. The skippers of these vessels were convicted but their cases were appealed. The court subsequently quashed the convictions on the grounds that the base lines from which the limits claimed were measured had not been made known either in Norway or in Britain. The local Norwegian police then declared its intention of appealing to the district court with the intention of driving the trawlers from the Norwegian Banks. This case was lost as well, which resulted in an award being made to the defendants against their costs.[13]

Another of the trawlers arrested in 1933 was the *St Just*. In August of that year the Norwegian Supreme Court delivered an important judgement that not only underlined the complexity of the matter but also how far the two sides were from reaching a satisfactory settlement to their differences. The court's verdict cited decrees dated 1869 and 1889 that had prescribed how the base lines had been drawn up on 'specified portions of the coast and these could be regarded as applying to the whole'. By that process of argument the *St Just* had properly been found guilty by the lower court of infringing territorial waters.[14]

In November 1934, the British Government protested against the Supreme Court judgement, predictably taking particular exception to the procedure whereby British fishermen were being arrested and prosecuted first with base lines established afterwards, apparently both in the course and purpose of legal proceedings.[15]

A royal decree and a red line

Finally, this long-running dispute seemed to be reaching a climax. But, unfortunately, it proved to be inconclusive. As 'incidents' continued, the British trawler owners became increasingly convinced that the Norwegians' ulterior motive was to make access to the lucrative waters of the Norwegian Banks untenable for its boats. They demanded naval protection. At last, at the end of 1933, the Norwegian Government was persuaded to suspend its actions against British vessels pending a declaration being made on the whole matter by the Storting regarding the 'line' that was used as a *modus vivendi* in accordance with the 1925 negotiations. This became known as the 'Red Line'.

On 12 July 1935 a Norwegian Royal Decree was announced, defining fishery (but not territorial) limits off the northern coasts from the Finnish frontier to Traener, in the county of Nordland. Crucially, this boundary used a method of drawing base lines according to the general trend of the coast line and not according to its intricate sensuosities.

Not only was that line a mile wider than Britain was willing to recognise but the low-water mark principle was also ignored. Instead, the limit was drawn from base lines, the longest 44 miles long, across fjords and between the innumerable islands of the Norwegian coast, the *skjaergaard*.[16]

The Inspector of Fisheries, in response to the Decree, stated, 'these were of such an extravagant nature as to be quite unacceptable to the British Government and the Trawling Industry'. As was feared, the ruling virtually excluded foreign vessels from the key Banks area and extended the Red Line to cover about 1,000 square miles of sea.[17] This issue of base lines was to prove to be of crucial significance later in the dispute.

The British Government lodged a strong protest in Oslo, refusing to recognise the Royal Decree. The trawler owners, meanwhile, were not in a conciliatory mood and refused to assist in any further discussions about finding a way to reach a settlement. Instead they continued to press for naval protection up to the 3-mile limit. HMS *Colne* was placed on standby duty at Lerwick but later told to stand down. The Captain FP & M, in his quarterly report, noted the unease in fishing circles concerning the Grimsby trawler *Monravia*, which had been working one mile outside the Red Line when it was ordered to cease immediately by a Norwegian Protection vessel. It was alleged that the *Monravia* was working within the limits laid down in the July Decree. This had caused confusion for the fishermen as they had previously understood from the Norwegian Government that it would not enforce this decree pending negotiations.[18]

Further incidents occurred. In his Quarterly Report for the period April to July 1936, the Captain FP & M in HMS *Lupin* reported that the trawlers S/T *Grampian* and *Preston North End* had both been harassed by Norwegian gunboats purportedly while fishing outside the Red Line. Both vessels were threatened with arrest if they did not leave the area and both complied reluctantly. The skipper of the *Grampian* was reported to be, 'highly indignant at the treatment received and felt particularly sore that no British gunboats to whom an appeal could be made was in the vicinity'.

By contrast, the next month, four Hull-based trawlers reported interference by the Norwegian gunboat HNoMS *Michael Sars*, again outside the 4-mile zone. This time no arrests were made. In one case, while three of the vessels were trawling together, they received W/T instructions from their owners to continue their work and the gunboat eventually left them alone.[19]

In order to avoid a situation that was rapidly becoming an impasse, the British Government proposed a bilateral Anglo-Norwegian Fisheries Convention that would avoid reference to the principle of the breadth of territorial waters. For a short while it appeared that some progress was being made with this idea and there was even talk on the Norwegian side of the country joining the North Sea Fisheries Convention.

But the matter once again was 'batted' back and forth to no avail. The British were persistent over the matter of access to the Banks and the Norwegians were reluctant about entering into a Fisheries Convention on the grounds that it might be a way of trapping them into a redefinition of their Red Line. There were other objections, leaving the British with the impression that their counterparts were being unnecessarily 'high-handed'.[20] The only positive outcome was a preliminary discussion about referring the whole matter to the Permanent Court of International Arbitration in The Hague.[21]

Resources and manning

As 1936 drew to a close the question was again raised as to whether or not the Fishery Protection Flotilla would be able to send its vessels to Norwegian waters in support of the trawlermen. MAF stated that it was highly desirable, if not necessary, to provide support during the key seasons February to April and September to November. The Admiralty countered that it had not been possible hitherto to find the necessary manpower. MAF added that it would be prepared to see a reduction of patrols in home waters if one or two vessels could be sent to Norway. It had been originally been envisaged that sloops or twin-screw minesweepers would be necessary for the task but it was thought that trawlers, shown to be more than capable during the Great War, would be equally acceptable.[22]

The Captain FP and M suggested that unemployed fishermen might be a suitable answer to the manning problem. However, the Director of Personnel Services (DPS), after some consideration, considered the idea was not feasible, remarking that maintaining the expected standards of naval discipline would present a 'virtually insuperable' problem. He was supported in that respect by the Head of the Naval Branch, who forthrightly dismissed the suggestion as 'out of the question'. Recent experience had shown it to be unsatisfactory. Undesirable recruits would have to be 'weeded out' and proper naval training organised, which at the present time the Navy did not have the resources to provide. The DPS, after further consideration, concluded that it would be impossible to accommodate the additional manning as it would have to come from existing budgets.

The situation was appraised to see if there was any way to assemble a presence in the area. The Fishery Protection and Minesweeping Flotilla for the next couple of years was expected to comprise:

1936
Sloops: *Harebell, Lupin*
Trawlers: *Boyne, Cherwell, Coyne, Dart,
Foyle, Doon, Kingfisher*

1937
Sloops: *Hastings, Lupin*
Trawlers: *Boyne, Cherwell, Coyne, Doon,
Sheldrake*, Kingfisher.*
* Sheldrake was a large Admiralty trawler, expected to complete in 1936.

It was acknowledged that, with respect to the 1937 fleet, a cut of £4,000 elsewhere would be needed in order to man the flotilla and even that figure would fall short of the actual cost by some hundreds of pounds.

There was, additionally, the question of which vessels to consign to the task. The Director of the Operations Division (DoD) considered that the old trawlers in the current flotilla were no longer suitable for the task where bad weather was to be expected. That left the Captain FP & M's ship HMS *Hastings*, plus three other vessels, one of which, HMS *Gossamer*, was assigned to LFNO Scotland and could not be included. *Hastings* would visit the area but could not be committed on a permanent basis on account of its primary role as the ship of the Senior Officer Commanding.

No progress had been made by December 1937, when it was concluded, on the British side, that further restrictions were being imposed by the Norwegians. Round-table talks were suggested for February 1938 and on eight further occasions during that year. By May 1939, with war looming, a further Convention proposal had still not been ratified and the inevitability of what was about to happen meant that the Norway problem had to be put to one side as preparations for visits by the RN Fishery Protection Squadron in time of war became the overriding priority.

Unresolved

Thus, a seemingly interminable dispute was left in disarray in September 1939. The 'Red Line' had been essentially a temporary compromise and the minutiae of the long-awaited Norwegian Royal Decree had never been accepted by the British Government.

A great deal has been written about Operation Weserübung, the German invasion of Norway in April 1940: the British response with all its controversial elements, the subsequent occupation of the territory by the Axis power, not to mention the several strategic consequences that had an impact for the duration of the war. A perceived key consequence of the German invasion was its ability to maintain access to high-grade Swedish iron ore, mined in the Kinuna-Gällivare district of Lapland and exported either through Luleå in the Gulf of Bothnia (which froze over in winter) or Narvik in Norway. Out of its total import of 22 million tons, the precious Swedish ore accounted for 9 million. At the time, the Allied side considered this to be a serious advantage for the Germans.[23]

But contrary to some commentators' judgements, Geirr Harr is fairly sanguine about the impact of the German occupation of Norway. He reasons that the German military resources were too scarce to exploit fully the potential of the Norwegian bases, the U-boat bases were of limited value compared with the French ones, while the Swedish iron ore exported through Narvik was useful on a seasonal basis, but found not to be indispensable, especially when iron ore mines in Lorraine in occupied France had been seized.[24] Harr concludes that despite the failures during the Battle for Norway, Britain gained a useful ally and benefitted, 'particularly in maritime terms – naval and especially commercial – through the gain of the vast Norwegian merchant fleet'.[25]

A final judgement in The Hague

In the first few years after 1945, as the Cold War loomed, international geopolitics predominated thinking across Europe. This was to have a bearing on the unresolved fishery dispute still hanging over relations between Britain and Norway. Norway initially chose non-alignment, or a policy of regional alliance if need be, conscious that its near-neighbour Finland had to accept Soviet limitations on its freedom of action. However, in early 1948, there were rumours that Stalin was about to ask the Norwegians to sign a defence treaty with the Soviet Union. Although this did not come about, it was a source of concern in Oslo. International tensions that year, including the Prague coup in Czechoslovakia and the Berlin Blockade, brought moves to include the Scandinavian countries in an Atlantic Pact. This gathered momentum and climaxed in April 1949 with the formation of NATO, which included both Britain and Norway among its list of members.

But despite their otherwise close and friendly relationship and the responsibilities inherent in a new strategic partnership, problems arose during the winter of 1947–48 when British trawlers again appeared off the Norwegian coast. There was disquiet expressed among the local fishermen at the so-called 'trawler plague'. In June 1948 there were calls in the Storting for the full imposition of the 'Blue Line', the terminology used by the Norwegians for the base line rule referred to earlier. A report by the SO Fishery Protection of a cruise he undertook in northern Norway in June and July in the modified *Black Swan*-class frigate HMS *Cygnet* detected anti-British feelings in Baas Fjord near Vardö.[26] There were complaints again about incessant British poaching and damage caused to Norwegian line fishing equipment. In September, the British Ambassador was informed that the Norwegian fishery protection force would prevent all trawling inside the Blue Line. Predictably, the British Government countered with threats to bring in the Royal Navy if the compromise Red Line was not adhered to, pending a more permanent settlement.

On 8 November 1948, a Foreign Office Cabinet Memorandum spelled out the uncomfortable position in which Britain found itself. There seemed no recourse but to refer the matter to the ICJ for 'an authoritative opinion on the relevant issues of international law'. The Memorandum stated:

> The only settlement, therefore, which could now be negotiated would be a settlement under which the United Kingdom accepted the Norwegian decree and that would be a step which would be politically almost impossible for the United Kingdom to take in view of the strong reaction of British fishery interests. If there is no settlement by judicial decision or otherwise, incidents by fishery protection vessels on both sides in the disputed area are inevitable.[27]

A quarter of a century earlier, as was demonstrated in the dispute with the Soviet Union, Britain would have had little compunction in deploying its fishery protection vessels (or even greater firepower) to the Norwegian coast. But these were different times and circumstances. If it was not immediately apparent at the time, this was probably due to what Henry Kissinger later ironically called Britain's 'extraordinary ability to adjust to changing circumstances'.[28] Within the confines of the Foreign Office, influential voices such as Sir Eric Beckett, the legal adviser, and Robin Hankey, Head of the Northern Department, cautioned against violent clashes in the disputed waters, particularly when the country was supporting efforts to include Norway in the Atlantic Pact. Thus, strategic considerations were perceived to be of greater importance than purely national interests. Then inevitably, in late November of that year, the first British trawler was arrested inside the wide Blue Line.[29]

This was the Grimsby boat *Welbeck*, arrested on the 8th of the month, followed the next week by the *Cape Palliser* on the 14th, *Nellis* on 7 December and *Etrurl* on 9 December 1948. The British fishing industry called for an injunction by the Hague Court to prevent the Norwegians from interfering with the British fleets outside the Red Line in advance of the decision reached by the International Court, which was not expected until 1951. The industry's plea was rejected by the Government's legal advisers despite the fact the *Welbeck* and *Cape Palliser* were allegedly 'close' but still outside the limit while *Nellis* and *Etrurl* were over 2 miles distant.

The Senior Officer FPS, in his letter to the Admiralty dated 5 January, could not offer any solutions. It was thought unlikely that one of his vessels would be in the vicinity when an incident occurred and the use of a danbuoy to mark the location was considered valueless as it was likely to drag. Moreover, the cost of maintaining a FP vessel continuously on station was of questionable value owing to the high operating costs and the fact that it was only of true value at certain times of the year. He could only suggest that the Norwegians could be persuaded to question the value of their actions by showing that there was a connection between their behaviour and the amount of fish Britain purchased from them. He offered what seemed an unworkable solution, ' ... we could stop out of our payments to Norway a sum equivalent to our claims for compensation which His Majesty's Government have stated, in their formal protests after each arrest, that they will make'.[30]

The Cabinet resolved to refer the matter to the ICJ in The Hague. The lawyers within the FO were confident of a positive outcome: that Britain, in accepting the Norwegian historic 4-mile zone, would be successful in getting the contentious base line rule rejected. Further negotiations were held in London both in December 1948 and in January 1949 and a new Yellow Line was proposed, 'roughly the Blue Line of 1935, with some dents to satisfy British interests'.[31]

Surprisingly, the Yellow Line idea found acceptance with the trawlermen and the Norwegian Government too saw it as a temporary *modus vivendi*. But the Storting was more reluctant to accept the proposal as the way forward. The Norwegian Navy also argued that the Yellow Line was too complex to be workable and, if accepted, 'Norway would have capitulated of her own will.'[32] In early May a Norwegian gunboat used gunfire to arrest the first trawler that year. *Lord Nuffield* was taken into the port of Vardø, then released on payment of a deposit pending proceedings in a Norwegian court.

The familiar diplomatic protest resulted. An Admiralty spokesman remarked, 'we cannot sit idly by while foreign gunboats fire on our fishermen'. The incident also provoked questions in the House of Commons. Christopher Mayhew, Under Secretary of State at the Foreign Office, was pressed by the opposition on the question of whether there was adequate protection for fighting vessels off Norway while negotiations were under way. Mayhew tried to justify his department's policy by stating that there was a difference between being firm and friendly, which was the approach being adopted, and being provocative. This drew a response from Vice-Admiral Ernest Taylor, the long-serving MP for Paddington South, which exposed the crux of the matter: the still unresolved international ruling concerning what actually constituted territorial waters, 'Is it not right to protect our fishing fleet operating outside territorial waters? There is no question of provocation attached to that. It is our right to protect them and we should do so.'[33]

Finally, Britain made a unilateral appeal to the International Court in The Hague for a ruling. In the meantime, arrests continued with four trawlers accused of poaching, which the fishing industry countered with calls for protection or retaliation in the form of an embargo on Norwegian exports. But despite the strong words and the flurry of protests, this was the reality of the new world order. If Britain was to unite with other countries under the NATO flag against the common enemy of what was to become the Warsaw Pact in 1955 it could not afford to risk the alliance for a lesser cause.

Confidence that it would win on the 'base line issue' was immediately dispelled when on 8 December 1951 the International Court of Justice surprisingly ruled entirely in favour of the Norwegian argument. The judges sanctioned the use of base lines, stating that the coastal population's dependency on fisheries for their livelihoods had constituted the deciding factor. Crucially, in a statement that had wider implications for future disputes of this nature, it was noted that, 'international law did not lay down any rule on the extent of territorial waters or fishery limits ... that every state was entitled to claim at least three miles'.[34] Britain chose not to contest the judgement, causing even the Norwegians to dub the country 'good losers'.[35]

The RN was instructed to follow The Hague guidance in the aftermath of the court's ruling. In future, potential poachers were to be warned that they were in danger of being arrested if close to the agreed limit. In the case of wrongful arrests, the trawlermen were told to inform the FP vessel; if the FP vessel was in the vicinity they should fix the position and if the trawler was arrested, the position should be reported. By contrast, which put the whole matter into perspective, there were instructions given to FP commanding officers to undertake exercises with Norwegian Navy submarines whenever possible – as good NATO partners![36]

Conclusion

The Hague Judgment of 1951 had far-reaching consequences for the future of the British fishing industry and what it considered to be its historic right to the freedom of the seas. The Declaration sent a clear signal to Iceland particularly and was to set in train a number of events that were lead to the outbreak of the first of the so-called 'Cod Wars' just seven years later. Britain's rather meek acceptance of the Hague ruling might well be construed as a small part of its much discussed post-war retreat from former imperial greatness and prestige.

In all this, the Royal Navy's fishery protection ships were basically passive bystanders. The slender resources available to provide support for the fishermen when the crisis was at its worst were crucially exposed in 1935 when details of the financial shortfall were revealed. On the other hand, one could argue that the top brass in the Admiralty did not care enough about the materiel requirements of a very minor branch of its service, especially at a time when the urgent needs for rearmament were preoccupying their thoughts.

Chapter Seven

In Home Waters
1815–2005

THE DUTIES OF THE Fishery Protection Squadron in the twentieth century, in general terms, remained largely unchanged from its historic charge to support and protect the nation's fishermen in what were described as coastal, intermediate and distant waters. The only difference was that by the middle of the century those directly involved were claiming that the task had become more important and complex.[1]

The primary aim in coastal or home waters was to ensure the observance by foreign fishing vessels of the British 3-mile exclusive fishing limits and the enforcement of international conventions regulating the fisheries outside the limit. This applied to all fishing vessels and included the regulations governing mesh size of nets, types of fishing gear, lighting of vessels and the prevention of collisions at sea. Fishery Officers were also expected to act in a quasi-judicial capacity in relation to disputes. They were guided in those matters by the Sea Fisheries Manual, which had grown in size exponentially. What is not included in this chapter is a comprehensive account of the everyday workings of the local UK fishing districts and obviously, because there have been too many individual incidents of poaching and other infringements by British boats or those of near neighbours across the Channel, the southern North Sea or the Irish Sea.

What *is* covered is the different arrangement that has historically applied to Scotland and the interface between the RN and what is currently called Marine Scotland, the organisation that has formed part of the core Scottish Government since devolution. Although legal procedures in the UK were in place for dealing both with national and international lawbreakers, there were inevitably individual cases

Trawling and Seine Fishing Methods

Purse Seining (primarily for pelagic fish – such as herring) in which a net is paid out in a large circle to enclose a shoal of fish. The bottom of the net sinks and is then drawn in to form a large purse or pouch trapping the catch.

Trawling (mainly for demersal – bottom living – fish, such as cod and haddock). A pair of otter boards keep open the mouth of a bag-shaped net when towed through the water. Wings of netting extend to herd the fish into the mouth of the net, and the catch is retained in the 'cod-end'.

Danish Seining (demersal fis The net, similar to a small tr net, is attached to two, very ropes, the warps. One end o warp is secured to a buoy. T boat then steams in a wide c 'shooting' warps and net and returning to the buoy. The tw warps are then hauled in, sweeping the fish into the ne

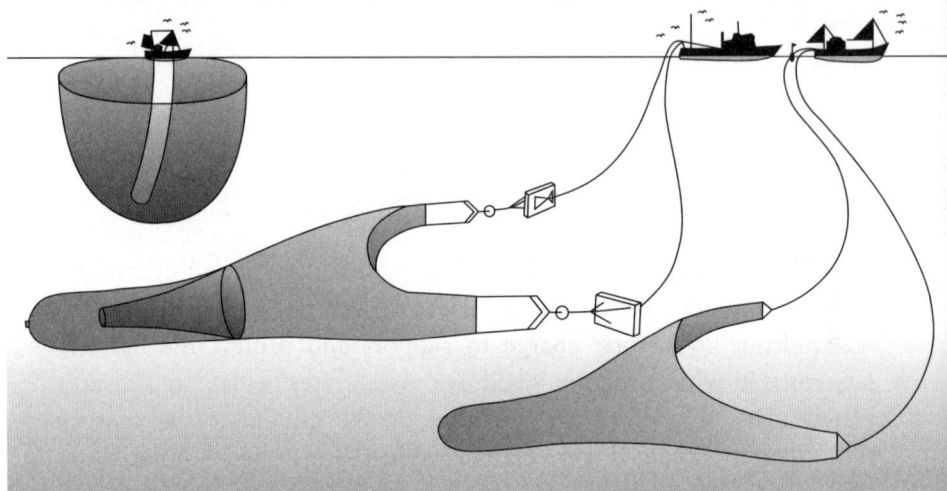

Figure 2: Types of trawler fishing. (Drawing by Stephen Dent, based on information in 1975 COI/HMSO leaflet 'Royal Navy Fishery Protection')

where the 'rulebook' was not helpful to the commanding officer 'on the spot'. The case of the attempted arrest of the trawler *Lucida* in 1933 is recounted as an example: a problematic incident exacerbated by the said differences between English and Scottish bye-laws.

There are sections on the first trials with aerial surveillance of fishing areas that were ahead of their time, and also on the importance of 'showing the flag' both in home ports and in those of near neighbours in the interests of maintaining good relationships. The notorious harshness of the weather conditions around the British Isles, particularly in winter, is a perennial factor in fishery protection. The tragic loss of two Hull trawlers, the *St Louis* in 1930 and the *Amethyst* in January 1937, illustrate the problems faced by the RN when responding to distress calls, particularly in an era before instant and continuous ship-to-shore communication. What is also underlined is the age-old requirement for FP vessels to be robust enough to cope with extreme weather conditions.

During the last part of the twentieth century, the coastal Fishery Protection Squadron ships became directly involved in Operation Grenada, the deterrent patrol of the waters off Northern Ireland that was principally aimed at preventing arms smuggling to the Province during the Troubles of 1969–2005. The routine presence of the Royal Navy in this area, ostensibly undertaking fishery patrols, masked the fact that the ships were also carrying out additional, covert duties and actions. Information about Operation Grenada was deliberately suppressed until well after its cessation in 2005.

The 'Ton'-class minesweepers played a major role in Operation Grenada; likewise they were the mainstay of coastal fishery protection from the 1960s through to the 1990s. Some of the recollections of those who served aboard the 'Fish Tons' are related in this chapter. Finally, any account of the history of sea fishing in the UK, which until recent years was essentially a 'man's world', would be incomplete without the 'voice' being heard of the women who lived and contributed year round in the fishing towns. The Grimsby Heritage Centre's Oral History Project 'The Women they Left Behind' provides a fascinating and invaluable glimpse into the life of a typical fishing community during the second half of the twentieth century.

Scotland

Historical perspective

Although Britain's sea fisheries have been controlled and protected by the Westminster Parliament for over 200 years, the arrangement with respect to Scotland has been different for the majority of the intervening years and this impacted on the work of the Fishery Protection Squadron during that time. Subject to a statute of 1815, which effectively lasted until 1994, the Royal Navy was required to allocate a naval vessel as a fishery protection ship exclusively to be deployed in Scottish waters. Historically, the commanding officer of the RN ship was recompensed to the sum of £100 per annum paid by the Scottish Office in recognition of the additional responsibilities involved with the task. In 1818 the Commissioners of the British White Herring Fishery acquired its own protection vessel.[2]

The same Commissioners were reconstituted as the Fishery Board for Scotland in 1882, principally because, with the introduction of the steam trawler and its impact on the traditional methods of fishing in Scotland, it was becoming harder to administer the various bye-laws appertaining to this region. In addition to the enforcement of the regulations in an area that stretched from 3 miles north of Berwick-upon-Tweed around the mainland and island coasts and westward, then south to the Solway Firth, the Board was also charged with investigating methods of fishing and with monitoring the state of domestic fish stocks. In order to undertake this considerable administrative task, the Scottish coastline was divided into twenty-six districts, each under the control of one of the Board's Fishery Officers.[3]

The Board's responsibilities were transferred to the Secretary of State for Scotland in 1939 and in April 1991 that office oversaw the establishment of the fisheries protection and enforcement services as an executive agency. This formed part of the British Government's move towards devolution. In 1994, it was decided that the Royal Navy's assistance was no longer required. The FPS was relocated from Rosyth to Portsmouth as a consequence. The Scottish Fisheries Protection Agency (SFPA) was created with the resources of 230 staff, twenty coastal offices, six protection vessels and two surveillance aircraft. Following devolution in 1999 the Agency was transferred to the control of the Scottish Executive Environment and Rural Affairs Department.

Marine Scotland currently operates three protection vessels (FPVs), two research vessels and two surveillance aircraft. The FPVs are not military ships and are therefore unarmed. They use the FPV prefix and fly the SFPA ensign. As well as providing a presence in coastal waters, the ships contribute to the UK's continuing commitment to NEAFC (North Eastern Atlantic Fishery Commission) and as such conduct annual patrols in the remote region west of Rockall.

The ships

The Scottish Fishery Board acquired its own vessel from the RN for the first time in 1882: the wooden-hulled sailing cutter *Vigilant*. Two more ships were taken up shortly and during the busy summer herring season these were supplemented by three or four others. The Board was also a pioneer of fishery research and in 1886 the steam trawler *Garland* was purchased. Although not powerful enough to undertake deep-water trawling, *Garland* was adapted to work a small-beam trawl. The research facilities at the Marine Laboratory at Aberdeen stemmed from this early initiative, and are internationally renowned, operating to the present day. The same year, due to the rapid increase in steam trawlers, the steam yacht *Violet* was purchased with the aid of a Treasury grant and was later renamed *Vigilant (2)*.[4]

HMS *Halcyon*: torpedo gunboat and senior naval officer command North Sea Fisheries, in 1905. (*Author's Collection*)

HMS *Godetia*: *Arabis*-class 'fleet sweeping vessel' or sloop, photographed in 1924. (*World Ship Society Photographic Library*)

HMS *Hastings*: 1930s sloop used extensively in the fishery protection role. (*Author's Collection*)

HMS *Mariner*: despatched to the Murman coast during a tense post-Second World War stand-off with the Soviet Union. (*World Ship Society Photographic Library*)

HMS *Hound*: the last Second World War vintage FPS vessel in active service. (*World Ship Society Photographic Library*)

The Fishery Protection Squadron base at Port Edgar in 1960. HMS *Russell* and probably HMS *Wotton* can be seen. (*UK MoD*)

Checking nets aboard a French trawler on the Dogger Bank. (*Courtesy of Adrian Wilkinson*)

The Fishery Protection Squadron operations room at Port Edgar in the late 1960s. (*MoD*)

HMS *Wotton*: originally a member of the FPS 'Home Division', this 'Fish Ton' had been fitted with an enclosed bridge by the time the photo was taken in 1983. (*Author's Collection*)

HMS *Lincoln* with prominent wooden protection in the bow area, which was fitted too late to see action during the last Cod War. (*UK MoD Crown Copyright, 1976*)

HMS *Palliser*: the Type 14 frigate played a central role in the *Milwood* incident in 1963 (*Author's Collection*)

HMS *Leopard*: the ageing Type 41 frigate was involved in the Second and Third Cod Wars and placed on the disposal list soon afterwards. (*Author's Collection*)

ICGV *Baldur* sheers away from HMS *Mermaid* after colliding on 6 May 1976. (*UK MoD Crown Copyright, 1976*)

CGV *Óðinn* just prior to a collision with the *Leander*-class HMS *Galatea*. (*UK MoD Crown Copyright, 1976*)

The RN's first purpose-built offshore patrol/fishery protection vessel, HMS *Jersey*, in the Bruges Canal in 1988. (*Courtesy of Mike Louagie, Ostend*)

RFAs *Wave Ruler* and *Wave Baron* were criticised for their poor performance and design in a Report of Proceedings during the First Cod War. (*UK MoD*)

ICGV *Óðinn* cuts across the bows of the trawler *Arctic Corsair* on 1 May 1976. (*UK MoD Crown Copyright, 1976*)

A third protection cruiser, *Brenda*, entered service in 1901; that summer was particularly busy with four other vessels flying the ensign of the Board, supplemented by a further three or four RN vessels.[5] *Brenda* had an extraordinarily long service, requisitioned in both world wars to act as a port examination vessel in the Firth of Forth: it was not disposed of until 1951. *Norna (2)* and *Freya* also completed over fifty years of service to the Scottish Board.[6]

The Mackenzie Committee was commissioned in 1923 to consider the best ways to improve fishery protection in Scottish waters. The Committee recommended establishing effective policing, preferably with more, and more modern and faster, cruisers. The Board reviewed its protection policy in 1933 and concluded that a fleet of ten vessels was required, consisting of four all-purpose vessels, four craft suitable for intensive patrol in local areas and two small boats for inshore, sheltered areas. *Vigilant (3)* and *Fidra* were both commissioned as a result of the building programme resulting from the Board's findings. Both ships had 'Q-Boat characteristics' in order to apprehend fishing boats suspected of breaking the law. Thus, to aid disguise until the last moment, *Vigilant (3)* carried a series of fishing boat registration letters and numbers to interchange both at bow and stern, together with false gallows and trawling lights. Even the funnel colour could be changed.[7]

The Scottish Home Department took over the responsibilities of the Fishery Board in 1939. At the time there were eight protection vessels in operation together with two research ships. These were supplemented at all times by one RN vessel. The same arrangement was reinstated following the Second World War and by 1964 there were still eight 'fishery cruisers' in service (as they were officially referred to by that time) plus one RN coastal minesweeper drawn from the Fishery Protection and Minesweeping Squadron then based at Port Edgar, North Queensferry, on the Firth of Forth.

Britain's dispute with Iceland in the early 1970s, when the latter unilaterally extended its fishery limit to 50 miles, prompted the Scottish Home Office to review the capabilities of its protection vessels as it was becoming likely that their areas of operation were to be considerably increased in the coming years. The outcome saw the commissioning of FPV *Jura* in 1975. As described in more detail in Chapter Eleven, the design of the ship was directly to influence that of the RN's 'Island' class and the succession of purpose-built protection vessels constructed thereafter. Crucially, *Jura*'s design was based on the seakeeping qualities demonstrated by the earlier fishery cruiser *Switha*. The *Jura* was constructed by Hall, Russell and Co. Ltd, Aberdeen, a company that had traditionally specialised in the construction of distant-water trawlers.[8]

Subsequently, the commissioning of FPV *Sulisker* in 1981 constituted a further milestone, having been specifically designed to undertake patrols up to the 200-mile EEZ limit. *Sulisker* was fitted with twin screws, a speed of 18 knots, a bow thruster, twin rudders and stabilisers to provide the crew with greater comfort. The ship displaced 1,250 tons and gave twenty-four years of service. One of its successors in the fleet, FPV *Hirta*, displaces 2,181 tons – in sharp contrast, for example, to the First World War-era *Vigilant (2)* (134 tons), mentioned above. In a depressing sign of the times, *Hirta* was built in Gdansk, Poland, rather than in Scotland despite the country's long and rich shipbuilding heritage.[9]

A bone of contention

The unusual Anglo-Scottish fishery protection arrangement was the cause of friction; in short the Royal Navy regarded the requirement to provide a ship for exclusive employment in Scottish waters both as a burden and as the source of unnecessary complication. For example, the commanding officer of HMS *Spey*, who was the Scottish Local Fisheries Naval Officer (LFNO), wrote a letter to the Captain FP and M in 1934 in the wake of the *Lucida* incident described below. He laid out the problems of coping with the Scottish bye-laws and the poor relationship that he claimed existed between the Scottish fishery cruisers and the Scottish fishermen.[10]

The matter was taken up with more urgency in the 1950s at a time when cutbacks in defence spending and the growing seriousness of the dispute with Iceland were making an impact. Captain F R Twiss, Captain 5th FP and M Squadron at the time, wrote a comprehensive report in 1954 on what he perceived as the 'functions and value' of his command. He addressed the matter of the 'continuous allocation of a naval vessel as fishery protection ship in Scottish waters'. Captain Twiss described the circumstances that had led to the *Algerine*-class minesweeper HMS *Welcome* being assigned to the duty in 1946 and still being used in that capacity eight years later. His frustration is evident:

Not only have we allocated a ship; it seems to be required also that the ship should be a Commander's command, because of the grading of the masters of the unarmed, civilian, vessels of the Scottish flotilla. ... Thus we have reached the ridiculous position where the civilian flotilla grows in size and importance (today there are no fewer than nine civilian fishery protection cruisers), so apparently must we continue to maintain an Ocean minesweeper to support them; whereas in 1945, when there were no civilian ships, a trawler would presumably have met our obligation.[11]

Twiss continues by criticising the Scottish Board for refusing to release HMS *Welcome* for service off Iceland on an occasion when, during the worst of the winter gales, its sister ship was in danger of foundering. He considered it, 'quite unsatisfactory that we should continue to be embarrassed by the modern interpretation of a Statute 150 years old'. He ends by suggesting that the Admiralty Board recommend to the Scottish Home Department that, because of manpower difficulties, *Welcome* should be used on patrols in the Faroes and off Iceland and Greenland. The Scottish Board did finally agree that the ship could be used for these additional duties the following year, 1955, but still quibbled over any increase in the historic £100 annual gratuity to be paid to the commanding officer.[12]

Finally, there was the matter of the burden to the taxpayer. It was pointed out that the Mackenzie Committee had calculated in 1924 that the whole fleet had cost £48,620; in 1960 one vessel alone cost £350,000 to build. Up until the 1920s the fleet had been more or less self-sufficient with the sum offset by the revenue accruing from fines etc. Since then there had been a progressive decline in the industry, particularly inshore fishing, which had become progressively uneconomic. The 1960 investigation had been prompted by the Scottish Home Department's proposal to build a new cruiser to replace *Freya (2)*, which had foundered in heavy weather.[13]

Test case: the saga of Skipper Jinks

The Head of the Admiralty Military Branch (M. Branch) observed in 1934 that, 'The Admiralty have always disliked the employment of Fishery Protection Cruisers to enforce the Scottish Acts and Bye-Laws which restrict the rights of British fishermen to fish within Scottish territorial waters.' He went on to state that the Admiralty had, 'only arranged to continue enforcing these Scottish enactments because it is known that the Scottish Office would refuse to agree with any alteration of the instructions'. He then referred, as a case in point, to the failed prosecution of the skipper of the trawler S/T *Lucida* that year.[14]

In the early afternoon of 14 November 1933, the *Mersey*-class trawler HMS *Doon*, patrolling near the southern reaches of the Outer Hebrides, encountered a group of trawlers apparently working illegally. Firstly, the Fleetwood trawler *Lucida* was sighted trawling with its port gear some 5½ miles from Barra Light. *Doon* ordered the trawler to stop and to haul its gear. The *Lucida* endeavoured to manoeuvre away, requiring the *Doon* to sail across its bows in order to compel the trawler to stop. The ship's boat was sent across and skipper Bert Jinks was charged with illegal trawling in contravention of the Herring Fisheries Act of Scotland, 1899.

Another trawler, the *Gwenlillian*, was then spotted, this time displaying the wrong lights in contravention of the Regulations for the Prevention of Collisions at sea. Lieutenant Commander Dalison took HMS *Doon* at full speed towards this second trawler, ordered it to stop, to haul its gear and to await his return. A third, unidentifiable trawler was then sighted but Dalison realised that he would be unable to catch it and so set about apprehending a fourth vessel, the *Tranquil*, which was also displaying incorrect lights. Following a short chase, during which a blank round was fired, the *Tranquil* came to a halt. This time, Lieutenant Commander Dalison boarded the vessel himself and, having concluded that the skipper was genuinely unaware that he had broken the law, returned to his ship. Dalison admitted that he had been able to catch more than one offender because he had been proceeding with no lights whatsoever, apart from an occasional use of his searchlight for identification.[15]

HMS *Doon* then returned to S/T *Lucida*, and, after leaving Leading Seaman Forrest aboard as the official boarding party, Lieutenant Commander Dalison ordered Jinks to proceed to Stornoway. However, as soon as *Doon*'s sea boat had cast off, the trawler made off southward with the FP vessel in pursuit. Repeated orders to stop were issued via *Doon*'s searchlight and three blank rounds were fired. These finally elicited a reply via the Lucida's whistle, 'Bound for Fleetwood'.[16] It was reported that Jinks had admitted earlier that he had been twice convicted for working inside the Scottish fishing limit and that when he had heard *Doon* firing its gun while apprehending the *Tranquil*, he had reassured his crew with, 'Go on, don't mind that f-----g gun, he daren't hit yer, it's only a blank.'[17]

The chase south continued all day. Dalison decided to keep close to the Mull of Kintyre in the hope of finding a more favourable tide than the *Lucida*, which appeared to be shaping course nearer to Rathlin Island off the coast of Northern Ireland. However, instead of gaining on the trawler, the *Lucida* steadily increased its lead. Meanwhile, *Doon*'s CO had to pin his hopes on closing Jinks's ship off the Mull of Galloway where, 'I hoped either to disable her by fouling her screw with a length of wire towed at the end of a grass line or, if the sea was sufficiently calm, by laying my ship alongside her and boarding.'[18]

As darkness fell, a rain squall off Tor Point temporarily blotted out sight of Jinks's vessel and when visibility improved it was described as, 'a smudge of smoke below the horizon to the Southward'. Dalison radioed for assistance, and despite delays, the 'W'-class destroyer HMS *Viceroy* managed to arrive off the Fleetwood Channel in time to intercept the *Lucida*, had it decided to return directly to its home port. However, thanks to the ingenuity of Leading Seaman Forrest aboard the *Lucida*, Jinks had decided to take his vessel instead into Ramsey Bay, where it lay overnight. Forrest had worked on Jinks's fears by pretending to read the Morse signals, which were audible over the *Lucida*'s loud speaker, purportedly relating to the movements of the pursuing RN ships.[19]

Having ascertained that Jinks's arrival in Fleetwood would be met by the police, Lieutenant Commander Dalison decided to station HMS *Doon* slightly north at the mouth of Lune Deep. The next day was calm but foggy. Dalison's hunch paid off when S/T *Lucida* was spotted among some twelve to eighteen other trawlers making their way slowly up the Lune Estuary in view of the weather conditions. When *Doon* signalled for the *Lucida* to stop, the trawler increased to full speed in spite of the fog. Dalison fired a blank round and set off in pursuit. He described the ensuing chase:

> The two ships proceeded thus in the most reckless manner up this narrow and tortuous channel packed with trawlers while the gloom of the fog deepened into night.

Later:

> At this time I was coming up on her starboard quarter: I could see that she hoped to edge me onto the mud as we overtook with some rapidity a peaceful trawler in mid channel. At the crucial

moment, however, I swung across her wake and dodged up on the opposite side of the peaceful trawler. This manoeuvre now brought me level and my boarding party now stood by to board at full speed while the remaining hands lined the side with fenders. The ships were now rushing neck and neck towards the right angle turn to port round the Knott End Buoy; ahead of us just about to take the turn was another trawler. There was just room between her and the buoy, and I pressed *Doon* into the gap, while *Lucida* had to take the wider sweep upon her opposite side. The next corner was to starboard and yet another trawler was going round it, but, by going close to this one, I was able to compel *Lucida* to reduce speed to avoid a collision; thus no boarding under way was necessary. Passing two more trawlers at full speed I rounded the next corner to starboard and was able to turn *Doon* across the entrance to the lock and prevent further entry.[20]

An armed party was then despatched to the *Lucida* in order to carry out the arrest of Bert Jinks. Dalison notes that, 'The display of the Sub-Lieutenant's revolver was, however, sufficient.' HMS *Doon* and S/T *Lucida*, with an armed guard aboard, then proceeded to Stornoway.

Undoubtedly to the immense chagrin of the Admiralty, Skipper Jinks was subsequently acquitted in the Scottish court through a combination of the intricacies of the Scottish Acts and bye-laws and what was described as 'bungling' on the part of the prosecution. He was charged with three offences: illegal trawling within territorial waters; refusal to comply with a direction made by a Sea Fishery Officer in pursuance of the Sea Fishery Act 1883; and wilfully obstructing a peace officer under Section 38 of the Offences against the Person Act. It was alleged that the first charge was not proceeded with because the court did not possess jurisdiction to deal with it. However, he was subsequently fined £65 by admitting the charge of illegal trawling and his gear was confiscated. The second, more damaging charge was dismissed on the technical grounds that the court was not allowed to examine the reason why Dalison ordered Jinks to put into Stornoway rather than a nearer port. *Doon*'s CO had refused to divulge his reasons on security grounds. The third charge was deferred for reference to the Crown Office in Edinburgh. The objections made by the defence were two-fold: that the Person Act did not apply in Scotland and Dalison's role as a peace officer was not recognised.[21]

The Navy, in considering the case retrospectively, thought it likely to diminish the prestige of the Fishery Protection Service and that Jinks's acquittal on a charge of disobeying a Sea Fishery Officer would create a very bad impression, which would likely undermine in future the authority of the commanding officers of FP vessels in the execution of their duties. An appeal against Jinks's acquittal was heard in Edinburgh on 15 March 1934. The Judiciary Appeal Court upheld the initial decision on the grounds that cross-examination on the question of whether Stornoway was the most suitable port to which Jinks could have been sent had been prematurely and improperly stopped. Thus, Lieutenant Commander Dalison's understandable reticence to divulge what he considered to be sensitive military intelligence had been outmanoeuvred by a legal technicality. However, in a postscript, it was reported late the same year that the owners of S/T *Lucida* had sold the ship in Aberdeen, while Bert Jinks 'was said to have been out of employment and in receipt of public assistance'.[22]

'The dangers of the seas'[23]

Inevitably, down the years, protection vessels have become involved in searches for missing fishing vessels. Two cases, seven years apart, highlight the perils brought about by the severity of winter weather around the coast of the British Isles, particularly in the higher latitudes to the north-east of the UK.

The S/T St *Louis*, 352 tons, was a newish vessel, built in 1925, when it was reported missing on 4 February 1930. The trawler had left Hull bound for the Murman coast on 8 January. It had been scheduled to pick up a pilot at Lødingen, north Norway, around the 13th of the month but had not arrived. The FP flotilla was alerted: the *Arabis*-class sloop HMS *Rosemary* was ordered to sweep southward from its patrol line on the Murman coast with the *Mersey*-class trawler HMS *Cherwell* (later joined by its sister ship HMS *Boyne*), approaching from the opposite direction searching the northern Norwegian coast. Additionally, HMS *Spey* was commanded to sail east from the Shetlands – depending on the weather.[24]

Initially, it was feared that the *St Louis* must have broken down and was drifting but there was no means of communicating with the vessel. Subsequently, two lifebuoys belonging to the trawler were found washed ashore on opposite sides of the channel leading to the port of Lødingen in the Lofoten Islands. Unfortunately, there was a fortnight's delay in reporting the discovery of the lifebuoys, so it was not until 15 February that HMS *Harebell* was able to visit Lødingen in order to make arrangements for the equipment to be returned to the ship's owners in Hull.[25]

The Captain FP & M learned there that local opinion was unanimous, that S/T *St Louis* probably went ashore on an outlying reef of the Lofotens and most likely sank immediately. Captain M C Goldsmith's report praised the manner in which HMS *Boyne* and *Cherwell* had conducted the search. It was, he wrote, undertaken, 'with the greatest determination and in a most conscientious manner', adding with typical understatement, 'in weather which might only too well be described as "unsuitable"'. He added graphically, 'The great danger to these small craft in a winter gale in high latitudes is the constant accumulation of ice. All spray freezes immediately it strikes the ship, and the mast and upperworks eventually weigh many tons, which is very likely to render the ship unstable.'[26]

On Monday, 25 January 1937, Captain FP and M, Captain V A C Crutchley, received a signal from the District Inspector of Fisheries that information had been received in Hull that the trawler S/T *Amethyst* was in difficulties about 120 miles east of Kinnaird Head in north-eastern Scotland. Signals had been received at approximately 2200 hours the previous night stating, 'Engine trouble, cracked cylinder head, position 120 miles East of Kinnaird Head', and then later, ominously, 'Boiler explosion, heavy list to Port, can do nothing'. The District Inspector had stated that the *Amethyst*'s owners, Kingston Steam Trawling Co. Ltd, had asked for assistance as they considered their boat might still be afloat and drifting helplessly.[27]

S/T *Amethyst* had been built in 1928 by the firm Cook Welton & Gemmell Ltd of Hull. It displaced 357 tons and had a triple-expansion engine and one boiler. Earlier the same month, the trawler had been lengthened by 11ft by Smiths Dock, Middlesbrough, and this was likely to have been the first voyage it had undertaken since the work was completed.[28]

HMS *Kingfisher*, commanded by the Aberdeen-based LFNO Scotland, Commander J H Pipe, was immediately ordered to sea from Invergordon and a wider, international call for assistance was broadcast through MAF in case other ships were in the locality. *Kingfisher* responded within two hours, proceeding to sea at 16 knots initially, then 14 knots as, 'the ship was bumping badly, weather conditions at the time being Wind

E.S.E., force 8, sea and swell 45'. Crutchley's report went on to state that *Kingfisher*'s speed had to be progressively reduced until during the Monday evening it was only making 3 knots with the propellers regularly out of the water. By midnight, Tuesday, 26–Wednesday, 27 January, with the sea and swell increased to 55, *Kingfisher* was hove to, unable to make any headway, and Captain FP and M ordered it to abandon the search at 1330 on the Wednesday afternoon.[29]

Meanwhile, HMS *Harebell*, Captain Crutchley's command, had sailed north from its base at Portland to Leith, where it was met by HMS *Kingfisher*. Crutchley was of the opinion that, unless the *Amethyst* had succeeded in riding some form of sea anchor 'such as her trawl gear shot forward', it had undoubtedly foundered. The trawler's owners disagreed, however, arguing that their boat was quite likely still to be afloat. Accordingly, the Admiralty ordered a further search. Having coaled, *Harebell* left Rosyth amid periodic blizzards at 1530 hours on 28 January, nearly five days after the *Amethyst*'s signal had been received. HMS *Boyne* and *Kingfisher* were also ordered to pass through the Fair Isle Channel in the most unlikely event that the trawler had meanwhile drifted north of the Shetlands.[30]

The sea had increased to such an extent that by mid-afternoon on 30 January it became obvious to Captain Crutchley that he would lose both whalers if the ship remained on course and the weather deteriorated further. He was still some 25 miles from Kinnaird Head. He decided to heave to with revolutions for a speed of 7 knots so as to maintain some steerage way. But early the following morning the wind and the seas were even worse. A bin on the *Harebell*'s forecastle containing a large manila head rope and wire spring had broken up. A bight (loop) of the rope was dangling over the port side, posing a danger if it became entangled in the propeller. Although that threat was averted, late in the evening a particularly heavy wave submerged the port whaler, causing the falls and gripes to part. The wind was measured as Force 11 and the sea 79.

Meanwhile, other ships had joined the search, including the veteran Danish Fishery Inspection Vessel HMDS *Islands Falk*. HMS *Kingfisher* was unable to leave Leith until 2 February as it was decided that it would make little headway in the prevailing weather conditions. Finally, late on the evening of 1 February, the wind had abated sufficiently for *Harebell* to resume its search. Sadly, despite best efforts, there was no trace found of the *Amethyst* and the search was officially abandoned by the Navy on 5 February.[31] An 'Admiralty regrets ...' notice was issued three days later.

Despite letters of commendation and appreciation from the Admiralty and the Hull Fishing Vessel Owners' Association for the efforts of the FP vessels, the fact remained that HMS *Kingfisher* had proved to be totally inadequate in coping with the weather. Accordingly, the CO and ship's company transferred to HMS *Sheldrake*, another of the *Kingfisher* class. *Kingfisher* was assigned to the less stormy Channel area.[32]

Inter-service co-operation

Much has been written about the creation of the RAF in April 1918 when it formally took responsibility for 2,949 seaplanes and aeroplanes from the Royal Naval Air Service (RNAS) together with 55,000 personnel. It is generally agreed that during the interwar period the move inflamed inter-service rivalry between the RN and the RAF. There was, supposedly, a general suspicion of air power within the Admiralty, which served to inhibit the development of strategies for the offensive use of carrier-based operations prior to it becoming a key feature of naval engagements during the Second World War.[33]

Therefore, it appears counterfactual to record that two amenable experiments in inter-service co-operation took place during the interwar period that tested the use of aerial reconnaissance to spot and track the movement of fishing vessels around the coast of Britain and to pass the information on to MAF officials and the RN.

In 1928 and 1929 RAF flying boats based at Felixstowe, Suffolk, undertook a series of patrols along the east coast to help identify French and Belgian fishing vessels encroaching within the 3-mile territorial water limit. It was noted that the 1928 patrols were particularly timely as the Fishery Protection Flotilla had been depleted by the combined effects of the demands of the Murman coast patrol, the Shetland patrol and various refits. Indeed there were periods when there were simply no patrol craft available.[34]

A pattern of communication between the flying boat on patrol and RAF Felixstowe was established whereby sightings of foreign fishing boats would be logged. It was noted that, with experience, the pilots were able to recognise the habits of individual skippers, 'to distinguish those with inclinations towards poaching'. An interdepartmental conference held in July 1929 at Pembroke Dock attended by the District Inspector of Fisheries, the RAF wing commander and the Captain

Fishery Protection to reflect on the lessons learned from the experiment emphasised the importance of establishing W/T communications between the protection vessel and the aircraft. As a result, a W/T set was loaned by the RAF but it was recognised that all of the RN vessels would need to be equipped with suitable sets if such joint operations were to be successful in the future.[35]

The presence of the flying boats over the fishing grounds clearly had an impact on the foreign fishermen. It was reported at the conference that the skipper of an Ostend boat later reported that he had experienced 'an air raid over us' and his agent had been warned that he had been fishing close to the limit off Winterton in Lincolnshire. But the climax of this experiment in co-operation came on 11 August 1929 when conditions favoured what was described as 'a concerted raid' by French and Belgian fishing boats on the inshore sole fishing grounds. In the afternoon, the French trawler DG.*901* was spotted a mile off Orfordness, Suffolk, with others close by adjacent to the 3-mile limit.

In the evening, the flying boat pilot landed near Lowestoft to discuss the matter with the Fishery Officer, who in turn telegraphed the LFNO at Sheerness. The LFNO summoned HMS *Selkirk*, an *Aberdare*-class minesweeper assigned to FP duties, which was at the time en route from Portsmouth to Lowestoft. *Selkirk* steamed straight to the fishing grounds and arrested DG.*916*, not the anticipated DG.*901*, inside Sizewell Bank and just over 2 miles off shore. A court case followed, the catch and one set of gear were confiscated and the incident was given widespread publicity. According to the MAF report, there were no further complaints about poaching during that summer season.[36]

The locals were highly impressed with the results of the experiment and their pleas for an extension into the autumn herring season were answered. George Atkinson concluded his MAF report:

> The question of flying officers engaged on fishery patrols being appointed Sea Fishery Officers is at present under discussion, and even if the proposal does not materialise, the important decision that a foreign fishing vessel seen fishing in territorial waters may be arrested on subsequently arriving in a British port, will add to the difficulties of those foreign fishermen who at present find our inshore waters as attractive as our markets are profitable.[37]

Although there was a successful prosecution in the case of DG.*916*, the convoluted workings of the communication 'chain' that finally brought

HMS *Selkirk* to the scene are obvious. It reiterated the point made earlier in the conference about the need for both the aircraft and the FP ships to carry W/T equipment.

The second experiment took place over the Bristol Channel in 1933. Prior to that, there had been discussions between the District Inspector of Fisheries and an RAF Wing Commander at Pembroke Dock that resulted in a combined operation between No. 210 Flying Boat Squadron and the FP vessel HMS *Doon*. A series of trials was undertaken. Again, effective communication between aircraft and ship proved to be the stumbling block. At first an Aldis lamp was used but this was later vetoed as being too conspicuous, and the subsequent report stated that, 'Wireless only was relied upon as far as possible.' A special type of buoy was devised to be dropped from the flying boat to mark the position of the offending fishing vessel.

In one operation the offending trawler was shadowed by the aircraft and its track was marked with calcium flares to enable *Doon*, which had moved out to sea, initially to give chase and then later to return inshore to ascertain exactly the position of the offence. However, the operation on that occasion had to be terminated abruptly after the aircraft was forced to land due to heavy ground mist.

Later, experiments were undertaken using parachute flares but effective real-time communication continued to prove a drawback. The CO of HMS *Doon* even went airborne during a night-time operation and later reported that he could appreciate the problems of close observation during the hours of darkness. It was decided to press on with the use of parachute flares dropped with HMS *Doon* in the vicinity but no positive results accrued.

Although no arrests for poaching resulted from this series of operations, a number of lessons were learned. These included the following recommendations:

- many flares needed to be dropped in order to be effective and the pattern of dropping was also of importance;
- the highest possibility of success rested with the illumination of a number of areas at the same time;
- the use of buoys was essential to mark the spot where the target vessel was fishing;
- similar combined operations should be undertaken more extensively in order to gain experience.

It was concluded that the experiment might have been proof that patrolling from the air constituted a useful preventative measure, as had been shown off the east coast four years earlier.[38] However, despite the positive comments above, the report ended on an equivocal note, 'Only the undoubted further value of the operations as training and experience for the time of war would justify their continuance under these circumstances.'

The 1933 exercise was revisited the following year when the CO of HMS *Doon* visited RAF Pembroke. It was agreed that both services had benefitted. The intelligence accrued by the Navy, for example regarding the type, number, position and speed of individual or concentrations of trawlers, was of considerable value to the Fishery Officers ashore and to the LFNO. Flying boats also had the speed to catch poachers. RAF observers had received valuable experience that, in time of war, would be applied to the identification of enemy ships. There were discussions about licensing all observers as Fishery Officers, although it was thought that the turnover of personnel and the constant demand for training would make such a move impractical.

Official visits

Official visits to overseas as well as home ports have long been in the general remit of naval vessels in peacetime. The arrival of a warship in a foreign port on a prearranged visit (even a small, lightly armed vessel displaying a fishery protection pennant) is 'the most obvious and visible demonstration of naval diplomacy in peacetime'.[39] A 'run ashore' in a foreign port has been recognised as a great recruitment and retention incentive; in the case of the crew of a fishery protection vessel it constitutes a welcome diversion from the inevitable monotony of a task often undertaken in unpleasant weather conditions. 'Showing the flag' both at home and abroad, in places unused to seeing the White Ensign, is a valuable public relations tool. Finally, on overseas visits, amid the civic receptions, cocktail parties on board ship, sporting fixtures and other entertainments, there are opportunities to forge important diplomatic and goodwill links with friendly nations as well as occasionally to accrue useful covert intelligence. This section gives some examples of port visits undertaken during the 1930s as described by the Captains Fishery Protection and Minesweeping in their quarterly reports of the period.

Captain MacPherson, in the sloop HMS *Harebell*, first led his ships into Ostend before arriving in Amsterdam on 20 May 1933. The SO paid courtesy visits to the British Consul General, the local Burgomaster and the Naval Commandant, and there was a football match with a local team. The next day, following Sunday services, a reception for British Society members was held aboard *Harebell*, while the crews of the British ships were taken on a canal trip. More entertainment followed during the next couple of days, including another football match, a trip to Amsterdam Zoo and a dance given by the British Society to honour the flotilla's arrival in Amsterdam. The diplomatic niceties were again observed with a luncheon held aboard *Harebell* for the Naval Commandant, the British Consul General and the Amsterdam Harbourmaster.[40]

Captain MacPherson notes that while at Amsterdam five German merchantmen were present in the harbour with all but one 'flying the Swastika flag in addition to the Ensign'. He adds, 'In all cases, the black, red and gold horizontal bars in the upper canton of the ensign were covered over with black.' Hitler had been sworn in as Chancellor a matter of weeks before on 30 January 1933, and already the impact was being felt across Europe. MacPherson relates that anti-Nazi feelings were very strong in Amsterdam owing to the high percentage of Jewish inhabitants. Local stevedores had refused to unload ships wearing the Nazi flag. Police had to be called to disperse a hostile crowd demonstrating in front of the German merchantman berthed next to *Harebell*.[41]

The flotilla then moved on to Esbjerg in Denmark for a similar five-day visit and then to Aberdeen, where MacPherson concluded, 'It was gratifying to observe the high standing of the ships of the flotilla and also the esteem in which their commanding officers are held in Aberdeen.' But Captain MacPherson's report did not just contain positive comments. A local newspaper report on 20 June stated that three of his FP vessels had been 'snubbed' by the Corporation of Manchester, which declared that, in view of an impending visit by nine RN destroyers, they were 'too busy' to entertain his flotilla.

A potentially more damning indictment was made in November 1933 by the Secretary of State for Scotland, who was reported to have said in a speech, 'British trawlers in Icelandic waters received small support from British cruisers, the cruisers paying more attention to social duties. This attitude compared unfavourably with the measures of support accorded German trawlers by German cruisers.' It appeared that the gist of the criticism had emanated from the President of the Trawler Owners

Federation. There was some retraction later on, including recognition that social duties ashore were part and parcel of the expected custom and courtesy to be demonstrated by commanding officers of HM ships while visiting foreign ports. But the damage had been done.

In contrast to the tense, anti-German atmosphere witnessed in Amsterdam in 1933, the welcome accorded HMS *Cherwell* by the naval authorities during a visit to Hamburg in June 1935 was described as 'noteworthy'. There was a lunch laid on at the City Hall that was attended by high-ranking German officers and civic dignitaries together with tickets to the State Opera for *Cherwell*'s officers and trips to the surrounding area for the crew. The warm reception seemed to reflect the Kriegsmarine's slower acceptance of Nazism in contrast to that of the German merchant marine two years earlier.[42]

On rare occasions the Reports of Proceedings stray beyond the confines of conventional reportage, betraying the attitudes and feelings of the writer. Lieutenant Commander Dalison's description of his pursuit of Bert Jinks's boat has already been related in this chapter; Captain E R Archer's visit to Antwerp as Captain FP & M aboard HMS *Hastings* in July 1937 is another. The tone of Captain FP and M's account on this occasion can be interpreted either as wittily ironic or artlessly patronising.

Archer describes how both Belgian and Dutch river pilots had raced each other in order to gain the privilege of bringing HMS *Hastings* up the Scheldt to Antwerp. 'In order to achieve this, the pilot had come away without his lunch, however he made up for that on the way up the river and managed to smoke eight of my cigars, which made me thankful the trip was only one of 48 miles.'

Wreath-laying ceremonies and official exchanges of visits followed the sloop's arrival. A regatta was arranged for the Sunday afternoon, with a crew from *Hastings* participating. Captain Archer described the event as 'a masterpiece of organisation'. 'No one quite knew how many crews were competing, no transport was provided as promised, to take the (*Hastings*'s) crew to the scene of the operations, the programme was two hours late.'[43]

Midweek, there was a further event organised by the international Ligue Maritime. Archer comments distastefully, 'Sweet champagne, sweeter cake and then coffee, coupled with an almost intolerable atmosphere, with every window shut and a room full of smoke may be enjoyed by some, but it is certainly not – at any rate the English-speaking Union's idea – of a pleasant afternoon.'

Hastings's captain concludes his narrative on a toe-curlingly condescending note, '... despite, at times, some pardonable exasperation there is something likeable about the Belgians – they are so friendly and want to please'.[44]

Backbone of the coastal patrol

The 'Ton'-class minesweepers were the mainstay of coastal fishery protection for a good deal of the second half of the twentieth century. When their predecessors, the steel-built *Algerine* class, were paid off, HMS *Belton, Soberton, Wasperton* and *Wotton* were allocated to what was called The 'Home Division', which was tasked to cover the entire UK coastline with the exception of the English Channel. They were based at Port Edgar. Rob Hoole notes somewhat sardonically, 'Only *Soberton* had an enclosed bridge and many were the times, soaked and frozen on a January night off the Shetland Isles, that bridge watchkeepers queried the wisdom of some civil servant who had sent the enclosed bridge versions to Singapore.'[45]

The 'Fish Tons' remained fully operational minesweepers: the crews regularly exercised that capacity in national and NATO exercises. Initially, the only visible difference between the original ships in comparison and the rest of the class was the substitution of the aft twin 20mm Oerlikon mounting with a 20in carbon arc searchlight. Fishing boat inspections were carried out initially via an inadequate 16ft motor boat, which was apparently liable 'to disintegrate on contact with a fishing vessel'. Fortunately, these were later substituted by Gemini inflatable dinghies.[46]

John Lippiett, who took command of HMS *Shavington* in February 1976, when asked about the suitability of the class for the demands of the task, remarked that the ships' 15 knots maximum speed meant that they could outpace most trawlers, which could manage around 12 knots. Their small size allowed the Tons to refuel in small harbours, which afforded the opportunity meet the local population at the same time. The minesweepers were not highly complex mechanically although, as records show, there were machinery breakdowns that sometimes seriously disrupted schedules. Their double-planked mahogany hulls on aluminium framing, originally selected to counter the introduction of new, highly sensitive magnetic mines in the Korean War, were straightforward to maintain.[47]

Ted Seath, who had command of HMS *Belton* in the early 1970s, recalls the almost complete freedom bestowed on a young officer to use both initiative and discretion. 'A six-week fishery protection patrol of the west coast meant she (*Belton*) could go anywhere and do virtually anything she liked in an area stretching from Cape Wrath to Land's End. She could choose her own ports for fuelling, re-provisioning and an occasional run ashore ... It was great fun.'[48]

Likewise, John Lippiett felt that he had been 'stretched' by the experience, especially being required to undertake the dual roles of FP as well as mine countermeasures – the 'war-mode'. Additionally, it served to test personnel for future promotion as responsibilities across all ranks were well above those to be found on larger warships. Lippiett likened the situation to the lean manning he experienced later in his career in Types 21- and 23-class frigates.[49]

Communication and intelligence were key. Informal discussions with fishing boat skippers were important sources of knowledge about the movement of the fish shoals. The vast majority of fishermen were happy to co-operate. Information was fed to HQ at Rosyth on a nightly basis during the routine 'fishrep'; in turn, headquarters provided guidance and intelligence about the latest movements, particularly of foreign fishing vessels.

A typical Commanding Officer's Report of Proceedings following a six-week patrol contained precise and detailed information:

A concentrated group of 35 Soviet stern trawlers and one mother ship was found 30 to 40 miles west of Trevose Head on August 15. Two Bulgarian stern trawlers were operating in this area. Catches appeared to be 2 to 3 times the size of trawls seen in the Channel, although it was not possible to identify the type of fish. The type of pelagic trawl in use appeared the same as those seen during the Channel NEAFC [The North East Atlantic Fisheries Commission, described in Chapter Eleven] inspections. ... Local fishermen in the Morecambe Bay area reported poor catches. No foreign activity was sighted in the area between Lynas Point and the Point of Ayr. ... Local and Northern Irish vessels were active throughout the period off of the west and south of the Isle of Man fishing for Prawns and outside the 12 mile limit to the west of the island for Herring. As Shavington left the Western Patrol there were indications that the herring were shoaling inshore around the Isle of Man.[50]

The mid-1970s saw the introduction of different national and international regulations concerning fishing. There were complicated rules governing types of fishing gear, areas to be fished and sizes of nets. The frequent changes even found the local District Fisheries Inspector at a loss. In one example, even after consultation with MAFF Headquarters, a French fishing boat was allowed to proceed after it had clearly been in breach of the latest regulations.

Reports of Proceedings often recorded negative results, where no contravention of the rules was evident. Less serious matters, such as small-scale poaching, had to be countered, although these were often met with a warning rather than an eventual prosecution. The unexpected arrival of a fishery protection vessel was intended to act as a deterrent. In one example, salmon poachers were known to be active in the waters off Eyemouth on the Scottish border. The CO of the 'Ton' class involved approached the area at dawn having arranged for an RN helicopter to over-fly the estuary at the same time. The operation lasted several days: illegal boats were boarded, nets hauled and illegal salmon confiscated. Some fishing vessels headed for harbour, their crews temporarily abandoning ship. The helicopter hovering overhead provided a running commentary describing the fishermen running through the town pursued by boarding officers who in turn were being assailed by insults thrown by the local inhabitants.

Operation Grenada

The Royal Navy has been involved in several peacetime 'deterrent' patrols in the years since 1945. Some are well known. The CASD (Continuous At Sea Deterrent), Operation Relentless, was instigated in April 1969 and continues to this day with one nuclear-powered ballistic missile submarine on patrol at any one time. The Beira Patrol, lasting a decade from 1965 to 1975, endeavoured to blockade oil shipments to Rhodesia (now Zimbabwe) through Beira, Mozambique, in the Indian Ocean. Some operations were comparatively short-lived such as the Palestine Patrol, 1946–48, the Royal Navy involvement in the prevention of illegal Jewish immigration into Palestine. Operation Grenada, devised to prevent illegal arms reaching Northern Ireland during what became known as the Troubles, is the least known although it lasted some thirty-six years between 1969 and 2005, and involved a succession of RN vessels mostly drawn from the Fishery Patrol Squadron.[51]

Gun-running by both Catholic and Protestant factions had become a serious enough issue by the autumn of 1969 for the General Officer Commanding (GOC) Northern Ireland to seek to enlist the support of the Navy both in detecting and seizing weapons but also as a means of deterrence. It was calculated at the time that without the Navy's assistance, the Army's efforts would be 50 per cent less effective.[52]

Operation Grenada itself was instigated the following month when the 'Ton'-class FP vessel HMS *Wotton* was despatched to Belfast at short notice to embark an element of the Royal Ulster Constabulary (RUC) with the intention of intercepting a fishing boat suspected of carrying arms.[53] The Navy's task at the time was defined as providing support for the land forces employed in the Province. The main area of operation was off the coasts of Counties Down and Antrim while keeping at least a mile outside the Irish Republic's territorial waters. The FP vessels employed would carry out their routine duties unless called upon to proceed to Belfast or Londonderry, where they would be '"chopped" (transferred) to SNONI Opcon'. It was felt at the time that the deterrent requirement for such arrangement would last some time.

That prediction turned out to be accurate. The operation was reviewed in late May 1970. The Secretary of State for Northern Ireland was advised then that a further six-month extension of the Navy's involvement should be sought. But there were to be significant alterations that were to impact on the FPS's involvement:

> It has been agreed that in future the crew of the HM ship involved will be responsible for conducting searches; they will already be well versed in the techniques of searching by virtue of their fishery protection experience, and from the security viewpoint there will be some advantage in not having to proceed inshore specifically for this purpose.

In other words, responsibility for boarding and possibly apprehending smugglers shifted to the Navy, obviating the necessity for the FP vessels involved to embark Army or constabulary personnel beforehand. Mention too was made of the Navy undertaking occasional overt coastal patrols that, by their very nature, would also serve to deter smuggling by sea.[54]

Thus, the Fishery Protection Squadron became inextricably linked with Operation Grenada, a fact that became well-known to both the

Unionists and Loyalists, to the extent that the connection could be used as part of an excuse. For example, in 1975 a covert operation was undertaken that involved an SBS unit being landed on the Northern Ireland coast from the submarine HMS *Cachalot*. The 'cover story', in case one of the party became isolated and captured, was to be, 'You are from a Fisheries Protection vessel out of the Clyde. Your vessel was called to assist a trawler which had snagged its screws in its nets. As one of the ship's divers you were ordered to free them. You and your companion were swept away by rough seas and after ditching equipment made for the nearest shore.'[55]

The FPS's involvement lasted for the duration of Operation Grenada. In 1990, the cutbacks resulting from Options for Change described in Chapter Eleven brought focus on the percentage of time afforded the patrol. By then, just two vessels were permanently allocated to *Grenada*. Analysis showed that on average 400 boardings per year took place. Although no arrests had been made in recent years, the overall deterrent value remained unaltered and was greatly valued.[56]

The Grimsby fishing community

Recollections, predominantly of the women who grew up and lived in Grimsby in the period from the Second World War through to the sharp decline in the fishing industry from the mid-1970s onwards, produced a rich variety of responses as a result of the Oral History project.

Most of the women, as was commonplace at the time, found themselves in almost sole charge of bringing up children. Some found jobs, 'I worked at Ross's gutting fish ... we was v-boning the fish, cold, cold job, not very good pay.' Others found employment as barmaids; a few had specialist skills, some hand-braided fishing nets to make them stronger:

> Even the materials are different now; then it was twine, sisal then so you used to get splinters and your hands would be red raw. At night when I got home I used to take all the splinters out and get a bottle of methylated spirit and put my hands in to harden the skin. Some of the braiders said to wee on them ... I said I'd pack it in when I'm 70, which is October, but I'd miss it. I get a sense of achievement, especially when I know where it's going. It's interesting to know.

Inevitably, long separation brought with it infidelities and a temptation for women to resort to sex work in order to supplement meagre incomes. There was a drinking culture among the fishermen on board the boats that continued ashore, where pay was often squandered as men simply spent their leave seeking the same male company as afloat. 'The drink was a problem for me. I could have been in a much better position if it wasn't for the drink. A lot was pissed up the wall. Even when he packed it in, he still liked his drink.' Alcohol also affected temperament, 'I think they were a breed of their own quite honestly – but we all admitted they were very moody people.'

Excess drinking on board ship inevitably led to tragedies:

> I said to him [her husband] 'John please don't go to sea drinking' and he never would listen. Apparently he was dogging the doors [securing the hatches to the interior] and he must have got a rope round his leg. The guy next door was in the ship behind him, he thought it was a sack of potatoes falling over, and they was all day looking for him. It was night time when the runners came to me and I just looked at them, I was poorly at the time, I looked at them and I said, 'It's John'.

Women did go to sea but it was actively discouraged as it was perceived as stealing jobs from men. When Alison Josefsen's brother broke his leg, she substituted for him but suffered the ignominy of being accused of incest as her father happened to be skipper. Life on board was not only tough but the facilities were primitive to say the least. 'There was a lad called Hewson, Alf, and when he first come [to sea] he were a decky-learner and he said ... "Where do I get a bath?" So I said "In a bucket" And it's the truth, he said: "I can't get in a bucket!" That is the truth and he was a smashing kid. A bit slow but he was a smashing kid.'

One woman recalled, 'There was a real stink from ten to fifteen trawlers at the same time unloading fish' and yet Angela McMullen stated that there was a tradition among the men that they left port in their best clothes. 'They all had their suits, they all went to sea in suits. Black suit, white shirt, red tie, they was the bees knees "You haven't ironed me socks!" "Er yeah" "My mother always irons my socks." "Take 'em round to your flipping mother then cause I aren't ironing your socks."'

Like traditions, superstitions were prevalent in an occupation where death came swiftly and totally unexpectedly. Washing clothes on the day of departure was banned due to a belief that it represented being washed out to sea. Whistling was disapproved of on board as it was supposed to conjure a storm. The colour green was almost universally feared as it was the colour of the sea and that was the last thing you wanted to have on board ship. This even extended to a 'Popeye the Sailorman' badge complete with its tiny tin of green spinach.

The swift decline of the industry, which coincided with the last of the Cod Wars, was met with bitterness and a deep sense of loss. One wife recalls, 'After the fishing industry broke up though Tom to a certain extent he was like a lost soul you know. I think he missed the sea strangely enough.'

Lastly, David Rimmer, in starkly simple and poignant words, describes the utter desolation of being told that his ship was going to be laid up for the last time. 'They told us in office, said we'd finished. It was the last trip we were going. And that were it.'[57]

This chapter is only intended to provide an oversight of some of the activities of the fishery protection service in home waters during the twentieth century. Some sections, such as those dealing with the extreme weather conditions across the British Isles in winter or the importance of overseas port visits are not, of course, exclusive to fishery protection. On the other hand, the interwar experiments with aerial surveillance and the long-running involvement with Operation Grenada during the last quarter of the century are unexpected yet important parts of the narrative that have been unremarked upon hitherto in historical accounts of fishery protection. Likewise, the Grimsby Oral History Project, based on local research, demonstrates the importance of investigations of this kind in capturing the precious experiences of ordinary people before they are lost forever.

Chapter Eight

A Settlement and a Gathering Storm 1930–58

THE 1930 ANGLO-SOVIET Temporary Fisheries Agreement was, as its title indicates, a stopgap measure. But, like the dispute over Norway's Royal Decree of 1935, the issue only came to a climax and was ultimately resolved in the decade following the Second World War. The reasons behind the Soviet Government's abrogation of the 1930 agreement in 1953 is analysed in this chapter together with the path to an eventual settlement three years later.

This chapter also examines the key events leading up to the first of the Cod Wars or in Icelandic, *Landhelgisstríðin* (the wars for the territorial waters), in 1958. The eighteen-year-long, increasingly antagonistic dispute with Iceland that was to follow was the climactic point of Britain's several battles with its fellow North Atlantic neighbours over its claims to fishing rights in coastal waters.

The Soviet Union

Fishing and intelligence gathering

The principal reason behind the British fishing industry's keenness to resume trawling in the Barents Sea after the Second World War can best be understood by looking at the numbers. The MAF Sea Fisheries Statistical Tables show that in 1939 the total weight of demersal fish landed from this area amounted to 1,551,916 cwt. By 1947 this figure had risen to 2,495,090 cwt, which represented 18 per cent of the total demersal fish landings in England and Wales. Two years later, the Barents Sea catch had reached 3,880,862 cwt or 27.4 per cent of the total catch.[1]

The decline of fish stocks available in home waters, coupled with the economic effects of the earlier 1930s Great Depression that had led to a crisis in the fishing industry, had been among the underlying reasons behind an increasing exploration of distant waters: that factor coupled with the heavy demand for fish in Britain following the stringencies imposed by wartime rationing and the shortages of fresh food.

On 5 January 1953 the Soviet Government formally announced that in six months' time it was abrogating the 1930 Bilateral Temporary Commercial Agreement, which had granted the right of the British fishermen to fish up to 3 nautical miles off the USSR coastline and in waters of the Barents Sea between meridians 32° and 48° and in the White Sea above the 68° 10′ latitude. It was claimed that the decision was made because the Agreement 'was out of date, no longer corresponded with the principle of reciprocity, and that it had been repeatedly violated by British trawlers, which had often penetrated the Soviet Union's territorial waters'.[2]

Indeed, a number of incidents had taken place leading up to this announcement together with an important shift in overall strategy adopted by the British Government and led by the Foreign Office. However, there was a further dimension to the phrase about violating territorial waters other than the obvious one relating to fishing. Throughout the Cold War there was intense interest shown by NATO allies in the activities of the Soviet Navy in the high north and particularly around its bases. Indeed it was correct for the Soviets to suspect that British trawlers and Fishery Protection vessels were being employed as intelligence gatherers. This role included taking photographs of naval movements and manoeuvring in the Soviet 'backyard', close to the growing cluster of naval bases for the Northern Fleet.

The RN Fishery Protection vessels were ordered not to show any overt signs of their intelligence-gathering role: their movements were to remain perfectly consistent with their primary task. There was to be no encroachment closer than 15 miles from the Russian coast except in an emergency. Additionally, rather mysteriously named 'Reception Trials parties' would be despatched occasionally in order to support the intelligence-gathering missions. If that happened, COs were instructed to arrange for their ships to visit Vadsø in Varanger Fjord as the port gave ready access to Russian fishing grounds where British trawlers were likely to be working.

The FP commanding officers were instructed to prepare a separate intelligence report following each deployment. This was expected to include any signs of communist activities noted during visits to north

Norwegian ports. The political sympathies of the civil authorities and any prominent Norwegian officers were also to be observed. The COs were also expected to quiz the trawler skippers about Russian naval and merchant vessel sightings but to do so with a view to the likely reliability of such evidence. Discretion in all the above tasks was to be observed.[3]

One commentator has alleged that intelligence gathering by trawlers commenced in 1948 at least, citing the so-called 'Spy-Log' of the trawler *Lancer*. He also interprets a rather enigmatic statement made in 1948 by Robin Hankey, a senior Foreign Office official at the time, that it was, 'undesirable ... we should refrain from showing the flag in a part of the high seas (the Barents Sea) where we have a perfect right to go out of fear of incidents which the Russians might create'.[4] Other sources suggest that the use of trawlers as spy ships started slightly later.

The first post-war covert entry into the Barents Sea by a RN submarine had been undertaken by HMS *Alcide* in September 1952, although earlier HMS *Andrew* had conducted an operation between Jan Mayen and Bear Island in 1948 in order to test the performance of 'A'-class submarines under the ice. When in April 1951 the Admiralty proposed to despatch a submarine deeper into the Barents Sea as 'a trial of communications', the FO agreed only if the Admiralty instructed the vessel to operate well out to sea.[5]

Ironically, as well as providing an inexpensive alternative to the deployment of a submarine, the use of a trawler, working legitimately close to the Soviet coastline, was in fact the safer option. Although any trawlers' contributions to knowledge of the Soviet Navy's capabilities in the very early stages of the Cold War were of fairly marginal value, they grew in importance and sophistication as the years went by in the same way as submarine intelligence gathering was to become one of the major roles undertaken by nuclear-powered fleet submarines by both sides in the Cold War. There was concern expressed by British naval intelligence in February 1953 that although the Soviet Navy was not comparable to Western navies it was, 'rapidly gaining in size, experience and efficiency'. The problem lay in measuring the pace of this development. In that respect, the Director of Naval Intelligence (DNI), Rear Admiral Anthony Buzzard, stated that, 'in the face of intense security arrangements it is becoming more difficult to gather intelligence on the Soviet Navy'. According to Richard Aldrich, Buzzard was, '... keen to find new ways and means. Confronted with anxieties about the dangers of monitoring the Soviet Navy from British aircraft or British naval vessels, he looked for alternative platforms.'[6]

Buzzard's quest for 'alternative platforms' resulted in him, supported by Patrick Dean, Chairman of the Joint Intelligence Staff, exerting pressure on a reluctant MAF to seek out British trawler owners and skippers willing to observe Soviet naval exercises and to gather 'valuable intelligence'. Whether or not there was worthwhile remuneration involved for this dangerous work is never mentioned. Aldrich states that, by September of that year, there had already been five quite ugly incidents when Soviet boarding parties had, 'threatened jail and sudden death if the trawlers misbehaved again'. Clearly, the stakes were high and MAF officials protested that Admiral Buzzard seemed prepared to sacrifice the trawlers for the sake of some fairly minor intelligence information.[7]

Tom Smith was a wireless operator aboard the S/T *Wellard*, a Second World War veteran trawler, which was working close to the Soviet coast on the Norwegian border. It was a risky business; the ship's insurers had to be informed once the boat left Norwegian waters as the insurance no longer applied. Smith developed a friendly relationship with the local Soviet wireless station that checked their position on a daily basis. However, one night the Navy sent a warship, 'It was a Russian naval ship, and I mean a big 'un.' The *Wellard* was searched but again they were reassured, 'They didn't have three heads or anything, they was like us,' and gifts were exchanged including chocolate and vodka.

However, when the *Wellard* was nearing Grimsby on its return journey they received a radio message stating that everybody was to remain on board when they reached harbour. They were despatched to a discreet area of the dock:

> There was naval intelligence came aboard, they wanted to know what this boat was that we had seen. God knows how they had known we had seen it. They said he's the only one who actually saw it. So I went into his berth and he brought this book out and it was all silhouettes, like you see in war films, of boats. So I said ... it had three funnels, 'Three Funnels?' And they were all looking at each other, so he got this other book out and turned it over. 'That's it,' I said. He went, 'It can't be.' 'Why?' I said. He said, 'Because that boat is near Australia.' Well if it is it's taken a shortcut and that's where it was, the intelligence was all wrong. You get a lot

of people saying about boats spying, but I never knew anything about any trawlers that spied at all.[8]

The use of trawlers as intelligence gatherers did not end there. The extent to which they were used in the 1960s and '70s has since come to light, although there are discrepancies between official records and the memories of those who participated that suggest the full story has not been fully revealed. But it would seem that the resulting Operation Hornbeam began in the early 1960s and was centred on the port of Hull. It involved a retired naval officer, Commander John Brookes, who recruited selected trawler skippers, probably on the recommendation of their employers. These skippers were equipped with warship recognition manuals, high-specification cameras and telescopes and were tasked with photographing warships and any other vessels of interest. Some of the ships' mates and radio operators were briefed to listen in on specific frequencies to monitor radio traffic. A few Royal Navy junior officers also joined the trawler crews both to gain sea experience and to take part in the surveillance exercises. Aside from Hornbeam, five more focussed deployments have been identified involving the trawler *Arctic Galliard* (1965–67), which undertook SIGINT operations with a RN liaison officer and coder specialists embarked. In the early 1970s the trawlers *Invincible* and *Lord Nelson* were employed, unsuccessfully as it turned out, to try to recover a Soviet missile that had landed in international waters.[9]

Be that as it may, it is common knowledge that both sides in the Cold War, and since, have spent a great deal of time and effort trying to gather information about the capabilities of enemy naval forces and their movements.[10] And both have been quite aware of what the other was doing. Back in 1952, the Soviet Naval General Staff informed the Defence Minister Bulganin that many British trawlers carried powerful radio transmitters and radar equipment designed for intelligence gathering. But when the Hull-based trawler *Etruria* was arrested near the mouth of the White Sea in May 1950 and subsequently fined for poaching, the reaction of Foreign Office was sanguine, 'I don't think we have anything to fear even if the Russian authorities spot it [the intrusion inside the 12-mile limit] and make some propaganda insinuations.'[11] This rather laid-back comment masked a more nuanced diplomatic scenario.

Etruria was arrested by an unidentified Soviet gunboat on the evening of 1 May while fishing off Sem Island. The next day the trawler was observed proceeding under escort in a westerly direction. The British Ambassador was subsequently asked to take the issue up with the Soviet authorities as a matter of urgency. Five days later this matter prompted questions to be asked in the House of Commons of the Secretary of State for Foreign Affairs, Ernest Davies. The further news that the *Etruria* had been 'boarded by a Russian crew' drew belligerent comments from the Conservative opposition. Anthony Eden called it 'an extremely high-handed action' by the Soviets, while another speaker questioned, 'Is there no action of a retaliatory nature which can be taken? Is there no Soviet ship in a British port at the present time?'[12] The Secretary of State's reply was equivocal, deliberately or otherwise:

> The position is that the Soviet Government claim that their territorial waters extend to a twelve mile limit, but because we do not accept that, or have not accepted it in the past, we have an agreement with them in a case such as we presume is now under consideration [that] it extends to only three miles.[13]

The British Government's 'paradoxical policy' towards the increasingly outmoded 3-mile rule in this case showed that in fact neither the Foreign Office nor MAF wanted British trawlers to intrude within the Soviet 12-mile limit, 'Then they [the British] could claim that the absence of incidents confirmed Britain's non-recognition of the Soviet claim for twelve-mile territorial waters!' The delicate balancing act between compliance by the unpredictable trawlermen and the Soviet authorities, who were rightly suspicious of British activities close to their naval bases, was unlikely to last.[14]

That the British Government at the time was anxious not to 'rock the boat' and to use the Temporary 1930s Agreement with the Soviets as the *modus vivendi* is made clear in the precise instructions issued by the Admiralty at the time, '... that fishing vessels registered in ports in the United Kingdom may fish within three miles of the Russian Coast between the meridians 32 to 48 East. Fishing vessels of all other nations must keep to the twelve mile limit.' The instructions go on to state that the Soviets considered that their gunboats did an adequate patrolling job in the 3- to 12-mile zone. Although the British Government continued to repudiate territorial claims in excess of 3 miles, it was considered that the Soviets would abrogate the 1930 arrangement should HM Government insist on its rights to patrol up to the 3-mile delimitation.[15]

Another trawler was arrested in September, a third in October and a fourth in November. In all cases the boats were detained in port, their catches confiscated and the skipper fined for encroaching on Soviet waters. HMS *Mariner*, one of four *Algerine*-class fleet minesweepers then attached to the Fishery Protection Squadron, was despatched to the Barents Sea with express instructions *not* to protect British trawlers from the Soviet gunboats but to ensure they did not fish in the disputed zone.[16]

Matters came to a head in spring 1951 when the Soviet Union ordered all Royal Navy protection vessels to stay outside the 12-mile limit. This followed an incident when HMS *Truelove*, another *Algerine*-class minesweeper, received warning signals from a Soviet gunboat to stop patrolling 4½ miles from the coast and to leave the 12-mile limit. A note from the Soviet Ministry for Foreign Affairs was forwarded to the Foreign Office making the point that Fishery Protection in the 3- to 12-mile zone was a Soviet responsibility and that foreign naval vessels were not permitted to be there. The CO of HMS *Truelove* sought clarification of his rights in view of the fact that he had one more patrol to undertake in the same disputed waters. At first, the Foreign Office was inclined to suggest that *Truelove* should follow its planned course, despite the fact that it would pass through a highly sensitive and thus prohibited area close to the mouth of the Kola Inlet. An official commented, 'I think we must stick to our normal programme if we are to avoid being pushed out altogether.'

Reacting to this matter, the FO's experienced official Gordon Etherington-Smith advised caution in view of the need to preserve the terms of the 1930 Agreement in order to maintain a hold on what were considered to be valuable fishing grounds. He advised that because of the short time left before *Truelove*'s next patrol, in mid-April, that the area should be avoided in order not to provoke the Soviets. Subsequently, *Truelove* was signalled, 'until further notice you should not repeat not enter within the twelve-mile limit off Soviet territory, and you should keep well clear of prohibited areas'.[17]

Etherington-Smith later admitted to both Admiralty and MAF officials that he strongly doubted that any action could be taken if the Navy continued to patrol up to the 3-mile limit and the Soviets decided to 'enforce their view on the matter'. He added:

> The Russians could no doubt make things very difficult for us, and there might be serious incidents. In the present world situation we

wished to avoid anything which would add to the existing tension. If an incident did occur, we should be in a peculiarly weak position vis-à-vis our own public opinion, since we should be virtually powerless to enforce our view, and probably to protect any British vessels which might be involved.[18]

The Foreign Office's cautious stance reflected the position the country found itself in as it struggled with the reality of coping with post-war economic reconstruction at home, which had to be the number one priority. Also, the Defence Committee of the Cabinet, when it held a series of meetings in 1948, realised that any decisions it was about to take relating to the future shape and size of the armed services had to be made in light of the fact that Britain could not expect to be fully prepared for war before 1957. Yet events that year, particularly concerning the USSR and the onset of the Cold War, served to undermine the chances of making any confident predictions a decade hence. The Committee concluded that, 'Soviet expansion would take place in forms short of war.'[19]

Three years later, when James Callaghan, the Parliamentary and Financial Secretary to the Admiralty, introduced the 1951 Defence Estimates to the House of Commons in March 1951, the forecasted 'expansion' in the Soviet submarine force had become a reality:

> We shall have to face a large number of Russian submarines if war should come. I have no hesitation in saying that they are Russian submarines because, apart from the Americans and ourselves, there is no other navy in the world constructing a large number of submarines … there is no doubt that they will constitute a grave threat, especially if they secure any Atlantic bases, and the building potential which the Russians have is extremely great.[20]

The eventual route to a settlement

The British sought to delay the upcoming Soviet abrogation of the 1930 agreement by threatening to annul a proposed bilateral trade agreement in retaliation for revoking the historic fisheries accord. But once again the Government was overtaken by events. Joseph Stalin's unexpected death in March 1953 changed the political landscape. An apparent thawing in East–West relations offered the prospect of an

Anglo-Soviet summit in which the 'small matter' of the fisheries dispute might be raised.[21]

Any hopes that this might lead to a long-awaited settlement were dashed as the Soviet Minister for Foreign Affairs, Vyacheslav Molotov, proved to be an elusive negotiator with a British Government still reluctant to concede ground despite the promise of possible trade agreements. The fact that the fishing industry still constituted a powerful lobby within the corridors of power, that 'a fishing trip up north' would not be as profitable without the excellent plaice grounds inside the 12-mile limit, not to mention the added benefits accruing from intelligence gathering, probably swayed the British into pursuing the matter relentlessly.[22]

The following year, 1954, brought no further progress and by the summer the British side was informed that the present agreement would run on until 6 July 1955. By the beginning of that year the British Government, exasperated by the endless temporary extensions and postponements, proposed to the Russians that a delegation should be sent to Moscow to negotiate a longer-term settlement. Again, the USSR dragged its heels and only at the end of June replied to the effect that when the old accord ended the following month, the Soviet Government would hold talks about a new treaty. It added the now familiar warning that fishing within the 12-mile limit would become illegal after the current agreement terminated on 5 July.[23]

Internally, the British Foreign Office was depressed by the perceived intransigence shown by the recent statement by one of Moscow's top officials, First Deputy Vasili Kuznetsov. Henry Hohler, of the FO's Northern Department, opined that nothing much could be done to shift the Soviets' position. He argued that the recent enlargement of their fishing industry, with new vessels being ordered by the Soviets from foreign shipbuilders, including British ones, was an indication that the country was becoming increasingly unwilling to share its resources. He further claimed that the Soviet fishing industry had failed to reach its target for 1954.

Whatever that target might have been, Hohler made an incorrect assessment of the recent achievements of Soviet fishing fleet. Robert Helin's examination of the Soviet fishing industry in the twentieth century shows that as a consequence of the first 'five-year plan', which resulted in the forced collectivisation of Soviet agriculture, and particularly the tragic deaths of millions of the population in the Great Famine of 1932–33, the authorities turned to marine resources and developed a new appreciation of fisheries both within and outside the country. The marine resources of the Barents Sea became a particular focus: the fishing grounds were exploited more intensively, yet rationally, supported by more sophisticated equipment, increasingly experienced crews and larger and faster craft. Soviet landings by the Barents Sea trawler fleet climbed exponentially between 1950 and 1956, when it reached an all-time peak of 725,000 metric tons of fish landed having started at just over 200,000 tons at the beginning of the decade.[24]

By the same token, the British stakes in the Barents Sea annual catch continued to be high. British catches in the region during the period 1951–54 averaged 680,000 cwt, valued at £1,557,000, representing 5 per cent of the industry's total catch in all waters. Significantly, denying access to waters up to the 3-mile limit would amount to a loss of up to a third of the catch.[25]

Discussions were finally convened in Moscow in July 1955. Kuznetsov proposed that British fishermen could be granted permission in a designated zone between the meridians 43° 17′ and 48° East, from 3 to 12 miles from the low-water mark. This proposal was rejected; it was realised that the new zones offered negligible concentrations of suitable fish, being largely a nursery of small cod and haddock that could not be deemed suitable for intensive fishing.[26] Once again, matters had reached an impasse. Cecil Parrott, the *chargé d'affaires* in Moscow who acted as chief negotiator, following dialogue with his Soviet counterpart, was left with the impression that Kuznetsov's insistence on the 12-mile limit stemmed principally from security concerns. Indeed, when Nikita Khrushchev visited Britain the following year he made a highly significant speech in front of an audience of senior naval officers at Greenwich. He divulged that the Soviets regarded guided-missile submarines with their ability to make 'defensive' attacks on the United States as the cornerstone of their future defence strategy. It is small wonder, therefore, that the Soviets were so sensitive about British fishing boats operating almost on the 'doorsteps' of their Northern Fleet naval bases.[27]

Gradually the two parties edged towards an agreement, which was finally signed at the Soviet Ministry for Foreign Affairs on 24 May 1956. Although the British side wanted a long-term agreement to assist their fishing industry to plan ahead with confidence, the Soviets insisted on a five-year period to be renewed automatically as long as neither side abrogated beforehand. Fishing would be allowed up to 3 miles in a limited zone on the Kola Peninsula west of the entrance to the White Sea. A second zone, east of Cape Kanin, stretched further eastward along the coast south of Kolguev Island. The Soviet Union's refusal to concede any fishing rights close to the entrance to the White Sea had far-reaching consequences in relation to Britain's negotiations with Iceland, which are discussed below.[28]

There was a subtle change in the British approach during the final phase of Anglo-Soviet fisheries negotiations, 'Cold war tactics gave way to considerations mainly dictated by economic interests, the views of domestic opinion and, above all, the need to enhance Britain's prestige and stance in other disputes on territorial waters and fishery limits.'[29] It meant at last a tacit acknowledgement of the Soviet 12-mile territorial claim that had been the key bone of contention for the past half century or more. This concession was not lost on the Icelandic Government, which was to extend its territorial waters from 4 to 12 miles just two years later. Finally, it should not be forgotten that, just two months after the agreement was signed, President Gamal Nasser nationalised the Suez Canal. This precipitated a chain of events leading to a strategic defeat, which in turn caused a crisis that brought about a historic, political setback for Britain that carried with it far-reaching consequences with regard to the country's future standing in the world.

Iceland

Treated with every consideration

The Danish–Icelandic Act of Union was signed on 1 December 1918, recognising Iceland as a fully sovereign and independent state with what was described as 'a personal union' with Denmark. The Act was deemed valid for twenty-five years. Defence and foreign affairs matters would be handled by Denmark subject to consultation with the Althing, the Icelandic Parliament. Therefore the Danish Navy was charged with the task of patrolling the Icelandic fishing limit. This was envisaged to be a temporary measure until the Icelanders took over but in fact it remained a shared responsibility throughout the interwar years. The Icelandic Coastguard itself came into existence in 1920 when the ex-trawler *Thór* was purchased. During the 1930s three Icelandic and one Danish protection vessels were regularly on patrol supplemented by some smaller craft during the summer months.

Illegal fishing by foreign trawlers remained a problem and figures for arrests in the period 1927–34, show that Germany was the biggest culprit with a total of eighty-four against Britain's fifty-nine. The Icelandic fishermen themselves were not exempt from poaching. Jon Thór concludes, however, that, 'the Icelandic skippers were much bolder and more unscrupulous at poaching than their foreign counterparts and that they had built up a network of contacts and communications all around the coast which made it easier and safer for them to fish illegally and helped them evade the coastguard vessels'.[30]

There is an important factor to consider, in the light of the number of arrests made during this period, which goes a long way to explaining the attitude of the Icelanders towards the fishing grounds around their shores. Considerable advances had been made in the understanding of marine biology in the interwar years and these highlighted the effects of heavy foreign fishing on the nation's most important and valuable economic resource; by the mid-1920s it was clear that fish stocks around Iceland were not an inexhaustible commodity. However, despite much concern and debate, the 3-mile convention agreed between Britain and Denmark in 1901 remained in force during this period. Nevertheless, it serves to explain the underlying discord that led to the continuing arrests, confiscations and fines, particularly along the borders of the limits where both the best fish were to be found and where the spawning and nursery grounds were located.

However, relationships on the surface at least appeared to be quite cordial. When Captain Goldsmith, Senior Officer Fishery Protection, paid a seventeen-day visit to Icelandic waters in his 'Flower'-class sloop HMS *Godetia* in August 1929 he reported, 'I am quite satisfied from information that I have received from all sources, that the British Trawler is treated with every consideration, and on equal terms with any other trawler fishing in Icelandic waters.' He added that any trawler caught infringing the 3-mile limit was dealt very fairly in the Icelandic courts and that the fines were 'the same as for any foreigner'.[31] Goldsmith concluded that while he thought it unnecessary to assign a protection vessel on continuous patrol, which, 'might appear that one was doubting the other's fairness and integrity', it would be advisable to pay a yearly visit, 'to maintain that entente which is so essential nowadays'.[32] On the British side there were complaints emanating from the east coast fishing ports that the RN was spending more time on social events than protecting the trawlers.[33]

However, in 1936, in what might be considered a growing atmosphere of mistrust between the Icelandic Government and the British fishermen, it was reported that five agents working ashore in Iceland on behalf of Hull and Grimsby trawler owners had been arrested on a charge of having communicated by W/T with trawler skippers, giving them the whereabouts of the Icelandic gunboats. The 'spies' were later convicted and fined.

It later transpired that spying on the movements of the Icelandic Coastguard vessels (ICGV) had been common practice for several years. So-called 'Grandmother telegrams' suggested an organised system of observation of the movements and activities of the ICGV was being undertaken:

> The telegrams derived their name from a code used by some of the people spying on the coastguard vessels, using the Icelandic word 'amma' (grandmother) for the patrol vessels. In a preamble to a bill of law on the control of the use of wireless sets aboard Icelandic fishing vessels motioned in 1928 it is stated that for three successive days a trawler had received the three following telegrams from Reykjavík: 'Grandmother is well', 'Grandmother is still well', and 'Grandmother is beginning to feel bad'. During the first two days when 'Grandmother' was well the coast guard vessel in question was at anchorage in Reykjavík but as the third telegram was dispatched it was just leaving the port.[34]

It appeared that this form of espionage had increased year on year during the 1920s and 1930s. Successive parliamentary bills to curb the use of W/T aboard trawlers were defeated until 1936, which led to the arrest of the agents who were allegedly in the pay of British trawler owners – although that was never proved. The whole issue also revealed a complicated information web of so-called 'code-societies' among Icelandic trawler skippers, who passed on intelligence to one another not only on the whereabouts of the ICGVs but about the fisheries in general.[35]

The account by the CO of HMS *Lupin* on a visit in April–May 1936 contained in the Quarterly Report of Fishery Protection Flotilla 1936–37, states, 'While there have been rumours that this activity (referring to the then recent arrests of the 'spies') has a political background it is also not unreasonable to assume that it is part of a campaign to enforce fishery protection legislation.' Quite what was implied by the comment about a 'political background' is not elaborated on but there is a further comment that the agents were using a 'government code' to communicate with the trawlers. Presumably he was implying involvement on behalf of the British Government.[36]

Lupin's CO also referred to the then recent arrest of the crew of the Grimsby trawler *Vambrey*. He seemed here to echo the fair-minded approach being adopted by the RN protection vessels to obvious transgressions by the fishermen on the agreed limits. The skipper of S/T *Vambrey*, when apprehended for poaching, was requested to take bearings that would have proved that he was encroaching within 3 miles. He refused to co-operate and received a heavy fine in the Icelandic court. The report concluded that only a large fine was likely to stop the trawlermen poaching for, 'if the fine is small it is worth taking the risk of only being caught occasionally'.[37] This underlines the narrow line the Fishery Protection COs had to adopt between remaining on friendly, co-operative terms with the fishermen and yet upholding the law.

However, the situation appeared to deteriorate the following year. There were further arrests prior to the arrival of the fishery protection vessel HMS *Boyne*. The Icelanders asserted that the trawlers were not stopping when ordered to; on the British side there was apparent confusion about the location of the exact delimitation of the territorial waters in some places. Additionally, there were reports in the British press that live shells had been fired by the Icelandic gunboat. After reviewing the situation, HMS *Boyne*'s commanding officer suggested such flashpoints could be avoided if the trawlers stopped when apprehended. Also, there needed to be clarification regarding the demarcation of territorial waters. He concluded that the problem was probably exacerbated by the fact that there was only one Icelandic patrol boat operating at the time. Finally, it was suggested that Britain should copy German policy, which was to fine the poachers when they returned home.[38]

Iceland joined Denmark in declaring neutrality on the outbreak of the Second World War. However, following the German occupation of Denmark on 9 April 1940, the Althing took control of its own defence and foreign affairs. Fearing a German invasion, British forces occupied the island, thereby violating its neutrality. A month later, in a skilful diplomatic coup, the Icelandic Government invited the still neutral USA to take over responsibility for the country's defence, thereby releasing British troops to fight elsewhere.

As agreed, the Danish–Icelandic Act of Union terminated on 31 December 1943 and the Icelandic people overwhelmingly voted in favour of independence from Denmark, which duly took place in June 1944 when Iceland formally became a republic. In 1946, the American forces left Iceland, only to return five years later and then remain until 2006 – such was the strategic importance of Iceland during the Cold War years. Although the island became a member of NATO in 1949, the politics within the country became divided between conformity to Western capitalist ideology and a left-leaning socialism that favoured stronger ties with the Warsaw Pact and the USSR in particular. Amidst a sometimes febrile political landscape, protection of its coveted fishing grounds became a key issue and was to come up against Britain's dogged determination to adhere to its age-old and increasingly challenged *mare liberum* principles.

Crucially, the 1901 Anglo-Danish agreement on the 3-mile limit off the shores of Iceland, the Faroe Islands and Greenland ended in 1951 and Iceland did not seek to renew it. Predictably, Britain protested this move, citing somewhat lamely perhaps historic claims to have fished the waters since the fifteenth century. This may have been the case but such assertions no longer carried the same weight in a changing world.

Cold War strategy

The international political tensions and ideological divides that developed rapidly in the immediate post-war period had been instrumental in the formation of NATO in 1949. The USA was insistent that this transatlantic alliance should include Iceland, Greenland (still at that time under Danish colonial rule) and the Azores (a Portuguese colony). The Western nations' geopolitical aim in including these territories was plain: to encircle the entire North Atlantic Ocean with allies who were willing to accept air bases and to contribute in other ways to the perceived threat from the East.

Iceland's geographical location astride the so-called GIUK Gap (Greenland, Iceland, UK), the naval 'choke point' through which the Soviet submarines had to pass to access the North Atlantic, became regarded as being of crucial strategic importance. In this respect, the US Naval Air Station located at Iceland's Keflavík International Airport on the Reykjanes peninsula on the south-west corner of the island developed into a key strategic base during the Cold War years before finally being handed back to Iceland in 2006.

Initially, Keflavík was used as an advanced base for the US Strategic Air Command. By the early 1960s, however, as the role of long-range bombers became of secondary importance to submarines and missiles in its nuclear strategy, the airport was transformed into an important listening post for Soviet submarines passing through the shallow waters of the GIUK gap.[39]

Yet Iceland in the late 1940s and afterwards was not as politically stable as the Western powers would have wanted. In 1946 elections, the pro-Moscow Socialist Unity Party polled 19.5 per cent of the votes. The party had been formed in 1939 through an amalgamation of the former Communist Party and a breakaway group of Social Democrats. In the end, the majority view prevailed, which admitted that although neutrality was the preferred option, the reality was that it would not be respected in any future war. Thus the Conservative Foreign Minister Benediktsson had been instrumental in leading the country into its alliance with NATO in 1949.[40]

Icelandic muscle flexing

Barely had the world emerged from the horrors of war than there were reports of 'interference' by Icelandic gunboats in Icelandic waters as the British trawlers returned after a six-year absence. In spring 1946 the trawlers *Nab Wyke* and *Cevic* alleged that they had been stopped by ICGV *Óðinn* when they were working 5 miles from the outer rock of the Westmann Islands. They were instructed that they were forbidden to fish within 10 miles to the east and south-west of the outer rocks of the islands, which lie to the south of the mainland. They were told that this was due to Icelandic net-fishing that was being carried out nearby. The Fishery Protection vessel HMS *Allington Castle*, on its way to the fishing grounds at the time, contacted MAFF for clarification. MAFF confirmed that while the trawlers had not been instructed to avoid fishing in that area, they had warned the skippers of the dangers of interfering with the Icelandic net-fishers but had also advised that the 3-mile limit was still in force.[41]

There were three reasons why the British trawlers were so anxious to return to the distant fishing grounds including Iceland. Firstly, soon after the outbreak of the Second World War almost all the big and modern trawlers had been requisitioned by the Admiralty. This had brought distant-water fishing practically to a standstill, almost at a stroke. Although a few older vessels were returned during the war they were deemed unsuitable for long voyages. Secondly, while the Iceland trawlers were able to monopolise their home waters from 1939 to 1945, 'under-fishing' allowed stocks to be hugely replenished. Thirdly, as stated above, the dearth of fresh food at the end of the war meant that every means had to be employed in order to feed the population and sea fishing off Iceland was an obvious choice.[42]

This early 'skirmish' shows that, like the other problems concerning the Barents Sea and the Norwegian coastline, the pre-war disputes had not gone away but remained unresolved. This was recognised and echoed in the discussions that were taking place within the Admiralty over wider manning issues, which led to scant resources being available for fishery protection.

The results of The Hague ICJ ruling regarding the Anglo-Norwegian dispute caused a great deal of soul-searching within the British Government during 1953 over the whole matter of the delineation of base lines.[43] In short, the Admiralty proved to be the body most opposed to the use of this measurement while the Foreign Office was the most progressive, seeing it as a way out of the current dilemma that was increasingly alienating Britain from other countries. Annoyingly for the British at the time, the USA, which might have provided a lead, was adopting a rather ambiguous stance on the matter. At the end of the year, the UK declared that, after considering the implications of The Hague ruling, it would not adopt base lines as a method of measuring delimitation nor would it accept that method anywhere other than off north Norway.

Iceland had declared its own 4-mile territorial limit in 1952 soon after the ICJ ruling. Undoubtedly, it felt its case had been strengthened by the unexpected turn of events in the Netherlands but also by the 1945 Truman Declarations and its own 1948 law on the Scientific Preservation of the Continental Shelf, which had been precipitated by the denudation of important fish stocks around its coastline due to over-fishing. Britain, Belgium, France and the Netherlands all protested against the Icelandic declaration but to no avail as the 1951 ruling had passed into international law. The Icelanders claimed that it was a conservation measure; angry British trawler owners said that it was a means of providing economic protection to Iceland's inshore fishermen. In that sense it is hard to blame the motives of the politicians in the Althing.[44]

Anglo-Icelandic talks were convened in 1952 but got nowhere; the Icelandic delegation left London angry and offended. On 19 March 1952, its government announced a regulation on the extension of its fishing limits to 4 miles around its shores. This was to be measured from base lines between the outermost headlands and islands. The declaration was seen as particularly inflammatory in London when it was pointed out that the important base line across the wide Faxa Bay in the south-west stretched some 78 miles, which was much longer than the longest coastline in north Norway.

A meeting of the National Joint Industrial Council was held in London on 15 May, with representatives from trawler owners, skippers and mates. The latter called for the Royal Navy to be involved as it had been in the Barents Sea in the 1920s. This time the argument fell on deaf ears; the Chief Inspector of Fisheries commented that the days of Nelson and Drake were past and Iceland was a NATO ally.[45] Despite the obvious acrimony, the Royal Navy's fishery protection vessels stationed off Iceland were ordered not to intervene. Instructions were passed to the commanders to avoid the use of force or threaten to resist the arrest of a trawler within the 4-mile limit used to mark territorial waters outside the base line. Unsurprisingly it was the shape of the base line across Faxa Flói that HM Government disagreed with but it was decided that in the event of an arrest the FP vessel would confirm the position of the trawler with the ICGV gunboat. If the gunboat chose to ignore that arrangement it would be notified that an arrest had taken place on the high seas and appropriate action would follow including a demand for compensation. If possible, the FP vessel would follow that gunboat and arrested trawler to port and later to court.[46]

The new Icelandic delimitation measure came into effect in the summer of 1952 in the face of unanswered protest notes from the British Government and by July the first trawler had been arrested for fishing within the new line. This further enraged the trawlermen, who felt that they had been abandoned by their leaders in Westminster. This time they retaliated by putting an embargo on the import of Icelandic fresh fish. The owners in Grimsby and Hull denied the Icelandic boats landing rights at their ports. Many in Iceland believed that the move was covertly backed by the Whitehall government, which made no moves to prevent it happening. It was believed that the embargo was aimed at forcing the Icelanders into a bilateral agreement that would have allowed the British trawlers to continue to fish inside the 4-mile limit.[47]

In some senses the move backfired. It forced the Icelanders to look for other markets for their goods. The most important was a long-term trade agreement with the Soviet Union, which very soon became one of Iceland's most important trading partners. Iceland was also the first NATO-aligned partner to sign an agreement with the Soviets. It is alleged that the new Soviet–Icelandic trade partnership gave impetus and support to the Socialist Unity Party.

Protracted discussions continued over the next three years. The Icelandic Prime Minister Ólafur Thors, a confirmed Anglophile who had private interests in deep sea fishing, tried his best, through a mixture of flattery and thinly veiled threats, to find a solution, but to no avail.[48] Finally, following protracted negotiations, the Organisation for European Economic Co-operation (OEEC) managed to broker a deal in 1956 and the damaging embargo on Icelandic exports to Britain was lifted.

Between the imposition of the 4-mile limit and the lifting of the embargo, some fifteen British trawlers had been arrested. On occasions, shots were fired across bows in the process and some trawlers escaped. An Admiralty letter dated 18 November 1953 cautioned that the current position regarding Icelandic territorial waters was, 'at present extremely confused and it appears the United Kingdom view in this matter may not be understood'.[49]

At the beginning of 1954, 400 trawler skippers had signed a petition demanding, yet again, that protection be provided by the Royal Navy – but to no avail. The previous year it had been calculated within the Admiralty that it would require at least three fishery protection vessels and an additional two frigates on permanent station in order to provide adequate cover. Ironically, the Royal Navy would have to consider withdrawing ships from NATO duties in order to take retaliatory action against a fellow NATO country.[50]

In December the next year a contingency plan was prepared for the Cabinet in the event of Iceland implementing further extensions to its territorial limit. It brought the prospect that the Royal Navy might have to fire in anger in the North Atlantic for the first time since the end of the Second World War – and against a NATO ally, to boot. These precautionary plans came just in time. On 24 June 1956 Parliamentary Elections were held in Iceland and resulted in the Social Democrats, the People's Alliance and the Progressive Party joining in a coalition to form the next government. This was a significant milestone as it was the first government of a NATO state that included ministers belonging to a Soviet Union-friendly party, the People's Alliance.[51] In the following November, on the day after British parachutists landed near Port Said at the start of the Suez Crisis, the *Algerine*-class minesweeper HMS *Bramble* arrived in Reykjavík Harbour to cries of, 'get off to Egypt, you murdering British pigs' from a crowd who also repeatedly attempted to detach the ship from its moorings.[52]

The new government in Reykjavík had two important international items on its agenda: a new defence agreement with the United States concerning its base at Keflavík and the extension of its territorial limit from 4 to 12 miles, which would bring it in line with some other nations. By the summer of 1958, because no progress had been made, the Icelandic Prime Minister threatened Iceland's resignation from NATO and the dismissal of US forces from Keflavík if Britain sent the Royal Navy inside the 12-mile limit.

Meanwhile, the first United Nations Conference on the Law of the Sea (UNCLOS) had taken place in Geneva from 24 February to 27 April 1958. This was the largest conference ever organised by the UN and brought together eighty-seven nations. Hrefna Karlsdóttir sums it up as, 'a mixture of defence, conservation, Cold War paranoia and economic interests'. Inevitably, a central issue concerned limits of territorial seas and contiguous zones. There was no agreement reached, although it did show continuing support for a limit wider than 3 miles, although an extension beyond 12 miles, which some countries were proposing, was not considered acceptable.[53] The Law of the Sea Conference constituted one of the last opportunities for Britain and Iceland had to come together and to try to reach an agreement.

Contingency plans

On 24 May 1958, the Icelandic Government forewarned that its new regulations on a 12-mile fishing zone would be issued on 30 June to take effect from 1 September. At the same time, the Royal Navy was drawing up detailed contingency plans for the protection of British trawlers should the Icelanders carry through with their threats. The Captain FPS, Captain Barry Anderson, issued detailed orders for Operation Whippet in June. The missions were threefold:

- To prevent interference with British fishermen on the high seas outside 4 miles and in particular between 4 miles and 12 miles from the Icelandic coast.

- To prevent the arrest of any fishing vessel on the high seas outside the 4-mile limit.
- To secure the release of any British fishing vessel so arrested.[54]

Detailed instructions to trawler skippers were also agreed and delivered by the British Trawler Federation through their owners. The trawlers were to report their arrival to the warship guarding their 'haven' (see below) and then not to fish outside their delegated area for three days. Additionally, they were not to fish within 4 miles of the Icelandic coast nor within 4 to 12 miles except within the haven. Advice was also given by the BTF on what to do if boarded by an Icelandic coastguard vessel, which was seen as the most likely threat. These included methods of avoidance that fell short of the use of real weapons and the infliction of actual bodily harm.

Three trawler 'havens' were to be established, somewhat quaintly named, 'Butterscotch', 'Spearmint' and 'Toffeeapple', between the 4- and 12-mile limits, each being 30 miles long to be guarded by one warship. The three protection warships would be supported by a fourth kept in reserve; a Royal Fleet Auxiliary (RFA) ship would also be on station to provide fuel and solid stores. Any sighting of an ICGV was to be reported to the duty warship. The havens would shift in accordance with the seasonal migration of fish and an experienced 'liaison' trawler skipper would be assigned to each warship to offer advice.[55]

Likewise the commanding officers of the RN protection ships were given precise instructions on how to react: 'when, what and how much force they could use to prevent the arrest of a trawler or to rescue a trawler once arrested'. As if to underline the true reality of the situation, orders were given that live rounds could only be employed in response to Icelandic gunfire after warnings had been issued. Moreover, the aim in such extreme circumstances should be to disable the IGCV's weapon, not to sink the ship. Although not called such at the time, these instructions were the beginnings of what became known as 'Rules of Engagement', which oversee the way in which the use of armed force is controlled in situations short of all-out war, such as UN embargo operations.

In another significant departure, this was the first time that single-band radios were employed, which meant that Captain Anderson (promoted to Commodore for the Operation Whippet Task Force in order to provide seniority in rank) was in direct contact with Whitehall. This meant that he could have instructions relayed to him, in real time, as to the constantly changing political picture. Although this did not diminish his responsibilities as the 'man on the spot', it did alter what had been for centuries the essential isolation of the senior officer in such a situation. Nearly a quarter century hence, the Falklands War was to highlight both the advantages and the inevitable pitfalls of a new world where instant, global communication was a reality.

As August 1958 drew to a close, the Royal Navy had assembled an impressive force off Iceland. Commodore Barry Anderson embarked his staff in the Type 12 *Whitby*-class frigate HMS *Eastbourne*. He was accompanied by the Type 14s HMS *Palliser* and *Russell*, together with the *Algerine*-class minesweeper HMS *Hound*. RFA *Black Ranger* arrived on station two days after the start of 'hostilities' on 2 September. HMS *Hound* was duly despatched to the *Spearmint* haven, HMS *Russell* to *Butterscotch* and *Palliser* to *Toffeeapple*. It is of note that only HMS *Hound* and the RFA tanker were more than five years old. However, as events were to demonstrate during the Cod Wars, the slim, thin-skinned frigates were built primarily for anti-submarine warfare in the wastes of the north-east Atlantic rather than the close manoeuvring and 'rough and tumble' engagements they were to encounter off Iceland.

In complete contrast to the professional and modern Royal Navy, the Icelandic coastguard fleet consisted of just seven vessels. These ranged from ICGV *Thór*, 700 tons with a maximum speed of 17 knots and a crew of twenty-eight, to the *Óðinn*, 75 tons and a crew of eleven. The slowest of the ICGVs could only manage a maximum speed of 11 knots, which meant that they could be easily outpaced by some of the British trawlers. Typically, the coastguard vessels were armed with one gun each. The crews had received no military training whatsoever, they were merely civilian sailors; the officers were enlisted policemen. In addition to the trawlers, the coastguard possessed a wartime Catalina flying boat, which provided a useful spotting service during the conflict by noting down names and registration numbers of encroaching trawlers, much to the annoyance of their crews.[56] ICGV *Thór*, *Albert* and *Ægir* were reported to be at sea on the evening of 31 August, having been warned by the Head of the Icelandic Coastguard, Pétur Sigurdsson, before they departed, 'to show the utmost caution at the outset when everyone is tense and the situation is a powder keg'.[57]

When it had become clear that protracted negotiations were getting nowhere, the Icelandic Minister for Fisheries, Lúðvík Jósepsson, had signed a regulation extending his country's fishing limit to 12 miles with immediate effect from 1 September 1958. Promptly on that date the British warships entered the 12-mile zone and the so-called First Cod War commenced.[58]

In the years prior to 1958, it had been customary for the FPS to patrol in the so-called Andanaer area for about fifteen weeks during the year. Regular visits were paid to Icelandic ports. In 1957 HMS *Hound* had visited in May, followed by HMS *Wave* in June. Despite the tensions over the fishing limit question, relations between the RN and the ICGV had been good and very professional. During the June visit the British Ambassador invited the Icelandic President Ásgeir Ásgeirsson to spend a day aboard HMS *Wave*, which was commanded by SO FPS Captain Eric Bailey. The President accepted the invitation and the *Wave* sailed up Hvalfjörður, which included the site of the wartime British and American naval bases. As they passed the still active but seemingly deserted American-run fuel jetty, the President asked where all the Americans were. Captain Bailey replied that they were probably enjoying an afternoon 'nap'. The President then suggested that they should be woken up – perhaps by firing a gun. No sooner had the idea been mooted than President Ásgeirsson was given a quick demonstration in using *Wave*'s 40/60mm Bofors gun. He duly fired five 40mm 'break-up' shells (made of Bakelite filled with shot) over the fuelling jetty, which had the desired effect, especially as it also roused around 50,000 ducks, which got airborne at the same moment.[59]

Conclusion

Unfortunately, on this occasion, 'diplomacy' between two otherwise friendly nations, in the form of a prank, albeit a potentially dangerous-sounding one, did not lead to the desired result. Just over a year later, Britain felt it had to employ its powerful navy against a NATO partner country in an attempt to get its own way. Similarly, whether it liked it or not, Britain had ultimately been forced to take a backward step in its long-running argument with the Soviet Union, as described earlier. It had come a long way in that dispute since the Admiralty had been prepared to despatch the cruiser HMS *Comus* to the Barents Sea in 1928.

In 1958 the UK was out of step with most of the rest of the world with regard to the delimitation of territorial waters. There had been suggestions made during the recent UNCLOS that seemed only marginally concessionary but ultimately were considered unacceptable to the British Government of the day. A huge amount has been written about this period in British history, a time when the nation found it exceedingly difficult finally to abandon its self-image as an independent world power. It had not done so when the Royal Navy entered the 12-mile zone around Iceland on 1 September 1958. That night, Prime Minister Harold Macmillan wrote in his diary gloomily, but prophetically, 'We shall protect our trawlers as best we can. But there is no future in it.'[60]

Chapter Nine

A War of Nerves – of Sorts[1]
1958–70

THE CHAPTER TITLE conveys something of the unreality facing the trawlermen, their Royal Navy guardians and the Icelandic Coastguard on the morning of 1 September 1958. The Force Seven of the previous day had abated and some seventy-five trawlers were gathered in the havens, the majority in *Toffeeapple* and *Butterscotch* to the north-west of the island and the rest in *Spearmint* to the east.

In one sense, the trawlers and their owners now had what they had consistently appealed for over many years: full protection for their boats in those distant waters, which would enable them to continue working, albeit within the strictures set out in the Admiralty instructions to skippers. Commodore Anderson was upbeat in his initial assessment of the reception by the trawlermen and there would be many heartening news items in the coming weeks and months about plentiful gifts of fresh fish received from grateful trawlermen for the Navy crews, much welcomed by a press corps anxious for some copy about those curious goings on in the far north.

A contradictory interpretation of the arrangement found the trawlermen complaining of bad catches and the rigidity of the system. They were obliged to use the havens for the first seventy-two hours initially, which were changed periodically according to catches and weather conditions. This was later reduced to forty-eight hours. 'The reduction was, it seems, caused by the fact that the fishing inside the "boxes" was poor, and that the trawler skippers, used to the freedom of roaming around looking for fish, were not at all happy with fishing in this way.'[2]

This chapter also covers the twelve-year gap in hostilities in the aftermath of the First Cod War. The settlement reached was not

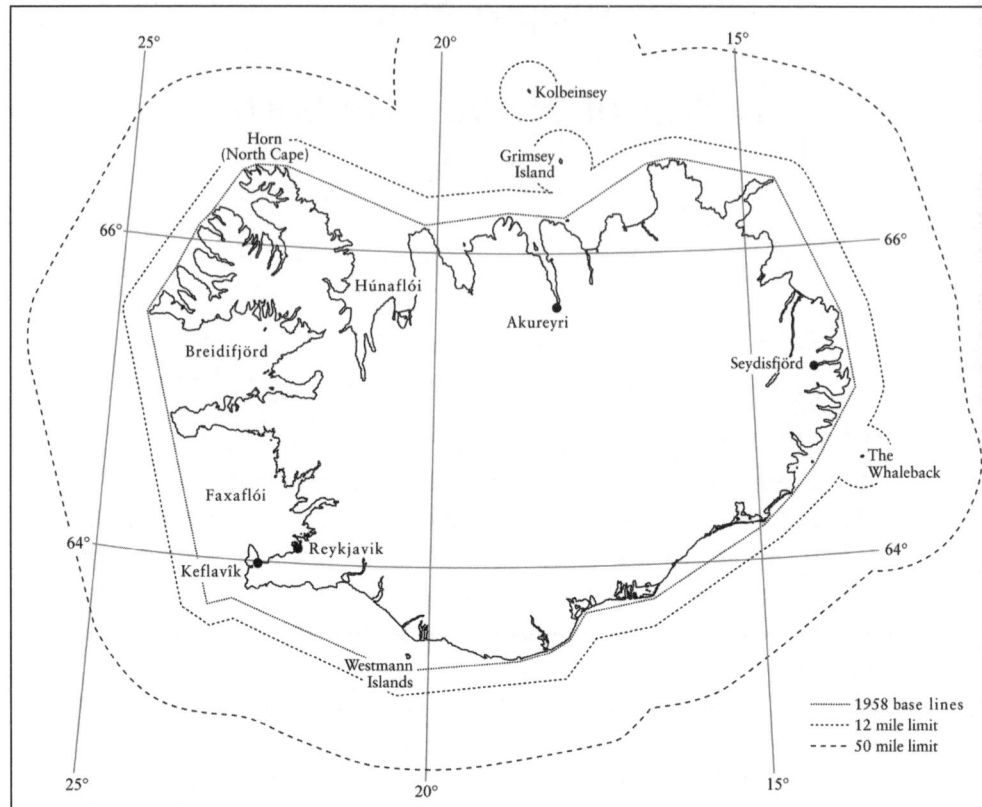

Map 4: Iceland. (Stephen Dent)

welcomed by all, least of all by the BTF. The strategic importance of the island to NATO during one of the most intense periods of the Cold War was another factor; commensurately Britain was coming to terms with the reality of no longer having superpower status. Finally, the so-called 'Milwood Incident' is described in some detail as it highlights the mentality of the independently minded fisherman, the shortcomings of the Royal Navy's chain of command and the fragility of Anglo-Icelandic relations at the time.

The wider significance of Whippet

Operation Whippet was, by some considerable distance, the largest and most comprehensive commitment undertaken thus far by the Royal Navy in its capacity as the primary provider of fishery protection for its nation. The sheer scale of the operation, which had at its outset no time boundaries, could not be undertaken by the FPS alone, although the squadron's Type 14s assigned to Whippet were ultimately to bear the brunt of the task.[3]

Why did the government of the day commit itself on such a grand scale? It has been suggested that Downing Street simply gave way to its powerful fishing industry lobby. There was the extra political pressure as Grimsby and Hull were both marginal parliamentary seats. Most tellingly, at the time, fish products accounted for 93–97 per cent of the value of Iceland's exports, whereas fishing only provided 0.5 per cent towards the British national income.[4]

However, these explanations do not convey the wider picture, taking into account the situation the country found itself in during the late 1950s. Britain's armed intervention in Suez less than two years earlier had ended in a humiliating diplomatic reversal and is now regarded as a significant milestone in the country's international post-war decline. In this instance, it needed to demonstrate that it might have been losing its long-running battle over the delimitation of territorial waters but its Senior Service could still put up an independent fight in support of its principles – even if its opponent was a tiny island nation like Iceland.

Yet, even if that is a correct interpretation it does not answer the question of whether the First Cod War at least was anything other than a short-term response to a minor crisis that might add to the growing world opinion that Britain was a major power in rapid decline. Commodore Anderson's recollection of his Downing Street briefing on the eve of the conflict, 'Standing no nonsense from anybody, neither the trawlermen nor the Icelanders, and do your best to avoid any incidents', is quoted as, 'an illustration, albeit a frivolous one, that a "holding operation" might suffice'.[5]

Peter Hennessy is of the opinion that the Suez Canal engagement impacted directly on the key Defence White Paper produced the following year, which was aimed at reducing expenditure on conventional forces in favour of the nuclear deterrence. He quotes Prime Minister Anthony Eden, 'we need a smaller force that is more modern and mobile in its equipment'. The overall aim was to bring defence expenditure down from 10 to 7 per cent of the Gross National Product (GNP) of the UK. The 1957 Defence White Paper was hotly contested between the tactically aggressive Minister for Defence, Duncan Sandys, and his three service chiefs, each determined to fight his corner and each independently at war with the other two.[6] The

Royal Navy suffered badly in the review, although it did manage to keep its precious aircraft carriers for another few years and contrived to carve out a role for itself in what was described as a 'limited war capability'.[7] Thus, although it could be argued that Whippet hardly registered on the grand scale of incidents of historical naval importance, it showed that the Royal Navy could still make an effort to execute an efficient and well-planned operation.

Early skirmishes

The gunboats duly appeared in some of the havens on 1 September, warning the trawlers by loudhailer and radio that they were fishing illegally within the 12-mile limit. Nothing dramatic occurred, although there were a couple of close passes made by the ICGV vessels.

The next day dawned calm with a notoriously dense 'east-fjord' fog descending over *Spearmint*. At 0800, Commodore Anderson in HMS *Eastbourne* received reports that the trawler *Northern Foam* had been arrested by an unarmed boarding party from ICGV *Thór* and *Maria Júlia*. The trawler had been fishing alone. The radio operator barricaded himself in his office before sending out the distress call. *Northern Foam*'s skipper was instructed to avoid doing anything rash but to resist arrest and immobilise his engines. *Eastbourne* reached the scene just as the boarding party managed to get *Northern Foam* under way again and put its own twelve-man boarding party aboard.

A futile exchange ensued between Commodore Anderson and Captain Kristófferson of ICGV *Thór*. *Thór*'s commander insisted that he was entitled to arrest the trawler, which had been fishing in contradiction of Icelandic law, while Anderson replied that Britain did not recognise the new legislation. In the end it was agreed that the Icelanders should be transferred to HMS *Eastbourne*.[8]

The official British reaction to this early, satisfactory resolution was little short of ebullient:

> To the British the firmly handled *Northern Foam* incident was a fine boost. The fishermen were delighted, morale was high and the navy's reputation was enhanced. The Icelandic Coastguard considered it a defeat and determined never again to put themselves into a position where such a defeat was possible. While continuing to make constant attempts to arrest trawlers, they never again kept a boarding party in a trawler once a British warship took

the initiative. The chance to carry out a counter-boarding did not recur for nearly two years.

Ashore in Reykjavik, as the news spread, there was a riot outside the British Embassy with stones and smoke bombs thrown, exacerbated by some bizarre behaviour on the part of the British Ambassador.[9]

Not everyone on the British side shared the euphoria over the British success. The diplomat Thomas Brimelow in Washington told his American counterparts in strict confidence that his country had made 'a basic mistake in the decision to protect their trawler fleet', while the man on the spot, Commodore Anderson, signalled the Admiralty a day later, 'I appreciate the political position but urge a face-saving interim solution be found quickly for both countries if only to save needless loss of life.'[10]

The first four months

Thereafter, the official Naval Staff History for 3 September–31 December 1958 summed up the autumn period as being relatively uneventful and routine. Patrol duties were shared between the Type 14s and escorts from the Home Fleet supplemented by what were described as 'other training and local squadrons'. One RFA tanker was kept permanently on station. The warships spent approximately eighteen days at a time off Iceland. Soon, the question of winter fishing arrangements had to be considered. Normally, the trawlers took shelter inshore during bad weather but to do that risked arrest, so it was decided to close the northern and western havens, leaving the two on the south and west coasts. Although gales were a year-round threat, in winter they occurred on over 50 per cent of the days and were often prolonged. There was too the ever-present threat of icing caused by the cold air and freezing spray.

About eighty trawlers remained until early December and there were still twenty at Christmas. The Staff History records that the gunboats made some 'close passes', some dangerously close, but no arrest attempts were successful. The appearance of a RN warship carried the necessary deterrent value. By the year end there had been thirty 'serious arrest attempts' and many other more tentative 'manoeuvring or buzzing' approaches. 'Icelandic tactics included coming alongside to allow the boarding party to jump, grappling the trawl warp to facilitate coming alongside, and latterly firing warning shots, both blank and solid shot, aimed off.'[11]

This is not to suggest an absence of potential flashpoints in the days that followed. ICGV *Maria Júlia* tried to arrest the Grimsby boat *Lifeguard* but the crew resisted, armed with boathooks, rope ends and an axe. The gunboat withdrew following a scuffle; fortunately there were no serious injuries. The gunboat *Ægir* collided with the trawler *Burfell* and then later made to ram the frigate HMS *Russell*. This drew a sharp retort from the latter's CO via loudhailer, '*Ægir*, if you try to ram me, I will blow you out of the water.' This incident had been preceded by an earlier clash between the two ships.[12]

The withdrawal of HMS *Hound* from the area of operations, very early on the proceedings, was a small and probably an unnoticed milestone in the Royal Navy's fishery protection history during the twentieth century. The immediate reason was a faulty radar set (which seemed miraculously to cure itself once the ship was Portsmouth-bound). However, the war-vintage *Hound* would not be employed again on Iceland service as the *Algerine*-class minesweeper, with a maximum speed of 16 knots, was simply too slow to be entrusted with the supervision of an entire fishing haven. From this point onwards, for the duration of the Icelandic dispute and later, fishery protection tasks in general would be undertaken mostly by modern vessels and later by ones built from the hull up exclusively for the task.

The weather continued to be the great levelling factor, for example for those who served aboard the 'Weapon-', 'Battle-' and 'Daring'-class destroyers, which had been designed with the traditional open bridge. Watchkeepers on those ships had to be woken a full thirty minutes before their duties in order to have time to don enough foul-weather clothing to endure a four-hour spell on the bridge.[13]

The uneasy stand-off continued, punctuated by a small number of incidents that threatened to worsen the situation. In late September, a sailor aboard the trawler *Paynter* developed acute appendicitis and HMS *Diana* arranged for its cutter to land the man in Patreksfjord but was obstructed in so doing. Meanwhile, Icelandic boarding parties from two gunboats attempted to arrest *Paynter*, which was loitering at the time 2 miles outside the 12-mile limit. The trawler's crew resisted and minor injuries were sustained on both sides. Meanwhile, *Diana*, having recovered its boat, returned to the scene at 25 knots. The Icelanders withdrew their boarding party on the personal instructions of their

Prime Minister, who deemed the incident to have been caused by a humanitarian crisis. He was widely criticised in Iceland, not least by the Coastguard, who claimed that they would have been able to take the arrested *Paynter* into port and thus achieve an important psychological advantage in the dispute. Later, the Icelandic authorities hardened their stance, stating that if such an incident recurred, the trawlers themselves would have to land their patients, which would almost certainly have led them to being arrested.[14]

On 25 November, there was another incident involving HMS *Russell*. The trawler *Hackness* was off the west coast of the island and not fishing when it was intercepted by ICGV *Thór*, which fired a warning shot. HMS *Russell* arrived on the scene and prevented an arrest taking place. When *Thór* indicated that another shot would be fired at *Hackness*, Lieutenant Commander Corson aboard the Type 14 repeated his threat of two months previously to sink the gunboat. The incident ended there. One of the commanders was asked later if in fact he would have carried out such a threat. He replied that using his 40mm gun would have been ineffective; his preferred, and indeed only choice, would have been to use a pattern of three ASW 550lb mortar bombs, which would probably have blown out the bottom even of the sturdily built ICGV. A chilling thought perhaps but also a reflection of the limited offensive options available aboard the Type 14 frigates built for a completely different purpose.[15]

A routine

New Year 1959 simply heralded a continuation of the stalemate and in fact established a routine that was to last throughout the year and on into 1960. The Official History records that normally seventy to a hundred British trawlers were working in the disputed waters in the period April to November, which reduced to fifteen to thirty during the winter months. The target area for the Icelandic Coastguard vessels was the 4- to 12-mile coastal belt, where they aimed to catch lone trawlers operating without nearby Royal Navy support. The trawler owners had been advised by HM Government to instruct their vessels not to venture beyond the internationally recognised 4-mile limit rather than the 3-mile zone that was still official British policy. This caveat was soon to be exploited, as will be described below.

The Report of Proceedings by Captain (D) 4th Destroyer Squadron, Captain E. Sinclair, for the period January to May 1959 provides an insight into the day-to-day problems involved in executing the Navy's task. TGG 334.0 was a 'mixed bag' comprising the 'Improved Battle'-class HMS *Agincourt* (Captain D4), the 'C'-class *Carysfort* and *Chaplet*, the 'Weapon'-class *Broadsword*, all late-war-built destroyers, and the nearly new Type 14 frigate HMS *Malcolm*.[16]

Firstly, Captain Sinclair was critical of the support provided by the Royal Fleet Auxiliary tankers during replenishment at sea (RAS) evolutions. He wrote, 'In future when our RAS fitted tanker strength is cut to the bare minimum, it is essential that they should be capable of operating in all weathers and giving a really efficient service.'[17] His words were heeded and Sinclair's later report notes that there were no further complaints made about the efficiency of the RFAs.

Sinclair, in his May 1959 report, commented on what he considered to be poor examples of seamanship displayed by the Iceland skippers, fearing, 'the careless skill-less tactics apt to be employed by the gunboats during close aboard work would be the cause of a serious accident'. He added:

> I do not think there is much we can do about it because it would be impracticable to order commanding officers not to get too close to them. It would result only in passing all the initiative to the other side. Cases are sure to arise in which the gunboats could be ridden off, legitimately, and HM ships must be given scope for action.

In the same note, he added that ICGV *Óđinn*, 'has been very persistent in her efforts to board and led *Chaplet* quite a dance'.

His final concern involved the recurring and historic problem of dealing with the independently minded trawler skippers:

> talk does not get anywhere with the trawlers; firm instructions are necessary and the failure to preserve precautions should carry a penalty. It is realised that the problem bristles with difficulties in that it is not the custom for owners to give decisive orders as in the Services, nor is the British Trawler Owners' Federation all powerful; how therefore are recalcitrant skippers to be made to toe the line? It is suggested therefore that a way may lie with the insurance companies who are both impartial and omnipotent.[18]

It should be added that Captain Sinclair's views were his own and were not necessarily shared by his fellow officers.

On 1 February 1959, the *Valafell* was approached by the gunboat *Thór* off the east coast of Iceland. A shot was fired across the bows of the trawler, which was ordered to stop on the threat of another round being directed this time *at* the fishing vessel. *Thór*'s CO accused the trawler of fishing within the 4-mile limit. HMS *Corunna* was in the vicinity and its CO countered the gunboat's threat with a similar warning that he would open fire. Captain Kristófersson then invited *Corunna*'s commander on board his ship to discuss the matter. Commander Gordon declined in lieu of the arrival of his superior aboard HMS *Agincourt*. After his arrival, Captain Sinclair ascertained that *Valafell* had been fishing five cables inside the 4-mile delimitation but he did not admit the fact to the Icelanders. A delicate, diplomatic situation ensued. Despite the transgression, the Commander Task Group (CTG) could not instruct the *Valafell* to be shepherded into an Icelandic port without permission of its owners. Four days of negotiations followed before the trawler owners gave way, allowing *Agincourt* to escort *Valafell* into Seydisfjord, where its skipper was fined and the trawler's gear was confiscated.[19]

Other, similar incidents occurred in March and April involving the trawlers *Carella* and *Swanella*. On 23 April, an allegedly recidivist 'poacher', *Lord Montgomery*, which was on the Icelandic Coastguard's 'blacklist', was apprehended by ICGV *Ægir*. HMS *Tenby* was on hand to prevent an arrest but the trawler's owners agreed that the boat's skipper could stand trial. When in court, in addition to the immediate charge of fishing within the limit, other historic charges were brought against the skipper. A £3,000 fine was imposed together with confiscation of gear and a three-month prison sentence. Payment of a bond quickly secured the release of the offending skipper but the severity of the judge's ruling in the case only served to harden the attitude of the trawler owners towards Icelandic justice.[20]

There was no break in the stalemate as the year wore on. The trawlers were urged to avoid the 4-mile delimitation but some chose to ignore the instructions. The Navy realised that the gunboats were now concentrating their attention on those who actually transgressed rather than attempting to capture vessels in the contentious 4- to 12-mile zone. Meanwhile, the trawler crews were preparing to repel boarders with a variety of weapons as diverse as broom handles and pepper![21] Despite a potentially nasty occurrence in late May when ICGV *Óðinn* allegedly cut across the bows of HMS *Chaplet*, causing a minor collision, that was a comparatively isolated incident. Welch concludes, 'In general, the First Cod War was conducted in a chivalrous way, with both sides trying to ensure that their actions would not be misunderstood and aiming to avoid direct confrontation.'[22]

Early in 1959 an attempt was made to monitor Icelandic voice transmissions in order to gather intelligence regarding the movements of the gunboats and their likely tactics. An Icelandic speaker called Edward Thomas embarked in the then brand-new *Salisbury*-class Type 61 frigate HMS *Llandaff* for the purpose. The subsequent report indicated that the main objective of the exercise was only partially achieved. The interception unit on *Landaff* failed to locate the main operational frequency used by the Icelanders and, until the last few days of the patrol, only picked up intermittent references being made to Icelandic gunboats. However, radio traffic was considered light and not much was happening, probably because it was the middle of winter. Some background news about the current situation in Iceland was acquired and this was considered useful.[23]

A year on

The first day of September brought the anniversary of the conflict and a fresh set of orders was issued by the Fishery Protection Office at Rosyth for the attention of Royal Navy ships taking part in Operation Whippet. In essence, little had changed but lessons had been learned in the intervening twelve months.

TG 334.0 was now distributed among six sub-groups numbered 35–40. Each comprised two or three ships. Apart from the same FPS Type 14 stalwarts *Duncan, Dundas, Malcolm, Palliser and Russell*, there was an interesting mix of warships including a sole 'Battle' class, HMS *Armada*, a couple of Cold War ASW destroyer conversions, *Paladin* and *Undine, Loch Fyne*, the nearly new *Whitby*-class frigate HMS *Torquay* and, something of an anomaly, the fast minelayer *Apollo*.[24] One RFA would continue to be attached to TG334.0 under operational command only but would not be officially attached to the task group.

The section in the instructions on 'Tactics' reminded the participating protection ships of the need to maintain a careful watch and to report on Icelandic Coastguard vessels entering or leaving the havens. It noted, 'The H.M. Ship should keep herself between the Coastguard vessel and any British trawler, where this is possible.' In order not to instigate any unnecessary trouble, it was advised that the ICGVs should not be prevented from closing the trawlers to take details of names or numbers and to issue warnings. Shadowing was to be considered sufficient if it was clear that no attempts at boarding were being contemplated.[25]

A new vocabulary had developed among the ships of the task group to describe some of the tactics used by the gunboats. When the Icelandic vessels steamed close by on the non-trawling side about 20 to 30ft off, the evolution was known as 'buzzing'. 'Super-buzzing' was the term given to a more threatening approach to a trawler and probably an attempt to board; a boarding party would be visible on deck and fenders would be rigged.

However, overall, caution and a low-key approach were the order of the day:

> Experience has shown that even when two Coastguard vessels simultaneously close a trawler in the fog with the Boarding Parties ready to jump, close shadowing and assurance to the trawler on Haven R/T – which is monitored by the Icelandic Coastguard vessels – that an H.M. Ship is closely watching the situation and all ready for immediate and firm action, will deter boarding. Whilst the primary aim is to prevent our trawlers being boarded, Commanding Officers should carefully consider the risks of physical obstruction before hazarding their ship when boardings are being attempted. A tow of nearly 1,000 miles in a damaged ship in an Arctic winter is an unwelcome thought.

The instructions about trawlers that transgressed the 4-mile limit were clear. It was reported that the owners were taking 'very severe disciplinary action' with skippers in those cases and the COs were told that if the skipper of a trawler was caught and held inside the limit he should not be protected from arrest and there should be no intervention. Moreover, consideration of the political delicacies of the situation had to be kept in the forefront of any decision-making. 'It is important that any H.M. Ship should not, in these circumstances, get into a position where the Icelandic authorities can claim that H.M. Government had "released" a trawler to go into an Icelandic port for trial.'[26]

The experience of Operation Whippet thus far meant that the individual personalities of the gunboat commanders became well known. The new ICGV *Óðinn*, about to enter service, would be commanded by Captain Kristófersson, who was described as 'A dour old Sea Dog.

No sense of humour'. *Thór*'s Captain Bjornsson was considered 'co-operative' but 'could be difficult', while *Albert*'s Captain Thorsteinssen was 'very aggressive'. On the other hand, Commander Jonnsen of *Ægir* was 'a nice friendly type'.[27]

A sobering assessment of the Navy's role off Iceland was prepared by the Head of M Branch in an internal memorandum in August 1959. He considered that the future of the commitment off Iceland was uncertain but there was no real prospect of it ending ahead of the next Law of the Sea Conference scheduled for the following March. 'We cannot hope to avoid a lot of political abuse about our activities off Iceland, but we shall make things easier for ourselves if we have stopped protection as a gesture of goodwill beforehand.' He considered that protection needed to be provided until the Conference, 'in the firm hope that we shall [then] be able to rid ourselves of this commitment'. Finally, the Head of M Branch remarked that recent experience had highlighted the need for purpose-built trawler-type vessels to be constructed for fishery protection duties with speeds in excess of 16 knots.[28]

The call for specialist vessels, similar in design to trawlers, was certainly not new, as earlier chapters attest. The utilisation of long, slim frigates and destroyers with thin, comparatively fragile hulls was implied in the call for more rugged, trawler-type designs and would become a glaringly obvious requirement during the increasingly rough clashes between the RN and the ICGV during the next two Cod Wars in particular. In the meantime, the discrepancy in tonnage and capability between the professionally manned Royal Navy ships and the non-military ICGV fleet was making Britain unpopular in the international community. The impression given by the report gives one a clear sense that March 1960 could not come round quickly enough![29]

Inching towards agreement

ICGV *Thór* made two attempts to secure arrests on the eve of the first anniversary of the 'hostilities', possibly to gain publicity for the Icelandic cause. Meanwhile, secret NATO-led negotiations took place during the autumn. It was hoped that an RN withdrawal could be arranged in exchange for Iceland dropping historic poaching charges against British vessels. The winter months passed fairly peacefully as both sides awaited the start of the second UNCLOS in Geneva in March 1960.

The Admiralty proposed suspending Operation Whippet ahead of the Conference as a peace gesture but this was opposed by the Foreign

Secretary Selwyn Lloyd. However, the Government did manage to persuade the BTF to withdraw its boats completely from the area during UNCLOS. It was agreed that to withdraw just outside the 12-mile limit would imply acceptance of the Icelandic ruling.

After a good deal of debate and some compromise, the USA, Canada and the UK finally proposed that there should be a 6-mile-wide territorial zone around Iceland plus a further 6-mile contiguous band where there would be what was described as 'time-limited historic fishing rights'. This meant that foreign fishing vessels would have access to those waters for a specified length of time, say five or ten years, following historical fishing precedence. (A shorthand description for this arrangement became known as '6 + 6 + historic rights'.) The UK had serious misgivings because of its fears about the impact on future employment in its fishing industry but eventually agreed. Iceland came to the Conference determined to keep to its demands for a 12-mile territorial zone and nothing else. In the end the Canada/UK/USA proposal failed by a single vote to get the necessary two thirds majority to achieve acceptance.

After UNCLOS, the British Government got the BTF to agree to try to prevent its boats from re-entering the 12-mile limit for a further three months in the hope that proper negotiations might take place. As far as the Navy was concerned, it would patrol only outside the contentious area and protect the trawlers if apprehended. If the fishing vessels disobeyed their owners and started working inside the zone, the RN would intervene if they were in the vicinity. However, only the owners had the jurisdiction to order their boats to leave; the Navy was there in an advisory capacity only. This 'softly, softly' approach was intended to aid what were likely to be delicate negotiations. Whether or not the Iceland Government appreciated the conciliatory approach adopted is not clear. To facilitate these arrangements, a new Operation Mint was established. Captain Hugo Bracken assumed command of the task force, which initially comprised HM ships *Battleaxe*, *Delight* and *Palliser* supported by RFA *Wave Ruler*. The Admiralty's M Branch produced another gloomy interpretation of the failure to reach agreement in Geneva, 'failure leaves in a very uncertain state the range and scope of duties which the Fishery Protection Squadron as a whole is likely to undertake in the future'.[30]

Somewhat unexpectedly, on 29 April, Iceland stated that it would drop all historic poaching charges and would allow fishing boats access to Icelandic ports during severe weather. These concessions seemed to indicate that FP could be suspended but again the FO cautioned that complete withdrawal might signal surrender. Unfortunately, the Icelandic move only encouraged some trawlers to venture again within the 12-mile zone and this, seemingly inevitably, led to no fewer than ten attempted arrests in late June.

One incident reached the notice of the press and also prompted a question in the House of Commons. It followed a complaint made by the Grimsby Trawler Officers' Guild to the Ministry of Agriculture, Fisheries and Food (MAFF) that the CO of HMS *Crossbow* had ordered a number of trawlers to leave the disputed zone. Ian Orr-Ewing (Civil Lord of the Admiralty) reminded the House that HMG was not in a position to give orders to the trawler industry and the trawler owners had themselves instructed skippers not to fish for the time being inside the 12-mile fishery limit claimed by Iceland. He went on, 'On 10th June a number of trawler skippers appeared to H.M.S. "Crossbow" to be unaware of their owners' instructions. Her Majesty's ships have orders to remind British trawlers of these instructions if, because of navigational difficulties or for any other reason, they are seen to be fishing inside the twelve mile limit and so running the risk of becoming involved in incidents.'[31]

A deteriorating situation later in June found ICGV *Albert* firing shots close to the trawler *Thuringia*. On the 28th *Thór* succeeded in getting a party on board *Northern Queen* and it required swift action from HMS *Duncan* to resolve the matter. Worse was to follow the next month. The trawler *Grimsby Town* recklessly attempted to ram the new ICGV *Óðinn* on 10 July. The gunboat replied with a shot fired through the trawler's superstructure. Although there were no casualties, this serious escalation prompted both sides to seek a resolution before there was loss of life.

But there were obstacles. In Iceland, the left-wingers were calling for the strategic NATO airbase at Keflavik to be closed and for Iceland to leave the Alliance. Britain was faced with the upcoming termination of the BTF truce and the prospect of the trawlers returning *en masse* within the 12-mile limit. Contingency plans for Operation Bailiff were drawn up for such an eventuality. Three fishing havens were to be assigned: *Partridge*, *Pheasant* and *Woodcock* within the 6- to 12-mile zone with a proposed five-year lifespan. Ironically, this arrangement in fact duplicated the recent moribund UNCLOS proposal.

In the meantime, the BTF agreed to a further two-month extension of its agreement not to sanction its trawlers to work inside the limit as the prospect of talks appeared imminent. Indeed, on 10 August Iceland signalled that it was ready to resume talks shortly on the grounds that it needed further time for its internal political unrest to subside. Summer gave way to autumn, then to winter, with intermittent discussions taking place but no substantial progress made.

At the year's end, Britain was insisting that the matter would have to be resolved by the International Court of Justice. The British Government realised that it had run out of room for diplomatic manoeuvre but could not contemplate sending in the Navy again to police inside the 12-mile limit. Iceland, too, had to concede it had pushed its opponent far enough. Jóhannesson writes:

> On the one hand, the rulers in Reykjavík had finally realised that they could not squeeze Britain further. On the other, they knew that they could only defend the outcome at home if they had demonstrably gone as far as they could in the negotiations. Once the authorities had pledged themselves to a settlement, the domestic pressure against concessions changed from a bargaining tool at the international level to a dangerous threat in internal politics.[32]

Both of the chief Icelandic negotiators were pro-West and NATO but were opposed by a very strong left-wing and nationalist lobby, which meant constant attention had to be paid to gauging public opinion both outside and within the Althing.

Finally, on 28 February 1961, a proposal to end the dispute was presented. It did make a key concession that the country would not seek to extend its limits again unilaterally. Both countries signed an agreement on 11 March. On that day, Operation Mint was formally suspended. HMS *Malcolm* and *Rhyl* remained on patrol supported by RFA *Tidepool*. The First Cod War had come to an end.

Retreat

The cessation of 'hostilities' brought an impasse. John Roberts, writing from the point of view of a career sailor, sums up the conflict on a positive note:

> Many of the incidents were very confused, with differing accounts resulting in claim and counter-claim. Different reports from commanding officers made it difficult for accurate assessment to be

made of the dangerous incidents. The fact that no lives had been lost was down to the great ship handling skills and seamanship on both sides.[33]

Paddy Johnston regards the First Cod War for the RN, 'as a simple matter of reinforcing the Standing Fishery Protection Squadron for a temporary extra protection task', adding that it was, 'a straightforward defensive presence, expected to be of short duration. Even when the operation continued for months and years, its success was apparent and, unpopular though it was with the British Admiralty, there were no differences between the Service and the politicians over the requirement and the method of fulfilling it.'[34] The second and third wars were to be of an entirely different nature.

One of the Grimsby fishermen, Jim Clark, experienced the First Cod War. His recollections appear somewhat cavalier in tone:

> The Icelanders moved the limit from three mile to twelve mile and obviously we objected as a big industry. We fished in boxes, like twelve mile wide and obviously up to the three mile limit. We had the big D Class destroyers there, the Icelanders just had a couple of little motor boats ... If one came and harassed you, you would just ring up and the massive big destroyer would come storming up at 30 knots and the wash was enough for the boat to clear off.

He then reflects:

> You can't blame the Icelanders for what they've done because that's all they've got. They've got nothing a few sheep and volcanoes. But what they've done for the fishing industry ... they've done it properly.[35]

Lieutenant Charles Wylie, aboard HMS *Russell*, had nothing but admiration for the ICGVs and their crews. They were, in his opinion, first-class seamen. Likewise, he developed excellent relationships with the trawlers; radio communications were conducted formally at first but became increasingly friendly and informal. Visits to the trawlers invariably included a measure of whisky in the tea, while excellent halibut-head soup was often served as well.[36]

However, although the ending of the Cod War brought a decade of stability, when viewed in the cold light of day, the actual terms of the agreement signed on 11 March could only be seen as a series of concessions amounting to a defeat for Britain. HMG would no longer object to a 12-mile fishing delimitation. Despite the fact that, shortly before the start of the conflict, Britain had been considering a grudging acceptance of that limit, it was, nevertheless, a final recognition that its historic insistence on the old 3-mile delimitation was now moribund. Secondly, Britain accepted the Icelandic plans for base lines that now denied access to some of Iceland's wider bays and fjords, which hitherto had been considered lucrative fishing areas. Even the permission to work in the outer 6-mile zone for a period of three years carried caveats regarding specified areas and times of the year. Finally, although the agreement was that Iceland would give the UK six months' notice of any further extensions and allow any new adjustments to be referred to the ICJ for arbitration, Iceland signalled its intention to stand by its 1959 Parliamentary resolution to extend its territorial waters.

Understandably the British Fishing Industry was not pleased with the terms of the agreement. Officially, the Conservative Government overrode the objections, arguing that the interests of Humber trawler owners and fishermen were secondary to NATO's North Atlantic defences. Meanwhile, the Icelandic left-wing opposition questioned the clause in the agreement that would allow future disputes to be referred to the ICJ and vowed to rescind it when it was next in power.

The threat that Iceland might leave NATO, deny access to its vital Keflavik airbase and develop closer ties with the Soviet Union put the whole matter into perspective, although there was no categorical proof that either the USA or NATO put any pressure on either the UK or Iceland to reach an agreement in March 1961.[37] What is unquestionable though is that for the Royal Navy, the decade following its arduous three years on Icelandic patrol has been seen perceived as the watershed period of its decline from greatness as a naval power. There is indeed a marked difference between the status of the Royal Navy and the country it served in 1958 at the start of the conflict and in 1976 when the dispute finally came to an end.

More directly pertinent to the 1961 agreement between Britain and Iceland over territorial waters were three other examples of 'retreats' or partial retreats by Britain over territorial waters. It seems likely that all were influenced at least in part by the headline events taking place off that remote island. Shortly after the close of the Geneva UNCLOS 2 talks, the Norwegian Government came under intense pressure from within to declare its own 12-mile limit. After months of fruitless discussions, principally with Britain, a '6 + 6 + historic rights arrangement' was agreed. The 'historic rights' clause would be phased out over ten years; thus Norway extended its territorial waters from 4 to 6 miles in April 1961 and to the full 12 miles in September of that year. Earlier, in 1958 in the wake of the UNCLOS 1 talks in Geneva, the Faroe Islands declared it would match Iceland in declaring a 12-mile limit around its islands. Britain was opposed to any change, citing that its waters were valuable, particularly for Aberdeen- and Grimsby-based trawlers. In the end, a settlement similar to the one with Norway was reached. The strategic value of the Faroe Islands astride the GIUK Gap was brought into focus at this point. Both Britain and the USA were anxious not to lose the Faroes as an ally at that point in the Cold War.[38]

Finally, on 2 March 1961, the Soviet Union denounced its 1956 agreement (see Chapter Eight), which had enabled British fishermen to work in certain areas in the Barents Sea up to 3 miles from the coast. Ten days later, a formal announcement was made that the agreement would be terminated one year from that date. This was a big blow for the British trawlermen and ended a historic link with the area that had been the focus of long and sometimes bitter dispute over the rights, again, to fish up to 3 miles from the coast.[39]

Meanwhile, Britain appeared to be increasingly isolated over the whole matter of territorial waters. The West German Government had been the only other European nation to dispute the Icelanders' unilateral declaration when it followed the British lead in July 1961 and signed an identical agreement.

The Milwood incident

However, Anglo-Icelandic relations did improve in the immediate aftermath of the March 1961 cessation of 'hostilities'. RN patrol numbers were reduced and throughout the 1962 fishing season only one Type 14 was kept on permanent duty in the area. The next year, a further reduction saw a 75 per cent presence only on the fishing grounds.

However, on the morning of 27 April 1963, a report was received at the Port Edgar Offices of the Fishery Protection Squadron that the Aberdeen trawler *Milwood* (*Millwood* in some references) had been caught poaching inside the 6-mile limit off the Westmann Islands by ICGV *Ódinn*. The details were both sketchy and garbled, even suggesting that shots had been fired. The sole Royal Navy FP vessel in Icelandic waters, HMS *Palliser*, was refuelling at Reykjavík at the time and was alerted.

It was a Saturday and the Captain FPS (Captain R J Trowbridge) was ashore and thus able to direct operations. The standard procedure, which had remained in place since the end of 'hostilities', was for the duty protection ship to make contact with the trawler and, if the commanding officer was satisfied there was a case to answer, to persuade the trawler skipper to obey the orders of the Icelandic gunboat.

However, when HMS *Palliser* (Lieutenant Commander N J S Hunt) reached the scene it soon became clear that the normal pattern of events would not be followed. It appeared that Skipper Smith of the *Milwood*, after he had been apprehended by *Ódinn*, decided to make a run for Aberdeen with the gunboat in 'hot pursuit' mode. Other accounts of what happened when *Ódinn* initially encountered *Milwood* also reached the Captain FPS at Port Edgar. These included claims that the trawler had deliberately rammed and sunk the gunboat's buoy marking the place where *Milwood* was fishing and may also have attempted to ram ICGV *Ódinn*. Earlier reports that live rounds had been fired were discounted at that stage, however.[40]

Captain Trowbridge contacted the owner of the trawler, Mr Wood, at Aberdeen and 'strongly advised' him to order his trawler to turn around and head for an Icelandic port. The narrative of Captain Trowbridge's account of the episode notes, 'At the time it was thought that the owner was being co-operative but subsequent events indicate that he acted with duplicity.'[41]

After some delays and further difficulty, the manager of *Milwood*'s company was located but despite being warned that the matter might precipitate an international incident, Mr Willox flatly refused to instruct Skipper Smith to reverse course until he had spoken to him personally and had verification of what had happened previously. Throughout the incident, the poor quality of radio communications between the ships and Port Edgar greatly hampered the chance of resolving the matter, which forced Captain FPS to switch to Maritime HQ, Pitreavie. Captain Trowbridge at Port Edgar was also urgently seeking further guidance from the Admiralty in London.

Lieutenant Commander Hunt decided to board the *Milwood* to try to persuade Skipper Smith to surrender. Crucially, he permitted a boarding party from the gunboat to also board the trawler while the furious Smith was away from his boat, having been taken to HMS *Palliser*. Meanwhile, the frigate's marine engineer officer, who had accompanied his commanding officer aboard *Milwood*, had succeeded in disabling the trawler's engines. Hunt's decision to allow the boarding party from Óðinn to accompany him was objected to by the Admiralty.

Mr Wood then called Pitreavrie to inform that Skipper Smith had been transferred to another trawler, the *Juniper* (owned by the same Aberdeen company), which was now heading for the UK. However, he omitted to say that HMS *Palliser* had strongly advised that *Juniper* be instructed to proceed to Reykjavík and Wood had taken the opposite action. Nevertheless, the Captain Fishery Protection now mistakenly believed that the incident was practically over. *Palliser*'s commander had prevented the real possibility of there being bloodshed and what he described as Smith's 'suicidal threat to sail *Milwood* home single-handed or even to scuttle her'.[42]

But, shortly afterwards, matters took a turn for the worse. Wood had just had a heated conversation with the British Ambassador in Reykjavík and had refused to order *Juniper* to head for an Icelandic port. Ambassador Basil Boothby then contacted the HQ of the Flag Officer Scotland and Northern Ireland (FOSNI) at Pitreavie Castle, informing that firstly Óðinn had established the right of hot pursuit on *Juniper* and was threatening to open fire, secondly that Mr Wood was refusing to order the trawler to Iceland, and thirdly that *Palliser* was reporting that the situation was becoming extremely critical.

Captain Trowbridge's main concern at this juncture was firstly to ease the pressure on Lieutenant Commander Hunt, either by contriving to stop *Juniper* or by persuading it to turn north, and secondly to give *Palliser*'s CO comprehensive instructions to afford *Juniper* maximum protection as it was being pursued illegally. However, at this point, the Admiralty in London intervened, informing Trowbridge that it was taking charge and would in future originate all future signals to HMS *Palliser*. Although relations between Pitreavrie and the duty officers in London were described as 'excellent throughout', it was clear that firm direction at a ministerial level was urgently required – never easily obtained at a weekend! Meanwhile, *Palliser* made an urgent call to the effect that unless *Juniper* was turned around it would not be able to keep the situation under control.

Finally, a temporary compromise was reached: *Juniper*'s course was reversed but for one hour only. The fear was that when this time elapsed and *Juniper* had turned again for Aberdeen, *Ódinn* would open fire. However, the Admiralty, communicating directly with the frigate, instructed Lieutenant Commander Hunt to invite Smith on board his ship. At the same time Mr Wood was on the telephone demanding that *Juniper* be instructed to set course again for Scotland. He was only dissuaded from contacting the trawler directly by the promise that a Foreign Office official was about to talk to him. At this stage, *Milwood*'s owner seemed to lose control. He managed to contact *Palliser* and using 'hysterical language' demanded the return of Smith to *Juniper*. He then remonstrated with Captain Trowbridge, claiming that he had been double-crossed.

Fortunately, the crisis point in the incident now passed – quite suddenly. *Palliser* reported that, with *Ódinn* in company, it was heading for *Milwood* to recover the ship's boarding party, which was still on board. This was duly effected; there was residual concern that when the gunboat realised that *Palliser* with Smith aboard was not returning to Iceland there would be further trouble. This did not materialise and it came as some surprise when *Ódinn* parted company with the frigate during the Sunday afternoon. Concern now switched to the frigate's dwindling fuel level. It eventually reached Lyness in Orkney with 19 per cent of burnable fuel remaining.[43]

Predictably, the whole business caused an outpouring of criticism in Iceland. Britain was accused of preventing a legitimate arrest. Fuelling facilities for RN and RFA vessels on patrol were temporarily withdrawn and the Icelandic Coastguard was reported to be unco-operative. Lieutenant Commander Hunt was ordered to appear before the ACNS to explain his actions, particularly why he had allowed *Ódinn*'s men to join his own when they boarded *Milwood*.[44] In the outcome, the ACNS supported Hunt's decision-making.

Reports provided for the resulting internal inquiry to be presented to the Board of Admiralty found the narratives provided by Captain Trowbridge and by his superior, the FOSNI, Vice Admiral Hezlet, differed in parts from the Admiralty's view, provided by M Branch II.[45] The latter defended its actions in response to a suggestion in Captain Trowbridge's report that responsibility in cases such as the *Milwood* incident should be delegated at a lower level. The Head of M Branch took exception to the paragraph in Trowbridge's report that read, 'Despite repeated representations to Admiralty for firm instructions as to what action should be taken to meet various difficult situations, nothing worthwhile has emerged and the warning sounded by the RED CRUSADER incident two years appears to have gone unheeded.' The charge was refuted on the grounds that M Branch claimed it had received no signalled or written representation on the matter from the office of Captain Fishery Protection.

The *Red Crusader* incident had occurred on 29 May 1961 when the trawler of that name was arrested by the Danish frigate HMDNS *Niels Ebbesen* while fishing in disputed waters off the Faroe Islands. Instead of heading towards the Faroe Islands' capital, Tórshavn, as instructed by the Danish protection vessel, the British trawler made for Scotland. The Danish frigate pursued the trawler, and fired warning shots, but to no avail. The Danish frigate then fired an aimed shot, damaging the trawler, which, nevertheless, made it home to Aberdeen.[46]

The Head of M Branch then addressed the contentious and still unresolved matter of the use of force in hot pursuit scenarios that lay at the heart of the matter concerning the *Milwood* incident. The Admiralty had pressed the Foreign Office for clarity but had merely been served with the nebulous response, 'we cannot say that international law absolutely forbids the use of force if, and to the extent that, it is necessary to effect an arrest'.

The official Admiralty view also differed from those of the Captain FPS on the question of affording commanding officers greater freedom of action, 'it would be difficult to separate naval authority over Skippers from Admiralty liability for their actions and their consequences, and it is wrong for the Admiralty to usurp the responsibilities of trawler owners'.[47]

Admiral Hezlet described his status during the incident as that of an 'interested spectator' but he gently reminded Their Lordships that it had taken place in his own operational area and involved a ship, HMS *Palliser*, under his full command. Thus, he had a direct interest as Lieutenant Commander Hunt's conduct had been called to question. Hezlet condemned the control of the operation as being 'most unsatisfactory', dividing the substance of his criticism between command and communication. He thought it fortuitous that Captain Trowbridge was ashore at the time, and not off north Norway for example, and thus able to exercise command. If he had been away, his deputy at Port Edgar would have been a duty lieutenant commander. In the event, responsibility was progressively removed from Fishery Protection HQ and invested in the Admiralty, bypassing FOSNI in the process – as Hezlet quietly mentions *en passant*. Although not openly critical of the move, the Vice Admiral did not consider, 'that operational control of a ship would be transferred at any time from a responsible naval authority to a consortium of duty officers [at the Admiralty] conferring by telephone'.

Hezlet also condemned the communications system that, despite great financial expenditure and effort, had failed to be reliable in terms of speed and efficiency. Instead, a totally insecure commercial network had to be employed because classified signals took so long to get through as to be worse than useless.[48]

Finally, Peter Carrington, First Lord of the Admiralty, gave his views, which embraced the wider, international dimension. He felt it inappropriate to apologise to Iceland for the Royal Navy's actions and more than anything else, a public expression of regret would have a negative effect on the morale of the FPS. He supported Hunt's actions in incorporating *Óðinn*'s boarding party and agreed that *Palliser*'s commander had no legal powers to compel Skipper Smith to remain on board *Milwood* or to submit to arrest. Moreover, in view of Smith's precarious state of mind at the time (threatening to sacrifice his ship, even to commit suicide), Carrington felt that Hunt had no alternative but to allow Smith to transfer to the trawler *Juniper*.[49]

The suddenness and rapid descent of the 'Milwood Incident' into a potentially damaging international crisis caught the FPS, the Admiralty and the Foreign Office 'on the hop'. It also raised wider issues as noted above. It highlighted the perennial problem facing the commander on the spot, which Carrington succinctly summed up as, 'reconciling national interests with international obligations'. Added to that was the awkward interface between military and civilian interests, perhaps unique to fishery protection, which meant that the Navy could only 'strongly advise' rather than issue an order.

A landmark Act

The near decade that followed passed without further, serious incidents in the waters around Iceland. The three years of 'historic rights' to fish up to 6 miles lapsed in March 1964 with little comment. The fears of the BTF that the industry would be ruined as a result of the 12-mile delimitation proved unfounded, as the statistics for the fish landings both before and after the First Cod War demonstrate.[50]

Later the same year, as a result of a European Fisheries Conference attended by all northern European nations including the UK, it was agreed that a 12-mile limit with ten years of historic rights up to 6 miles would be established.[51] This decision served to alter the profile of the FPS as there was a decreasing demand for distant-water patrols but a requirement for more inshore protection. Thus, the number of Type 14s in the FPS was reduced to three, with five 'Ton'-class minesweepers added. A further alteration was made in 1967 when the Type 14s were moved to general fleet duties. Britain had finally abrogated its historic adherence to a 3-mile territorial waters limit when the 1964 Sea Fisheries Act passed into law.

The second reading of the associated Bill was introduced by the Minister for Agriculture, Fisheries and Food on 15 June 1964. Christopher Soames remind the House of Commons that the country's fishery limits had remained unchanged since the Sea Fisheries Act of 1883, when, rather than being innovative, it had merely reflected international law at the time. Soames said that since the Second World War this legislation had been increasingly challenged and although the UK had consistently favoured the 'narrow seas' doctrine, its change of thinking had been made in, 'the wider interests of our fishing industry'. Thereafter, with a typical politician's manoeuvre to explain an abrupt policy change in the best possible light, he asserted that some extension to the limits could not be denied to the country's fishermen. He added, most emphatically, that the decision had not been reached in the interests of conservation, rather to, 'secure some scope for our fishermen around the coast'.[52]

This was indeed a landmark moment in the history of British fisheries and fishery protection. It marked the diminution of Britain's distant-water fishing fleet and a shift in emphasis for the Royal Navy's Fishery Protection Squadron, symbolised, perhaps, by the move ashore by the Captain FPS into HMS *Lochinvar* on the Firth of Forth, where his role became more focussed on providing information and advice on protection matters rather than actively supervising his squadron while afloat. This was intended to set a pattern for the future running of the FPS but was to be interrupted in the meantime by a general election in Iceland in 1971.

Chapter Ten

The Last Gasp of *Mare Liberum* 1971–76

BRITAIN HAD EXTENDED its exclusive fishing zone to 12 miles in 1964, dispensing with its historic adherence to a 3-mile territorial limit but by the 1970s was becoming increasingly isolated within a world community that was inexorably moving towards a 50- or even a 200-mile delimitation. Not only was there an increasing interest in claiming the waters adjacent to the coastline but also the right to exploit the same area of the seabed.[1] Britain was adopting a seemingly contradictory position, on the one hand supporting a 200-mile economic jurisdiction on an international level by securing oil rights in the North Sea but, at the same time, attempting to deny the Icelanders those same rights on their fishing grounds.

Britain, and initially West Germany, became embroiled in two further disputes with Iceland between September 1972 and November 1973 and again between November 1975 and June 1976. Both of these confrontations developed into increasingly acrimonious affairs and threatened a rupture in the NATO Alliance. UK protection of the trawlers was principally handled by some of the most modern frigates in the fleet, which had the speed, agility and command and communications facilities to counter the experienced and capable Icelandic coastguard vessels. This drew the RN frigates away from their primary Cold War tasks and became increasingly expensive undertakings when they collided with their robust opponents, particularly during the final phase of this unfortunate conflict.

Thus, during the first half of the decade, Britain contested two 'wars' it could not hope to win as the tide of international opinion moved in favour of the 'plucky underdog' Iceland, which skilfully held the upper hand in the propaganda battle. At home the UK, enduring a series of internal economic crises, found itself caught between defending one of its oldest and most cherished industries while facing the reality that the days of distant-water fishing were numbered and that it no longer carried the clout on the international stage to influence, let alone change, world opinion.

A key election victory

The Icelandic General Election in June 1971 brought to power a coalition between the People's Alliance and the Liberal Left that subsequently called itself 'the Second Leftist Government'. Prior to victory it had tabled a motion in the Althing calling for an extension of Iceland's fishery limit to 50 miles. Therefore it came as no surprise that in September of that year it issued a policy statement that read, 'the 1961 agreement with Great Britain and West Germany will be terminated and Iceland's fishery limit extended to fifty miles from base lines, not later than on the 1st September 1972'.[2]

Why did the Icelandic Government decide on a 50-mile limit rather than follow the lead of some South American Pacific coast countries and push the claim to 200 miles? The probable answer is that the shallower waters in the 12–50-mile continental shelf zone were the most profitable in terms of fish stock and a resolution to extend to 200 miles would be more difficult to defend than a 50-mile claim. The British Government's position was clear: any decision on international law of that kind had to be decided by the United Nations at the next Law of the Sea Conference. When it was apparent that the Icelanders would act unilaterally over the matter, both the British and the West Germans referred the matter to the ICJ in The Hague.[3] Essentially, this was a delaying tactic, in the hope that other nations with similar claims would render support at the next UNCLOS deliberation. Long gone were the days when Britain would have ignored international convention and taken the matter into its own hands when dealing with a small nation such as Iceland.

During the twelve months that followed, the ICJ offered alternatives but these were rejected by the Icelanders; likewise talks failed to reach an agreement despite the efforts of the Icelandic Minister for Foreign Affairs, who travelled to London and to Bonn in search of a compromise. When it was pointed out that Britain had already taken over natural resources on the North Sea seabed, far beyond the continental shelf, Iceland was told that international law drew a clear distinction between resources *in* the waters and those lying *on* the seabed and within the subsoil beneath the sea.[4]

On 30 August 1972 Iceland notified Britain of the abrogation of the 1961 Exchange of Notes that had brought the previous conflict to an end, stating that the earlier agreement had achieved its purpose and that the country would assert its rights to a continental shelf fishery jurisdiction, which would come into effect immediately. Two days later, Iceland duly extended its fisheries limit to 50 miles.[5] Meanwhile, preparations were well under way in Britain for the re-establishment of the havens used in the First Cod War that had proved generally unpopular with the fishermen. Andrew Welch comments, 'Although haven fishing had only reduced the catch by 15 per cent in the First Cod War, much of the fishing had actually been outside havens, outside the 12 miles. There was comparatively little fish outside 40 miles, hence the assumption that there would be a 50 per cent reduction from haven fishing this time round.'[6]

When the new ruling came into force, all countries complied with the exception of Britain and West Germany. The West German trawlers, which were supported by three tugs by this time, tended to fish further out because the home market favoured saithe (coley) and redfish rather than the traditional British favourites, cod, plaice and haddock.[7]

Earlier in the month, some sixty to seventy British trawlers, together with ten to twenty West German boats, had left harbour for Icelandic waters. Some skippers painted over the names and home ports of their boats in order to prevent the ICGVs from identifying them. A further number, purportedly, flew the 'Jolly Roger' as if to publicise their independent spirits. While there was still some hope of a negotiated settlement, the British Cabinet agreed to deploy the civilian support vessel *Miranda*, equipped with a doctor, medical supplies and facilities for the repair of radar and sonar; the ship duly left Hull on 26 August. Additionally, the MAFF 1,600-ton research vessels *Cirolana* and the DAFS *Scotia* were despatched in the spirit of providing low-key but practical support for the trawlermen. Britain would only commit to providing naval assistance as a last resort in order not to jeopardise the use of Keflavik as a key NATO base.[8] Iceland's left-wing government was already rumoured to be considering leaving the alliance. Following an internal debate within the government in Whitehall, a decision was reached to station one or two frigates outside the 50-mile limit in order to establish a presence and as a possible deterrence.

A 'secret weapon'

Prior to 1958, two Icelandic blacksmiths had secretly developed what they called a 'trawl wire cutter'. The warp cutter was very simple and very effective, just a pair of jaws with a cutter in the throat – akin in many ways to the paravanes of the First World War or to the minesweeping gear before the advent of the explosive cutter. The gunboat towed the cutter on a wire so that the cutter would catch one, or both, of the trawl warps. With the momentum involved, this action would force the warp into the cutter and so sever the wire.[9]

Very skilful, close-quarter manoeuvring was required for a successful cutting run and this was to become a major bone of contention between the two sides as the number of collisions between the RN ships and the Coastguard vessels increased during the latter stages of the Second and during the Third Cod War.

The wire or warp cutter had been developed prior to 1958 and by 1959 all ICGV vessels had been equipped. But it had never been used during the 1958–61 period for fear of disrupting negotiations that were then under way, although all the crews had received training. It proved very successful. Nine British and one West German trawlers had their wires cut during the last four months of 1972 and between eighty-two and eighty-four during the whole 1972–73 conflict.[10]

There were five successful warp-cutting attempts during the first month of the new delimitation. The most serious incident occurred when the Grimsby trawler *Aldershot* clashed with the OCGV's *Óðinn* and *Ægir*. Both sides claimed the other caused the subsequent collision. The rate of incidents increased in January of the New Year, which led to fresh demands from the skippers for naval protection. However, on this occasion, the BTF held off, merely stating that restrictions in movement would inevitably lead to smaller catches. Britain joined the European Economic Community (EEC) on 1 January, which led in turn to adherence to the Common Fisheries Policy (CFP), the significance of which is discussed in the next chapter. However, these matters had no immediate effect on the events off Iceland.

In the meantime, further diplomatic attempts to resolve the dispute had taken place during September and October 1973 with proposals and counter-proposals, but to no avail. Gallingly for the British, bilateral agreements were reached between Iceland and both Belgium and the Faroe Islands on quotas and permission to fish within the 50-mile zone.[11] In the meantime, there had been a fatality on board a West German trawler. On 25 November, two trawlers had their wires cut; one crew member was severely injured by the trawl cable as it snapped back and he died shortly afterwards. The West Germans registered a strongly worded protest but took no further action.[12]

Discussions had been under way in late 1972 between MAFF and the BTF about the use of civilian tugs to provide a bulky presence between the gunboat and the trawler to try to prevent further collisions or wire-cutting attempts. Each tug would carry a 'defence commander', either a fisheries officer or retired naval officer, answerable to MAFF and directed to work in a liaison capacity.

Ministerial approval was granted in January 1973 for the 1,666-ton ocean-going tug *Statesman*, on long-term charter to United Towing Company of Hull, to be seconded and deployed and it left Leith on the 20th of the month. A second tug, the smaller *Englishman*, 573 tons, joined *Statesman* in February. The problem with both vessels was their lack of speed and manoeuvrability (*Statesman* 16 knots, *Englishman* 15 knots), which meant that neither tug was capable of 'marking' the gunboats. The Royal Maritime Auxiliary Service (RMAS) salvage tugs *Roysterer* and *Rollicker* were considered for a time, but at 15 knots they too were not fast enough. The RMAS boats were also marginally less powerful than *Englishman*, while their Mirrlees diesel engines had been liable to break down and were thus considered unsuited for the rigours of the task. Finally, as military vessels, they would become the target for adverse publicity in the propaganda 'war'.[13]

Icelandic commentators were dismissive of the effectiveness of the tugs. The MAFF evaluation however, as might be expected, was more ambivalent. It was considered that they were useful but did not provide the complete solution to the problem of harassment faced by the trawlers. Although, in MAFF's opinion, the tugs had, 'considerably limited the freedom of manoeuvre for the gunboats and their effectiveness', they lacked the speed to 'head off the gunboats and keep them clear of the trawlers'.[14]

The MAFF report includes a description of a passive tactic adopted by the trawlers and tugboats to keep the gunboats at bay:

The trawlers fish in echelon, with the tug protecting the trawls of the vessels at the rear of the formation. The tugs have sufficient speed and manoeuvrability to outwit attempts on the warps of the vessels on either wing of the echelon, and the forward vessels leave insufficient space for the gunboat to get between them and cut the warps. Not all grounds, however, are suitable for echelon fishing.

The report continues, rather soberly, with the comment that only two tugs were known to have the ability to outpace the gunboats but even they lacked the speed to be completely effective. It ends prophetically, as is related in more detail below, 'Naval frigates have the speed, but lack the required manoeuvrability – for instance "Aegir" or "Odinn" (or a tug) can stop and turn more quickly, and should be able to win any confrontation or manoeuvre with a frigate.'[15]

It was becoming increasingly likely by March 1973 that the RN would be called upon again to render support within the contested 50-mile zone. A document that amounts to the Navy's 'position paper', and intended for internal consumption only, sets out the role the protection vessels were likely to have to play in the event of an escalation in the dispute. In an echo of many such statements made in the event of an impending international crisis when the Royal Navy was called upon to take action, the report titled 'Behind the Cod War' concludes, 'What is important is that it should be realised that the use of naval force is merely a means of preserving British interests pending a negotiated settlement. The decisions to intervene and the form and level of that intervention are political, not naval …'.

The document firmly establishes the British position as well as the role the Navy would be expected to undertake; the philosophical rationale would be debated at a future date. It states that, 'We have traditionally fished in the disputed area, and whole communities of British fishermen depend on these fishing grounds for their livelihood.' However, the assertion that things should remain unchanged for the future is qualified in the next sentence, 'underlying these considerations are important and long-term questions about national sovereignty over the sea and its resources, freedom of movement for shipping on the high seas and about conservation of fish as an important source of food for this and future generations'.[16] The sub-text acknowledges that the historic adherence to *mare liberum* was under increasing threat.

Predictably, the number of clashes increased during May. Nevertheless, Britain and Iceland engaged in negotiations, optimistic of a settlement at the outset over the size of catches that might then form the basis for an interim agreement. However, cautious hope turned to frustration as neither side could agree; in the meantime more warp-cutting runs were made in the middle of the talks, which hardly helped matters. On 16–17 May, some forty trawlers conducted what amounted to an industrial 'walk-out', withdrawing outside the 50-mile limit and refusing to resume fishing unless the Navy came to their assistance. The owners spent three days trying to persuade the skippers to return. The resolve among the fishermen was not unanimous, however; there were some who wanted to soldier on without military support.

Matters came to a head on the 19th of the month when a second ultimatum was delivered: the boats would leave for the Faroe Islands or for their home ports unless naval protection was provided by 1600 hours that day. At 1535, HM ships *Plymouth* (relieved by *Jupiter* three days later), *Cleopatra*, *Lincoln*, RFA *Wave Chief* and three tugs led about thirty trawlers back inside the 50-mile limit.[17]

Strategic command of what became Operation Dewey was exercised by FOSNI, who in turn was responsible to the C-in-C Fleet and then the MoD for the overall conduct of the operations. FOSNI also dealt directly with the BTF over fishing matters. The tactical aspects of Operation Dewey were executed by the Senior Officer on patrol, the OTC (Officer in Tactical Command), who was usually a captain in rank, often with previous experience as a senior frigate squadron commander. He assumed day-to-day command of the warships, RFAs and defence tugs. The civilian support ships, meanwhile, remained under MAFF control; neither the OTC nor the British Government exercised any authority over the fishermen.[18]

The fishermen were instructed by the BTF to work within the designated fishing areas (DFAs), which were approximately 100 miles in length and situated along the inner margins of the 12–50 mile zone. They were expected to co-operate with the Royal Navy and the civilian-manned support and to report their movements when entering or exiting the zone. In turn, the RN frigates were instructed to operate under RoE 'Option Charlie', which included permission to use the 'riding off' tactic (i.e. presenting a physical presence) in order to deter the gunboat from attempting a warp-cutting run at the trawler. The use of jamming both of radar and radio, 'buzzing' by their helicopters, searchlights, and boarding and counter-boarding, were also permitted. Gunfire was only to be sanctioned in self-defence.[19]

Tactics

Iceland had a maximum of just six coastguard gunboats at their disposal: *Óđinn*, *Ægir*, *Thór*, *Týr* (due to be returned shortly to its owners for whaling duties), the unarmed *Árvakur* and the elderly *Albert*. The first three only could be described as front-line units. The Icelandic perception of the tactics employed by the British, once the Navy entered the dispute, is summed up thus:

> On the approach of an Icelandic Coastguard vessel to the protected area, the frigates would sail towards it and for several hours sail parallel, and very close to it, preventing it from sailing into the boxes (the DFAs). Then, often, the frigate would suddenly speed ahead of the Coastguard vessel, and steer across its bows without giving any notice of a changed course, and then slow down in front of it, causing a collision with the object of damaging the vessel and making it inoperative.

Inevitably, the Icelanders blamed the Royal Navy for many of the inevitable collisions, 'there were many incidents where the British "protection forces" made direct attempts at sending coastguard vessels to the bottom'.[20]

There is nothing, at least in the official British documentation of the period to support the claim that specific instructions were given to sink the gunboats or even suggestions that such attempts were made by commanding officers acting alone. Nor is there any evidence that the relevant files of the period have been redacted on this subject. The orders for commanding officers of Royal Navy ships in the contested zone, repeated in several different documents, appear to be unequivocal on this point: to avoid provocative action or the escalation of tensions; to use minimum force in execution of the Government's aims.

From the British point of view, there are a number of references made in various reports of proceedings during both the Second and Third Cod Wars to a possible lack of understanding by the Icelandic coastguard skippers of the pressure and suction effects between ships operating in close company. The RN had gained a great deal of experience, over the post-war years especially, from alongside replenishment at sea serials. Ships have 'pressure zones' fore and aft with a low-pressure zone amidships. Another ship, steaming at close quarters, can get sucked in if its bow gets within the low-pressure zone – resulting in a collision before evasive action can be taken.

The tactic that evolved during the conflict required the RN frigate to 'mark' the Icelandic gunboat positioning the ship astern and at a short distance from the ICGV. If the trawlers were considered to be at risk, 'the frigate would move up onto, or maybe just ahead of, the gunboat's beam, between the gunboat and the trawlers. The aim was to stop the gunboat from getting either across the frigate's bows or around her stern'.

This course of action necessitated steaming often at high speeds on a parallel course with the ever-present danger of the suction effect precipitating a collision. Frequent changes of speed often demanded a fast response to otherwise emergency engine orders for 'full ahead' or 'full astern'. The gunboats held the advantage in that respect: their diesel-driven, controllable-pitch screws meant that they were able to react more quickly and thus evade the opponent. 'If the gunboat managed to slip past the frigate, it might become necessary to get back onto the gunboat's "up-threat" beam and then "ease her over" by altering a degree or so towards her at a time.' At this stage the frigate's superior speed came into play.[21]

The time that had elapsed between the First and Second Cod Wars meant that communications had become more sophisticated and effective. Two maritime 'Rear Links' were enacted that enabled rapid ship-to-shore information to be effected. The method of communication between the warships on station was left to the discretion of the OTC. HM ships were briefed prior to departure to use trawler procedure when communicating on the trawler networks. A discrete circuit was also established in order to allow the defence tugs to communicate with the OTC.

Keeping track of the exact location of the gunboats was a constant problem for the Royal Navy forces. In that respect, Outfit UA8/9 proved to be the most effective electronic countermeasures set for tracking and identifying gunboats, as did the RAF Nimrod's ARAR/ARAX10. ICGV tactical talk was monitored on the trawler network and elsewhere but although it was recognised that Icelandic-speaking interpreters were needed, suitable personnel completed their training too late to be of use. 'Spoofing' and 'Jamming' techniques were also employed.[22] A key feature of the Cod Wars as a whole was the ability of both sides to listen to the other's communications traffic.

The surveillance provided by the Nimrods was considered to be excellent despite the controversy caused by its use, which will be described later. FOSNI's report notes that their radar and navigational ability provided constant, useful and accurate intelligence of own and Icelandic forces. The aircraft were tasked with locating the gunboats, compiling the trawler 'plot', reporting trawlers working outside the DFAs and tracking the presence of ice floes and fog. Additionally, the 'mail-drop' service they provided proved to be a great morale-booster for the ships' crews. However, thick fog in June and July 1973 inhibited their use. Naval Wasp and Wessex 3 helicopters were used extensively, flying from the frigates and the RFAs although it was noted that they were susceptible to icing in the northerly latitudes and were sometimes harassed by being 'buzzed' by Icelandic Coastguard aircraft.[23]

The Navy enters the fray

The first phase of the Second Cod War had lasted eight and a half months, during which the British and West German trawlers had been under civilian protection. The second phase of four and a half months, including in the busy summer months, was to become increasingly fractious and controversial, with claim and counter-claim of reckless seamanship by the frigates and gunboats amid varying degrees of co-operation and compliance to the rules shown by the trawlers.

The West German Government did not follow the British in providing military support for the trawlers despite it being reported that they were landing smaller catches and making less money than before the conflict. This caused unrest among the fishing communities of Bremen and the district coastal *länder* in the north of the country, who believed their dilemma was not appreciated in distant Bonn. Their trawlermen had been instructed to haul their nets if an Icelandic challenge looked likely. As a result, by late August, they had only fifty warps cut, although warp cutting had been threatened on over 150 occasions. But the exercise of premature hauling and then later deploying nets wasted time and was, of course, a major factor in the reduced size of the catch. The German Trawler Owners Federation was of the opinion that the German Government was 'being wet' about not sending in the Bundesmarine. However, those closer to the administration in Bonn realised the impracticability of such a move as it might well be construed as an example of German militarism and bring back uncomfortable memories of the Second World War.[24]

The first serious incident occurred on 25 May 1973 when the trawler *Everton*, a serial poacher according to the ICGV, was found fishing alone by *Ægir*. The *Everton* was told to stop and submit to arrest or risk being fired on. The trawler skipper refused, the gunboat opened fire, firstly with blanks and then a 57mm live round across the bows, followed by seven more, one of which punched a 4 x 10mm hole below the waterline, which started to flood the lower hold. *Ægir* was shortly ordered to stand off. Overnight, a repair party from HMS *Jupiter* managed to save *Everton* from sinking, amazingly, 'to the apparent complete lack of interest of her skipper and crew'!

The *Everton* incident prompted calls for changes to be made to the RoE but no action was taken. The British Government made a formal complaint; the Icelanders replied that *Ægir* had adopted accepted procedure in firing on a vessel that failed to stop when ordered. Meanwhile, the Secretary General of NATO, Dr Joseph Luns, visited London and remarked somewhat injudiciously that in the view of the organisation, 'Britain was paying much too much attention to fishing and that it didn't matter.' Prime Minister Edward Heath replied curtly that, 'It did matter, a great deal.'[25]

The BTF's response was to urge their skippers to obey instructions and to work in loose groups but this suggestion was rejected with a declared intention to follow *Everton*'s example: to resist arrest and to ram the gunboats if necessary. This 'go it alone' declaration may well have been prompted by an incident that had occurred on 23 April, a month before the reintroduction of the Navy. The defence commander aboard the tug *Statesman* had reported that trouble had started when ICGV *Árvakur* had arrived in an area where British, German and Icelandic boats were fishing and had cut the warps of a German vessel. The coastguard vessel had not been recognised immediately, so normal defensive positions had not been adopted. It was then claimed that *Árvakur* fired on the trawler *Portia* (this was rifle fire as the gunboat was unarmed), which prompted a group of three British trawlers to surround the ICGV and escort it into the 12-mile limit. *Portia*'s skipper claimed that no warning had been given and that the fire had been deliberately aimed at his crew, who were standing about on deck. Furthermore, when he protested to the *Árvakur*'s captain over the radio, he was told that the next rifle shot would be aimed at his head![26]

After a short interlude, the gunboat *Thór* arrived and promptly cut the trawler *SSAFA*'s warps before cutting across the bows of the

St Leger, firing blank rounds. The *St Leger* maintained its course and struck *Thór* on the portside, causing minor damage to the railing area of the bridge. The remainder of the British trawlers, apparently frustrated at being prevented from fishing, variously took up station astern of the Icelandic boats. The trawler *Macbeth* then 'became involved with the Thor', which chased it. Shots were fired, forcing the crews of the other British boats to take cover.

Later, an Icelandic coastguard plane, displaying the fishery pennant on its side, 'buzzed' the trawlers, reputedly flying dangerously low between the masts of the boats. The fishermen also reported that, 'the captain of the "Thor" was seen at one time during the fracas stomping up and down, shaking his fist, threatening to fire live rounds at such English bastards'.

Subsequently, both governments protested very strongly about the other's behaviour. How much of the above account was hearsay is hard to assess as it only gives the trawlermen's version of events. The defence commander aboard *Statesman* was of the opinion that the unexpected arrival of the small gunboat *Árvakur* encouraged the fishermen to feel that they could handle a vessel of that size. The use of gunfire by *Árvakur* only served to exacerbate an already incendiary situation. Hannes Jónsson presents convincing evidence of the aggression shown by the support tug *Irishman* in an incident on 1 June, again involving *Árvakur*. An image of the radar plot and photographs of the tug colliding at 90 degrees to the stern of the gunboat appears pretty conclusive.[27]

The dispute worsens

There were further flashpoints during June and July 1973. On 21 June, *Lloydsman* turned across the bows of *Óðinn*, causing the latter to strike the tug's port quarter. Understandably, the Icelandic media made a great deal of the unequal encounter between the 910-ton gunboat and Britain's '3,100 ton super-tug'. By early July there were some eighty British trawlers in the area making the most of the summer fishing season.

HMS *Leopard* and ICGV *Ægir* were engaged in a tense stand-off on 1 July and the next morning the gunboat entered the DFA, detected first by the tanker RFA *Olwen*, and was subsequently 'marked', again by *Leopard*. During the early afternoon, *Ægir* commenced harassing a group of German trawlers. The German support ship *Frithof* managed to deter the gunboat from its intended warp cutting enough to cause

Ægir to fire two shots towards the east across the support ship's bows. HMS *Leopard* had stationed itself about one mile further to the east of the incident and within 10 degrees of its bearing. The frigate went to action stations with her gun crews closed up and watched the gunboat continue to menace both *Frithof* and the trawler *Teutonia*.

It then warned *Ægir* by radio that if the gunboat continued to fire in its direction, it would be returned. During the next quarter of an hour, it appeared to *Leopard* that *Ægir* made an attempt to board the German trawler and then began to close the RN frigate at an estimated 20 knots. Shortly afterwards the tension suddenly subsided as the gunboat withdrew to the south.

Meanwhile, the OTC in HMS *Charybdis*, some 100 miles further east, marking ICGV *Thór* and listening to events unfold, sent a request to FOSNI for *Leopard* to lend support on humanitarian grounds. FOSNI denied permission that would have allowed the frigate to open fire in defence of the Germans. The orders for Operation Dewey were clear on that matter, 'No operations in the area are conducted under any NATO agreements; it is important that the Icelanders should be given no excuse for accusing the British of carrying out operations in concert with West Germans through NATO. HM Ships while marking gunboats must keep well clear of West German trawlers.'[28]

This encounter raised two matters. Firstly, the British were understandably hypersensitive in avoiding any grounds for accusation that two NATO partners were collaborating against a third. This would provide the communist-leaning elements in the Icelandic Government with the excuse they needed to press for a vote to leave the organisation and thereby strengthen the country's ties with the Soviet Bloc. Secondly, the timing of communications between *Leopard*, the OTC and FOSNI left a lot to be desired and was another public relations reversal for the MoD.

Information about the warning delivered by *Leopard* to *Ægir* was sent at 1527 (Zulu time) but was not received in the Naval Operations room ashore until the frigate's full account of the incident, in the form of a signal from HMS *Charybdis*, was acknowledged at 2215 hours. Earlier, following enquiries from the Duty Press Officer as to whether *Leopard* had, 'threatened to open fire on *Ægir*', the duty Commander stated that he had received no information that this was so. At 2045, the Duty Press Officer again enquired if further information was available or confirmation had been received concerning the Icelandic version of the incident that was being circulated. Once more the reply was negative. Subsequently the Icelandic report that HMS *Leopard* had threatened to open fire on ICGV *Ægir* was rather lamely denied and the opportunity to explain the full course of events was missed.[29]

On the evening of 12 August the trawler *Lord St Vincent* (H-261) was reported by some Icelandic trawlers fishing inside the old 12-mile limit. *Ægir* arrived on the scene shortly before midnight and observed that *Lord St Vincent*'s trawl wires were lying 'through the gallows into the sea'.[30] Captain Sigtryggsson ordered the trawler to stop and to haul its gear, and informed the skipper that he was sending a boarding party across and that he would be arrested. *Lord St Vincent* did not obey these instructions and, 'At 2237 hours the H-261 had got the trawl doors in the gallows. At 2239 hours propeller wash from the trawler was observed and a blank shot was fired at her.' Two more blanks were fired by *Ægir*, which were ignored by *Lord St Vincent*.

HMS *Sirius* had arrived by that time and Commander Coward and Captain Sigtryggsson, having ascertained that *Lord St Vincent* had been fishing within the 12-mile limit, agreed that it would be best if *Sirius*'s commander negotiated directly with the trawler skipper, Robert Turner. Meanwhile, a group of around ten British trawlers, in addition to HMS *Plymouth* and the tugs *Statesman* and *Englishman*, came down from the north; the trawler skippers threatened to defend *Lord St Vincent* from all comers, including the RN.[31]

Commander Coward explained to Turner that under the International Law of the Sea, *Ægir* had the right to make an arrest as long as it remained in company with the offender. The trawler promptly set off in a south-easterly direction in the company of the RN frigates, the ICGV and one trawler, *Kingston Emerald*. Sigtryggsson promised not to intervene for seven hours to allow for reflection on all sides (and to receive further advice from the Coastguard Directorate ashore).

By 1800 hours on the 13th, the little convoy was just 12 miles from the Faroe Islands coast. Earlier there had been a difference of opinion between Coward and Captain Weir, the OTC aboard HMS *Andromeda*, over the action to take in the event of *Ægir* firing on *Lord St Vincent*. Commander Coward had signalled his intention, in such an event, to warn the gunboat that he had authorisation to place himself between *Ægir* and the trawler and to return fire. Weir disagreed, emphasising that the instruction not to interfere with a legal arrest was 'paramount' and that fire should not be opened. Confusingly, the MoD at first agreed with the OTC and then later reversed its verdict in favour of Commander Coward.[32] Finally, *Ægir* turned back towards Iceland.

Predictably, a diplomatic 'spat' followed. *Sirius* remained in company with *Lord St Vincent*, which, obtusely under the circumstances, recommenced fishing for a further twelve hours. Robert Turner was suspended for six months by the BTF for disobeying orders not to fish alone and for his boat being found to be within the 12-mile limit.

The *Lord St Vincent* affair was unsatisfactory for the British from all perspectives. Robert Turner was shown to be prepared to break the law, to disobey clear BTF instructions and openly to defy the Royal Navy, which was there in order to afford protection. Again, in this case, there was the threat of anarchy on the part of at least some of the other trawler skippers. On the other hand, it can be argued though that as the fishermen's livelihoods depended on the size of the catch there was the inevitable temptation to seek the best fishing grounds – and not to share that information.

For the Navy, the MoD and the chain of command, the incident showed, yet again, the problems associated with the interpretation of 'hot pursuit'. The inevitable 'winner' was the Icelandic press, which claimed that the RN had deliberately prevented the coastguard from making a lawful arrest. Andrew Welch sums up the whole matter cynically, but probably truthfully, 'The Royal Navy was being used by politicians, who were not prepared to acknowledge that they were fighting a losing battle in order to buy time in the hope that some other solution would turn up.'[33]

The death of an Icelandic engineer on 29 August, who was electrocuted while repairing a damaged section of railing aboard *Ægir* after a minor collision with HMS *Apollo*, was followed by a perilous incident less than a week later when the gunboat *Albert* tried to cut *St Alcuin*'s warps. In attempting to free its cutter, *Albert*'s device caught in *St Alcuin*'s heavy trawl door, which then swung across the trawler's deck, mercifully missing its crew.

These two occurrences underlined the everyday, hazardous nature of the dispute in which extreme weather conditions inevitably played a part. In late October, HMS *Jaguar* reported on its experience of the ever-dangerous effect of severe icing, after one of the autumn storms:

> Most of ice accumulated during three hour period when Force 11/12 winds combined with air temperatures minus 5 degrees to

minus 8.5. It took sixty men three hours whilst running down sea in Force 7 to clear 70 per cent of accumulated ice. A further three hour session today in calm sea has cleaned most of the remainder. Director and platform max 12 in. (of ice?). Bridge wings max. 18 in. solid ice. Forescreen 18in. solid ice overall. GDP area max. 18in. frozen snow and ice. A Turret max 12in. solid ice.[34]

During September, further warp-cutting incidents took place amid accusations and counter-accusations that threatened to worsen the situation and to diminish the chances of reaching a settlement. Iceland banned the landing of sick and wounded British personnel on their soil. FOSNI, in an effort to reduce the number of collisions and near collisions, instructed his ships to use a systematic gradation of 'marking' and only to close mark when a direct threat was posed.

In the end, successive resolutions by the Icelandic Cabinet on 11 and 27 September to break off diplomatic relations with Britain by 3 October, exacerbated by a widely publicised clash between *Lincoln* and *Ægir*, finally brought the politicians to the negotiating table.[35] It could well be construed that the tussle between the two vessels on 21 September was not only 'stage-managed' by the Icelanders for the immediate benefit of the TV cameras aboard the gunboat and in the Fokker Friendship aircraft that flew overhead, but was also intended to become a lever towards reaching a settlement in their favour.

Commander Howard of HMS *Lincoln* described events on that day as, '24 hours of action overshadowed by a maniacal determination on *Aegir*'s part to cut a trawl at any cost'. Howard remarks that Captain Sigtryggsson apparently waited near to the working British trawlers for *Lincoln* to approach before taking any action. A stand-off period ensued with the frigate marking *Ægir*, which sometimes approached within 20ft before heeding *Lincoln*'s warning on the ship's siren.

The frigate commander then stated:

> As we cleared the trawler group he again moved in close and I waved a bottle of whiskey towards him. His first officer indicated that Aegir would accept it and I was about to transfer the bottle by heaving line when Aegir suddenly shot ahead trying to cut under my bow. One of his guardrails stanchions just touched my bow but there was no damage to either ship. Aegir's TV cameras recorded this incident.

Howard added dryly, 'Aegir then stopped for lunch which obviously disagreed with him for in the afternoon he went berserk.'[36]

The description that follows is not short on sarcasm and emotive language, yet the Commander does make plain his interpretation of the true purpose of Sigtryggsson's actions:

> I now had Whitby with me and there followed a maniacal rampage through the trawler fleet which lasted several hours. Aegir again had his embarked TV camera running and TV cameras in the Fokker Friendship now circling also covered events. Aegir was determined to give them a scoop. In his hysterical efforts to cut a warp he rammed me twice and very nearly rammed Whitby. When he rams he means business. He uses his flared bow and holds his wheel on after impact trying to rake down my side and get his strengthened stem into me amidships where my freeboard is lower.

The gunboat finally departed the area at 1800 hours and headed for port but returned shortly afterwards, 'presumably having landed his TV film'. Commander Howard finished his report glumly, 'The weather forecast promises severe gales. It looks like being a memorable weekend.'[37]

Having had time to take stock of the day's tumultuous events, Howard's later signal was more reflective and analytical in tone:

> After his relative docility this morning his savage behaviour this afternoon was surprising. If the TV cameras on Swedish [unclear] he may well have lost face over the whiskey incident. Alternatively, it may have taken time to arrange the more elaborate TV filming from the Fokker Friendship. TV equipped trawlers have reported seeing some of this afternoon's events this evening. ... The question of when to haul off and sacrifice a warp is always to the forefront in my mind.

Howard ended by praising the behaviour of the trawlers and, 'The plucky little tug Welshman ... a qualified member of the Lincoln/Whitby gang.'[38]

Subsequently, the Icelandic Cabinet rejected their Prime Minister's suggestion that they accept the British Government's offer of a *modus vivendi*, which would see the frigates and tugs withdrawn on the understanding that the ICGV would not interfere further with the trawlers. The British also suggested that an offer of an annual quota of 130,000–150,000 tons of fish taken from Icelandic waters might be negotiable.

The Icelandic Government kept to its threat about breaking off diplomatic relations and the Second Cod War ended with the Royal Navy withdrawing from the disputed area and Iceland agreeing not to harass the trawlers. A two-year provisional agreement was reached that would allow the British a 130,000 tons catch per annum within a restricted area inside the 50-mile limit. Crucially, they were to be banned from the key conservation area. One of the Icelanders' principal concerns had been extraction of immature cod, which was popular on the British market but not elsewhere.

Restrictions were also placed on the numbers and the size of the trawlers permitted to work within the 50-mile zone. The Icelandic Parliament finally ratified the plan and on 11 November, HMS *Phoebe* (OTC) led two frigates, an RFA and three defence support tugs back to their bases in the UK. The RAF was permitted to use Keflavik airbase again for national and NATO surveillance flights with the support of Icelandic air traffic controllers.

The agreement was welcomed by the BTF but tempered by the realisation that it was temporary and that the UN Conference on the Law of the Sea (UNCLOS3) was due to begin less than a month later and was expected to advocate a 200-mile fishing limit. But the UNCLOS discussions duly proceeded at a snail's pace, and were spread across several sessions, a year apart. In the meantime, the ICJ finally ruled that Iceland's exclusion of foreign fishing vessels from the 12- to 50-mile zone was unlawful. But events had moved on. On 15 July 1975, Iceland declared a 200-mile delimitation around its shores, which would come into effect on 14 November of that year. Talks proved fruitless, the MoD prepared for the inevitable and resurrected orders for Operation Dewey.

The propaganda battle

There can be little doubt that Britain lost the propaganda battle during the 1972–73 conflict. Officials of the Icelandic Ministry for Foreign Affairs travelled extensively during 1973 in order to elicit support for its country's cause. Meanwhile, as in earlier disputes, the Icelandic embassies conducted a vigorous propaganda campaign. 'Publications on the Icelandic position were distributed; emissaries spoke with influential people and tried to influence them.'[39] Not only various left-wing and more radical student groups across Europe were lobbied, even

Harold Wilson of the opposition Labour Party in Britain was contacted via letter.

Essentially, Britain was 'on the back foot'. James Goldrick notes that in the important area of what he calls 'information management', Iceland, 'made much play of the fact that what became known as "white hulls" (the popular term for coastguard vessels) working for Iceland were facing warships. This contributed to the Icelandic narrative that the British were escalating the conflict, despite the cause being Iceland's claims and actions.'[40]

The Icelanders possessed shorter and more direct lines of communication and exploited modern technology to issue both still and moving images quickly – importantly before the British could hope to process them. They often had control of the 'story' and were able to portray the British as aggressors. Even if journalists and camera crews were embarked in the RN ships they lacked the technical resources at the time to transmit camera footage (which had to be 'landed' ashore before being broadcast), which meant that the British side was invariably 'a response to an already shaped narrative'.

Crucially, the British press lost interest. Despite opportunities to join Nimrod reconnaissance flights or to take passage on one of the frigates, the chances of witnessing a ramming incident or a firing incident were pretty slim, so it did not seem worthwhile for editors to despatch a reporter for what would probably turn out to be a two-week assignment.

The *Lincoln*/*Ægir* encounter towards the end of the Second Cod War became a *cause célèbre* for the FCO and the MoD as they seemed to awaken, at the eleventh hour, to the importance of propaganda. It appeared that the Foreign and Commonwealth Office (FCO), as it was now known, had vetoed the issue of an MoD press statement being made about the incident. Both the MoD and the FCO news departments were apparently in agreement that as the Iceland Government intended to ease pressure on the conflict at the time (presumably in lieu of possible talks), it would be unwise to risk the UK being accused of provoking a 'slanging match'. It later transpired that the Icelanders *did* publicise the event and to their advantage. The FCO then advised that the British Press Association be informed by the MoD that the allegation that HMS *Lincoln* deliberately attempted to ram *Ægir* on 21 September was inaccurate. But, although the MoD press officer subsequently spoke to the Press Association, they chose not to use the information.

There was mutual agreement that the matter had been handled correctly, despite the obvious signs of an unco-ordinated approach, concluding, 'But nonetheless we are taking steps to try to ensure that our procedures are speeded up in future. We have, as you will be aware, a built-in disadvantage that the Icelandic approach to these matters is distinctly less scrupulous than our own.'[41]

Four days later, at a meeting in the MoD titled 'The Icelandic Dispute – Publicity', which was attended by representatives of the Navy, the FCO and MAFF, there was a resolution advanced by the chair that, 'everything possible should be done to sharpen up publicity given to the British version of events'. There were a number of suggestions made but the overall tone of the meeting suggested that it was a battle already won by the Icelandic publicity organisation. Crucially, the British were not prepared to deviate from presenting what they saw as a fair and factually accurate version of events in contrast to what was described, quite tactfully, as the Icelanders', 'less than scrupulous attitude towards the truth'.[42] When it was suggested that a film be produced using models, showing the movements of HMS *Lincoln* and ICGV *Ægir* during the encounter, the idea was rejected by the Director of Naval Warfare (DNW), who had undertaken a thorough analysis of the ship movements leading to the collision. Captain Hepworth concludes:

> DNW doubts if a convincing case can be made to show LINCOLN'S actions to be justified internationally. Details of the movements of ships can only show that LINCOLN did place herself across AEGIR'S bows and that AEGIR did not take sufficient action to avoid her. But LINCOLN'S action is only justified if she was preventing AEGIR from an illegal act, the harassment of trawlers, not in Rules of the Road terms. (Under the latter, LINCOLN was probably the overtaking vessel and thus should have kept out of AEGIR'S way until she was past and clear).[43]

In short, the dispute meant so much more to the people of Iceland and this was reflected in their sharp grasp and very modern attitude to the importance of the media. The British response, in contrast, appears cumbersome and lacking co-ordination, with the press itself not fully engaged. It was, most likely, distracted by the start of a two-year recession at home and the looming prospect of the 'three-day week'.[44]

And so to 'war' – again

The Third Cod War lasted from the middle of November 1975 to the end of May 1976. By some considerable distance, it included the most serious and dangerous clashes between the ICGV gunboats and the Royal Navy warships and accompanying civilian-manned defence vessels. Numerically, it dwarfed the number of individual incidents that had occurred in the 1958–61 and 1972–73 phases of the dispute, as is shown in the summary below.

Summary of Iceland Incidents – Third Cod War

	Collisions		Other Dangerous Manoeuvres		Warps Cut Inside DFA		Warps Cut Outside DFA	
	Involving HM ships	Involving other vessels	Involving HM ships	Involving other vessels	Gear lost	Gear recovered	Gear lost	Gear recovered
Before naval patrols 15 Nov–25 Nov	0	0	0	1	2	2	1	2
First patrol period 25 Nov–20 Jan (8 weeks)	3	5	12	0	2	4	2	1
Interval between patrols 20 Jan–6 Feb	0	0	0	0	3	0	0	0
Second patrol period 6 Feb–30 May (16 weeks)	46	3	38	2	13	9	0	0

(Source: TNA, DEFE 69/675: Fishery Protection off Iceland during the Cod War 1976)

It is beyond the scope of this book to describe more than a representative sample of the more serious engagements that took place, especially during the intense second patrol period during the spring and early summer of 1976.[45]

The interim agreement between Britain and Iceland expired on 13 November and almost immediately two trawlers lost their gear and the close presence of three of the gunboats caused the trawlermen to stop work. Further harassment during the next few days included warp cutting and a near collision. Despite the establishment of a DFA and the presence of the tug *Lloydsman*, frustration among the fishermen increased, exacerbated by poor fishing conditions, and on 23 November they voted to leave unless assurance was given on naval protection.

The first Nimrod LRMP sortie was undertaken a day later and HMS *Leopard* was diverted from its homeward passage to Rosyth following a distant-water FPS patrol off north Norway. Two more frigates, HMS *Falmouth* and *Brighton*, together with RFA *Tidepool*, joined it off Iceland a week later and the familiar pattern of 'close marking' by the frigates and intimidating manoeuvring by the ICGVs resumed and continued into the New Year during the eight-week period referred to by the MoD as the 'first patrol period'.

There followed a brief respite in January and early February when the Navy withdrew from the 200-mile delimitation while a deliberate attempt was made by both sides to avoid incidents. The trawlers were asked to haul their gear if requested and were promised compensation for loss of earnings if required to do so. The uneasy truce lasted until 5 February when ICGV *Baldur* cut *Loch Eribol*'s warps. This prompted the return of the frigates to guard the DFA. Diplomatic relations between the two countries were briefly severed in February, only to be restored in the spring.

The long, sixteen-week, final phase of the war was marked by almost daily efforts by the coastguard vessels to interrupt the fishing boats using what was interpreted by the British as deliberate intimidatory tactics. The frigates countered this with an equally resolute determination to prevent their opponents from gaining the upper hand. This was very often perceived by the Icelanders as provocative, that the RN frigates were using their superior size and speed either to conjure situations where collision was inevitable or by deliberately ramming their ships.

Although, mercifully, no lives were lost, considerable material damage was inflicted as a result of the sheer number of the collisions that took place. The RN's frigates suffered most and the resulting repair costs were considerable. The Type 12 frigate HMS *Yarmouth*, as a result of two, bruising encounters with ICGVs *Thór* and *Baldur* had to be withdrawn to the UK immediately as a result of the damage it suffered over the space of four days.

According to the *Yarmouth*'s CO Commander Mike Jones, he had just completed a RAS on the morning of 24 February when he was alerted by a trawler to the presence in the vicinity of ICGV *Thór* some 25 miles north of his current position. The weather was fair, with sea state 3 and what was described as a 'confused' swell from the south. Jones then received a report from a patrolling Nimrod that *Thór* had passed close to the only trawler currently fishing out of a group of seven British boats. Closing, the CO warned *Thór* unequivocally over VHF radio, 'My instructions are, that I will tolerate no interference with British trawlers fishing legally in International Waters.'[46]

Commander Jones subsequently stationed his ship on the starboard side of the gunboat at about 100ft and claims that he, 'steered him round to the south east to firmly establish my position and attitude'.

Shortly, he relates, 'Thor then commenced a back and fill operation for 3 minutes during which I kept pretty much abeam. I was always fighting to maintain my bow by his bridge both for psychological reasons and as his whaler bow has the most devastating razor edge.' Two collisions followed. Perhaps as a sign of the increasing atmosphere of hostility, Jones notes, in relation to the second one, 'In similar situations, however, with other Icelandic Coastguard Vessel's collision, even at this late stage, has been avoided (sic.).'[47]

Four days later, HMS *Yarmouth* was involved in a more serious incident, this time with ICGV *Baldur*. *Baldur* was a new 740-ton, ice-strengthened, stern trawler that had been built in Poland for an Icelandic fishing company and had only commissioned in 1975. It had been requisitioned by the Coastguard in December of the previous year under the command of Captain Höskulder Skarphéöinsson. *Baldur* gained a reputation, according to the British, for employing particularly aggressive tactics including, 'a trick of swinging her stern into frigates' sides and causing more damage to the Royal Navy than any other Coastguard vessel'.[48] Inevitably there were conflicting claims as to the perpetrator of the numerous clashes that ensued.

On the morning of 28 February, *Baldur*, hitherto undetected, entered the southern end of the DFA but was then spotted by a Nimrod. Two hours later HMS *Yarmouth* took up a marking station to starboard, shielding a group of seven trawlers. *Baldur*, in demonstrating its exceptional manoeuvrability, executed a tight 360 degree circle, managing to set a course towards the trawlers, which were now only 3 miles distant. Commander Jones attempted to ride the ICGV off *Baldur*'s warp-cutting course, the trawler refused to give way and collision became inevitable.

Chris Handley, an aircraft artificer with 829 Naval Air Squadron and member of the ship's flight servicing the single Wasp HAS Mk. 1 helicopter aboard *Yarmouth*, was eyewitness to events that day:

> It took a long time until finally *Baldur*'s captain made a fatal error but the day of judgement was upon both ships. As she slipped across our bows the *Yarmouth*, doing a full 23 knots at the time and still coming out of a sharp turn just could not miss. An almighty thump as our prow buried itself deep into the port side of the ICGV amidships. When the two ships finally parted company the resultant dent in the heavy plating of the *Baldur* was immense.

With other deck damage and, it is thought, the unseating of one of its two prop shafts the engagement was promptly terminated as she turned for home at about 12 knots.

An initial, internal assessment of the bow section of the frigate revealed that HMS *Yarmouth* too had suffered severe damage and that some of the forward compartments had flooded up, although the watertight bulkheads were holding. Later that day, a further examination was undertaken by the senior squadron engineer from HMS *Andromeda*, who confirmed that the ship should return to the UK accompanied by RMAS *Rollicker*. Ironically, the two ships encountered a severe storm on their way to Rosyth, reducing speed to some 4 knots, which delayed their voyage.[49]

ICGV *Baldur* was involved in another serious incident on 27 March, this time with the *Leander*-class frigate HMS *Diomede*. The official MoD 'Iceland Incidents' summary records no fewer than twenty-five attempts to collide with *Diomede* made by the converted stern trawler that day, of which four succeeded. Damage to the RN ship included a 13 x 3ft hole that wrecked the ship's wardroom.[50]

Earlier, the two ships had clashed on 10 March, resulting in minor damage to the frigate. This time, *Baldur* was initially held at bay by Captain McQueen, *Diomede*'s CO, co-ordinating the movements of the defence tugs *Euroman* and *Lloydsman* in the process in order to prevent the gunboat from closing the trawlers. However, in the early afternoon, as McQueen notes in his report, 'there followed a series of manoeuvres by the ICGV which were extremely dangerous and which resulted in four collisions between the two ships, in the last of which BALDUR tore its starboard quarter into DIOMEDE's vulnerable midship section'. He adds, somewhat ruefully, 'There is no doubt that BALDUR was taking full advantage of the restrictions imposed on the Frigates because of the present Rules of Engagement and used DIOMEDE as a "Punch bag".'[51]

Countering the Baldur problem
There can be little doubt that the commanding officers 'on the spot' felt constrained by the fact that, however skilful they might have become in their use of marking and riding off tactics, the Operation Dewey 'Oporder' clearly stated that collisions were to be avoided even at the expense of the trawlers having to haul their gear. In other words, and understandably, all actions should be subservient to the overarching

need to reach a diplomatic settlement to the dispute. Following the *Diomede/Baldur* incident described above, the First Sea Lord, Sir Edward Ashmore, instructed the MoD on 27 March to signal the OTC to the effect that there would be no change to the RoE and that, pending further ministerial considerations, frigates were to avoid sustaining action damage if at all possible and that that should take priority over continuity of fishing.

Despite this directive, Ashmore was fully aware that circumstances at sea had worsened. The above incident, in addition to another serious one the previous day involving ICGV *Baldur* and HMS *Galatea*, persuaded the First Sea Lord that the then current RoE needed to be reviewed urgently. It had been agreed back in mid-January that if the Icelandic gunboat actions became more aggressive, consideration would need to be given to reducing the effectiveness of protection. Admiral Ashmore believed that that point had been reached:

> The collision on 26 March between BALDUR and GALATEA in which the latter suffered a hole 2 feet square, and the four collisions on the 27 march between BALDUR and DIOMEDE (which received extensive damage, including a tear some twelve feet long, bringing our total of badly damaged ships to three), persuade me that a new pattern of deliberate ramming of ships by ICGVs, and particular by BALDUR, has emerged clearly enough to warrant a review of the Rules of Engagement for naval protection off Iceland.[52]

Ashmore summarised the options open to Government: to make no changes to the RoE; to continue to accept damage to HM ships and thus risk casualties; to escalate the RoE. He ruled out sanctioning the use of gunfire (Option Delta of the RoE) 'against so important an ally'. He considered the only form of escalation viable was the adoption of deliberate counter-ramming tactics solely in the case of ICGV *Baldur* to be undertaken by the CDVs (Civilian Defence Vessels) *Lloydsman*, *Euroman* and *Statesman*. The First Sea Lord did concede that the tactic might not prove successful owing firstly to the slow speed of the tugs, secondly that it might be open to criticism from NATO allies and lastly that it was inherently risky, essentially uncontrollable, and could lead to loss of life.[53] The Minister of Trade strenuously opposed any plans to employ the CDVs in counter-ramming. He considered it illegal. He also questioned the legality of using the tugs to interpose themselves as shields between the ICGVs and the RN ships, citing the Collisions Regulations Act, 1965.[54]

In the end, Admiral Ashmore recommended that the Secretary of State should advise Cabinet colleagues that, as a result of the deliberate ramming tactics adopted by *Baldur*, the effectiveness of naval protection had been temporarily reduced. Thus it was to be expected that the Icelanders would take more frequent advantage of the fact that British fishing could be easily interrupted. If the Ministers desired that effective naval protection be restored they would need to sanction the adoption of deliberate counter-ramming tactics against *Baldur* by the CDVs.

Carry on as before

In the event, no alterations were made to the RoE at that stage and the Government was prepared to accept the consequential interruptions to fishing in the meantime. Ashmore concludes his paper by supporting the Defence Secretary, Roy Mason, 'about the desirability of seizing any opportunity to reach a short term agreement with the Icelandic Government'.[55]

HMS *Salisbury* collided with ICGV *Tyr* on five occasions on 1 April. *Salisbury* had been close marking the coastguard vessel in an effort to deflect it from two separate groups of British trawlers. In the course of the first four of the encounters, the frigate, under the command of Commander Hugo White, positioned his ship about 200ft on *Tyr*'s starboard beam and, in a series of 5 degree course alterations to port, endeavoured to head off the gunboat. In reply, *Tyr* would resort to using, 'violent sternboard and accelerating manoeuvres', attempting to get ahead or astern of *Salisbury*.

The frigate was ready for these tactics to be adopted. Special orders appropriate to the ship's diesel propulsion had been prepared. Commander White related, 'With her diesel propulsion and high minimum shaft revolutions, SALISBURY has good brakes and was able on nearly all occasions to prevent TYR from crossing her stern. However TYR's subsequent accelerations and use of wheel was more than SALISBURY could match, and this movement had to be contained by anticipation.'[56]

White regarded the fifth collision that day to be 'potentially disastrous'. Having been frustrated in his attempts to get among the northern group of trawlers, *Tyr*'s captain turned his attention to the main southern group. As the gunboat closed the trawlers, the familiar pattern of manoeuvring was adopted. Eventually, however, 'Tyr achieved a rapid acceleration after a sharp sternboard which left SALISBURY temporarily behind.'

A stern chase ensued. Eventually, the frigate's 4-knot advantage began to tell but as *Salisbury* drew abreast of *Tyr*'s stern, Captain Kjærnested apparently deliberately altered course 30 degrees to starboard across the frigate's bows. Collision was now simply unavoidable, 'and a very serious accident was only averted by rapid application of full starboard wheel. Impact was sharp but not severe as SALISBURY's bow was lifted by a swell and dropped down on to TYR's starboard quarter.'

The frigate sustained several minor splits and dents in its port bow just above the waterline, while *Tyr* received slight crushing to its starboard quarter. Commander White adds caustically, 'She also obtained what must have been spectacular photographs of a collision which would look convincing in any newspaper over a caption "Frigate rams gunboat".'[57]

The small number of gunboats were proving remarkably resilient in contrast to a rapidly growing list of severely damaged RN frigates, which often required urgent dockyard repairs.[58] Therefore, it became important on the British side to exploit every advantage, as with the use of *Salisbury*'s diesel propulsion. The Type 81 'Tribal' class, for example, were fitted with exceptionally large stabilisers, and these too were utilised as a deterrent; the Icelandic vessels were explicitly warned not to approach too close to these ships.[59]

HMS *Gurkha* was involved in five minor collisions with *Óðinn* on 6 and 7 May. Late on the evening of the 6th, the Type 81 adopted a marking position close on *Óðinn*'s quarter as the ICGV ventured within 5 miles of the trawler group. The weather was quite poor and the sea rough with a visibility of three miles:

> During this initial pass down the flank of the fishing fleet ODINN closed to within 8 feet on a number of occasions, often attempting to swing her stern into GURKHA's ship side on disengaging. These attempts were accompanied by some joviality on the bridge of ODINN, but it was apparent that ODINN was very cautious lest he should place his hull too near GURKHA's stabiliser about which he had been warned, and these forays served to forewarn me of his likely tactics in a really determined ramming attempt.[60]

These tactics, requiring precise timing in view of the ship's limited close manoeuvring capability, carried obvious hazards, as Commander T R Lee explained:

> During this close manoeuvring period I found that ODINN could be dissuaded from approaching too close by my accelerating to pose a threat with my stabiliser to his point of maximum beam. However against this had to be weighed the more dangerous possibility that from such a position where his bow was aft of GURKHA's, he could inflict serious damage with his bow by a rapid acceleration towards. Acceleration to pose a threat with the stabiliser therefore had to be delayed until ODINN had closed to about 60 feet. Many such manoeuvres were carried out, and miss distances for about ten such approaches that did not end with collisions varied from six inches to 15 feet.

However, almost inevitably, luck ran out. Late in the afternoon of the next day, in an effort to deflect Óðinn from cutting the warps of the trawler *Ross Ramilles*, the ICGV and frigate collided and as they disengaged Óðinn's port quarter struck *Gurkha*'s starboard stabiliser.[61]

Tipping point

The collisions between Óðinn and *Gurkha* formed only part of a quite extraordinary series of events that took place over the two days, 6 and 7 May, with numerous collisions and attempted collisions involving HM ships *Mermaid*, *Falmouth* and *Gurkha* and ICGVs *Baldur*, *Ver* and Óðinn. The Icelandic gunboats strived to cut the warps of several British trawlers, which had resumed fishing following what seemed to be a more decisive directive from the UK stating that the Government was resolved to support fishing that it considered to be lawful on the high seas. The RN was mandated to allow this to happen. In addition to the collisions between *Gurkha* and Óðinn recounted above, HMS *Mermaid* collided with ICGV *Baldur* following seven near misses. Two trawlers had their warps cut and the OTC in HMS *Galatea*, Captain Gueterboek, requested that the RoE be changed on three occasions in the course of the two days asking permission for the use of gunfire. This was denied each time.

By far the most violent encounters were between *Falmouth* and *Tyr*, resulting in three collisions and serious damage that required both ships to be withdrawn from the area. In his report, Vice Admiral Troup (FOSNI) stated, 'The CO of HMS FALMOUTH was unfortunate in encountering possibly the most aggressive gunboat that night.'[62]

Commander Gerald Plumer, in his Report of Proceedings, describes how he was close marking the gunboat on the afternoon of 6 May. *Tyr* slowed suddenly when abreast of the frigate before turning to port. Plumer sought to mirror the move but *Tyr*'s bow caught his starboard side. Minor damage was caused, buckling the frigate's flight deck nets and deck fairleads.

This fairly minor incident was followed by a far more serious one late the same evening. *Tyr* was closing a trawler at 20 knots with its cutter streamed and *Falmouth* was in a marking position some 100ft from the gunboat's port quarter. Then, with the trawler just six cables away, Commander Plumer felt he had no option left in order to prevent the trawler's warp being cut except to order a turn to starboard. The result was that his ship struck the ICGV amidships on its port side, about 40ft from its stern. Plumer recounted:

The effect of the collision was awful. TYR heeled over 70° to starboard as she rapidly pivoted round my stem until the two ships were lying stem to stern, our port sides grinding past at 3–4 knots. While I appreciated that my bow must be damaged I was concerned about the hull of the TYR and whether any lives had been lost. TYR pulled away quickly astern and I searched the sea for any men who might have been thrown overboard – there appeared to be none.

Just ten minutes later, *Falmouth* was again close marking on *Tyr*'s port quarter. The gunboat still had its cutter streamed and was again approaching the unnamed trawler at 20 knots. Plumer ordered three blasts of the siren as a warning. 'I turned to starboard and as TYR did not turn away the two ships collided in almost similar circumstances to the first occasion. TYR again heeled sharply to starboard and swung round to port moving slowly down my port side as the two ships stopped or went astern.'

Falmouth's commander was even more concerned this time that he had caused serious damage and that men were in the sea. He signalled *Tyr* on VHF offering assistance but received the abrupt reply, 'I want no help from you.' The gunboat then departed in the direction of Iceland.

Plumer concluded his report by regretting the damage he had caused to both vessels but believing it to be his only option if the new RoE was to be followed.[63]

Predictably, the accounts of the clashes between the two ships were reported very differently in the Icelandic press. Oli Tynes had been invited on board HMS *Falmouth* on 6 May to witness events as a 'neutral' journalist and his account was published the next day under the headline, 'Order to ram Tyr'. His opening paragraph read, 'I thought twice yesterday that Tyr would turn over when British frigate Falmouth attacked her in wildest rammings of the Cod War up to now. Tyr listed to 70° to starboard and turned 180° degrees off course. I saw her port screw come up and I also saw her keel.'

Tynes reported that both vessels were steaming close to one another. He did not know if any trawlers were in the vicinity. He deduced that the captain of ICGV *Tyr* was 'somewhat peeved' at being hemmed in by the frigate, which explained why he, Captain Knaernested, made a sudden turn to starboard and manoeuvred his stern close towards the starboard side of *Falmouth*, which moved away. Tynes does not reference the first minor collision that resulted.

However, he does report the second occasion when the ships were again in close proximity. *Falmouth*, he reckoned, was only 100m away from *Tyr*, which reversed and turned towards the frigate. *Falmouth* also reversed at full speed and moved away. Tynes writes, 'I heard captain of Falmouth give order to turn 30° to starboard, which was direct ramming course. Frigate hit Tyr near stern, and she listed so horribly that I have never seen anything like it. British officer on bridge cried, "My God, my God, she is going over."'[64]

He then describes the last of the clashes:

> Later frigate repeated move and rammed her (Tyr) at full speed on port side. Frigate's loud speaker announced, 'Tyr is badly damaged. She is holed and may be in need of assistance.' There were cries of rejoicing on board. It is obvious that British Government have now decided to use tougher measures to protect trawlers and that orders have been given for direct rammings to prevent clipping. When I was on bridge yesterday I heard that tug Lloydsman was approaching. She called up 'I have received orders to dent gunboat.' When asked from whom she had received orders, she replied 'From Galatea'.[65]

Very hostile encounters continued to occur after 6 and 7 May but none quite equalled the intensity of those two days. ICGV *Ægir* attempted to board the trawler *Primella* on 12 May, which was operating off the west coast of Iceland and outside the DFA. The gunboat fired three blanks and one solid shot. A week later, *Salisbury* and *Ægir* collided twice and on the 22nd, which proved to be another busy day, the same ICGV was involved in a minor beam-to-beam collision with HMS *Tartar*, which was attempting to ride it off. *Baldur* and *Eastbourne* and *Leander* and *Ver* were also involved in incidents on 22 May but, with the exception of a collision between *Ægir* and *Tartar* on 26 May, there were no further serious incidents, although the ICGVs continued in their attempts to disrupt the fishing with their warp-cutting runs. The defence forces commenced their final departure from the DFA at 2100 hours on 30 May. The Cod Wars were over.[66]

An end to a 'nasty little war'

Finally, it would seem, there was enough impetus on both sides to bring an end to 'the nasty little war'.[67] The British Foreign Secretary, Antony Crosland, met in Oslo with his Icelandic opposite number and later with the Prime Minister Geir Hallgrimsson. They were present for a NATO Ministerial meeting that presented 'cover' for secret negotiations to take place. The resulting agreement was signed on 1 June 1976.[68] Britain would accept the 200-mile delimitation following what Jón Thór describes as a short, six-month 'phase out' period during which twenty-four British trawlers would be permitted to work within a small, restricted area between 20 to 30 miles from the Icelandic shore.[69]

Crosland, new to his post, made a statement in the House of Commons on 7 June, explaining the strategy adopted by the country. The fishing industry, while recognising that the writing had been on the wall for some time regarding distant-water fishing, nevertheless was said to be shocked by the suddenness and the extent of what was immediately dubbed a 'sell-out'.[70] They set about lobbying both at a local and at national level, '[We would be] interested in the prospect of EEC aid for any re-structuring of the fishing industry i.e. vertical and/or horizontal integration, substantial investment in new vessels, and the retraining of those declared redundant as a result of any imminent contraction in the fishing industry.'[71]

MAFF, as the fishing industry/government 'go-between', had been heavily involved throughout the final phase of the war, basically in preparation for the inevitable that was to follow. Back in March they had been commissioned to produce a wide-ranging report offering an interim future policy for the industry. This was published on 6 May. Later in the month, the Government's ministerial group on fisheries requested the same department to investigate with the Treasury if additional Government aid could be allocated to deal with the problems associated with the inevitable redundancy of both workers and ships and the effect on subsidiary industries such as fish processing and fish meal producers.[72]

Antony Crosland wrote a memo to the Prime Minister in the aftermath of his statement in the House on 7 June. He admitted that what he had said would not mollify the fishing industry but he now wanted to shift some of the responsibility to the EEC, who needed urgently to ameliorate the Common Fisheries Policy and particularly the formal declaration of a 200-mile delimitation. This would bring to a halt the current plundering of the North Sea by what he described as 'refugee trawlers and factory ships'. He also wanted the Community to take the initiative with Iceland in drawing up a long-term plan, although he conceded that larger mesh sizes and smaller numbers of trawlers being employed would be the inevitable outcomes. He added, significantly, 'Prophesies are dangerous but I cannot see how we could ever again fish off Iceland under naval protection.' Crosland gives a typical politician's upbeat conclusion, describing the recent conflict and settlement as a 'Dunkirk', 'We have had heavy but unavoidable losses but we have also secured a breathing space for refurbishing our forces to meet new situations.'[73]

Debrief

Meanwhile, letters of appreciation were received for what was regarded as the Navy's stoic efforts during the recent conflict, including ones from the BTF and the National Federation of Fish Fryers. Although many of the encounters between the Icelandic Coastguard vessels and the Royal Navy had been contentious and bruising in the long period between 1958 and 1976, the latter had remained faithful to its overall brief, which was to protect the trawlers from interference and to provide an environment in which fishing could continue uninterrupted. In truth though, they achieved varying amounts of success in that regard.

The Navy was, for the entirety of this period, entirely subservient to the deliberations and policies of whichever government was currently in office. Lawrence Freedman's recent publication makes it clear that military decision-making cannot be separated from civilian priorities and that commanders have to demonstrate that they can navigate both politics and warfare.[74] However, the Cod Wars were hardly conflicts on a grand scale. For instance, Admiral Edward Ashmore was First Sea Lord at the time and was personally involved during the climactic events of March to May 1976, but does not afford a single line in his memoir to what was happening between the NATO partners in the North Atlantic.

Without doubt, the RN senior commanders felt constrained and frustrated by the RoEs, which prevented them from taking decisive action during the final months of the Third Cod War – witness Captain Gueterbock as OTC, thrice requesting permission to use gunfire over a twenty-four hour period. Andrew Welch writes of a private, pre-patrol briefing between FOSNI and Commander James Weatherall in which Vice Admiral Troup had told him to 'get stuck in'.[75] Indeed, the admiral invariably stood by his frigate captains in their patrol reports, invariably praising their skills and waiving the necessity for any further investigation into the causes of the damage incurred to their ships.

Charles Wylie was the Navigation Desk Officer in the Directorate of Naval Warfare at the Ministry of Defence during the Second Cod War. His duties were to receive all reports of damage to HM ships such as those resulting from the collisions that took place off Iceland. Under normal circumstances these could result in a Board of Enquiry being convened, which might then lead to a court martial. However, 'It was commonplace during the Cod War for FOSNI to recommend NFA [No Further Action] to C-inC Fleet, who usually concurred. My consequent recommendation usually followed the same line.'[76] An unofficial Nelsonic 'blind eye' policy appears to have been adopted.

The Icelandic Coastguard vessels and their crews were undoubtedly the heroes on the 'winning side' and understandably have made the most of their successes against powerful, professional opponents. To this day, ex-ICGV *Óðinn* has been preserved as the proud centrepiece of Reykjavik's Maritime Museum – Iceland's equivalent of the Royal Naval Museum complex in Portsmouth with HMS *Victory* at its heart, perhaps. In 2017, the Hull Maritime Museum was gifted an original warp cutter, donated by the Icelandic Coastguard and the Club of Retired Coast Guard Personnel. This weapon, which proved so decisive during the Second and Third Cod Wars, must serve as an uncomfortable reminder to local people of one of the causes of the hardships that emanated from the loss of a vital part of their fishing industry.

Ultimately, it was the fishermen who had most to lose. The effect on the prosperity of Grimsby, for example, can be measured by the fact that in the early 1960s 25,000 of the town's 57,000 population depended on the fishing industry. When the initial 12-mile limit was declared, catches within the contested area alone were estimated to contribute £4 million of the £11 million net worth of fish landed in Grimsby each year.[77]

Memories of the Cod Wars varied among the fishermen who took part, including where responsibility lay for the outcome and the part played by the Royal Navy. David Rimmer recalls:

> Cod wars? Well a lot of it was just a laugh, to most of us. Not to my son-in-law when they got four shots put through them in the Arsenal but I never got a gear chopped or anything. I got fired on plenty of times like. You know you'd be chased, a gunboat would chase you and put a shot across your bow ... But most of the Cod War it was, I remember the gunboats colliding with them and the tugs colliding with them like.

Others echoed the frustrations felt by the RN at the political restrictions that had been imposed on them:

> The Navy down there but they couldn't do anything because their hands was tied they had to get permission to do this from the government, permission to do that. They were just like that skipper said on one of those videos, they were HMS useless ... They couldn't open fire on a gunboat from Iceland, they'd be in trouble. It was the same with the cutting gear, the gunboats at Iceland would come across your stern, cut in between the British gunboats and they would come in and cut you off, and they couldn't do anything to stop 'em.

Richard Wright considered that the root cause of the problem lay with American access to the air base at Keflavik, 'what the Americans did, they come under pressure from the Icelandic government; they said if we can't get this sorted out, we're going to kick you off Iceland, that's what this was all about, nothing to do with fish'.

THE LAST GASP OF *MARE LIBERUM* 247

Finally, amidst the frustration and acrimony, humour inevitably surfaced. During the First Cod War, the trawler *Vivaria* was being pursued by ICGV *Ægir*, which was closing fast. Its increasingly anxious skipper kept contacting a nearby Royal Navy destroyer, HMS *Broadsword*, which was under orders at the time simply to trail the Icelandic gunboats:

> 'I tell you this Aiga's is chasing on me and he's gaining on me all the time, it's gonna run right into me!' ... So then a bit later Roy (the skipper) comes on again and he's panicky then cause he's very close to him. 'Broadsword Broadsword this is the Vivaria. This Aiga's so close to me that if he gets much closer he'll disappear right up my arse!' So Broadsword come back and he said 'Vivaria this is Broadsword, Captain speaking. Skipper if rape is inevitable enjoy it.'[78]

Chapter Eleven

The Offshore Tapestry
1976–99

WHEN THE ROYAL NAVY emerged from the imbroglio of the last of the Cod Wars, its core Fishery Protection Squadron was faced with an enlarged set of duties different from those it had faced in the late 1950s, some eighteen years previously. The Defence Estimates for the year 1975–76 used the term offshore patrol vessels (OPV) for the first time to identify those ships involved in the generic task of policing what had become known as 'the Offshore Tapestry'. These were now listed as follows:

– Fishery protection, surface patrols and aerial surveillance;
– protection of offshore energy installations;
– policing of safety zones around, and reporting of oil pollution from, offshore energy installations;
– maintenance of a general defence presence.[1]

Additionally, it was stated, for the first time that fishery protection would be shared between surface and aerial surveillance.

The changes had been brought about because the task in the waters around the British Isles was no longer limited to supervising a 12-mile limit, occasionally gathering fishery intelligence further offshore and inspecting fishing vessels permitted by the Joint Enforcement Scheme of the North East Atlantic Fisheries Commission. Since 1964, this area had come under progressively expanded and enhanced forms of domestic jurisdiction. The measures had been introduced principally to extend criminal jurisdiction to cover the increasing numbers of exploration and production platforms in the North Sea. The inshore fisheries limit had also been widened to 12 nautical miles in October the same year as a result of a European Fisheries Conference. While the fishing industry welcomed the resulting extension of their 'exclusive' zone from 3 to 6 miles, it would have preferred the coverage to have been applied to the entire 12-mile area.

On 10 December 1976, Britain enacted its own 200-mile limit, ironically only ten days after the last of its trawlers finally left Icelandic waters. On 1 January 1977, a 200-nautical mile extended fisheries zone (EFZ) was established as a result of the European Economic Community's agreement (to which Britain was party, having become a member in 1973) to establish an Exclusive Economic Zone (EEZ) of the same dimensions. This meant that 320,000 square miles of water (previously 192,000) now constituted the area of sea to which the term Offshore Tapestry would be applied.

This chapter covers the last quarter of the twentieth century. It was a period in which the traditional approach to fishery protection came under quite intense scrutiny. There were repeated calls for the entire task to be privatised and made accountable to the growing number of government departments with vested interests in the Offshore Tapestry. To that end, it was proposed that fishery protection itself could be administered by the fisheries departments more cost effectively and efficiently by using civilian-manned vessels. Likewise, the additional air surveillance role was analysed along the same lines.

At the same time, Britain's new role as a member of the European Community brought fresh demands in a working environment in which, hitherto, it had been able to make its own decisions; there was now a shared responsibility to uphold a new set of rules and regulations. Additionally, the policing of an ever widening area of sea was being tested, particularly by fishing vessels from Eastern Bloc countries. Perennial problems, such as those associated with the legality of 'hot pursuit', also re-emerged.

Finally, the declaration of 200-mile EEZs by many nations including the USA, Canada, Russia and Norway, together with the legacy of the dispute with Iceland, meant that all the traditional distant-water fishing grounds were now covered by 200-mile exclusion zones. The British Fishing Industry was forced to move with the times to become far more EEC oriented. 'Distant-water trawlers were laid up and paid off in huge numbers from 1977 and within a year or so, the British distant-water fishing fleet had all but disappeared.'[2] The impact on the fishing towns particularly was nothing short of disastrous, as was illustrated in Chapter Seven. The impact was felt not only by the fishermen themselves but also by the support sectors upon which the individual fleets depended.

A global re-alignment

A great deal has been written about the decline of Britain as a world power in the twentieth century, a process that can be traced as far back as the early 1920s. After the Second World War, the three 'defeats' in its disputes with Iceland had followed successive concessions over fishing rights off the coasts of Norway and the USSR in particular. These can be interpreted as evidence of the weakening grip of a nation also in the process of dismantling its empire. Domestically, the country was suffering a succession of economic crises and was dogged by rising unemployment, frequent strikes and severe inflation, which exceeded 20 per cent twice during the decade and was rarely below 10 per cent. Unemployment exceeded one million by 1972 and was to rise even higher, passing the million and a half mark in 1978. It climaxed in 1978–79 during the so-called Winter of Discontent with a series of public sector strikes, leading to the collapse of the Labour government in March 1979.

By the same token, after 1960, a number of political decisions had been taken at home that adversely affected the way in which the Royal Navy contributed to Britain's continuing worldwide involvement. During the period 1965–68, the requirement and the means by which the RN would continue to undertake this role was to be undermined as never before by the decisions of a Labour government resolute on making reductions in defence spending to below 6 per cent of the gross domestic product (GDP) of the country. This included the cancellation of the order for a new aircraft carrier, code-named CVA-01, along with its global capability.

The monumental decision to withdraw all British armed forces from east of Suez by the middle of the following decade was taken in January 1968, a few weeks after the devaluation of the pound. This crisis caused the date for withdrawal to be forwarded to 1971, although in the outcome it was not to be fully implemented until the middle of the 1970s. Meanwhile, due care was taken to assure the public that the Navy would continue to play a leading part in the defence of the country. Attempts were made to 'sugar the pill'. According to Eric Grove, the Supplementary Statement on Defence Policy announced in

July 1967, 'made clear that the Royal Navy's future was still secure. It would "continue to play a leading part in the maritime shield forces of NATO" ...'[3]

Nevertheless, in reality, this would mean that the major function of the senior service would be confined principally to an anti-submarine warfare role in the north-eastern Atlantic, while the main striking power of the future would rest with the routinely 'invisible' ballistic nuclear submarine. The effect of this decision, in the eyes of the rest of the world, is summed up by the Argentinian writer Jórge Boveda, writing about the Falklands War of 1982 from his country's perspective:

> This formidable enemy [Britain] was at the time devoted to planning and preparing for the Third Battle of the Atlantic against the Soviet Union. This single threat and single scenario were forced on the Royal Navy by the political necessity to justify their continued existence in terms of their contribution to the Atlantic Alliance's strategy. This had the unfortunate result of eroding the flexibility and autonomous capability of the Royal Navy and of gradually reducing it to the auxiliary role of a specialised ASW force.[4]

A re-examination

Thus, the future focus of the nation and its economy was turning inwards to Europe. Understandably, a good deal of attention was to be paid to the successful exploitation of the oil and gas fields, which offered some prospect of fiscal relief from a succession of world energy crises during the 1970s.

In an uncanny reprise of what happened in the aftermath of the two world wars, all aspects of fishery protection, together with its new security tasks in the North Sea, were subject to intense scrutiny following the end of the Cod Wars. As had happened before with these 'reviews', they concentrated mainly on the way forward rather than analysing the lessons to be learned from past events. The preamble to the Parliamentary Expenditure Committee's written report of the investigation into the fishing industry in 1975–76 gives a detailed insight into what was involved on a typical fishery protection patrol. There is nothing novel in this, except, despite being an operational task currently undertaken by a military force, the nature of FP meant that it was not normally subject to the kind of redaction for security reasons that would have been routine procedure with other aspects of the Royal Navy's work.

A searching 'examination of witnesses' by six MPs who sat on the Expenditure Committee followed the preamble. The witnesses comprised members of the Naval Staff including the then Captain Fishery Protection, Captain M H Livesay, representatives from the Department of Agriculture and Fisheries for Scotland (DAFS) and its England and Wales counterpart, MAFF.[5]

The questions posed were wide-ranging. Inevitably the annual cost of running the Offshore Tapestry was raised. It was asked, with respect to the policing of the offshore rigs, whether 'in terms of public accountability if the capital cost of performing a function which is largely of commercial origin ... fell on the sponsoring department rather than the Navy'. Although the logic of that argument was undeniable, it was sometimes difficult operationally to separate it from the core FP task. The cost of the 'Island'-class programme, which was under way at the time with the first of class HMS *Jersey* about to be commissioned, was defended with respect to pricing in the current highly inflationary environment, 'because we went for a proven design'.[6] The matter of cost was also raised, not for the first time and certainly not for the last, in relation to the use of the RAF Nimrod. The panel questioned whether or not there were cheaper alternatives, such as the Fokker Friendship or the Hawker Siddeley 748.

It was the Navy's opinion that the combination of the 'Island'-class OPVs and the Nimrods would constitute 'the right mix between sea and air' and the 'right quality of resources' for the forthcoming task of patrolling the 200-mile zone. The Nimrod could cover an enormous area in a short time. However, by travelling quickly and usually at a great height it needed to be supplemented by Navy helicopters and sea patrols. It was being proposed that a number of these aircraft should be withdrawn from their normal long-range maritime patrol role and that they would not be fitted with sonar gear.

The MPs also wanted to know why the 'Island' class would not be fitted with helicopter platforms. Captain Livesay stated, 'So far as carrying helicopters is concerned, our experience has been – and this is reinforced by the experience of the Icelandic coastguard ships, that the smaller type of ship has great difficulty in operating helicopters around our island and it tends to be a bit wasteful to install a helicopter platform.' It was later stated that attempts to land boarding parties from helicopters onto fishing vessels had yet to be trialled but it was agreed that it would be a risky and difficult operation and a roundly unpopular manoeuvre for the crew members involved.[7]

A separate investigation into the use of helicopters in fishery protection work was undertaken by the MoD in 1977, particularly with regard to their usefulness in routine patrols, reactions to requests for urgent assistance and hot pursuit. Studies of helicopter-equipped frigates on FP patrols had shown that the aircraft could make useful contributions, leading to the conclusion that autonomous helicopter capabilities should be investigated in future OPV designs. However, boarding operations were 'not viewed with enthusiasm' by crews (echoing Captain Livesay's words earlier). Although the addition of a helicopter did increase patrol effectiveness, it bore an additional cost. The overall assessment was that it carried only a marginal benefit.[8]

It was confirmed that the new 'Island' class had been ordered specifically in relation to the anticipated extension to the 200-mile zone. The fact that the top speed of these ships was limited to 16 knots drew much attention. It was noted that the Russian 'Atlantic'-class trawlers were capable of 17½ knots. One panel member asked, 'Could it be suggested that the Island Class were designed in a hurry and nothing had been prepared for the new task [protecting the oil and gas rigs] and they are basically a JURA design taken off the shelf and into production?' In replying, the MoD confirmed that the design was indeed based on the *Jura*. The advantage had been that it was a ready-made design that could go straight into production and the builder, Hall Russell of Aberdeen, was constructing the vessels to the planned dates while maintaining a very satisfactory standard of workmanship. It was admitted that more speed 'would have been desirable'. However, having taken advice from the MoD Ship Department we 'had learnt that had we required a further four or five knot speed from the Island Class we should have put production back by about two years and we should certainly have increased the cost by probably half as much again to possibly even doubling it'. Thus, a proven design, with good sea-keeping qualities, made speed of secondary importance although, admittedly, it would have been advantageous.[9]

The panel posed further questions to the DAFS representatives concerning the *Jura* design and was told that the overwhelming factor behind it was the vessel's ability to keep the sea in all weather conditions, and certainly when other fishing boats were present. This was particularly pertinent to the sea conditions found off the west coast of Scotland. It had been concluded that, 'Like everybody else, of course, we are limited by financial constraints, but we are satisfied that the speed which was obtained and the sea-keeping qualities provide the best combination of attributes.'[10]

The discussion included other classes of vessels currently used by what was still referred to officially as the Fishery Protection and Minesweeping Squadron. It was noted that the 'Ton' class, which were employed extensively in coastal waters, would be coming to the end of their service lives over the next ten years and would need replacing. It was admitted that the *Kingfisher* or 'Bird' class had not proved to be 'man enough for the job'. Likewise, HMS *Tenacity*, which had so-called 'dash capacity', was too small and uncomfortable in rough weather, making it of limited use beyond a strictly inshore role.[11] Hydrofoils had yet to be examined in relation to the fishery protection task, although it was concluded that the current Boeing design was unsuited to weather in the North Sea.

It is a measure of the importance attached to the new offshore task that the employment of so-called 'high-level wartime capability' warships was also examined. These included the soon to be commissioned Type 22 frigate and 'Hunt'-class MCMVs. Unsurprisingly, both designs were rejected.[12] Finally, the panel asked whether the surplus of laid-up trawlers had been considered for conversion. The MoD stated that, when examined, they had been found to be in a poor physical state, 'we were also very concerned that taking on a series of different kinds of trawlers would pose serious support problems with mixed spare parts and this type of thing'.[13]

This conclusion about the viability of utilising the laid-up trawler fleet was also raised in a long letter in February 1977 from the MoD to the Foreign and Commonwealth Office. Although it was conceded that those vessels could be adapted quite quickly for the task, 'through life costs' would exceed that of the 'Island' class. Interestingly, it was also admitted that the trawlers would be effective for so-called 'harassment tactics' and 'provide a useful additional capability' in that respect.

The methods of harassment were defined as gunfire, ramming, warp cutting, towing appliances to foul trawlers' propellers or fishing gear, close manoeuvring to hinder fishing operations, the use of searchlights at night, likewise to disrupt fishing, and electronic devices to scare away fish. The MoD considered gunfire to be the most effective technique as it carried an immediate impact and its use could be easily calibrated to suit the occasion. Ramming was the second best option, although the effect on the rammed ship was less controllable. Although both of the above techniques were considered the most effective options, their uses were equally difficult to justify in international law and fell into the category of 'disproportionate response'.[14]

The next most effective form of harassment was 'warp cutting' but this was considered to be extremely dangerous if the target ship continued to resist. 'One practical problem is that most RN ships other than minesweepers would have to be modified to enable them to stream and recover the cutter rapidly and this would involve the installation of special high-speed winches; these are not immediately available and would cost in the order of £5,000 each.' The fouling of trawler gear etc had mixed chances of success and increased the likelihood of retaliation. Close manoeuvring was considered to be disproportionately time-consuming, while the use of searchlights and sonic devices were non-discriminatory with little chance of achieving success.[15]

The letter warned of the political implications inherent in the use of any of the above aggressive harassment techniques. One can only speculate on the reasons why these matters were being discussed at the time. The tactics obviously refer back to the experiences of the very recent Cod War, when warp cutting and ramming in particular came to the fore as the conflict worsened. But why was the RN even contemplating an entirely different approach to the fishery protection task? As will be discussed below, the most likely threat to Britain's fishing waters during this period would be from Eastern Bloc vessels. One would have thought that any additional escalation to the already tense relationships in the form of aggressive harassment by fishery protection vessels at the height of the Cold War would have been most unwelcome politically. One can only conclude that this was a reaction to the recent climbdown in the dispute with Iceland, coming as it did at the end of a long succession of political reversals as a world power. The fact that the MoD's remarks were made to the FCO suggests that, in future, the UK would contemplate employing, in the manner of a cornered animal, extreme forms of harassment in defence of its declared EEZ.[16]

Government documents of the period point to a concern that Britain was unprepared for the full implications of its new responsibilities in policing this much-extended sea area. Matters discussed included the current practice of apprehending and arresting a suspected offender, including the firing of warning shots and the use of live ammunition – all within the context of adherence to international law. In the meantime, incidents at sea both illustrated and tested the legislation brought into force following the newly declared 200-mile limit, as in the so-called '*Daniel Roger* incident'.

On 18 March 1977, a boarding party from the FPS minesweeper HMS *Brinton* was carried off by the French fishing vessel *Daniel Roger*, which had been apprehended 4 miles inside British territorial waters. The skipper had been invited to follow the *Brinton* into Dover, had refused and had headed home to Boulogne with the RN boarding party still aboard. The minesweeper had fired four blank rounds as warning and set off in pursuit, obstructed on the way by the manoeuvring of nine other French fishing vessels. Meanwhile, the boarding party had been twice threatened by one of the trawler crew with a knife; later a metal bar had been thrown in the direction of the RN personnel.

The CO of HMS *Brinton* called off the pursuit at the 12-mile limit, having been unable to fire a 'shotted' round across the bows of the *Daniel Roger*, the accepted next step in the procedure for 'hot pursuit'. The RN party was released at Boulogne and returned to the UK, somewhat ignominiously, by public ferry. Formal protests were subsequently lodged with the French with the threat of court action.[17] This incident tested the efficacy of British jurisdiction under the Fishery Limits Act it had passed into law late the previous year.

Admittedly, it was not surprising that misunderstandings should occur when new international legislation was introduced. By the same token, the EEC laws concerning so-called 'third countries', those outside the community, proved to be complex following the 200-mile agreement. It was expected that there would shortly be reciprocal fishing agreements with Norway and the Faroe Islands but Iceland remained a problem. No agreement with Reykjavik meant no return of British boats to their distant-water Icelandic fishing grounds. The USSR, Poland and the German Democratic Republic (GDR) agreed for the first three months to accept average fishing catches equivalent to 1965–74 levels, less 15 per cent. Thereafter Poland and the GDR would lose their right to fish, while the Soviet Union would be limited to a level that took into account a reciprocal agreement that allowed British trawlers to access its historic fishing grounds in the Barents Sea. The special concession to the USSR was a ploy to bring them to the negotiating table. In the event it was to be many years before such an agreement was reached.

Other 'third countries' such as Bulgaria and Romania were informed that fishing would not be permitted with effect from 1 January 1977, although it was proposed that a licensing system would be introduced in due course.[18]

There were a number of articles in the press during the first couple of years, highlighting the problems associated with managing the extended zone and the associated bureaucracy involved in working with the new Community regulations.[19] One article described the RN's task as a 'nightmare', listing no fewer than nine statutory orders that officers had to cope with including licences, quotas, geographical limitations, kinds of catch and sizes of nets. The licensing system restricted the numbers of Eastern Bloc countries working in the North Sea and this had to be managed, while the responsibilities of the boarding officers now included considerable technical knowledge about fish types and net sizes.

Another report in the *Sunday Telegraph Magazine* in 1976 estimated that between 120 and 150 Russian trawlers were using 'vacuum-cleaning methods' to harvest mackerel shoals off the West Country. Worryingly, a separate letter from Flag Officer, Sea Training at Portland stated that forty modern Russian trawlers supported by four mother ships were interfering by incurring on the clear ranges for gunnery serials and delaying submarine resurfacing drills. Certainly Reports of Proceedings and other accounts by COs of FP vessels during the mid-1970s frequently refer to the presence of large Soviet trawlers with their attendant 'mother ships' operating in the English Channel and elsewhere around the coast. As an indication of the attention being focussed on the presence of these vessels, a Navy Minute in July 1976 by the Captain Fishery Protection noted that in 1975 alone seventeen Soviet trawlers had been boarded, while a further 102 had been subjected to what were described as 'lesser investigation' by sea and air.[20]

Of 'donkeys' and 'panda cars'

The purpose-built ships that entered service in the 1970s and '80s, which were to constitute the backbone of the OPV force, were subjected to intense scrutiny by Parliament, by the press and later, more widely, in books and articles relating to naval matters. This could be argued as being disproportionate both to their military importance and certainly to their size. After all, they could only be classed as minor war vessels.

The five, later seven, 'Island' class received the widest coverage, and the most opprobrium. One backbencher in Parliament was notably dismissive. 'The characteristics of the Island class are somewhat dull. These vessels are certainly slow, having a maximum speed of 16 knots. They are equipped with only one Bofors gun. I should describe them as Donkey class ships.' Earlier, Frank Judd, Under-Secretary of State for Defence (Navy), had been kinder, but, nevertheless, he too alluded to their nondescript appearance. 'That precept [referring to the protective task undertaken by the OPV] has led to the creation of what I have described as our "panda car" patrol force in the North Sea.'[21]

The MoD had been under considerable political pressure in the early 1970s to provide suitable defence for the EEZ, including the valuable oil and gas platforms. It instigated a thorough investigation into the best sea-keeping characteristics for the new construction. This in turn established criteria including length, beam, freeboard and sub-division. The focus was directed at commercial designs and the most favoured solution appeared to be the trawler-type fishery protection vessels *Jura* and *Westra*, currently operated by the Scottish Department of Fisheries. *Jura* was subsequently chartered in 1975, commissioned into the Royal Navy and its performance was successful enough for the MoD to order five vessels to be built by Hall Russell of Aberdeen to the same design.[22]

The 'chunky' profile of the 'Island' class stood in marked contrast to that of their immediate predecessors in the more distant-water category of fishery protection ship, the *Blackwood* or Type 14 frigates. In some respects the 'Island' class bore closer resemblance to the *Algerine*-class ocean minesweepers that were widely employed before them on distant-water FP duties during the 1950s. Despite the defence of the 'Island' class mounted by the MoD, that speed was not *the* determining factor and that endurance and sea-keeping qualities counted for more, the adverse criticisms seemed to stick. Likewise, the lack of airborne facilities, at a time when the naval uses of helicopters was growing, continued to be perceived as a shortcoming. Eric Grove sums up, 'Nevertheless, it was recognised that the "Islands" were something of a "quick fix", and in the late 1970s Naval Staff Target (NST) 7040 was drawn up for a more capable and flexible vessel with helicopter facilities that would displace almost 1,500 tons.'[23] The 'Castle'-class design is discussed below.

By the mid-1970s the ubiquitous and numerous 'Ton' class had become the mainstay of the coastal FP division and four were tasked to be at sea at any one time, selected from a pool of between eight to ten of the class. However, serviceability was becoming an increasing problem with these ageing vessels.[24] Readily available alternatives, particularly the 'Bird' class (another 'off the shelf' design), had proved unsatisfactory in the key sea-keeping capability, as noted earlier.

In 1975 it was decided that the roles of Captain Mine Countermeasures and Captain Fishery Protection should be separated, with a Captain RN appointed to each task. This was officially described to be as a result of 'severe overloading'. The separation took effect on 1 May 1975 with the Captain FP exercising day-to-day control of the FPS through the Maritime HQ at Pitreavie under the operational control of FOSNI. Officially Captain FP was also appointed Chief Staff Officer (Fishery Protection) to FOSNI. Significantly, in terms of the blurring of distinction in some areas of the Offshore Tapestry task, it was noted that, 'Inevitably there must be close links between the ships of the Fishery Protection Squadron and those of the MCM squadrons not only in their primary role as MCM vessels but in such operations as the Northern Ireland Patrol.'[25]

Of Tons and Castles

The policing of the new extended fishing limit (EFL) was described in 1977 as a 'two-tier system'. Officially it was conceded that this reflected more of a recognition of the limitations of the available vessels rather than an acceptance that it was the best way of achieving the RN's current and future protection patrol tasks. Therefore, in the immediate future, the 'Tons' would be used exclusively in the 12-mile inshore zone, while the 'Islands' would be assigned to the new EFL. Describing the general unsuitability of the minesweepers for fishery protection, it was stated, 'In addition to some erosion of their War Role efficiency caused by this type of employment, these ships are barely adequate for the tasks because their designed endurance and sea-keeping qualities were not intended for prolonged open water patrol activities.'[26]

It was further recognised that a detailed evaluation of the 'two-tier' system was required. This was undertaken and it was concluded that in the long-term a 'one-tier' system was the better option, with one design of vessel undertaking the 'total patrol task'. This would result in greater operational flexibility, thus crucially leading to a reduction in the number of vessels required despite the total cost of the one-tier choice being marginally higher.[27]

The chosen option to meet the one-tier requirement resulted in the 'Castle' class (OPV Mk. 2). It was expected that six ships initially would be ordered for the Royal Navy. The design was first shown to the public at the Royal Navy Equipment Exhibition in 1979, unveiled as a project aimed at the export market in addition to meeting the needs of the Royal Navy, having been designed by Hall Russell and Co. Ltd as a development of their 'Island'-class OPVs. This was partly true; the detailed ship design was in fact undertaken by a team from the Royal Corps of Naval Constructors under the leadership of David Brown.[28] Eight commercial designs had been considered in the 54–86m range, costing between £3.3 to 8.5 million for what was described as the 'basic ship'. Brown notes, 'We had an elaborate marking frame against which submissions were judged as a result of which we chose my design to be built by Hall Russell.'[29]

Brown researched his subject thoroughly. He concluded that it was unprofitable to put effort into making improvements to the 'Island' design. Consultations with Navy personnel convinced his team that high speed should not be a dominating factor, in reality, 'the required success rate in catching poachers was lower than that in full-scale naval warfare. A moderate number of arrests and convictions would make illegal fishing unprofitable.' The number of trawlers capable of speeds exceeding 12 knots was very small. Although there was pressure on Brown's team to produce a 25-knot ship, in the end 19.5 knots was accepted.[30]

Great emphasis was placed on tackling the problems of discomfort and nausea caused by the rough seas in which the 'Castles' were expected to operate. By producing a longer ship, 81m as opposed to 59.5m for the 'Island' class, Brown was able to incorporate a flight deck aft large enough to accommodate a Merlin helicopter and to bring the living and working spaces to the centre, where ship motion was least. The resulting profile was distinctive and unusual, with a long, flared prow, high freeboard and superstructure concentrated amidships.

Despite frequent references made during the period 1980–85 to the ordering of 'Castle'-class ships Nos 3–6, no orders were forthcoming. Disagreements about capital cost sharing between the MoD and the other Government departments were at least partly the cause of the prevarication.[31] In the meantime the first two Castles, HMS *Leeds Castle* and *Dumbarton Castle*, were both sent to the South Atlantic in 1982 as part of Operation Corporate, the retaking of the Falklands

Islands, where they successfully undertook the role of dispatch vessels, transporting vital supplies south from Ascension Island. A rather bald statement made in the House of Commons in June 1985 brought to an end plans for the 'one-tier' fishery protection ship as a long-term replacement for the 'Tons' and eventually the 'Island' classes: 'OPV3 has not secured a place in the forward defence programme when set against competing priorities for the Royal Navy and for the other services.'[32] The repercussions firstly of the Parliamentary Statement on the 1981 Defence White Paper, the infamous 'Nott axe', and then the lessons of the Falklands War had profoundly affected the future priorities for the Navy. The 'Ton' class was not to be replaced in the immediate future. The impact of that decision was to be felt most acutely in the next decade.[33]

Another factor also began to receive ever greater attention – the question of who should pay for fishery protection. The MoD argued that the relevant civil departments should bear the running costs because the FPS was involved in the peacetime policing of civil regulations, the policy responsibility for which lay with the civil departments. This was not a defence function, therefore those 'stakeholders' should be expected to pay for the running costs of the prospective 'Ton' class replacements and, arguably, to contribute to their building costs. However, in the absence of any ministerial agreement, none of the civil departments had made commensurate provisions in their budgets.[34]

An unexpected interlude

There exist what are probably apocryphal tales of senior RN officers reaching for their copies of *Jane's Fighting Ships* and for hydrographers' maps of the South Atlantic when the Falklands War commenced on 2 April 1982 – such was the unexpectedness and short preparation time for a conflict against a little-known opponent in an infrequently visited part of the world.[35] Amidst the extensive preparations for the launch of Operation Corporate there was a vital need for minesweepers. 'History repeated itself. ... The Admiralty turned to the very vessels which had provided such stalwart service in two world wars – the fishing trawlers.'[36]

Admiral Sandy Woodward, the commander of what became known as the Falklands Task Force, wrote in his memoir, 'One of our submarines (HMS *Spartan*) had already watched the Args laying mines to the east of Port Stanley harbour entrance ... which was after all the most obvious place for us to land. So we knew well enough that they were perfectly capable of laying mines across the northern end of Falkland Sound as well.'[37] Knowledge that the Argentinians possessed the capability to lay both moored and ground mines had been recognised over a month before Woodward's note. Duly, three days later, the Argentinian landing ship ARA *Cabo San Antonio* laid the moored mines that were to exercise the mind of Admiral Woodward as the date of the counter-invasion drew ever closer.

The 'Ton' class were unsuited for the long passage and the heavy seas expected to be encountered in the late autumn in the South Atlantic, moreover the first two ships of the new 'Hunt'-class MCMVs, which might have been employed, were barely operational at the time. The situation demanded that commercial trawlers needed to be used for the task in an uncanny throwback to the two world wars.

Consequently, five deep sea trawlers, *Northella*, *Farnella*, *Junella* and *Cordella* from J Marr and Son Ltd, Hull, and *Pict* from British United Trawlers, were taken up and sailed initially to Rosyth, where military communications equipment was fitted along with the necessary Extra Deep Armed Team Sweep gear (EDATS). The fact that the five ships could be fitted out so quickly was due to the availability of war stocks of minesweeping gear. The trawlers, all between 1,200 and 1,500 tons, were described as 'robust ships and excellent sea boats well used to keeping the seas in all weathers with speeds up to 17 knots and fuel for 60 days at sea'.[38]

It was fortunate, perhaps, that ARA *Cabo San Antonio* had been observed laying 'moored' mines because those could be swept fairly easily, albeit still dangerously, by two minesweepers steaming parallel courses with a wire sweep with cutters suspended between them. The mine, having been cut from its mooring, would float to the surface, where it could be disposed of with rifle fire. Such had been the procedure used extensively in the Second World War. The trawlers were manned by naval crews drawn from the 'Ton' class ships of the coastal Fishery Protection Squadron. Despite protests by many of the trawlermen, the deployment was considered too dangerous to risk civilian life. Nevertheless, some of them managed to get as far as Freetown while training the RN personnel to operate their equipment.[39]

Although the minefield near to Port Stanley had been identified, there was a risk that the enemy had laid further fields in the shallow waters close to the proposed landing areas. The trawlers' steel hulls, noisy engines and deep draughts made them unsuitable for the task, putting themselves at risk of being blown up by magnetic or acoustic mines. The first of the trawlers finally left the holding area at South Georgia on 3 June to start their operations. Admiral Woodward ordered *Cordella*, *Junella* and *Pict* to undertake 'an early MCM check of Berkeley Sound and approaches plus adjacent harbours'. The Amphibious Force commander, Commodore Mike Clapp, expressed concern that the sweepers with their wire sweeps and limited acoustic capability 'could not by themselves reduce the threat to an acceptable level'. But Woodward was adamant, 'the present circumstances require the acceptance of risk to find out if Berkeley Sound is mined. The employment and loss of an MSA (Auxiliary Minesweeper) for this purpose is infinitely preferable to that of a frigate, LPD or hospital ship.'[40]

After Port Stanley had been recaptured on 14 June, copies of the Argentine minefield plans were discovered. Ten of the twenty-one moored mines had been cleared off Port Stanley and the EDATS trawlers were close to completing their work when two of the 'Hunt' class arrived from the UK on 10 July. The five trawlers returned to a heroes' welcome at Rosyth late the same month, bringing to an end a totally unexpected interlude in the life of the nation's fishing fleet.

Privatisation

The pressure on government department financial budgets became ever more acute in the 1980s, as noted above. Firstly, the high cost of providing aerial protection by Nimrod LRMP aircraft came under the spotlight. A Treasury report on the Fishery Protection Service noted that the RAF provided 180 hours of surveillance while RN Sea Devons contributed 100 hours per month in the 12-mile coastal zone. The Nimrods were paid for by MAFF, DAFS, WOAD (the Welsh department) and the Department of Energy (DEn). The ageing Sea Devons were due to be phased out and replaced by a three-year contract awarded to a civilian operator. This would be paid for by reducing the Nimrod provision to 160 hours per month. The attitude towards the use of these highly sophisticated aircraft had changed with a decade's worth of experience. It was noted that the aircraft, 'in many ways are too sophisticated ... for the service required by the fisheries department'.[41]

The UK's commitment to the European Common Fisheries Policy brought into question whether it was necessary for the country to maintain a protection force at the then current level, which in 1982 consisted of seven 'Islands' and twelve other 'patrol craft'. Was this purely to satisfy an EC requirement or did the force have an additional, exclusively national, task to protect home waters against all comers? The answer to the question was 'yes', carrying with it all the wider implications of loss of sovereignty if the answer had been negative and the UK had instead joined some kind of federal European naval force. However, doubts remained about the charging policy. Naturally the MoD needed to continue to carry the burden of the defence task, so what proportion of the total budget should be paid for by MAFF etc.? This matter was becoming contentious and would continue so for the rest of the century.

In the summer of 1984 Michael Jopling, the MAFF Minister, mounted a powerful argument in favour of privatisation. He proposed that on the grounds of cost-effectiveness, the entire fisheries protection operation should be taken over by a commercial enterprise. 'Civilianisation' would, he argued, provide up to 200 additional merchant marine jobs in the private sector and over £27.5 million of prospective orders for the shipbuilding industry, as opposed to £13.5 million if MoD naval contracts were awarded instead. It was estimated that it would save the fishing industry £4 million and the Exchequer £1 million to £1.5 million annually. Jopling added that the arrangement would result in 40 per cent extra seagoing time for RN OPVs, with a similar saving for the RAF Nimrods, and still leave eight vessels available for the ongoing OILSAFE counter-terrorist commitment.[42]

In summation, the options were firstly to allow the Offshore Tapestry arrangements to remain unchanged. This would have the advantage of leaving the task under the operational control of one agency, the MoD. The disadvantage would be that the fisheries departments would not have control of the operations for which they were responsible. The second option was to privatise, which would bring financial savings but would lead to a reduced military presence with possible adverse consequences for deterrence, although it would broadly meet the offshore presence requirement. Thirdly, there was the opportunity to civilianise either the seaborne or the airborne element. Both were operationally distinct but to do so would not fully meet the objectives of the fisheries departments.[43]

A Government press statement, distributed in September 1985, concluded that the last option had been chosen:

> They [the Government] have concluded that the main surveillance and enforcement service provided by the Royal Navy Fishery

Protection Squadron, which complements other, naval tasks should remain with the Royal Navy. Aerial surveillance, where the role is more observation and collection of evidence rather than direct enforcement, can be carried out effectively and at a lower cost by using civilian aircraft of a lighter type than the RAF Nimrods at present employed on this task. In consequence, the use of Nimrods will be phased out as soon as arrangements can be made for the employment of suitable civilian aircraft.[44]

In the meantime, two long-running international agreements were settled during the 1980s. Firstly, the European Common Fisheries Policy (CFP) had been subject to what the Conservative Government claimed had been three and a half years of intense negotiations with Britain's partners, following the failure of its Labour Party predecessors to reach an agreement. The Government stated that the CFP, which had come into force in January 1983, gave Britain better domination of its coastal waters than at any time in its history. One of the key demands had been to ensure that a sensible system of enforcement could be in place so that overfishing or the infringement of access provisions could be avoided. The agreement also made the UK solely responsible for enforcement within its home fishing ports and territorial waters.[45]

A second international settlement was concluded in 1989 when, in the spirit of 'glasnost', reciprocal agreement was reached over fishing rights between the Soviet Union and the European Community. Britain gained access to parts of the Barents Sea and other EC members to the Baltic Sea. In exchange, the Soviet fishing fleet was allowed to fish within European EEZs. Nonetheless, the MoD retained misgivings about the resulting arrangement.[46]

Falling short in the face of cuts

In 1990, in the midst of the collapse of the Warsaw Pact, the MoD commenced a far-reaching study of future defence requirements and policy under the umbrella title of Options for Change. Personnel were to be reduced by 18 per cent, bringing the number in the Navy down to 60,000 by around the middle of the 1990s. Despite the intervention of the First Gulf War and the successful completion of Operation Granby, with a leading part played by the Royal Navy, the 1991 Defence White Paper brought confirmation of the planned reductions together with the loss to the Navy of a further 5,000 men and women. In the words of one writer, 'The overriding requirement was to deliver the Peace Dividend by whatever means possible.'[47]

The disbandment of the Royal Navy's Fishery Protection Squadron by April 1991 was one of the measures considered by the MoD itself in answer to the call for reductions in spending stemming from Options for Change. The RN was requested to contribute and this resulted in a comprehensive and searching analysis report compiled by the Assistant Chief of Naval Staff (ACNS), Rear Admiral Hugo White.[48] The immediate impact of the measures being contemplated would see the paying off of ten minor war vessels and the redeployment of the remainder.

White's report stated that the FPS provided MAFF/DAFS with a total of 1,690 ship days per year.[49] Additionally, the DEn was provided with monthly deterrent patrols with an additional RN vessel on standby within twenty-four hours of steaming from the oil and gas installations. To that end, the Navy allocated one 'Castle' class, seven 'Island' Class and one 'River'-class minesweeper (MSF), plus four 'Ton' class drawn from 3 Squadron MCMV.[50]

However, the ACNS conceded that the FPS had been unable to fully meet this commitment in recent times owing to upkeep overruns and the loss of one 'Castle' to Falklands Guardship duties. The 'overruns' mainly applied to the 'Tons' and even by replacing them with three modern MSFs, as had been suggested in LTC 90, it would result in a 40 per cent reduction in FP capability. Moreover, the Naval Staff considered the other, newer MCMV vessels, the 'Hunt' and 'Sandown' classes, were generally unsuited to FP work owing to their sophistication, lack of speed and requirement for specialist support, currently available only within their base ports.

Admiral White outlined the considerable monetary gain that would accrue from withdrawing from the historic task. A total of £49 million would be saved in the period 1990–95, together with a further £14 million from the scrapping without replacement of three further vessels associated with the task. In addition, if MAFF/DAFS inherited the role, they would seek to purchase 4 (+1) 'Island' class, providing a welcome reimbursement for the MoD.

On the other hand, what had been a significant factor in the RN's wish to retain the task since the matter had been last reviewed in 1985 were the extra roles undertaken by the FP ships in counter-terrorism, dealing with emergency humanitarian incidents, pollution control as well as providing additional assets in time of war.[51] Interestingly, in a true sign of the times, the ACNS drew attention both to the issue of the public perception of the Navy in the modern world and of the importance of morale within the service. Considering the latter point with respect to the FP service itself, he wrote that it was, 'a motivating task with tangible and self-evident results which the RN does well with a high PR profile. Withdrawal from the task, with its obvious implications of a shrinking navy ... would be likely to shrink morale and adversely affect retention fleet-wide at a time of continuing manpower crisis.' He added that, 'minor war vessels provide important, productive and enjoyable training and broadening opportunities for junior officers'.[52] The small size of the fishery protection vessels enabled them to maintain a 'high profile' in many ports around the country. Although public perception was difficult to quantify, it was highly likely that the FPS was also aligned with conservation measures in the eyes of the public. Moreover, they were the only naval vessels with pollution control equipment permanently installed, which again would be visible to the public gaze at Navy Open Days etc.

The ACNS concluded this important section of his assessment:

> The primary arguments in support of retaining fishery protection must centre partly on degradation of the RN's preparedness for its contribution to defence of the UK base, but in particular on the likely adverse impact on naval personnel at a critical moment of high outflow, as well as the likely public perceptions. Withdrawal is unlikely to be understood except as a further signal that the Royal Navy is in an apparently unwarranted decline.

In conclusion, White recommended, 'that the measure in LTC 90 to withdraw the RN from the fishery protection task be rescinded'.[53]

The matter of the charging policy for the services provided by the Royal Navy had been a major source of disagreement during the 1980s but during the last decade of the century an agreed method of calculation had been reached. It was based on an analogue using a tender obtained by MAFF from a commercial shipping company who would be prepared to offer a comparable service to that provided by the MoD. This was updated on a regular basis.

However, the problem remained of the ability of the RN to meet their target of providing 1,690 ship days on duty. A recent decision to cancel orders for three more 'River' class further exacerbated the existing problems, mentioned by Admiral White, caused by the upkeep overruns and loss of one 'Castle'-class OPV. Matters were likely to get worse after the end of the current fisheries agreement in April 1991, when the Navy would be required to prune a further £6.5 million from its budget.

Each of the options considered seemed beset with problems. The 'gap' could be filled by using 'Hunt'-class or the newer 'Sandown'-class single-role minehunters (SRMH). However, concerns existed in both cases over lack of speed. The 'Hunts' could only be considered for the coastal role, thus replacing the remaining 'Ton' class. Moreover, if those vessels were used they would be at reduced readiness in time of crisis or war: it would take two months for them to be 'reconstituted' for their primary MCMV task. Consideration was also given to utilising larger Royal Maritime Auxiliary Service vessels, as had been the case during the Falklands War and the Cod Wars. But this idea was condemned as being impractical, while employing the Royal Navy Reserve, at a time of cutbacks in personnel, was also considered but found not to be a solution, at least in the short term, owing to the provisions of the Reserve Forces Act. Despite the reservations about suitability, it was decided that the 'Hunt' class should be recommended for future service in the FPS. Almost inevitably, the MoD would seek a further reduction in the tasking level from 1992–93 onwards.[54]

The prospect of the Fishery Protection Squadron ceasing to exist must have been on the minds of some rank and file officers within the Navy. The July 1992 edition of *The Naval Review* carried an article with the provocative title, 'Whither or Wither Fishery Protection'. Lieutenant Commander B G Wainwright began, 'The Fishery Protection Squadron is in grave danger of becoming extinct. The Navy's oldest squadron could disappear without a shot being fired unless it is decided that it is in the national interest for the RN to continue the fishery protection task. How can this be, and do we care anyway?'

Wainwright's warning was made in the light of MAFF's latest investigation into the cost-effectiveness of renewing its contract with the Navy. The options were stark, 'If our political masters decide in favour of one of the "privatisation" bids then the RN will either have to undercut the lowest tender, or lose the MAFF contract.' He suggested a third way that would see the creation of a US-style Coastguard force, combining the roles of FP with those of the Customs cutters. However,

Wainwright proceeded to rule out this option because it would be non cost-effective to create a separate small force of that kind.[55]

His solution turned again to the construction of a purpose-built class of vessel. Based on experience with the 'Island' and 'Castle' classes over the previous fifteen years, this would require a vessel of approximately 1,500 tons, approximately 75m long and diesel-electrically powered. His design would include a flight deck, if that was affordable, but he felt it essential that the ships should have global positioning system (GPS) equipment, 'very affordable, and fitted to nearly every fishing boat in the EC'. Finally, Wainwright stressed that ships' complements should be kept to the minimum, which included the provision for an unmanned engine room. He concluded that it was in the 'national interest' to retain some form of coastal patrol and that the RN should continue to exercise the task.[56]

When the five-year contract came up for renewal in 1999, MAFF recommended that it should be awarded again to the Royal Navy. The Fisheries Department was not by any means satisfied with the service it was receiving, however, what was noticeable in comparison with earlier reviews was that the criticism was constructive rather than concentrating simply on the savings that might accrue from privatisation.

It was pointed out that in 1995 a total of 229 ship days of patrolling had been lost due to bad weather, caused either by the FP vessels being unable to leave port or being at reduced effectiveness, which meant they were unable to undertake boardings. The 'Hunt' class was considered slightly more susceptible to bad weather than the 'Islands' and generally performed less well than the OPVs, but both were considered superior to the 'River'-class MSFs. The length of postings for RN officers, which was currently between eighteen months to two years, was thought to be too short, providing an unnecessary burden on initial training for what was a demanding and complex task.[57]

The tone of the criticism was not severe, however, instead it suggested ways in which the service might be improved in each case. Evidence that the quality of the provision provided by the Navy could not be adequately replicated by another body had been recognised in an earlier internal memo entitled 'Combining anti-harassment with surveillance and enforcement duties'. That memo argued that the actual frequency of incidents involving fishing vessels was insufficient alone to justify the maintenance of an RN ship at sea if it was not also carrying out fishery enforcement duties. Nor could the timely presence of an RN ship be assured at a time of crisis. The system only functioned through a combination of the two factors.

Two examples were given of this argument. The 'Cherbourg Incident', which took place in March 1993, began when two fishing inspectors from the local Guernsey fishery protection launch *Patriot* were abducted by the French fishing boat *Impatiens*. An exclusive 6-mile delimitation around the Channel Islands had been recognised by the EU the previous year but the regulation had not been accepted by some of the French fishermen who had traditionally worked those waters. The situation became tense as the *Impatiens* headed for the port of Barneville-Carteret and the fishery officers reported that they were being threatened with knives. HMS *Pursuer*, whose complement included twelve university students, was in the area and set off in pursuit. Its CO, Lieutenant Kingwell, partially bluffing, requested permission to board the *Impatiens* if the threats to harm the fishery officers continued. This ruse worked and the two men were recovered by the French coastguard before entering territorial waters.[58]

Two days later, the 'Hunt'-class MCMV, on regular FP duty, intercepted the trawler *La Calypso* in the disputed waters and ordered the French fishing boat to Saint Peter Port. As had occurred with *Impatiens*, *La Calypso*'s skipper ignored the instruction and set off for Cherbourg with three RN sailors aboard, which were landed when the boat reached harbour. However, HMS *Pursuer*'s sister ship *Blazer* happened to be in Cherbourg at the time and received the full brunt of the French fishermen's frustrations. A mob boarded the ship, dragged it from its moorings and ringed it in mid-harbour. The Union Jack was seized dramatically and burned, and it was feared that *Blazer* might run aground.

The situation was calmed somewhat by the arrival of the French Navy and HMS *Blazer* was able to sail for Guernsey. A flotilla of thirty-six French trawlers had steamed to Saint Peter Port in the meantime amid threats to blockade the port. Kingwell brought *Pursuer* to the Guernsey capital and *Blazer*, together with the French boats (including *Impatiens*) in close attendance, spent a tense few hours in an uncomfortable 'stand-off'. 'Overnight we planned for trouble: the upper deck was manned and we prepared to prevent protesters coming aboard in a repeat of the Cherbourg incident.' Having made their point, the French boats departed the next day. Following further minor incidents the matter was settled after a diplomatic exchange of notes the following year.[59]

'Dutch herring busses on the fishing ground' by W V Velde. (*National Maritime Museum PAH 1711*)

HMS *Champion*: HM sloop on the North America & Newfoundland Station in the late 1820s. (*National Maritime Museum PW6107*)

'Fleeting': the face of fishing's increasing industrialisation in the 1870s. (*North East Lincolnshire Museums Service*)

HMS *Hearty*: fishery protection vessel in the 1890s. (*Author's Collection*)

HMS *Doon*: *Mersey*-class trawler. (*Abrahams, Devonport*)

S/T *Lucida*: HMS *Doon*'s adversary during the Skipper Jinks 'saga'. (*Author's Collection*)

HMS *Harebell*: *Anchusa*-class sloop, which undertook extensive service on the Murman coast in the 1920s. (*Abrahams, Devonport*)

Nova Scotia and Newfoundland, and the much-contested fishing grounds, are pictured in this late nineteenth-century print. (*Author's Collection*)

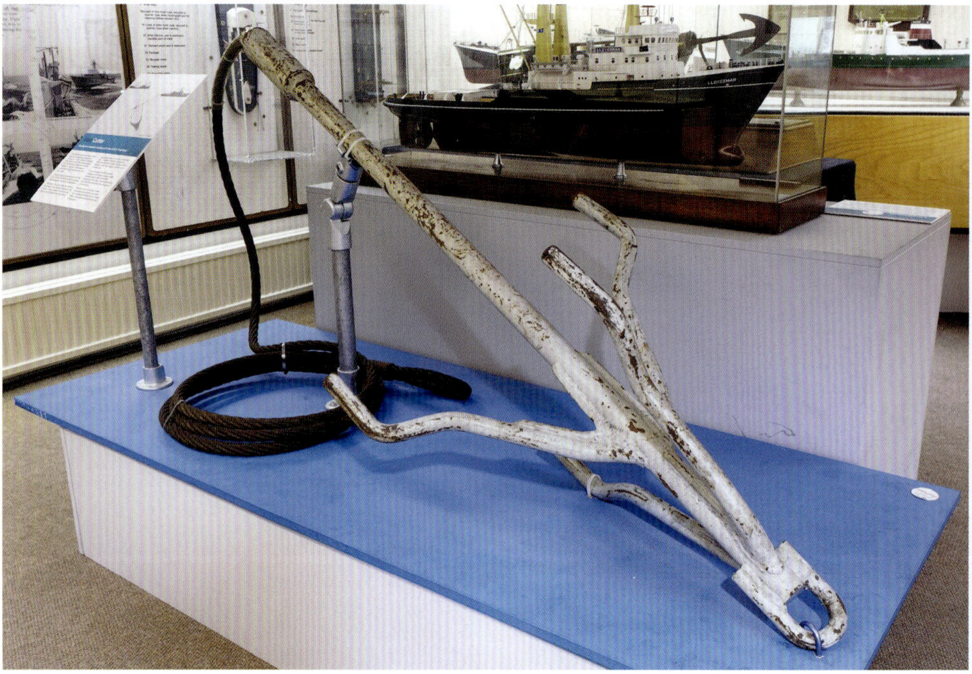

The infamous trawl cutter gifted by the Icelanders to the Maritime Museum at Hull. (*Courtesy of Maritime Museum: Hull Museums*)

The reactivated Batch 1 'River'-class HMS *Tyne* at Falmouth in January 2019. (*Author's Collection*)

Neither the 'River'-class MSF HMS *Blackwater* nor the 'Bird'-class HMS *Kingfisher* proved adequate for fishery protection work. (*Author's Collection*)

The innovative 'Castle'-class OPV HMS *Leeds Castle* entering Portsmouth Harbour. (*Courtesy of John Jordan*)

A brand-new Batch 2 'River'-class HMS *Medway* photographed in 2019 with HM Naval Base Portsmouth in the background. (*Courtesy of Stephen Dent*)

There were also problems in the Bay of Biscay in 1993 following reports of damage to gear and harassment by Spanish fishermen. Once HMS *Anglesey* arrived in the area to check that the UK tuna fleet complied with EU net size regulations, the disturbance ceased. The MAFF was of the opinion that, without the intervention of the RN, it was unlikely that the tuna fishermen would have been able to continue their work.[60] The report concluded that prospects for 'good order' in the fishing grounds were not encouraging over the next four or five years. There were likely to be problems because of the pressure over declining fish stocks, market instability and the integration of Spain and Portugal into the European CFP fraternity, which allowed increased access to waters around Ireland. Therefore, it was vital that the UK retained the ability to react decisively and effectively when interests were threatened. The Royal Navy was in the best position to offer the necessary support. 'The outstanding feature of the FPS is the degree of respect it commands from UK fishermen and those of other countries, both for its authority and the impartiality with which it undertakes its enforcement responsibilities.'[61]

The final submission to the Parliamentary Secretary entitled 'Fisheries Enforcement: Surface Surveillance' was made in January 1998, ahead of the renewal of the contract in March 1999, and importantly it accepted a reduction in patrol days from 1,140 to 1,030. It was felt that the reduction was acceptable because of the diminishing size of the UK fishing fleet. However, it was on the proviso that every effort would be undertaken to make more extensive use of the 'Island'/'Castle'-class OPVs, better use of officer training and improved levels of effectiveness and efficiency, including the introduction of satellite monitoring.[62]

In the spotlight

Historically, it could be argued, the Fishery Protection Squadron had been the embodiment of the 'silent service'. It had carried out its routine duties mostly out of sight of land, the minutiae of its work only familiar to those directly involved with the nation's fishing fleet. Its vessels might have been recognisable in some of the smaller ports around the country and it was possible that one of its number would be present at a fleet review, distinguishable by virtue of its bright blue and yellow squadron pennant. This was not the case during the last quarter of the twentieth century when the *raison d'être* for the FPS came sharply into focus because of its crucial role as part of the Offshore Tapestry, and its continuing existence as a duty performed by the Royal Navy was questioned as never before.

In the 1970s, as has been shown, the UK was in the process of adapting to a new set of international circumstances in the midst of a series of internal economic crises. The fishing industry was in decline, its lucrative distant-water presence had all but disappeared and it now worked in partnership with the other signatories to the European Common Fisheries Policy.

The matter of how best to 'police' a vastly expanded EFZ containing a large number of precious oil and gas rigs became a central debating point during the late 1970s and early '80s. There was also the issue of which government departments should pay. This was complicated because the Offshore Tapestry encompassed the security of the oil/gas installations, routine fishery protection and the need for both surface ships and aircraft to also be available to deal with national and international military crises.[63]

The key debating point, towards the end of the century, centred on the suitability of the Royal Navy to undertake the core fishery protection task. The MoD, MAFF, the Treasury and the Home Office each contributed its point of view. Following the last review of the century, MAFF, the leading 'customer', concluded that the RN should continue to provide the service by virtue of the authority, respect and impartiality it demonstrated in its work among the fishing fleets.

In reality, however, coping with the demands of the Offshore Tapestry had been a struggle for the Royal Navy. It had been made worse by the need to spend less money on defence owing both to the parlous state of the UK economy in the early years of the period under question and later to the effects of the 'peace dividend' at the end of the Cold War. Inevitably, fishery protection was not seen as a priority in terms of defence spending, as had happened so often in past times. Although some progress seemed to have been made with the building of the 'Island' and the 'Castle' classes towards proving the FPS with suitable, purpose-built vessels, the force was still dependent on being supplemented either by the obsolete 'Ton' class or the newer MCMVs – increasingly specialised ships that had not been designed for fishery protection. This unsatisfactory state of affairs would not be addressed until the beginning of the next century.

Chapter Twelve

What's in a Name?
2000–22

THIS CHAPTER BRINGS the long narrative of the Royal Navy's association with protecting the nation's seawater fisheries to the present day. Spending on defence so far this century has been subject to quite alarming cutbacks, notably in the Strategic Defence and Security Review 2010, but post-Brexit there has been a re-evaluation, particularly in the light of the country's global ambitions in a post-Brexit world that has seen various pledges to increase spending and commensurately the size of the Navy. In the midst of this, the RN has continued to undertake its traditional fishery protection tasks, although these have now been reduced to minimal proportions along with its status as the principal provider of this service. The Fishery Protection Squadron lost its unique identity in 2020. Its vessels were reassigned, confusingly becoming part of the Overseas Patrol Squadron. However, the issue of privatising the whole operation, which was a major topic of debate during the 1980s and '90s, has apparently receded for a while – at least publicly.[1]

The reason why there are currently just three ships assigned to UK fishery protection duties in 2022 can be understood, at least in part, by analysing the relevant fishing industry statistics for the period. It has also been to the RN's advantage in coping with the few vessels at its disposal that the current 'River'-class vessels were purpose-built for the role, unlike in the past when suitability for the rigours of operating under extreme weather conditions seemed to be continually in question.

From 2005 to 2010, the Royal Navy worked in partnership with the Marine and Fisheries Agency (MFA), a civilian executive branch of the British Government charged with controlling sea fishing around England and Wales. The MFA was superseded by the Marine

Management Organisation (MMO) in 2010, which to this day functions as an executive, non-departmental public arm of the Department for Environment, Food and Rural Affairs (DEFRA). Currently, the RN has contractual arrangements with the MMO to provide a fixed number of days of fishery protection. The relevant airborne maritime surveillance capability is also delivered by the same organisation.

The numbers of boardings of both national and foreign fishing boats by FP vessels and the numbers of convictions and fisheries administration penalties arising from them are both indicators of the workload undertaken by the squadron's ships in any given year. Historical, statistical comparisons have shown a decline in both of the above categories.

There have been no major international fishing disputes during the last two decades. However, in 2012, 2018 and 2020, there were altercations between French and UK fishermen in the Bay of Seine, which was immediately dubbed 'the Scallop Wars' by the media. As already noted, one of the final stumbling blocks in the Brexit agreement related to fishing licences. The matter was not settled satisfactorily when Britain formally left the Union and erupted again in May 2021 when French fishing boats attempted to blockade St Helier amidst claims that the terms of the EU–UK trade deal were not being met in the waters surrounding Jersey.

Fishery protection currently forms just a part of the role undertaken by the Overseas Patrol Squadron, not entirely dissimilar to the state of affairs when it constituted a minor unit within the 'Auxiliary Patrol', which included in its brief a plethora of tasks in the immediate aftermath of the First World War.

What the numbers tell us

In October 2021, the Office for National Statistics calculated that the fishing industry contributed around 0.03 per cent of the total UK economics output and around 5 per cent of the broader agriculture, forestry and fishing sector. There were 17,988 full-time equivalent jobs in the 348 fish processing plants around the country. In 2022 there were approximately 11,000 fishers working at sea, representing nearly half the 20,000 in the mid-1990s.[2] Currently, there are some 4,150 fishing businesses in the UK, of which 90 per cent have fewer than five employees. To put the employment numbers into context, historical analysis of the statistics shows that there has been a near continuous decline in the post-war period. This has seen a 55 per cent reduction in numbers between 1948 and 1970 and the overall downward trend has been maintained ever since. Although there were slight fluctuations during the 1970s and '80s, numbers have fallen progressively since 1984.[3]

Commensurately, the size of the British fishing fleet has also fallen since the mid-1990s, by approximately 33 per cent, from just over 8,000 boats to just under 5,000. In 2021 this amounted to 120,286 gross tonnes in Scotland, 60,286 in England, 16,584 in Northern Ireland and 2,206 in Wales.

Britain has been a net importer of fish and related products since 1984. The UK fishing fleet lands approximately 400,000 tonnes of fish in the UK and around 200,000 to 300,000 tons in foreign ports. However, this amount does fluctuate when calculated on a year-on-year basis. For example, there was a distinct dip in pelagic and shellfish landings in 2018–19, a situation that has since corrected itself. In 2019, the UK had the second largest catch total and the seventh largest fleet size in comparison with other EU countries.

It has to be remembered that just under 70 per cent of the current industry output is generated by Scottish fishing, aquaculture and fish processing. None of the remaining areas of the UK contributed as much as 10 per cent to the total.[4] Therefore, in terms of assessing the extent and importance of the RN fishing protection task in this century, one has to bear in mind that the Scottish Fishery Protection Agency took full responsibility for the protection of Scottish fishing boats in the aftermath of Devolution in 1999. Therefore, in making any overall assessment of the level of support required of the Royal Navy, it has to be borne in mind that it now only applies to 30 per cent of the total UK fishing industry output.

In 2013–14, 575 vessels were boarded by the FPS within British fishing limits. This was the lowest annual figure since at least 1997–98. It represented a 36 per cent decrease over the previous year and 59 per cent compared with 2011–12, which had seen the highest number of boardings since 2004–05. Why was this? A likely explanation is that under a new agreement made in April 2013 between the RN and the MMO, the FP ships were no longer exclusively tasked with fishery-related enforcement and therefore were able to undertake other RN activities. They were only expected to be on FP tasking for twelve hours per day while on patrol. Non-marine enforcement duties tended to be concentrated in the south-west of the country due to the concentration of RN training areas, ranges and trials areas in the vicinity. Previous chapters have shown the significance of the North Sea: it is pertinent to state that by the second decade of the twenty-first century 70 per cent of the boardings took place in the Bristol Channel, Celtic Sea, English Channel, Irish Sea and Western Approaches, with the remaining 30 per cent in the North Sea.[5]

Another change that in one sense improved the lives of the fishers was the introduction in 2008–09 of the Fisheries Administration Penalty (FAP), which streamlined the legal process connected with law breaking and removed the necessity for most of the crews of vessels who would previously have been sent to court from having to attend in person. The numbers of convictions and FAPs have fluctuated considerably since the turn of the century, from nearly sixty in 2007–08 to just eight in 2013–14. Since the FAP system was introduced, 39 per cent of convictions have been French nationals, followed by the UK with 21 per cent, Belgium 13 per cent and the Irish Republic 9 per cent.[6]

The Military Aid to Civil Authorities bulletin published in June 2017 showed that the downward trend in boardings and convictions had been maintained; just 278 vessels were boarded (the lowest in at least eighteen years) in the financial year to April 2017, a drop of 40 per cent over the previous year. There were just six convictions resulting, either executed or pending. Nearly three quarters of the boardings (73 per cent) were in the south-west region and 33 per cent of the convictions and FAPs were issued to UK nationals.[7]

This was the last year in which the MoD published the information in this format.[8] Thereafter, there has been a noticeable diminution in the importance attached to the Royal Navy's role. Recently, the Government and MoD have popularised the use of the acronym 'MACA' (Military Aid to the Civil Authorities) as the collective term for all operational deployments of the armed forces of the United Kingdom in support of the civilian authorities, other government departments and the community as a whole.

For a short time there were references made to fishery protection under the list of MACA activities. But in a paper published on 4 August 2016 entitled, *2015 to 2020 Government Policy: Military Aid to the Civil Authorities for activities in the UK*, amidst various references to the way in which the armed forces are utilised in that capacity, it was noted that, 'The Royal Navy's Fishery Protection Squadron *supports* [author's italics] the Marine Management Organisation with fishery patrols and inspections.' In other words, the RN had been relegated to a secondary role. Four years later, fishery protection was merely referred to as one of several 'niche capabilities' undertaken by the armed forces in its MACA role.[9]

New ships for new millennium

By 2000 the ageing and apparently increasingly unreliable 'Island'-class OPVs were in the process of being sold, principally to the Bangladeshi Navy. During the last years of their service, support of these ships had been taken over by Vosper Thornycroft (VT). The same company, in the first agreement of its kind, contracted in May 2001 to construct, lease and support three 'River'-class OPVs, to be named HMS *Tyne*, *Severn* and *Mersey*, over an initial five-year period to cover the replacement phase of the 'Island'-class vessels. Late the previous year, the MoD had set up a Future Offshore Patrol Vessel (FOPV) programme in response to an unsolicited bid made by VT to replace the 'Island' class. Subsequently, the Solent-based firm won the circa £60 million contract following a process of competitive tendering.[10]

The contract introduced a novel leasing arrangement whereby the shipbuilder financed the design and build of the new ships and chartered them to the Navy for an initial five-year period. A second and key element, negotiated under a separate contract, was a Contractor Logistic Support (CLS) package guaranteeing a minimum level of operational availability. 'This arrangement effectively committed VT to making each "River"-class vessel available for 320 days each year compared with around 160 days for the ships they were replacing.' It will be remembered that, at the end of the previous century, MAFF's major bone of contention regarding its contract with the Royal Navy was the latter's inability to achieve its target number of days on fishery protection duties due to vessel breakdowns and shipyard maintenance overruns. It also serves to explain why it was possible to replace the previous five OPVs with just three ships.[11]

Construction of the vessels proceeded at pace. HMS *Tyne* was laid down in September 2001, just six months after the contract was signed. It was launched nine months later and handed over in January 2003. *Severn* and *Mersey* followed at regular intervals and all three vessels were in commission by early 2004. The five-year leasing arrangement was renewed and a further five-year extension was negotiated in 2007 valued at around £50 million. Vitally, the accompanying CLS contract had also proved to be successful in practice and was similarly renewed.

Conrad Waters describes the modern purpose-built OPV as the 'day-to-day workhorses of naval forces across the globe', adding, 'They range from relatively simple vessels built largely to commercial standards and focussed on low-intensity constabulary missions through to more sophisticated ships incorporating the weaponry and command systems necessary for higher intensity war-fighting.' The 'River' class definitely fall into the first category. In keeping with their original requirement to undertake 'policing' duties in coastal waters, the ships were constructed to commercial shipbuilding standards with, as Waters describes it, 'a minimal overlay of Ministry of Defence specifications in areas such as damage control and stability'. The ability to 'keep the sea' has long been a prerequisite for, and a perennial criticism of, some of the Royal Navy's FP vessels and the 'River'-class OPVs were fitted with a fine ram-bow and a larger full-load displacement (1,700 tons as opp,osed to 1,250 tons), both of which were aimed at improved durability in heavy weather.[12]

Interestingly, there are no marked differences between the machinery fit of the 'River' class and its predecessor. Both classes were fitted with MAN (formally Ruston) diesels, albeit with different specifications, which provided sustained speeds of 16 knots in the 'Islands' and a marginally faster 16.5 knots in the three 'River'-class ships. It is of note that the range of the 'Island' class at 12 knots was 11,000 nautical miles, whereas the 'River' class attain a much shorter 7,800 nm at the same speed. The bow thruster fitted to the three VT boats was aimed at improved manoeuvrability. A major criticism levelled at the 'Island' class related to its minimal weaponry. Essentially, the philosophy did not change in the intervening twenty-five years; the 'River' class are fitted with a single 20mm gun, although provision has been made for the installation of a medium-calibre gun if that is deemed necessary at some future stage.[13]

The previous chapter showed that the importance of what is described as the 'human factor' had begun to make an impact on ship design in the 1970s. The VT OPVs are fitted with high-standard accommodation in keeping with the need for the modern sailor to have a suitable environment in which to work. In order to meet the 320 day per year target for availability, it was necessary to introduce a three-watch manning system. Forty-five crew members are allocated to each ship, with only thirty embarked at any one time. These are rotated in a twelve-day handover period. There are sufficient stores carried for up to twenty-one days without replenishment.[14]

The novel leasing arrangement for the three fishery protection vessels was terminated in 2013 when the three ships were purchased outright for the Navy at a cost of £39 million with the aim of keeping them in service for a further ten years. Initially, the MoD announced that it was running a competition to replace the CLS package. The purchase of the ships came about as a result of a decision to devolve the naval budget, including the future equipment programme, to the separate services. This provided the Navy with more flexibility to use any underspend in an imaginative way. Rear Admiral John Kingwell, in his memoir recalling his time as Head of Naval Resources and Plans, stated:

> In 2012 DNRP (Directorate of Naval Resources and Plans) was able to make the case to both the First Sea Lord and the Centre for the Navy to use the underspend to purchase the River Class offshore patrol vessels SEVERN, MERSEY and TYNE which were leased from Vosper for £39m ... I also saw the running on of the River Class as providing another opportunity for the Navy (and Defence). The MoD had a contract with BAE Systems that guaranteed a certain number of days between the completion of the QUEEN ELIZABETH class and the build of five new Batch 2 offshore patrol vessels. Some argued that these would simply replace the existing River Class but in DNRP we believed that they should be used to supplement the existing ships and be available to deploy worldwide.

The apparent turnaround in policy was explained away in 'politician speak' by the Defence Secretary at the time, Philip Hammond, who did have the courtesy to credit the MoD with the plan, 'Buying these vessels is a shrewd move by the MoD ... this contract not only saves money in the long term but ensures the Royal Navy is able to continue to conduct a wide range of operations to protect the UK.' The 'wide range' of operations was a key reference to the extended brief for the vessels, which were now expected to embrace not only maritime security, and counter-terrorism, particularly around the oil and gas fields, but also criminal activities such as smuggling, including people smuggling, and the monitoring of foreign naval vessels as they pass through British waters.[15]

Commonly referred to now as the Batch 1 design, the 'River' class was subjected to exactly the same general criticism as the 'Island' class, for their lack of speed and the absence of an on-board helicopter facility. The latter shortcoming was also aimed at the slightly later 'Castle' class, although the innovative design of HMS *Leeds Castle* and *Dumbarton Castle* addressed the matter of speed, the lack of a helicopter landing platform and also paved the way for higher standards of habitability.

If the Batch 1 'Rivers' represent the more austere end of the OPV 'spectrum', the same cannot be said of the Batch 2 ships, the initial contract for which was signed by BAE Systems in August 2014.[16] It was originally proposed that the Batch 2 vessels would replace the Batch 1s on a one-to-one basis. In May 2018, HMS *Tyne* entered Portsmouth ahead of its pre-planned decommissioning, which was to take place on 24 May 2018. Confusingly, by July 2018 the ship was reportedly still flying the White Ensign sign and therefore still in active service. The Royal Navy subsequently clarified that a formal decommissioning ceremony had not in fact taken place, confirming the ship was still commissioned due to delays in the delivery of the ship's planned successor.[17]

Subsequently, an official announcement of the retention of the three OPVs was made towards the end of 2018 by the Defence Secretary Gavin Williamson. As if to cement this fresh commitment, he spoke in Newcastle aboard HMS *Tyne*, stating that in future each ship would forward operate from its namesake river: in Newcastle, Liverpool and Cardiff respectively. Williamson remarked that the connection with the ships' affiliated locations was intended not only to provide a quick response at a possible time of tension as the country exited the European Community but also more generally it would serve to strengthen the bonds between the RN and the local community.[18] This attractive idea for forward basing was later abandoned due to the complications in logistic support requirements.

This apparently abrupt change of mind resulted from a complex chain of events involving the management (or mismanagement) of naval shipbuilding strategies and schedules during the second decade of this century. A National Audit Office (NAO) report found there had been significant quality issues with the build of the first of the Batch 2 vessels, HMS *Forth*. This had much delayed its entry into service, which did not take place until November 2019 having been ordered more than five years earlier. At the time, the delays were attributed, erroneously as it turned out, to the need to keep the Clyde workforce intact between the completion of the *Queen Elizabeth*-class carriers and the start of the Type 26 frigate programme.[19]

It is unsurprising that much opprobrium has been levelled at the MoD regarding the apparent lack of a discernible strategy and the high cost of the five Batch 2 'River'-class ships, which were initially dubbed by some as superfluous and expensive 'white elephants'. However, one could argue that their value and purpose in the Fleet has been rescued as a result of a fortuitous change in political direction resulting from Brexit.

Following the decision to extend the tasking of the FPS beyond just fishery patrols, HMS *Severn* and *Mersey* demonstrated their capabilities to operate successfully beyond UK coastal waters during deployments to the Caribbean and Mediterranean in 2015 and 2016.[20] After the Brexit vote was announced, a paper entitled *Integrated Operating Concept* was published in September 2020, which explained how the UK armed forces would be rebalanced to provide a more proactive and regular presence around the world. The much more capable Batch 2 class neatly fitted into this new strategy. 'The Batch 2 "River" class will play a prominent part in a new Royal Navy policy of international forward presence, particularly in lower-threat areas. As well as providing greater scope for defence diplomacy, the new approach will reduce some of the pressure on the Navy's overstretched force of surface combatants. The change in the OPV's operational forces has been reflected in the assigning the Fisheries Protection Squadron ships to the Overseas Patrol Squadron in 2020.'[21]

Thus the Batch 2 'River'-class HMS *Forth* is now officially assigned as Atlantic Patrol Tasking (South), based principally in the Falklands, and HMS *Medway* is Atlantic Patrol Tasking (North), in the Caribbean. HMS *Trent* is permanently stationed at Gibraltar, working with NATO in the Mediterranean and on the western seaboard of Africa as far south as the Gulf of Guinea. Meanwhile, HMS *Tamar* and *Spey* have received a good deal of media coverage, having been deployed to the Far East for at least the next five years as part of the Conservative Government's so-called economic and defence 'tilt' towards the Indo-Pacific region. In an interesting twist of fate, HMS *Spey* took part in Operation Island Chief during August 2022 as part of a seventeen-nation exercise focussing on the deterrence of illegal fishing in the south-west Pacific. Currently, it is planned that, 'as the Type 31 frigates enter service, the Batch 2 OPVs will return to the UK, thereby replacing the three Batch 1s'.[22]

Everyday working

Advances in technology, including improved communication channels and the liaison with the MMO, can be identified as significant influences in the way in which fishery protection tasks have changed in the period covered in this chapter. This was summed up recently in an interview with an officer with extensive experience of fishery protection:

> There used to be far more manual eyeballing, and now it's far more electronic, linked to databases to record events and through the vessel monitoring system (VMS). The whole of the regulatory system is far more automated. I personally think this is a good thing, and every fisherman who works within the rules will want to know that the regulations are there to protect them and the industry.[23]

The MMO provides a conduit for information about a particular sea area and the types of vessels working there – identified as low or high risk. The night before, and into the next morning, the MMO monitors their movements using the VMS at the operations room in Newcastle. This gives the FP vessel more in-depth information, such as where a particular boat of interest has been fishing, how long it has been in a specific area, its history, past reports etc. – in other words a complete picture of that vessel.

Lieutenant Commander George Storton, commanding officer of HMS *Mersey*, describes a typical routine:

> In the morning, before boarding there will be a brief by the marine enforcement officers as to which vessels they wish to board and why. Communication plays a very important part. With the introduction of electronic logbooks we can see what type of gear they are using and what a vessel has on board; this plays a vital part in our decision-making process.
>
> Prior to boarding we then go through a complex brief, before putting our officers into the sea boat and sending them toward a vessel. Legislation that they could encounter is taken into consideration, as well as what they might find on board and what they need to specifically look at. They will also highlight any legislation changes with those on board, just in case they are unaware of such changes.[24]

The old analogy of the 'policeman on the beat' still appears to hold true in the general approach underpinning the work of the squadron. As in the past, there needs to be a symbiosis between the fishers, the Navy and MMO personnel. 'We like to be seen by the fishing community, not only as a deterrent but also being able to meet members of the local fisheries agencies and communities – this helps us gain a proper appreciation of the areas we work in.' There is a recognition that inevitably some fishers will look to break the law but there are others who do not deliberately set out to do so. Therefore, it is up to the Navy to make sure that the skippers of the boats that are boarded are fully commensurate and up to date with sometimes quite complex and changing legislation.

Sea boat operations are pivotal in the everyday work of the squadron ships. The Navy began to be fitted with new Pacific 24 RIBs from 2017 onwards. The RIBs have a top speed of 42 knots and can carry up to eight passengers. This provides the ability to undertake the core task for the boarding crews, which is to conduct inspections of hauls day or night, in rough or calm conditions in either summer or winter.[25]

'Albacore', writing in the November 1953 edition of *The Naval Review*, remarked that in the years 1919–39, all but two of the Fishery Protection Squadron commanders had later attained flag rank. The same seems to be true some seventy years later for all ranks, not only those with aspirations to become squadron commanders. Working on small ships brings extra responsibilities in sometimes unforeseen circumstances, 'People in the squadron are conducting roles in the Royal Navy that would be done by a rank or two above elsewhere in the Navy.'[26]

Clashes with an old adversary

It is unsurprising that, given both geographical proximity and a history of disagreements, there were serious incidents concerning British and French fishers that took place either side of Britain's withdrawal from the EU. One 'flashpoint' appeared to be the Bay of Seine where, as noted above, clashes between French and British scallop fishers took place during the second decade of the century.

The scallop fishery is not governed by the quota regime applied to most fin-fish species but instead by the so-called Western Waters Regime, which seeks to place limitations on the work undertaken by vessels over 15m. These vessels are limited by 'kilowatt-days', and these measures of units of effort can be traded between producers in the same way as quotas. The regulations do not apply to vessels under 15m.

In October 2012 French fishing boats surrounded five British vessels and, according to the latter, attempted to ram them, threw rocks and nets and tried to cause damage to propellers and engines. On that occasion, the French coastguard vessel *Esteron* had been present, but had not intervened because the attacks had taken place in international waters.

An apparently amicable agreement had been reached after 2013 but that was placed in jeopardy when the French decided in early 2018 that the regulation should be extended to include the under 15m boats. On 27 August, 'Some 35 French boats confronted a smaller number of UK vessels, with reports of rocks and stones being hurled at UK mariners.'[27] Britain at the time was still a signatory to the EU Common Fisheries Policy, which afforded the right of member countries to fish within each other's EEZs but handed the responsibility to member states to control the activities taking place in its waters.

Marine Management Organisation VMS tracking for 27 August showed that there were sixteen British vessels in the Baie de la Seine area at the time. Although HMS *Mersey* was subsequently despatched to the waters off the south coast, it did not enter the French EEZ as it had not been invited to do so and British lives were not at risk. The UK scallop fleet voluntarily agreed to withdraw from the bay while discussions to resolve the issue were ongoing.[28]

Naturally, *Fishing News* reported the matter on behalf of its principal readership. It was rumoured that the 27 August assault was premeditated; the fact that a TV crew was aboard one of the French vessels appeared to support that claim. According to the British scallop fishers, 'the French were armed with rocks, flares, petrol bombs, lumps of chain, shackles and ropes to foul propellers. Two vessels, *Golden Promise* and *Joanna C*, had windows smashed, and another, *Honeybourne III*, experienced a minor fire that had to be extinguished.' As a consequence, the Scottish dredger attempted to ram a number of French boats following the fire. Three French vessels were damaged in the course of the fracas.

Inevitably, there were calls for the Fishery Protection Squadron to intervene, especially as the vessels were working legally outside French territorial waters. Meanwhile, the French pledged that its navy would intervene in the case of further troubles. Just over two years later there was a further incident. In October 2020, two Brixham-based boats,

Golden Promise and *Girl Macey*, were in the same troubled area, again close to the territorial limit. It was reported that one of the boats was surrounded by five French adversaries, the other by fifteen, and flares, oil and frying pans were thrown at the British boats by the French.[29]

Tortuous EU–UK trade negotiations over fishing quotas, timescales and an industry-specific transition period threatened to become the major obstacle in reaching an agreement ahead of Britain's exit from the European Union, scheduled for the last day of 2020. Again, Anglo-French disagreements lay at the heart of the dispute. Philip Stephens writes, 'Europe held all the cards, as it demonstrated during angry exchanges over fishing rights. [Prime Minister] Johnson had pledged that the UK would regain control of the coastal waters. The fishing industry accounted for only a small fraction of the UK's economic output and many of its trawlers were under – usually European – ownership.'[30] There were rumours that the Royal Navy was strengthening its patrol force amid bellicose calls for tough action in the case of trouble. 'I would seek to make an example and take a [EU fishing] boat or two into Harwich or Hastings. Once you had impounded them, the others would not be so keen to transgress without insurance.'[31]

Lingering tensions between Britain and France over fishery matters had persisted from as far back as the June 2016 referendum result. A seemingly insignificant bureaucratic delay in the issuing of licences to French fishermen to work in the waters off Jersey in May 2021 threatened to escalate into a serious international incident following attempts by French fishing boats to blockade the entrance to St Helier harbour.

A change in regulations had caused a delay in the issuing of licences to seventeen fishing boats. Britain had ceased to be a member of the Common Fisheries Policy at the end of 2020, so it was perhaps inevitable that problems of this kind would occur. The new independent rules specified details such as areas where vessels were permitted to fish, on how many days and what gear could be used. Apparently, forty of the new licences had been issued by the time of the dispute but the French Government accused the British of 'dragging their feet' over the matter and had apparently threatened to cut off power supplies to the island via its three undersea cables.

French fishing boats had entered St Helier Port and were prepared to prevent the cargo ship *Commodore Clipper* from docking. Crews had set off flares and there were reports of one British boat being rammed. HMS *Severn* and HMS *Tamar* were despatched to Channel

Islands waters as a precautionary measure while the French authorities countered by sending the 'Militare Gendarmerie' vessel *Athos*.[32]

Endgame?

The French fishers' accusation that the Jersey authorities were limiting access to the waters around the Channel Islands, and thus were in breach of the post-Brexit arrangements agreed between the EU and the UK, seemed to lie at the heart of the matter. Meanwhile, the Royal Navy's fishery protection ships provided a classic peacekeeping presence, as in the 2018 Scallop Wars dispute described above:

> Several times in the past it has been argued that this kind of role could be undertaken just as effectively, and more *cost*-effectively, by forming a separate, non-military authority. A uniformed, United States-style Coastguard Force has also been suggested which might encompass all forms of border patrol, customs and coastguard work as well as the policing of Britain's very large territorial waters. The on-going migration problem, together with Britain's new requirements as an independent state ready to respond quickly and effectively to crises such as those described above, does lend some credence to the argument. Certainly the Royal Navy might welcome any easing on tasking that would accrue if it was free of protection duties. On the other hand, it would result in a further diminution of opportunities for junior officers to gain early seagoing command experience: a real headache which will be worsened once the Hunt and Sandown MCMV Classes are replaced with unmanned surface and sub-surface vessels.[33]

The protection and supervision of the British nation's fishing fleet has been part of the responsibility of its Navy from long before the service added 'Royal' to its title. But it has been invariably positioned on the fringes and largely ignored or sidelined in historical accounts of all kinds. It has been denied adequate funding and sometimes equipped with ships clearly unsuited to the roles they have been expected to play in some of the harshest of weather conditions.

And yet, as this narrative relates, fishery protection has exactly mirrored the changing fortunes of the Royal Navy itself from an uncertain, rather haphazard beginning, through increasing prosperity and power in the seventeenth to nineteenth centuries to the long decline over the last 100 years. Although the country's fishers have often demonstrated cussedness, and an independence of spirit bordering on and sometimes embracing lawlessness, relations between the 'protectors and the protected' have been good, importantly recognising that the Navy exists only to serve whoever governs the country at the time. By the same token, the benefits of working in a small ship environment, learning very different skills and taking on responsibilities not expected of those who work on larger warships, is appreciated by those who have served aboard the RN's fishery protection squadron ships.

'What's in a name?', Juliet muses rhetorically on the Veronese balcony. 'That which we call a rose/By any other word would smell as sweet.'[34] Juliet is right, of course – the title 'fishery protection squadron' *is* immaterial. However if, at a future point, the last vestige of this role passes out of the hands of the Royal Navy, then regrettably the longest thread in the rich tapestry of this country's naval history will be broken forever.

Appendix 1

Royal Navy Fishery Protection Ships 1896–2022

A statistical comparison of some of the vessels mentioned in the text.

HMS *Galatea* (date mentioned in text: 1896) *Orlando*-class armoured cruiser
Built: Robert Napier, Govan; *completed* 1887; *standard displacement* 5,620 tons; *dimensions*: 300 x 56 x 24 (figures rounded to nearest foot); *machinery*: 2 triple-expansion steam engines, coal-fired; *speed* 18 knots; *complement* 484; *principal armament*: 2 x 9.2in, 10 x 6in guns.

HMS *Skipjack* (1905) *Sharpshooter*-class torpedo gunboat
Chatham dockyard; 1891; 747 tons; 252 x 27 x 11 ft.; 2 x triple-expansion; 19 knots; 91 crew; 2 x 4.7 in.

HMS *Godetia* (1923) 'Flower'-class sloop
Connell, Scotstoun; 1916; 1,250 tons; 268 x 33 x 11ft; 1 x 4-cylinder, triple-expansion; 16.5 knots; 85–116 crew; 1 x 4in.

HMS *Hastings* (1937) *Hastings*-class sloop
Swan Hunter, Tyneside; 1930; 1,045 tons; 266 x 34 x 12ft; Parsons geared turbines (oil-fired); 16 knots; 100 crew; 2 x 4in.

HMS *Allington Castle* (1946) 'Castle'-class corvette
Fleming & Ferguson, Clyde; 1944; 1,060 tons; 252 x 37 x 13ft; 1 shaft VTE (vertical triple-expansion); 16½ knots; 120 crew; 1 x 4in.

HMS *Hound* (1958) *Algerine*-class minesweeper
Lobnitz, Clyde; 1942; 950 tons; 225 x 35 x 15ft; 2 shaft VTE; 16½ knots; 85 crew; 1 x 4in.

HMS *Palliser* (1963) *Blackwood* or Type 14 frigate
Stephen, Clyde; 1957; 1,180 tons; 310 x 35 x 15ft; 1 shaft geared steam turbines; 27 knots; 140 crew; 3 x 40mm.

HMS *Wotton* (1976) 'Ton'-class coastal minesweeper
Philip, Dartmouth; 1957; 360 tons; 140 x 29 x 8ft; 18-cylinder Napier Deltic diesel; 15 knots; 29 crew; 1 x 40mm.

HMS Leeds *Castle* (1981) 'Castle'-class offshore patrol vessel
Hall Russell, Aberdeen; 1981; 1,427 tons; 265 x 38 x 11ft; 2 x Paxman diesels; 20 knots; 40 crew; 1 x 40mm.

HMS *Tyne* (2002) 'River'-class offshore patrol vessel
Vosper Thornycroft, Southampton; 2002; 1,700 tons; 262 x 45 x 23ft; 2 x MAN 12RK 270 diesels; 20 knots; 30 crew, 1 x 20mm.

HMS *Tamar* (2021) Batch 2 'River'-class offshore patrol vessel
BAE Systems, Clyde; 2020; 2,000 tons; 297 x 43 x 12ft; 2 x MAN 16V 28/33D diesels; 25 knots; 50 crew; 1 x 30mm.

Appendix Two

The Icelandic Coastguard Vessel Fleet

Vessels used by Iceland during the Landhelgisstríðin (the wars for the territorial waters)

ICGV *Ægir* I In Service 1929 (rebuilt 1953); Displacement 507 tons; Speed 14 knots, Crew 23, Armament 1 x 3pdr gun (first war)

ICGV *Ægir* II 1968; 1,150 tons; 20 knots; crew 22; 1 x 57mm, 1 x 47mm (second and third wars)

ICGV *Albert* 1957; 200 tons; 13 knots; crew 15; 1 x 47mm (all three wars)

ICGV *Árvakur* 1962; 380 tons; 12 knots; crew 15; nil armament (second and third wars)

ICGV *Baldur* 1975; 740 tons; 18 knots; crew 20; 1 x 47mm (third war)

ICGV *Hermodur* 1947; 208 tons; 12 knots; crew 13; 1 x 47mm (first war)
(Foundered and lost with all hands, February 1959)

ICGV *Maria Júlia* 1950; 138 tons; 12 knots; crew 12; 1 x 3pdr (first war)

ICGV *Óðinn* I 1938 (rebuilt 1954); 100 tons; 11 knots; crew 11; 1 x 3pdr (first war)
(Renamed *Gautur* when *Óðinn* II commissioned)

ICGV *Óðinn* II 1960; 1,000 tons; 20 knots; crew 22; 1 x 57mm (all three wars)

ICGV *Suborn* 1937; 100 tons; 11 knots; crew 11; 1 x 3pdr (first war)

ICGV *Thór* 1951; 920 tons; 18 knots; crew 22; 1 x 57mm (all three wars)

ICGV *Týr* I 1952; 630 tons; 14 knots; crew 15; 1 x 3 pdr (second war)

ICGV *Týr* II 1975; 1,150 tons; 20 knots; crew 22; 1 x 57 mm, 1 x 47 mm (third war)

ICGV *Ver* 1951; 740 tons; 18 knots; crew 20; nil armament (third war)

Appendix Three

'Voices'

Inducement

'The runner would say "Have you got a match?" You'd say, "Yeah I've got a match for ya." You'd put two pound in this matchbox and hand it over. So next thing you know, he says, "Here's a job for ya." 'Cos he's got his two pound hasn't he. Everybody knew it went on. ... Down the fish docks, we used to stand there nine in the morning, might be twenty of you and all of a sudden the runner's come forward and picked you out.'

Distant Water: Stories from Grimsby's Fishing Fleet

Recruitment

The last season's fishing has been a wonderfully good one, some boats earning as much as £500, consequently the temptation to follow the calling of their fathers must be strong in the rising generation, and the parents would also probably prefer to employ their sons themselves, than to allow them to seek service elsewhere. It is not, however, to be expected – the life of a fisherman is notoriously a precarious one, accidents occur, boats are lost and many lives with them, so that it is not improbable that the attentions of the islanders will be turned to the more sure and certain employment offered in her Majesty's Service and that 'stout healthy boys' will in time be induced to offer themselves.

British Naval Documents 1205–1960

Checking

> When the signs in the sky say 'Its' going to blow,'
> And you notice the first of white horses,
> Then its high time to put all your crew in the know,
> And carefully review your resources.

Fuel levels OK? Have you done engine checks?
Is the storm jib right ready to hoist?
Prepared all the sandwiches? Soup on the go?
Are your radio checks fully voiced?

Is everybody briefed? All life jackets on?
Emergency cards at the ready?
Have you ensured the best hand's at the con?
Is the atmosphere calm now, and steady?

From 'Before the Low' by Charles Wylie

Acknowledgements

PRECIOUS LITTLE HAS BEEN written about fishery protection and consequently this book has demanded a large amount of primary source research. Therefore I am most grateful for the kind assistance I received, particularly from the staff at the National Archives at Kew and at the Caird Library at the National Maritime Museum in Greenwich. I would also record my thanks to Adrian Wilkinson, Archivist at the North East Lincolnshire Archives in Grimsby, and his staff who helped me during my visit. I am also grateful to Louise Bowen, Collections Officer, Grimsby Fishing Heritage Centre, and Susan Capes at Hull Maritime Museum.

I consider myself extremely fortunate to have made contact with the 'Ton'-class Association, whose stated aim is to bring together in mutual friendship those who served in 'Ton'-class ships and those who served in support of them. Although a complete outsider, I have received a great deal of assistance, initially through contact with Lieutenant Peter Down JP, FBCS, Royal Navy, the Association Vice Chairman and Editor, TON Talk magazine and website. Peter introduced me to Rear Admiral John Lippiett CB CBE DL, Royal Navy, President of the Association. In addition to contributing the foreword to this book, John Lippiett gave me access to his private papers and to some of his fond memories of serving in the 'Fish Squadron'. I am equally grateful to Commander C G Wylie OBE, FCMI, Royal Navy, who in addition to serving in 'Ton'-class minesweepers, also spent time aboard the Type 14 frigate HMS *Russell* in the early 1960s and experienced the First Cod War as well as fishery protection duties in the Barents Sea. Charles is also a poet and I am delighted to include a snippet from his work in the book.

I also wish to record my thanks to former staff and fellow students at the Greenwich Maritime Institute (GMI), Greenwich University. Dr Martin Wilcox, now at the University of Hull, was very helpful at an early stage of this project. I am grateful too to Dr Byrne McCleod. I would particularly like to thank Professor Roger Knight, who read parts of the manuscript and applied the kind of intellectual rigour I fondly remember from my time at the GMI.

I am grateful to Dr Ian Buxton and to the World Ship Society for providing access to their renowned photographic archive. Additionally, I would like to thank my good friend Mike Hill for volunteering to compile the index, thus relieving me of a task I look upon with both trepidation and dread.

Most of all, I want to record my sincere gratitude to Julian Mannering and Steve Dent of Seaforth Publishing, who have guided me from the start of this project and provided me with support, advice and encouragement at every stage. Finally, I am indebted to my wife Lindsay for her patience over countless hours while I was hunched over a laptop.

Jon Wise, Ross-on-Wye, January 2023

Glossary

A/S	Anti-Submarine
ACNS	Assistant Chief of Naval Staff
ASDIC	Anti-Submarine Detection Investigation Committee (later Sonar)
BoT	Board of Trade
BTF	British Trawler Federation
CASD	Continuous At Sea Deterrence
CDV	Civilian Defence Vessel
CFP	Common Fisheries Policy
C-in-C	Commander-in-Chief
CLS	Contractor Logistic Support
CO	Commanding Officer
CTG	Commander Task Group
DAFS	Department of Agriculture and Fisheries for Scotland
DCNS	Deputy Chief of Naval Staff
DEFRA	Department for Environment, Food and Rural Affairs
DFA	Designated Fishing Area
DEn	Department of Energy
DMS	Director of Mine Services
DNC	Director of Naval Construction
DNI	Director of Naval Intelligence
DNW	Director of Naval Warfare
DoD	Director Operations Division
DoP	Director of Plans
DPS	Director Personnel Services
EDATS	Extra Deep Armed Team Sweep
EEC	European Economic Community
EEZ	European Economic Zone
EFL	European Fishing Limit
EFZ	Extended Fisheries Zone
FAP	Fisheries Administration Penalty
FCO	Foreign and Colonial Office
FdU	Führer der Unterseeboote (Senior Commander U-Boat Service)
FMS	Fisheries and Minesweeping Flotilla
FO/FCO	Foreign Office/Foreign and Commonwealth Office
FOPV	Future Offshore Patrol Vessel
FOSNI	Flag Officer Scotland and Northern Ireland
FOST	Flag Officer Sea Training
FP	Fishery Protection
FP and M	Fishery Protection and Minesweeping (Flotilla)

GLOSSARY

FPS	Fishery Protection Squadron
FPV	Fishery Protection Vessel (Scottish)
GDP	Gross Domestic Product
GDR	German Democratic Republic
GIUK	Greenland, Iceland, UK Gap
GNP	Gross National Product
GOC	General Office Commanding
GPS	Global Positioning System
HA/LA	High Angle/Low Angle
HDML	Harbour Defence Motor Launch
HMG	Her (His) Majesty's Government
ICGV	Iceland Coast Guard Vessel
ICJ	International Court of Justice
LFNO	Local Fisheries Naval Officer
LRMP	Long range Maritime Patrol (Aircraft)
M Branch	Military Branch (Admiralty)
MACA	Military Aid to the Civil Authorities
MAF/MAFF	Ministry of Agriculture and Fisheries/Ministry of Agriculture, Fisheries and Food
MCMV	Mine Countermeasures Vessel
MFA	Marine and Fisheries Agency
MFV	Motor Fishing vessel
MMO	Marine Management Organisation
MoD	Ministry of Defence
NAO	National Audit Office
NATO	North Atlantic Treaty Organisation
NEAFC	North Easter Atlantic Fisheries Commission
OEEC	Organisation for European Economic Co-operation
OPV	Offshore Patrol Vessel
OTC	Officer in Tactical Command
R/T	Radio Telegraphy or Morse
RAS	Replenishment at Sea
RCNC	Royal Corps of Naval Constructors
RFA	Royal Fleet Auxiliary
RMAS	Royal Maritime Auxiliary Service
RNAS	Royal Naval Air Service
RNR	Royal Naval Reserve
RNR(T)	Royal Naval Reserve (Trawler)
RNRPS	Royal Naval Reserve Patrol Service
RNVR	Royal Naval Volunteer Reserve
RoE	Rules of Engagement
RUC	Royal Ulster Constabulary
S/T	Steam Trawler
SBS	Special Boat Squadron
SFPA	Scottish Fishery Protection Agency
SIGINT	Signal Intelligence
SNONI	Senior Naval Officer Northern Ireland
SO	Senior Officer
SRMH	Single Role Minehunter
TGWU	Transport and General Workers Union
UNCLOS	United Nations Convention on the Law of the Sea
VMS	Vessel Monitoring System
VT	Vosper Thornycroft
W/T	Wireless Telegraphy

Notes

Introduction
1. Philip Stephens, *Britain Alone: The Path from Suez to Brexit*, Faber and Faber, London (2021), pp. 409–10 & 417.
2. Jan Rüger, *The Great Naval Game: Britain and Germany in the Age of Empire*, Cambridge University Press, Cambridge (2007), pp. 170–71.
3. Op. Cit., Stephens, *Britain Alone*, p. 171.
4. Newly installed as Poet Laureate, Alfred Tennyson wrote a poem in honour of Queen Victoria that ended: 'By shaping some august decree, Which kept her throne unshaken still, Broad-based upon her people's will And compass'd by the inviolate sea' (To the Queen, March 1851)
5. Steve R Dunn, *The Power and the Glory: Royal Navy Fleet Reviews from earliest times to 2005*, Seaforth Publishing, Barnsley (2021), pp. 267 & 290.
6. N A M Rodger, 'The Naval Service of the Cinque Ports', in N A M Rodger, *Essays in Naval History, From Medieval to Modern*, Ashgate Publishing, Abingdon (2009), p. 646.
7. John B Hattendorff, R J B Knight, A W H Pearsall, N A M Rodger and Geoffrey Till, editors, British Naval Documents 1204–1960, Scolar Press, Aldershot (1993), pp. 11–12. From the *Libelle of Englysche Polyce* (c.1436).
8. E E D Day, 'The British Sea Fishing Industry' in *Geography*, Vol. 54, No. 2 (1969), p. 165.
9. Colin Waters, 'Fisher Folk: Masters, Mates and Kedgers' in *Your Family Tree*, August 2007, p. 46.
10. Chapter Seven shows, by example, that women did work at sea in fishing boats through family connections rather than as a result of a deliberate gender equality policy.

Chapter One
1. N A M Rodger, *The Safeguard of the Seas: A Naval History of Britain, 660–1649*, Penguin Books, London (2004), p. 115.
2. Julian Gwyn, editor, *The Royal Navy and North America: The Warren Papers, 1736–1752*, The Navy Records Society, London (1973), p. 255.
3. Robb Robinson, 'The Common North Atlantic Pool', in David J Starkey, Chris Reid & Neil Ashcroft, editors, *England's Sea Fisheries: the Commercial Sea Fisheries of England and Wales since 1300*, Chatham Publishing, London (2000), p. 9.
4. Brian Lavery, *The Island Nation: A History of Britain and the Sea*, Conway Maritime Press and The National Maritime Museum, London (2005), p. 97.
5. Robb Robinson & Ian Hart, *Viola: The Life and Times of a Hull Steam Trawler*, Lodestar Books, London (2014), p. 16.
6. Adrian G Osler and Katrina Porteous, '"Bednelfysch and Iseland Fish": Continuity in the Pre-Industrial Sea Fishery of North Northumberland, 1300–1950' in *Mariner's Mirror* Vol. 96 No. 1 (February 2010), p. 11.
7. Salt was a valuable commodity in itself in medieval times, being used as a preservative or as a means of flavouring food. Local industries prospered in certain parts of the country, where they collected salt water in pans on a rising tide before leaving it to evaporate. It was also imported. Alan C Jenkins, *The Silver Haul: Trawling and Deep-Sea Fishing*, Methuen and Co. Ltd, London (1967), p. 30. Attempts were

made during the reigns of Queen Elizabeth I and King Charles II to make Wednesdays and Saturdays 'meatless' days as well, a practice referred to as 'Political Lent'. In 1563 legislation was passed requiring the populace, on threat of prison or a fine, to eat fish to the total exclusion of meat, on Fridays and Saturdays, and to content themselves with 'one dish of flesh to three dishes of fish on Wednesdays'. See, Gerald S. Graham, 'Fisheries and Sea-Power', *The Canadian Historical Association* Annual Meeting, Vol. 20, No. 1, 1941, p. 25. https://doi.org/10.7202/300216ar
8. John B Hattendorff, R J B Knight, A W H Pearsall, N A M Rodger, Geoffrey Till, editors, *British Naval Documents 1204–1960* (Scolar Press, Aldershot, 1993). Op. Cit., Hattendorff, et al, *British Naval Documents 1204–1960*, p. 10. 'King Edward III to the Authorities of Great Yarmouth, 6 February, 1344' (in Latin).
9. Op. Cit., Rodger, *The Safeguard of the Seas*, p. 117.
10. Wendy R Childs, 'Fish Production, Trade and Consumption *c*.1300–1530: Control, Conflict and International Trade', in David J Starkey, Chris Reid & Neil Ashcroft, editors, *England's Sea Fisheries: the Commercial Sea Fisheries of England and Wales since* 1300, Chatham Publishing, London (2000). Op. Cit., p. 32.
11. Ian Friel, *Henry V's Navy: The Sea Road to Agincourt and Conquest 1413–1422*, The History Press, Stroud (2015), p. 19.
12. Ibid., Friel, *Henry V's Navy*, p. 22. Rodger notes that 'the king's ships' did not necessarily mean that they were owned by the Crown but might well have been chartered or arrested in order, later, to undertake a particular mission. He adds, 'The suffix "of Westminster", later "of the Tower" was attached to the king's ships, almost in the manner of the modern "H.M.S.", but "ship of the Tower" soon came to be used as one of the phrases for "warship" (in the sense of a merchant ship fitted for war), and ceased to distinguish the king's own ships with any precision'. See, Op. Cit., Rodger, *The Safeguard of the Seas*, pp. 117–18.
13. Op. Cit., Steve R Dunn, *The Power and the Glory*, p. 8.
14. Op. Cit., Wendy R Childs, 'Fish Production, Trade and Consumption *c*.1300–1530', p. 32.
15. Op. Cit., Friel, *Henry V's Navy*, pp. 46, 83–4, 92.
16. Ibid., p. 102.; Op. Cit., N A M Rodger, 'The Naval Service of the Cinque Ports', in N A M Rodger, Essays in Naval History, From Medieval to Modern, Routledge, Abingdon (2018), p. 637.
17. Ibid., Friel, *Henry V's Navy*, p. 102. The balinger *Gabriel* was slightly larger than *Peter* and *Paul* with a crew size of between twenty-eight and forty-three. Strategically, 'sea-keeping' voyages were defensive by nature and did not mean the same as exercising control of the sea.
18. Op. Cit., Hattendorff, et al, *British Naval Documents 1204–1960*, p. 15. 'The Governance of England' by Sir John Fortescue, *c*.1470.
19. Rodger, *The Safeguard of the Seas*, p. 106.
20. Ibid., p. 157.
21. Robb Robinson states that the medieval Icelandic economy largely consisted of farming but by the late thirteenth century the dried cod trade had overtaken homespun cloth in importance. Op. Cit., Robb Robinson, 'The Common North Atlantic Pool', in Starkey et al, *England: Sea Fisheries*, pp. 10 & 11.
22. In 1380 the Norwegian monarchy had entered into a union with the Danish crown that, with the addition of Sweden, became the Kalmar Union in 1397 under a single monarch – an arrangement that would last until 1523. Dependencies of the three states included Greenland, the Faroe Islands and Iceland.
23. By 1586, the Admiralty had invested in a 'wafting ship' that would be used on an annual basis to escort the fishing fleet to Iceland and would remain until the season end in early autumn. It was specifically tasked to provide protection against pirates, privateers and the more renegade elements among the fishing community itself.
24. Op. Cit., Rodger, *The Safeguard of the Seas*, pp. 192–93; Op. Cit., Wendy R Childs, 'Fish Production, Trade and Consumption *c*.1300–1530', p. 33.
25. Op. Cit., Rodger, 'The New Atlantic: Naval Warfare in the Sixteenth

Century' in *Essays in Naval History*, p. 233.
26. Op. Cit., Rodger, *The Safeguard of the Seas*, pp. 221–22.
27. Op. Cit., Robinson, 'The Common North Atlantic Pool', pp. 12–13.
28. John D Grainger, *The British Navy in Eastern Waters: The Indian and Pacific Oceans*, The Boydell Press, Woodbridge (2022), p. 7.
29. Op. Cit., Rodger, *The Safeguard of the Seas*, p. 351.
30. Op. Cit., Rodger, 'The Naval Service of the Cinque Ports', pp. 646–7.
31. Rodger, *The Safeguard of the Seas*, p. 384.
32. Danny Buck, 'Great Yarmouth's Battle against Herring Piracy during the English Civil War', *Norfolk Record Office*, September 2019. www.norfolkrecordofficeblog.org
33. Ibid.
34. Ronald Barback, *The Political Economy of Fisheries: From Nationalism to Internationalism*, University of Hull, Hull (1966), p. 4.
35. Charles Wilson, *Profit and Power: A Study of England and the Dutch Wars*, Martinus Nijhoff, The Hague (1978), pp. 20 & 22.
36. Ingo Heidbrink, 'Fisheries', in N A M Rodger & Christian Buchet, *The Sea in History – The Modern World*, Boydell Press, Woodbridge (2017), p. 366.
37. Jeroen ter Brugge, Fish Promotion in the Netherlands, *c.*1690–1983, in David J Starkey & James E Candow editors, *North Atlantic Fisheries: Supply, Marketing and Consumption, 1560–1990*, University of Hull (2006), p. 110.
38. Op. Cit., Wilson, *Profit and Power*, pp. 33–34.
39. Ibid, pp. 36–37.
40. Op. Cit., Barback, *The Political Economy of Fisheries*, p. 3.
41. Op. Cit., Rodger, *The Safeguard of the Seas*, p. 382.
42. Op. Cit., Wilson, *Profit and Power*, p. 38.
43. Ibid., Wilson, *Profit and Power*, p. 59.
44. Ibid., p. 68.
45. Ibid., p. 122.
46. Op. Cit., Hattendorff, et al, *British Naval Documents 1204–1960*, p. 379. 'J Collier to Andrew Stone', 21 April and 14 May 1747.
47. David J Starkey, 'The Newfoundland Trade', in Op. Cit., Starkey et al, *England: Sea Fisheries*, pp. 100–101. Peter E Pope, 'The Scale of the Early Modern Newfoundland Cod Fishery', in David J Starkey & James E Candow, editors, *The North Atlantic Fisheries: Supply, Marketing and Consumption, 1560–1990*, University of Hull (2006), p. 9.
48. Ibid., Starkey, 'The Newfoundland Trade', pp. 102–104; Ibid., Pope, 'The Scale of the Early Modern Newfoundland Cod Fishery', p. 10. The post of 'fishing admiral' ceased to be relevant after 1729 when a governor for the whole island was appointed. Prior to that, since the early 1600s, governors for particular English colonial settlements had been in office.
49. Op. Cit., Graham, 'Fisheries and Sea-Power', p. 25.
50. (No stated author), *The Fundamentals of British Maritime Doctrine BR1806*, HMSO, London, 1995, p. 66.
51. Op. Cit., Gwyn, *The Warren Papers*, pp. 10–13. Letter: Warren to Burchett (Secretary to The Admiralty Board), 9 July 1739.
52. Ibid., Gwyn, *The Warren Papers*, pp. 33 & 38. Letters: Corbett to Warren and Warren to Corbett.
53. Op. Cit., Gwyn, *The Warren Papers*, p. 50. Letter: Shirley to Warren, 27 January 1745.
54. Ibid., Gwyn, *The Warren Papers*, pp. 44–5 and 62. Letters: Admiralty Board to Warren, 2 January 1745 and Warren to Corbett, 10 March and 18 June 1745.
55. Ibid., Gwyn, *The Warren Papers*, p. 240. Letter: Warren to Vice-Admiral Townsend 16 May, 1746.
56. Ibid., Gwyn, *The Warren Papers*, p. xviii.
57. Olaf U. Janzen, 'The French Raid upon the Newfoundland Fishery in 1762: A Study in the Nature and Limits of Eighteenth Century Sea Power' in Olaf Janzen, *War and Trade in Eighteenth Century Newfoundland*, Liverpool University Press, Liverpool (2013), pp. 133–34.
58. Op. Cit., *The Fundamentals of British Maritime Doctrine*, p. 73.
59. Op. Cit., Janzen, 'The French Raid upon the Newfoundland Fishery', p. 142.
60. Olaf Janzen, 'The Royal Navy and the Defence of Newfoundland during the American Revolution', *Acadiensis*:

Journal of the history of the Atlantic Region, University of New Brunswick, New Brunswick (1984), Vol. 14, No. 1, p. 30.
61. Ibid., Janzen, 'The Royal Navy and the Defence of Newfoundland', p. 36.
62. Roger Knight, *The Pursuit of Victory: The Life and Achievement of Horatio Nelson*, Allen Lane, London (2005), pp. 69–71.
63. Ibid., pp. 71–72.
64. Roger Knight, 'British North Atlantic convoys, 1812–14, and the subsequent rejection of the convoy system' in Paul Kennedy & Evan Wilson, editors, Navies in Multipolar Worlds: from the age of sail to the Present, Routledge, Abingdon (2021), p. 48.
65. Ibid., Knight, p. 51.
66. Roger Knight, *Convoys: The British Struggle against Napoleonic Europe and America*, Yale University Press, New Haven & London (2022), p. 28.
67. Ibid., pp. 47 & 250.
68. Op. Cit., Rodger, 'Mobilizing Seapower in the Eighteenth Century' in *Essays in Naval History*, pp. 3–5.

Chapter Two
1. The 'Long Eighteenth Century' is a phrase used to cover a more natural historical period rather than the usual use of the calendar division by centuries. The expansion of the eighteenth century connects the Glorious Revolution of 1688 with the Battle of Waterloo in 1815.
2. David Cannadine states of this period, 'British ships were unchallenged by any western power. For the first time, that proudly boastful claim, made in 1745, that Britannia rules the waves, had serious and global substance to it.' Quoted in, Op. Cit., Dunn, *The Power and the Glory*, p. 55.
3. Admiral Sir R. Vesey Hamilton, *Naval Administration: The Constitution, Character, and Functions of the Board of Admiralty, and of the Civil Departments It Directs*, Forgotten Books, London (2018), p. 1. Paul Kennedy qualifies this assessment of Britain's world dominance by stating that its naval supremacy was due to the fact that no other nation could build and man the same number of warships, provide the mercantile support in time of war and the string of interconnecting naval bases. See Paul Kennedy, *The Rise and Fall of British Naval Mastery*, Penguin Books, London (2001), p. 157. The country's position as the foremost world economy was severely dâmaged in the course of the intermittent depression it suffered from 1897 until the 1890s. Peace and harmony did not prevail throughout the vast British Empire, certainly during the middle years of the twentieth century. Writing of the Far East, John Grainger claims that the period 1838–1863, '… were the most violent of all, even more so than the preceding French wars'. Op. Cit., Grainger, *The British Navy in Eastern Waters*: p. 205.
4. Neil Ashcroft, 'The Diminishing Commons: Politics, War and Territorial Waters in the Twentieth Century' in Op. Cit., Starkey et. al, Chris Reid and Neil Ashcroft, editors, *England's Sea Fisheries*, p. 217.
5. Op. Cit., Robinson & Hart, *Viola*, p. 18.
6. Ibid., p. 25.
7. National Maritime Museum, Caird Library (NMM), ADL/Q/76, *Service Documents of Captain William Henry Webb 1929–1857*. Letter: British and French Fisheries – permission to inspect.
A similar document to the above, authorised the 'chief boatman in charge of Stan(d)gate Creek Coast Guard Station' to undertake similar, more localised, boardings. See, NMM MSS/70/027, *Papers of Joseph Andrew Ford, Coast Guard 1832–1872*.
8. Op. Cit., Hamilton, *Naval Administration*, p. 102.
9. Ibid., p. 104.
10. Hansard, *House of Commons Debate Vol. 303, 5 March 1886. The Fishing Industries (England and Wales): Institution of a Fishery Board – Observations*.
11. Hansard, *British Parliamentary Papers (BPP)*, Vol. XIV, 1833. Select Committee Report.
12. Ibid., Hansard, *BPP Report*, p. 1.
13. Ibid., Hansard, *BPP Report*, pp. 1 & 2.
14. Hansard, *House of Commons Debate, Vol. 31, 11 February, 1836*. Fisheries of England.
15. The National Archives (TNA), ADM 116/866A, *Sea Fisheries: Protection by H.M. Ships 1884–1904*. Admiralty Memorandum: Officers employed in carrying out the duties connected with the Sea Fisheries, May 1884.

16. Nick Thriplow, Tina Bramhill & Sophie James, *Distant Water: Stories from Grimsby's Fishing Fleet*, North Wall Publishing, Grimsby, (2011), p. 56.
17. Op. Cit., Robinson and Hart, *Viola*, p. 22.
18. Ibid., pp. 18–19.
19. The first experiments with steam power took place in 1870s when paddle tugs were used to tow sail trawlers out of the Humber Estuary. This was followed by the fitting of steam engines in existing sailing trawlers. Some paddle tugs were also fitted for fishing. Eventually, in 1881, the first purpose-built steam trawler, the *Zodiac*, was launched at Earles Shipyard in Hull. See, Jón Th. Thór, *British Trawlers and Iceland 1919–1976*, University of Goteborg Press, Ebsjerg (1995), p. 45.
20. Robb Robinson, Fishermen, *The Fishing Industry and the Great War at Sea: A Forgotten History?*, Research in Maritime History No. 54, University of Liverpool Press, Liverpool (2019), p. 6.
21. Op. Cit., Thór, *British Trawlers and Iceland 1919–1976*, p. 45.
22. FO83/714 *Conflicts between British and Foreign Fishermen in the North Sea Vol. 1*. Letter: Board of Trade to Under Secretary of State, Foreign Office, 25 July 1979.
23. Ibid., FO83/714, *Copy of Telegram with Enclosures from Collector of Customs*, Lowestoft to Assistant Secretary, Board of Trade, London: Statement of Joseph Spooner, Master of the Fishing Smack *Henry & Lydia* of Great Grimsby.
24. FO83/715 *Conflicts between British and Foreign Fishermen in the North Sea Vol. 3*. Petition by Lowestoft Fishery Boat Owners, 9 December 1879. Account by Master of the Fishing Lugger *Alliance*. Ninety-four years later, the Icelandic Coastguard used a 'warp cutter' to great effect during the Second Cod War, causing the tactics by both sides to become more heated and aggressive during the rest of the conflict.
25. Op. Cit., Ashcroft, 'The Diminishing Commons', p. 218.
26. Op. Cit., ADM 116/866A, *Sea Fisheries*: Regulations for the Protection of the Sea Fisheries, 15 April 1889.
27. Ibid.
28. Ibid.
29. MAF 12/10 *Fishing in Foreign Territorial Waters 1892–93*. Letters: November 1891.
30. Ibid., MAF 12/10 *Fishing in Foreign Territorial Waters 1892–93. London Gazette*: Board of Trade Department Statement, 20 October 1892.
31. MAF 12/8 *Outrages on Dutch and German Vessels, 1891*.
32. Ibid.
33. Ibid.
34. *Hansard House of Commons Debate, Vol. 320, 26 August 1887*. North Sea Fisheries: Outrages by Belgian on English Fishing Vessels. The word 'outrage' carries far more emotional weight today than it did in the nineteenth century, when it was used widely simply to describe a perceived wrong-doing. A question about *Lady Godiva* had been asked earlier in the month in the House of Commons. It had been alleged that the fishing smack had been pursued by a German protection cruiser, which had fired a ball cartridge that had struck *Lady Godiva*'s mast and then had collided with it, causing considerable damage. The Secretary of the Board of Trade replied that the Grimsby boat had been within German territorial waters and the North Sea Fisheries Convention applied only to international waters. Details of the subsequent trial of the skipper in the German court had yet to be received by the Board of Trade. This had no doubt prompted Sir Edward Birkbeck's reference to the case on 26 August. See, *Hansard House of Commons Debate, Vol. 318, 2 August 1887*. North Sea Fisheries Convention, 1883 – The smack 'Lady Godiva'.
35. *Hansard House of Commons Debate, Vol. 2, 24 March 1892*. Destruction of Nets on The North Sea Fishing Grounds.
36. Ibid MAF 12/8 *Outrages on Dutch and German Vessels, 1891*. Letter: Commander Russell to Admiral Commanding Naval Reserve, 25 November 1891.
37. Edward Luttwak describes two forms of 'latent suasion' – deterrent and supportive. Both are apposite in the case of the presence of the Royal Navy off the American coast in the early nineteenth century. The Navy's 'deterrent' to a possibly 'antagonistic'

38. United States was, 'as a shadow that impinges on the freedom of action of adversaries, because the capabilities can be activated at any time, while the formulation of the intent to use them can be both silent and immediate'. The supportive nature of latent suasion, applicable in this case to the fledgling Canadian state, lay in the fact that, 'The deployment of naval forces is a continuous reminder to allies and clients of the capabilities that can be brought to their aid.' See, Edward N Luttwak, *The Political Uses of Sea Power*, The John Hopkins University Press, London and Baltimore (1974), pp. 11–13.
38. Andrew Lambert, *The Challenge: America, Britain and the War of 1812*, Faber and Faber, London (2012), p. 3; Op. Cit., Kennedy, *The Rise and Fall of British Naval Mastery*, pp. 149–175.
39. NMM SOT 5, *Official Letters relating to George Scott's naval service 1804–1830*. Letter from Sir Charles Ogle, Rear Admiral of the Red and Commander-in-Chief North American and Newfoundland Stations, 26 August 1829. HMS *Champion* was a 456-ton, 18-gun sloop, launched at Portsmouth in 1824. It was disposed of in 1867.
40. John A Wolter, David A Ranzan & John J McDonagh, editors, *With Commodore Perry to Japan: The Journal of William Speiden Jr, 1852–1855*, Naval Institute Press, Annapolis (2013), p. 20.
41. In what were called the 'Alabama Claims', the United States in 1869 claimed direct and collateral damage against Britain, alleging that it had violated neutrality by allowing five warships to be constructed, especially the CSS *Alabama*, knowing that they would eventually enter into naval service with the Confederacy. On the British side, the Civil War caused a 'cotton famine' in Lancashire in particular, while the Union side's indifference to active Irish Republican groups operating out of the United States was the cause of further friction in the immediate post-war period.
42. NMM MDY/103 *Instructions of H.M. Vessels employed in the protection of the North American Fisheries, 1866–1869*.
43. Ibid.
44. Ibid., MDY/103 *Instructions of H.M. Vessels, 1866–1869*. Report to Admiral C-in-C American Station by Captain Kennedy, HMS *Druid* 1881.
45. NMM, JOD/95/3, *Memoranda relating to Captain John Masterman RN while serving on HMS* Bullfrog, *1886–1888*. HMS *Bullfrog* was a *Banterer*-class gunboat, 465 tons, built at Pembroke Dock in 1881.
46. Robb Robinson, 'The Common North Atlantic Pool', pp. 11–14, in Op. Cit., Starkey et al, *England's Sea Fisheries: The Commercial Fisheries of England and Wales since 1300*.
47. Op. Cit., Ingo Heidbrink, 'Fisheries', in Rodger & Buchet, *The Sea in History*, p. 368. Robb Robinson describes the extraordinary efforts made by Icelandic farm workers living in the interior of the island to reach the sea in time for the winter fishing season. Ibid., Robinson, 'The Common North Atlantic Pool', p. 12.
48. MAF 12/4 *Complaints, Offences etc: Fishing Vessels in Foreign Territorial Waters, 1887–89*. Letter: Admiralty to Secretary of the Board of Trade, 28 September 1872. HMS *Valorous* was a wooden-hulled, second-class paddle frigate launched at Pembroke Dock in 1851.
49. Ibid., MAF 12/4, *Complaints, Offences etc*. Lloyd's List announcement May 1877.
50. The accusation that the evidence about *Corvos*'s intrusion into territorial waters was based on hearsay was raised in the House of Commons on 20 April 1899.
51. *Cod Wars – 1893*. Hullwebs History of Hull. www.hullebs.co.uk/content/1-20c/industry/fishing/cod-war/cod-war.1893
52. *Hansard: House of Commons Debate*, Vol. 70. Arrest of British Trawlers by Danish Gunboats.
53. ADM 116/100, *Faroese and Icelandic Fisheries, 1899*. Letters: Foreign Office to Secretary of the Admiralty, 24 March and 5 May, 1899.
54. Ibid., ADM116/100, *Faroese and Icelandic Fisheries, 1899*. Letter with instructions for Captain, HMS *Galatea*, 12 May 1899.
HMS *Galatea* was an Orlando Class armoured cruiser, first commissioned in 1889.
55. Ibid., ADM116/100, *Faroese and Icelandic Fisheries, 1899*. HMS

Galatea – remarks by Captain Cross, 19 June 1899. KDM *Heimdal* was a 1,342-ton 'Hekla'-class light cruiser, a comparatively new ship having been launched in 1894.
56. Ibid., ADM116/100, *Faroese and Icelandic Fisheries, 1899*. Report of Proceedings, Commander Dare, 27 August 1899.
57. Ibid., ADM116/100, *Faroese and Icelandic Fisheries, 1899*. Letter: British Legation, Copenhagen to Foreign Office, 9 May 1899.
58. William E Butler, *The Soviet Union and the Law of the Sea*, The John Hopkins Press, Baltimore & London (1971), pp. 28–29.
59. Ibid., Butler, *The Soviet Union and the Law of the Sea*, p. 31.
60. The measure called for a navy to maintain a number of battleships at least equal to the combined strength of the next two largest navies in the world.
61. This should have heralded an era of prosperity and growth for the industry. However, Martin Wilcox argues otherwise. 'Britain's failure to develop an economy based on the principle of vertical integration [the combination in one firm of two or more stages of production normally operated by separate firms] was a prime cause of the relative decline that began in the last quarter of the nineteenth century'. Wilcox states that although many firms within the fishing industry adopted vertical integration initially, by the 1890s the process began to go into reverse largely due, ironically, to the introduction of the steam trawler, 'which cost at least twice as much to buy, and far more to operate, than the best sailing trawlers ... .' See, Martin Wilcox, 'Concentration or Disintegration? Vessel Ownership, Fish Wholesaling and Processing in the British Trawl Industry 1850–1939', in David J Starkey & James E Candow, editors, *The North Atlantic Fisheries: Supply, Marketing and Consumption 1560–1990*, The North Atlantic Fisheries History Association, University of Hull, Hull (2006), pp. 50, 52, 56.
62. Op. Cit., ADM116/100, *Faroese and Icelandic Fisheries, 1899*. Letter: British Embassy, Copenhagen to Foreign Office, 17 May 1899.

Chapter Three
1. 'Albacore', 'Fishery Protection', in *The Naval Review*, Vol. XLI, No. 4, November 1953, p. 425. The Naval Review can be described as the Royal Navy officer's 'in-house journal'. First published in 1913, its primary purpose was, and still is, to encourage serving officers to debate relevant professional matters without fear of censure – although for many years most of its contributors opted to use pseudonyms as in the case quoted.
2. Ibid.
3. Robert Gardiner, editor, Conway's *All the World's Fighting Ships, 1860–1905*, Conway Maritime Press, London, 1979, p. 87.
4. Ibid., pp. 89 & 113.
5. TNA, ADM1/8553/74 Admiralty Responsibility for Protection of Fisheries. Paper by Captain Dugmore RN, 1919.
6. Ibid.
7. ADM1/8576/339 *Captain Auxiliary Patrols, appointment, 1919*.
8. Ibid.
9. ADM1/8760/226 *Replacement of the title Captain FMS by Captain Fishery Protection and Minesweeping, 1932*. 'Confidential Office Acquaint, October 1928.
10. Ibid.
11. Ibid., ADM1/8760/226; Memorandum: Captain F.M.S. to Secretary of the Admiralty, 16 November 1932.
12. Op. Cit., 'Albacore', *The Naval Review*, p. 425.
13. T1/11012 *Report: Interdepartmental Conference: Protection of Sea Fisheries, 1908*. The Admiralty's case had been put by Sir W Graham Greene, uncle of the famous twentieth-century writer. Greene had recently worked as Principal Clerk in the Department of the Secretary of the Admiralty under Jacky Fisher, thus had been at the heart of the naval reforms undertaken prior to the Great War.
14. Ibid., T1/11012; Letter: Admiralty to Treasury, 20 April 1909.
15. Op. Cit., ADM1/8553/74 *Paper by Captain Dugmore RN, 1919*, Section 2. The early history of the Royal Navy's involvement has already been discussed but, somewhat surprisingly in view of the resources at its disposal, Captain Dugmore's report failed to pin down exactly *when* the protection of fisheries was 'imposed upon the British Navy'.

16. Ibid., It is only in the past fifty years or so that the importance of the benign use of naval power or naval diplomacy (not to be confused with 'gunboat diplomacy') has been properly recognised and articulated in naval literature. Its significance was spelt out officially, as far as the Royal Navy was concerned, with its inclusion in *The Fundamentals of British Maritime Doctrine (BR1806)* first published in 1995.
17. Ibid. It is unsurprising that Captain Dugmore's argument about sharing the cost of fishery protection should receive such prominence. The cutbacks in spending following the Great War were particularly severe on the low- and middle-ranking naval officer cohort at the time, as well as affecting the numbers of ships in commission, so this matter was highly topical.
18. Ibid., Section 3.
19. ADM1/8700/128, *Fishery Protection Vessels: Use of force by, 1926.*
20. Ibid.
21. ADM1/27623 *Fishery Protection Flotilla: Proposals for post-war Fleet, 1944–59.* Memo PAS(S) to Head of MI and MII, July 1945.
22. Ibid., ADM1/27623 Memorandum by Director of Operations Division, 4 February 1944.
23. ADM1/19339 Fishery Protection Flotilla – report on activities ending 31 December 1945. Quarterly Report ending 31.3.46 by SO Captain C B Tidd. The report notes that the 'Castle'-class corvettes were not suitable for FP work. Their single screw and comparatively deep draught generally prevented them from entering smaller ports. Moreover, the commanding officer's quarters were 'entirely unsuitable for entertaining a most necessary part of their duties'. On the other hand, the HDMLs were very successful in coastal ports such as Rye and provided a better counter to poaching than larger vessels. Captain Tidd concluded what was his final report as SO Fishery Protection on an optimistic note, 'Great satisfaction has been shown by the entire fishing world as the reincarnation of the Fishery Protection Flotilla, and every possible assistance has been offered by both trawler owners and fishery officers.'
24. Op. Cit., ADM1/27623, Admiralty Memorandum, 9 November 1945. Anti-submarine escorts had previously been called sloops by the Royal Navy and these were reclassified as frigates after the war, as were the remaining smaller war-built 'Castle'-class corvettes.
25. Desmond Wettern states that in addition to their FP duties, the MFVs had the task of 'guiding shipping away from those areas which still had to be swept for mines'. See D Wettern, *The Decline of British Seapower*, Janes's Publishing Company, London (1982), p. 5.
26. ADM1/27623, Memorandum: Director of Operations Division, 7 July 1947.
27. MAF209/76 *Fishery Protection Service: organisation, composition and administration, postwar revival, 1945–48.* Fishery Protection Periodical report, 14 October 1947.
28. Ibid.
29. Ibid.
30. Ibid.
31. Op. Cit., ADM1/27623 Strength of the Fishery Protection Flotilla, 30 October 1948.
32. Ibid., ADM1/27623 Proposals for post-war Fleet, 1944–59. Enclosure to Captain, 5th Fishery Protection and Minesweeping Squadron, 26 November 1954.
33. Ibid., ADM1/27623, Enclosure by Captain F R Twiss to Captain, 5th Fishery Protection and Minesweeping Squadron, 26 November 1954.
34. Ibid.
35. Op. Cit., 'Albacore', *The Naval Review*, p. 429.
36. Eric J Grove, *From Vanguard to Trident: British Naval Policy since World War II*, The Bodley Head, London (1987), p. 64; D K Brown & George Moore, *Re-building the Royal Navy: Warship Design since 1945*, Chatham Publishing, London (2003), p. 130.
37. Op. Cit., ADM1/27623, Enclosure by Captain F R Twiss.
38. The term 'Cod War' was the invention of a Fleet Street journalist in 1958.
39. Prior to the Second World War, HMS *Challenger* was originally built in 1930–31 as a fishery protection vessel with survey ship capabilities. It was paid for by MAF, to be administered and run by the Hydrographer of the Navy and RN manned. A specific task, as originally conceived, was to seek out new fishing grounds in northern waters.

However, it never served in the FP role. After completion, MAF announced it could no longer afford the ship and it was taken over by the RN, which used it for survey work exclusively and later escort duties during the war. See, Simon Matthews, 'HMS Challenger', *Warship World Magazine*, 2021, Vol. 17, No. 2, p. 46.
40. MAF 209/78 *Fishery Protection Service: organisation, composition and administration; post-war revival 1953–60*. A total of sixteen coastal minesweepers were in full commission in 1957, with thirteen more on trials and training duties along with seven inshore boats. A further thirty-one coastals and eighteen inshores were still under construction, with fifty-two coastals and fifty-nine inshores held in reserve. See, Op. Cit., Grove, *From Vanguard to Trident*, p. 207.
41. Op. Cit., Brown & Moore, *Re-building the Royal Navy*, p. 81. Bryan 'Tiny' Height served on The Type 14 HMS *Palliser* off Iceland in the 1960s and recalled, 'These ships really pitched in heavy seas and to sit down on the heads [toilets] was some experience, it was a good job you had these handles on each side of you to hang on to.' Quoted in, Andrew Welch, *The Royal Navy in the Cod Wars: Britain and Iceland in Conflict*, Maritime Books, Liskeard (2006), p. 87.
42. Email exchange with Commander C G Wylie OBE FCMI, Royal Navy, 29 December 2022.
43. Hannes Jónsson, *Friends in Conflict: Anglo-Icelandic Cod Wars and the Law of the Sea*, C Hurst & Co., London (1982), pp. 38–41.

Chapter Four
1. Steve R Dunn, editor, *British Trawlers and Drifters in Two World Wars: From the John Lambert Collection*, Seaforth Publishing, Barnsley (2021), p. 17.
2. Corbett's words are quoted in Robb Robinson, *Fishermen, The Fishing Industry and the Great War at Sea: A Forgotten History?*, Liverpool (2019), p. 33.
3. Mines had posed a threat log before that, as Steve Dunn explains in a succinct history of the weapon. Op. Cit., Dunn, *British Naval Trawlers and Drifters*, p. 18.
4. Ibid., Robinson, *Fishermen*, pp. 17–18.
5. John Greenacre, 'The Admiralty's interwar planning with the British fishing industry, 1925–1940', in *Journal for Maritime Research*, Vol. 22:1–2 (2020), p. 140.
6. The British were technologically inferior to the Germans in the development of the mine as a weapon owing to some within the Admiralty who were opposed this form of warfare on principle.
7. Op. Cit., Robinson, *Fishermen*, pp. 25–26. A contract was drawn up between the owners and the Admiralty that allowed the latter to requisition the vessels where necessary. The terms of the agreements were calculated according to the vessel's tonnage. By 1916, such was the demand for both trawlers and drifters, three classes of supplementary, purpose-built 'Admiralty trawlers' started to be constructed. Steve Dunn notes that the major English fishing ports of Grimsby and Hull bore the brunt of the requisitioning drive, contributing some 829 trawlers and 9,000 crew members between them. Op. Cit., Dunn, *British Naval Trawlers and Drifters*, p. 24.
8. Ibid., Robinson, *Fishermen*, p. 29.
9. Douglas d'Enno, *Fishermen Against the Kaiser: Shockwaves of War 1914–1915, Vol. 1*, Pen & Sword, Barnsley (2010), p. 81.
10. Op. Cit., Dunn, *British Naval Trawlers and Drifters*, pp. 42–44.
11. Op. Cit., Greenacre, 'The Admiralty's interwar planning with the British fishing industry', p. 140.
12. Ibid., Greenacre, 'The Admiralty's interwar planning with the British fishing industry', p. 140.
13. Op. Cit., Robinson, *Fishermen*, pp. 47–52.
14. TNA, ADM131/70, *Auxiliary Patrol: Orders and Memoranda issued to vessels, 1914–1918*. Memoranda: Remarks on Submarine Patrols: Distribution of Enemy's Submarines, 28 June 1915. Later, evidence collected from captured U-boat crews, stated that the Channel barrage was much less effective than thought. See, Derek Nudd, *Castaways in Question: A Story of British Naval Interrogators from WW1 to Denazification*, Grove Cottage Editions, UK, (2020), pp. 47–48. This point is reinforced by Admiral Rosslyn Wemyss, who was soon to become First

Sea Lord. According to John Johnson-Allen, he 'made the point very forcibly' at a meeting in the Cabinet Room on 20 December 1917, 'that the existing measures in the Dover Strait allowed submarines to pass through the strait successfully and unchallenged'. See John Johnson-Allen, *'Rosy' Wemyss, Admiral of the Fleet: The Man who Created Armistice Day*, Whittles Publishing, Dunbeath (2021), p. 181.
15. *U-34* was commanded by Käpitanleutnant Claus Rücker during the June 1915 patrol. In all, *U-34* undertook seventeen wartime patrols before being lost in 1918, sinking a total of 117 vessels.
16. Ibid., ADM131/70, *Auxiliary Patrol*: Remarks on Submarine Patrols.
17. Andrew Boyd, *Naval Intelligence through the Twentieth Century*, Seaforth Publishing, Barnsley (2020), p. 129.
18. Op. Cit., ADM131/70, *Auxiliary Patrol: Remarks on Submarine Patrols*.
19. Op. Cit., Robinson, *Fishermen*, p. 69. The General Orders for the conduct of the Auxiliary Patrol included the note, 'As far as possible, among the ship's company composing the gun's crews, a coastguard man is drafted who has some knowledge of signals. It is important that, where this has not been possible, one or two of the men should be practised in semaphore or Morse signalling.' See Ibid., ADM131/70, *Auxiliary Patrol: Orders and Memoranda issued to vessels, 1914–1918*. General Orders for H.M. Trawlers and Drifters of Auxiliary Patrol, 1915.
20. Op. Cit., d'Enno, *Fishermen Against the Kaiser*, pp. 95–97.
21. Op. Cit., Robinson, *Fishermen*, p. 86.
22. Ibid., Robinson, *Fishermen*, p. 87. U-boats were also fitted with hydrophones. They required the submarine's engines to be stopped before being used, drawing this sceptical assessment when interrogated by the captured crew members of *U-48* in November 1917, 'It was stated that very little use is made of sound signalling apparatus, and that, almost as good results can be obtained by placing the ear against the pressure hull in the fore torpedo compartment as by using the apparatus. For this purpose, however, all noise must of course be stopped in the boat.' See, Op. Cit., Nudd, *Castaways in Question*, p. 50.
23. Op. Cit., ADM131/70, *Auxiliary Patrol: Orders and Memoranda issued to vessels, 1914–1918*. Southern Patrol Force Operations Orders, 24 July 1918. Paravanes were evidently still in short supply. Senior officers were told to economise and not to use them in bad weather.
24. Ibid., ADM131/70 *Southern Patrol Force Operations*: Orders, 24 July 1918. What would now be described as low-frequency passive sonar was used extensively during the First World War but overall it proved to be relatively ineffective. See Norman Friedman, *British Submarines in the Cold War Era*, Seaforth Publishing, Barnsley (2021), p. 43; Gerald Toghill, *Royal Navy Trawlers Part 2: Requisitioned Trawlers*, Maritime Books, Liskeard (2004), p. viii.
25. Op. Cit., Robinson, *Fishermen*, pp. 97–110; Ibid., Robinson, *Fishermen*, pp. 110–112.
26. Op. Cit., Greenacre, 'The Admiralty's interwar planning', p. 141.
27. Op. Cit., Robinson, *Fishermen*, p. 139.
28. Op. Cit., d'Enno, *Fishermen Against the Kaiser*, pp. 167–168.
29. Ibid., d'Enno, *Fishermen Against the Kaiser*, pp. 169–175.
30. Roger Chesneau (editor), *Conway's All the World's Fighting Ships 1922–1946*, Conway Maritime Press, London (1980), pp. 55 & 63–64.
31. Stephen Roskill, *Naval Policy between the Wars: II, The Period of Reluctant Rearmament 1930–1939*, William Collins, London (1976), p. 228.
32. Stephen Roskill, *Naval Policy between the Wars: I, The Period of Anglo-American Antagonism 1919–1929*, William Collins, London (1968), p. 536.
33. Op. Cit., Greenacre, 'The Admiralty's interwar planning with the British fishing industry', p. 141.
34. ADM 116/3504 *Fishery Protection Flotilla: Quarterly Reports 1936–37*. Report by Senior Officer, Fishery Protection.
35. ADM 116/3805, *Fisheries and Fishery Protection (22): Control of fishing fleet, merchant shipping etc. in time of war and expansion of Fishery Protection and Minesweeping Service, 1936–39*. Report by Director of Plans; Report

on Organisation and Expansion of FP & M Command in time of war by Captain FP & M, 19 August 1936.
36. Ibid., ADM 116/3805, Report: Organisation and Protection of Fishing Fleet, 1936.
Steve Dunn makes the point that the Abyssinian Crisis (1936) 'proved to be the catalyst for increases in the Naval Estimates', which resulted in purchase from trade of twenty modern A/S and minesweeping trawlers. Op. Cit., Dunn, *British Naval Trawlers and Drifters*, p. 74.
37. Op. Cit., Greenacre, *The Admiralty's interwar planning*, pp. 148–151; Op. Cit., Robinson, *Fishermen*, pp. 172–174.
38. Op. Cit., ADM 116/3805, Report: The Control and Direction of the Operation of the Fishing Fleet (other than coastal fishing) in War, 15 December 1938.
39. Simon Matthews, 'Royal Navy Anti-Submarine Trawlers and Whalers in World War Two', in *Warship World* Vol. 17, No. 7, MCI Media, (2021).
40. Op. Cit., ADM 116/3805, Report: The Control and Direction of the Operation of the Fishing Fleet (other than coastal fishing) in War.
41. ADM1/10042 *Conversion of trawlers for anti-submarine and minesweeping duties, 1939*. Memo by Captain A/S: Fitting of Type 123 asdic set for trawlers, 6 June 1939.
42. Ibid., ADM1/10042, Memo: Director of Plans, 3 July 1939.
43. Op. Cit., Dunn, *British Naval Trawlers and Drifters*, p. 77.
44. ADM1/10045 *Merchant Navy (64): Minesweeping Trawlers: command, disposition, complementing, etc. 1939*. Memo: Director of Local Defence Division, 22 September 1939; Memo: Captain Extended Defences Officer, Sheerness, 11 September 1939.
45. ADM1/10039 *Trawlers purchased for anti-submarine and minesweeping operations, 1939*. Memo: Captain A/S HMS Osprey, Portland, 18 August 1939.
46. ADM1/10511 *Fisheries and Fishery Protection, 1939–40*. Letter: General Secretary Transport and General Workers Union to First Lord of Admiralty, 10 October 1939; First Lord Minute, 26 October 1939.
47. ADM1/16994 *Requisitioning of trawlers from Grimsby and Hull: requests and suggestions regarding release, 1939–44*. Draft Report of Conference re: problems of fishing industry in war time, 19/20 October 1939.
48. Ibid., ADM1/16994, Statement by ACNS to Fishery Advisory Committee, 19 December 1939.
49. Ibid., ADM1/16994, Admiralty Memo regarding deputation by Hull and Grimsby MPs: The Fishing Industry in Hull. 4 October 1939.
50. Ibid., ADM1/16994, Letters: Mayor of Grimsby to First Lord of Admiralty, 6 October 1939; Bishop of Lincoln to First Lord of Admiralty, 19 September 1939; Skippers of Cardiff deep sea fishing boats, 11 October 1939.
51. Paul Lund and Harry Ludlam, *Trawlers go to War*, W Foulsham & Co. Ltd, Harrow (1971), p. 20.
52. Ibid., pp. 20 & 36.
53. Ibid., p. 81.
54. Op. Cit., Dunn, *British Naval Trawlers and Drifters*, p. 120.
55. Ibid., p. 105.
56. ADM1/16398, *Fisheries and Fishery Protection: Post-war position and problems for Herring Industry, 1942–43*. Memo by Head of Military Branch, 27 March 1942; Undated and unattributed memo: Herring Industry: post-war condition; Memo by DMS, 8 April 1942.
57. ADM 1/12092, *Fisheries and Fishery Protection: requisitioning of fishing boats – shortage of fish, 1942*. Memo by Director of Trade Division, 20 October 1942.
58. ADM 1/14947, *Possibility of release of fishing vessels from war duties, 1943*. Letters: Minister of Food to First Lord, 16 July 1943; First Lord to Minister of Food, 28 July 1943.
59. Op. Cit., Lund and Ludlam, *Trawlers go to War*, p. 177; Op. Cit., Toghill, *Royal Navy Trawlers, Part 2*, p. xiii.
60. Op. Cit., ADM1/16994, Memo: DSVP regarding the dilemma of Hull, 14 September 1944.
61. Ibid., ADM1/16994, Letter: MAF to Admiralty Military Branch, 22 September 1944.
62. ADM 1/17785, *Cabinet Fish Committee: Formation of Reports, 1945*; ADM1/19128, *Release of trawlers from Royal Navy, 1945*. Various Admiralty memos and reports, May–June 1945.
63. Op. Cit., Dunn, *British Naval Trawlers and Drifters*, p. 118.

64. Op. Cit., Toghill, *Royal Navy Trawlers*, Part 2, p. x.
65. Op. Cit., Lund and Ludlam, *Trawlers go to War*, p. 250.

Chapter Five
1. TNA, ADM116/2179 *Fishery Protection in North Russian Waters 1922–23*. Extract from trawler log, 28 April 1923.
2. Op. Cit., Butler, *The Soviet Union & The Law of the Sea*, pp. 93–4.
3. Grennady P Luzin, Michael Pretes & Vladimir V Vasilev, 'The Kola Peninsula: Geography, History and Resources' in Arctic, Vol. 47, No. 1 (1994), p. 1.; Ronald A Helin, 'Soviet Fishing in the Barents Sea and the North Atlantic' in *Geographical Review*, Vol. 54, No. 3 (1964), p. 387.
4. Paul R Josephson, 'When Stalin Learned to Fish: Natural Resources, Technology, and Industry under Socialism' in Jeffry M Diefendorf & Kurk Dorset, editors, *City, Country, Empire*, University of Pittsburgh Press, Pittsburgh (2005), p. 165.
5. Op. Cit., Helin, 'Soviet Fishing', pp. 387–88; Op. Cit., Luzin, Pretes, Vasilev, 'Kola Peninsula', p. 3.
6. Ibid., Luzin, Pretes, Vasilev, 'Kola Peninsula', p. 4. A small news article in *Scientific American* at the time, 'Completion of Murman Railway in Russia', celebrated the event. What was not known then was the fact that it had been constructed by slave labour with the aid of 40,000 Austrian prisoners of war and several thousand Chinese workers.
7. C J Webster, 'The Economic Development of the Soviet Arctic and Sub-Arctic', in *The Slavonic and Eastern European Review*, Vol. 29, No. 72 (1950), p. 185; Op. Cit., Helin, 'Soviet Fishing', p. 390.
8. Op. Cit., Josephson, 'When Stalin Learned to Fish', p. 169.
9. Ibid., Helin, 'Soviet Fishing', p. 390.
10. William E Butler, 'Soviet Territorial Waters', in *World Affairs*, Vol. 130, No. 1 (1967), p. 17.
11. Op. Cit., Butler, *The Soviet Union & The Law of the Sea*, pp. 28–31.
12. Ibid., p. 31.
13. Op. Cit., Butler, 'Soviet Territorial Waters', p. 18.
14. Josephson, 'When Stalin Learned to Fish', pp. 165–67. Other writers acknowledge the work and influence of Knipovich in this respect.
15. Op. Cit., Butler, *The Soviet Union & The Law of the Sea*, pp. 90–91.
16. Patrick Salmon, 'Foreign Policy and National Identity: The Norwegian Integrity Treaty 1907–42', in *Forrsvarsstudies* No. 1 (1993), pp. 47–48.
17. ADM 116/2178 *Protection of British Fisheries in North Russian Waters, 1922–23*; O Parkes & F McMurtie, editors, *Jane's Fighting Ships 1924*, David and Charles Reprints, Newton Abbott (1973), pp. 80–81.
18. Randal Gray editor, *Conway's All the World's Fighting Ships 1906–1921*, Conway Maritime Press, London (1985), p. 94; Ibid., Gray et al, *Jane's Fighting Ships 1924*, p. 81.
19. ADM204/16 Fisheries General: Protection of British Fishing Vessels off the Murman Coast of Russia, 1923; Hansard, House of Commons, Vol. 152, Oral Answers, 'Fishery Protection', 22 March 1922.
20. Ibid., ADM 116/2178 Protection of British Fisheries, 1922–23. Letter: Captain A/P Harebell to Secretary of Admiralty, 3 June 1922.
21. Ibid., ADM 116/2178 Protection of British Fisheries.
22. Ibid., ADM 116/2178 'Remarks on Recent Patrol of HMS "Godetia" in North Russian Waters,' 3 December 1922.
23. Ibid. The 'discontent' felt by *Godetia*'s crew fell far short of mutiny but perhaps reflected the deeper wave of social and political unrest and division that was sweeping across Europe at the time. Steve Dunn speculates on this matter in his account of the spate of minor mutinies that took place almost contemporaneously aboard RN ships serving in the Baltic in support of the newly independent states of Latvia and Estonia, 1918–20. See, Steve R Dunn, *Battle in the Baltic: The Royal Navy and the Fight to save Estonia and Latvia 1918–20*, Pen & Sword, Barnsley (2020).
24. T161/204/16 *Fisheries General: Protection of British Fishing Vessels off the Murman Coast of Russia, 1923*.
25. Ibid., T161/204/16, Statement by Deputy Chief of Naval Staff (DCNS).
26. Ibid., T161/204/16, *Protection of British Fishing Vessels, 1923*. There

had been a meeting with representatives of MAF, the FO, the Admiralty and the Trawlers Federation in January 1923, which reached an impasse. See TNA, MAF41/705, *Russia: Naval Protection of British Fishing Vessels*, (1923). Predictably, the press exploited the story. When HMS *Harebell* finally departed for the region in May 1923, an article in was published with the provocative headline: 'Hull's Grievance: "Illusory Government Promises"'. The *Daily Telegraph*, 11 May 1923.
27. Op. Cit., ADM116/2179. HMS *Godetia*, Letter of Proceedings.
28. Ibid.
29. Ibid., ADM 116/2179. HMS *Harebell*, Confidential Letter to Captain Auxiliary Patrols, 28 May 1923.
30. Ibid.
31. Ibid.
32. Ibid.
33. Op. Cit., Gray editor, Conway's All the World's Fighting Ships 1906–1921, p. 318; Graham Watson, *From Tsar to Commissar: Russian Naval Organisation and Warships 1914–1922*. www.naval-history.net/xGW-RussianNavy1914-1918.
34. Ibid., Gray editor, Conway's *All the World's Fighting Ships 1906–1921*, p. 318.
35. Admiral Timirev, an ex-officer in the Tsarist Navy, gives an excellent first-hand account of the monumental changes to everyday life brought about by the Soviet takeover of the Russian Navy at the end of the First World War. It echoes the eyewitness account given by Skipper Greaves, albeit on a much smaller scale. See, Stephen C Ellis, *The Russian Baltic Fleet: in Time of War and Revolution 1914–1918: The Recollections of Admiral S.N. Timirev*, Seaforth Publishing, Barnsley (2020).
36. ADM 116/2179. Report of Interview with Skipper Samuel Greaves of the S/T 'Lord Astor', 31 May 1923.
37. Ibid., ADM 116/2179. HMS *Harebell*, Report of Interview. The estimations regarding the *Yaroslavna* were mostly correct. In fact, it was built by William Denny & Bros. Ltd, Dumbarton, for the US newspaper millionaire James Bennett and completed in 1901. Its displacement was 3,315 tons and it was armed with 2 x 120mm guns. The ship was subsequently renamed *Vorovsky* in 1924. See, Siegfried Breyer, *Soviet Warship Development: Vol. 1, 1917–1937*, Conway Maritime Press, London (1992), p. 106.
38. Ibid., ADM 116/2179. HMS *Harebell*, Remarks by Director of Naval Intelligence.
39. See Andrew Gordon, *The Rules of the Game: Jutland and British Naval Command*, John Murray, London (1996).
40. Op. Cit., Boyd, *British Naval Intelligence*, p. 136.
41. CAB 24/196/35 Protection for British Trawlers on the Murman Coast, 13 July 1928. Foreign Office Memorandum.
42. Ibid., CAB 24/196/35. Foreign Office Memorandum.
43. Ibid., CAB 24/196/35. Memorandum by Minister of Agriculture and Fisheries.
44. Elise Uberoi, *UK Sea Fisheries Statistics*, House of Commons Briefing Paper 2788, 2017, p. 4.
45. Ibid., CAB 24/196/35. Memorandum by First Lord of Admiralty
46. Ibid., Breyer, *Soviet Warship Development*, p. 179.
47. HMS *Comus* was a *Caroline*-class light cruiser that saw extensive active service during the First World War and thereafter. At the time it belonged to the 2nd Cruiser Squadron as part of the Atlantic Fleet. The *Caroline* class were considered to be 'grossly overweight' at the close of the war as a result of wartime additions to their armaments and were subsequently lightened. This would have been crucial for *Comus* in view of the role it was expected to play in the stormy waters of the Barents Sea. See Op. Cit., Gray ed., *Conway's All the World's Fighting Ships 1906–1921*, pp. 56–7.
48. ADM 116/2649 *British Fishing Trawlers off the Murman Coast: Naval Protection of*.
49. Op. Cit., MAF41/705 Foreign Office Letter to MAF, 22 May 1930. There had been suggestions in the communist press that the RN had been adopting Kirkenes as a British naval base, which had embarrassed the Norwegian Government. At the same time, the FO felt that the negotiations under way between the Russians and the British over an agreement about the 3- to 12-mile fishing zone might be compromised if there was further publicity on the subject.

50. Op. Cit., ADM116/2179, HMS *Godetia*, Letter of Proceedings. Norway, as well as having some left-wing sympathisers, also found itself trying to arrive at a delicate diplomatic decision about the timing of its official recognition of the USSR state. These issues are described in Op. Cit., Salmon, 'Foreign Policy and National Identity', pp. 47–50.
51. ADM 116/2640 *Fishery Protection Duties 1928–30*. Report for 1928 by Captain M E Goldsmith, Captain Auxiliary Patrols aboard HMS *Harebell*.
52. Ibid., ADM 116/2640, Report by C.O. HMS *Doon*.
53. Op. Cit., ADM 116/2649, Report of Proceedings.
54. Op. Cit., ADM 116/2640, *Fishery Protection Duties 1928–30*. Report of Proceedings, Captain FMS July 1929.
55. Uri Bar-Noi, 'The Cold War and Britain's Dispute with the USSR over territorial waters and fishery limits, 1953–1956', in *Journal for Maritime Research*, Vol. 17, No. 2 (2015), p. 199.
56. Op. Cit., MAF41/705 Letter: Admiralty to MAF with enclosure giving statement of F Norton, 24 January 1930.
57. ADM116/2767 *Fishery Protection Flotilla 1930–31*. Report, Captain FMS.
58. Ibid., ADM116/2767, Report, Captain FMS.
59. Gudni Johannessón, *Troubled Waters: Cod War and Britain's Fight for Freedom of the High Seas, 1948–1964*. University of London PhD thesis www.academia.edu./255so64/Troubled_Waters_Cod_War_Fishing_Disputes_Britains_Fight_For_Freedom, p. 18; James Cable, *Gunboat Diplomacy: Political Applications of Limited Naval Force*, Chatto & Windus, London (1971); James Cable, *Diplomacy at Sea*, The Macmillan Press, London and Basingstoke (1985), p. 19.

Chapter Six
1. Op. Cit., Jóhannesson, *Troubled Waters*, p. 14.
2. Norwegian Institute for Defence Studies (NIDS), *From Unspoken to Outspoken Alliance: Norway Between Britain and Germany*, www.jstor.com/stable/resrep 20312.4 (1994), p. 2.
3. Robb Robinson, *Fishermen, the Fishing Industry and the Great War at Sea*, p. 6.
4. E E Prince, 'Territorial Waters and a Suggested Extension of the Three Mile Limit', in *Transactions of the American Fisheries Society*, Vol. 146, No. 6 (2017), p. 175.
5. HNoMS *Heimdal* carried out the first ever sortie of a Norwegian fishery protection vessel on 12 March 1908. It also became the first Norwegian ship to apprehend a ship for illegal fishing when it arrested S/T *Lord Roberts*.
6. Steve R Dunn, *Southern Thunder: The Royal Navy and the Scandinavian Trade in World War One*, Seaforth Publishing, Barnsley (2019), pp. 76 & 264; Op. Cit., NIDS, *From Unspoken to Outspoken Alliance*, p. 3.
7. Ibid., Dunn, *Southern Thunder*, pp. 77–78.
8. Kristine Offerdal, *The 1920 Svalbard Treaty*, Center for Strategic and International Studies (2016), pp. 14–15.
9. TNA, ADM 116/3930, *Anglo-Norwegian Fisheries Dispute*. Foreign Office Memorandum, 1 December 1936.
10. Ibid., ADM 116/3930, Chief Inspector of Fisheries Report.
11. Op. Cit., Patrick Salmon, 'Foreign Policy and National Identity', p. 48.
12. Op. Cit., TNA, ADM 116/3930, Chief Inspector of Fisheries Report.
13. Ibid.
14. Op. Cit., ADM 116/3930, Foreign Office Memorandum.
15. Ibid.
16. Op. Cit., Jóhannesson, *Troubled Waters*, p. 31.
17. Op. Cit., ADM 116/3930, Chief Inspector of Fisheries Report.
18. ADM 116/3079 *Report of Proceedings of the Fishery Protection and Minesweeping Flotilla 1935–1936*. Quarterly Fishery Report.
19. ADM116/3504, *Fishery Protection Flotilla: Quarterly Reports 1936–1937*. HNoMS *Michael Sars* was a 1,300-ton sloop that together with another sloop, *Heimdal*, shared fishery protection duties at the time. See, Op. Cit., Roger Chesneau, *Conway's All the World's Fighting Ships, 1922–1946*, p. 379.
20. ADM 116/3930, *Anglo-Norwegian Fisheries Dispute: Negotiations 1936–1939*.

21. Op. Cit., ADM 116/3930, Foreign Office Memorandum.
22. Ibid., ADM 116/3930, FO Confidential Memorandum, 1 December 1936; Op. Cit., Robinson, *Fishermen, the Fishing Industry and the Great War at Sea*, p. 131.
23. Gierr Harr, *The German Invasion of Norway: April 1940*, Seaforth Publishing, Barnsley (2009), p. 27.
24. Ibid. p. 2.
25. Gierr Harr, *The Battle for Norway: April–June 1940*, Seaforth Publishing, Barnsley (2010), p. 369.
26. MAF 209/76 *Fishery Protection Service Organisation, Composition and Administration: Post-war revival 1945–48*. Report by Senior Officer Fishery Protection Flotilla, June/July 1948.
27. ADM1/28914. *Fishery Protection: Instructions relating to patrols in Northern Waters, 1952–1956*. Memorandum by the Secretary of State for Foreign Affairs: The Anglo-Norwegian Fishery Dispute.
28. See, Saki Dockrill, *Britain's Retreat from East of Suez: the Choice between Europe and the World?*, Palgrave Macmillan, Basingstoke (2002), p. 1.
29. Op. Cit., Jóhannesson, *Troubled Waters*, p. 34.
30. ADM1/27623 *Fishery Protection Flotilla: Proposals for Post-War Fleet 1944–59*. Senior Officer Fishery Protection Letter: Anglo-Norwegian Fishery Dispute, 5 January 1949.
31. Op. Cit., Jóhannesson, *Troubled Waters*, p. 36.
32. Ibid., p. 37.
33. Hansard, *House of Commons Debate, Norway (British Trawler, Arrest)* Vol. 465, 1 June 1949.
34. Hrefna Karlsdóttir, 'Fishing Rights in the Post-war Period: The Case of the North Sea Herring', in Gordon Boyce & Richard Gorki, *Resources and Infrastructure in the Maritime Economy, 1500–2000*, Liverpool University Press, Liverpool (2002), p. 108.
35. Op. Cit., Jóhannesson, *Troubled Waters*, p. 59.
36. Op. Cit., ADM1/28914, Instructions relating to patrols in Northern waters 1951–56.

Chapter Seven

1. Captain F R Twiss, in the conclusion to his review of the work of the 5th Fishery Protection and Minesweeping Squadron, wrote, 'The operations of the Fishery Protection Squadron today differ widely from those of pre-war and immediate post-war years. These operations are more important and more complex than hitherto, and as the Squadron is also an operational minesweeping squadron the emphasis on fighting efficiency is greatly increased.' TNA, ADM1/27623, *Fishery Protection Flotilla: Proposals for Postwar Fleet 1944–59*. Review of the Functions and Value of the Fifth Fishery Protection and Minesweeping Squadron. 26 November 1954.
2. The relevant extract from the Act of Parliament in question reads, 'It shall be lawful for the Lords Commissioners of the Admiralty, upon the application of the Commissioners for the Herring Fishery, from Time to Time to appoint a commissioned officer of His Majesty's Navy as Superintendent of the British Herring Industry carried on in the Lochs and upon the coasts of Great Britain, not in the deep sea, for the purpose of preserving order among the fishermen and other purposes engaged in the said Fishery …' 55 George III, Chapter 54. Powers to regulate sea fisheries predated this Act by seven years. In 1808 the Commissioners of the British White Herring Fishery were charged with the responsibility to regulate the industry and assigned two Royal Navy ships to assist them. The task was imply to maintain law and order on the inshore fishing grounds.
3. Graeme Somner, *Scottish Fishery Protection*, World Ship Society Monograph No. 7, Kendal (1983), pp. 3 & 4.
4. Ibid., Somner, *Scottish Fishery Protection*, p. 4.
5. The short-lived career of *Brenda* (1) ended when it was found to be unsuitable for the rough weather conditions found in the Moray Firth. See, Ibid., Somner, *Scottish Fishery Protection*, p. 5.
6. www.gov.scot/binaries/content/documents/govscot/publications *Marine Scotland Vessel List 1882 – Present Date*, pp. 4–5 & 9.
7. Op. Cit., Somner, *Scottish Fishery Protection*, pp. 8 & 9; Ibid., *Marine Scotland Vessel List*, p. 9.

8. Ibid., Somner, *Scottish Fishery Protection*, p. 39.
9. Op. Cit., *Marine Scotland Vessel List*, pp. 21 & 26.
10. ADM 116/3361 *Fishery Protection in Scottish waters*, 1933–36. Letter LFNO Scotland to Captain FP & M, February 1934. At the time, Scottish Sea Fisheries was in general subject to the UK Sea Fisheries Act but differed in relation to certain bye-laws. Fishery Protection was carried out by the Fishery Board (Scotland) as constituted by the Act of 1882. The Act had been amended in 1928. A fishery officer was appointed to each of Scotland's twenty-six districts by warrant from the Board of Trade and were employed in execution of the historic Herring Fishery (Scotland) Acts. The officers were instructed to co-operate with the Scottish fishery cruisers and the RN LFNO in the enforcement of the local laws and regulations.
11. Op. Cit., ADM 1/27623, Review of the Functions and Value of the Fifth Fishery Protection and Minesweeping Squadron. 26 November 1954.
12. Ibid., ADM 1/27623, Review. This was the second time that Captain Twiss had brought the matter to the attention of the Admiralty. His letter, 'Provision of an HM Ship for Scottish Fishery Protection Duties', covering the same arguments, was addressed to the Admiralty Secretary in June 1954.
13. Ibid., ADM1/27623, Report: Scottish Home Department's Fishery Protection Fleet, 29 March 1960.
14. Op. Cit., ADM 116/3361, Minute by Head of Military Branch, June 1934.
15. Ibid., ADM 116/3361, Letter: LFNO Irish Sea to Secretary, Fishery Board for Scotland, 14 November, 1933.
16. Ibid.
17. Ibid.
18. Ibid., ADM 116/3361. Letter LFNO Irish Sea. On paper, HMS *Doon* and S/T *Lucida* were of similar size, displacement and age and both were classed as trawlers. Officially, the RN vessel had a maximum speed of 11 knots, the *Lucida* a slightly slower 9 knots. HMS *Doon*'s inability to overhaul *Lucida* during the chase southwards was remarked on in a subsequent exchange in the House of Commons. It was disclosed that the *Doon* had a superior speed, but this was not divulged for security reasons. The Opposition called for the employment of 'up-to-date cruisers' for fishery protection and for the employment of seaplanes in a chase. See, Hansard, House of Commons Debate 'Fishery Patrol Vessel (Speed)', Vol. 283, 23 November 1933.
19. Ibid., ADM 116/3361. Letter LFNO Irish Sea.
20. Ibid. One can detect a degree of relish in the tone of this vivid account of the chase up the River Lune as though Lieutenant Commander Dalison, smarting at the inability of his ship to overhaul the *Lucida* during the chase south, had derived satisfaction from getting the better of Jinks in the hair-raising manoeuvring in the narrow channel.
21. Ibid., ADM 116/3361. Minutes by Head of Military Branch: June and November 1934.
22. ADM 116/3070 *Quarterly Reports of the Fishery Protection and Minesweeping Flotilla, 1934–35*. Fishery Protection Quarterly Report April–June 1934.
23. 'YE gentlemen of England
That live at home at ease,
Ah! little do you think upon
The dangers of the seas.
Give ear unto the mariners,
And they will plainly show
All the cares and the fears
When the stormy winds do blow.'
Martin Parker d. 1656
24. ADM1/8742/102 *Search for the missing Hull trawler St. Louis by HM Ships of the Fishery Protection Service, 1930*. A weather report summary for the week beginning 10 January 1930 was later produced and showed that there were almost continuous south-westerly gale force winds in the North Sea with frequent rain and snow showers. HMS *Spey* (ex-P38), built in 1916–17, had been assigned to the Fishery Protection Flotilla in 1925 and thus became the only one of its class to be named. These 20-knot, 613-ton vessels had been designed to replace destroyers in coastal operations. Its hardened steel ram bows and sharply cutaway funnel betrayed the class as linear descendants of the late nineteenth-century steam torpedo boats and coastal destroyers. *Spey*'s very low

freeboard would not have been suited to the harshest of conditions in the North Sea in winter, which probably accounts for the somewhat circumspect order to proceed with some caution in account of the weather. On the 6th, *Spey* reported it was making just 10 knots in strong N.E. winds in a high and rough sea.

25. Ibid., ADM1/8742/102, *Search for the missing trawler St Louis*.
26. Ibid., ADM1/8742/102, Letter: Captain Goldsmith to Secretary to the Admiralty, 25 February 1930.
27. Op. Cit., ADM 116/3361, Report: Search for the missing trawler 'Amethyst' H.455, 6 February 1937. Captain Victor Crutchley was already a distinguished naval officer prior to his appointment as Captain FP & M. in 1936. He was awarded the V.C. during the Zeebrugge Raid in 1918 and also served throughout the Second World War, attaining flag rank in 1942. The first message picked up by Wick Radio Station sounded slightly more optimistic: 'In dangerous position east of Kinnaird Head. Do not think lifeboat will get through to us. Think we shall be OK if we can get anchor out, but chains fouled.' *Daily News*, 25 February 1937.
28. www.wrecksite.eu, FV Amethyst (H455) (+1937).
29. Op. Cit., ADM 116/3361, Report: Search for the missing trawler 'Amethyst' H.455. The *Kingfisher* class was designed for coastal convoy work in wartime. Ordered in the wake of the 1930 London Naval Treaty, it was an attempt to build a patrol vessel under 600 tons but its small displacement, 510 tons, and short range made it unsuitable for open-ocean work and clearly for the rough seas off north-east Scotland in January 1937. See, Op. Cit., Chesneau, *Conway's All the World's Fighting Ships, 1922–46*, pp. 2 & 62; Roskill, *Naval Policy Between the Wars II*, p. 73.
30. Ibid., ADM 116/3361, Report: Search for the missing trawler 'Amethyst' H.455. HMS *Harebell* was, by 1937, nearly twenty years old and had seen much service in the FP flotilla. Although considerably larger than the *Kingfisher* at 1,250 tons, it was a single-screw ship, described as lively in a seaway (see Chapter Five). HMS *Boyne* was a *Mersey*-class trawler, again dating from the end of the First World War. It was based at Lowestoft.
31. Ibid., ADM 116/3361, Report: Search for the missing trawler 'Amethyst' H.455. It was reported later that wreckage, including two lifebuoys bearing the name *Amethyst*, had been washed up on Fetlar Island, off the Shetlands. *Aberdeen Press & Journal*, 15 February 1937.
32. Ibid., ADM 116/3336, *Fishery Protection Flotilla, 1937*. HMS *Sheldrake* was in turn replaced on LFNO duties the following year by the brand new *Halcyon*-class minesweeper HMS *Gossamer*.
33. See Grove, Eric J, *The Royal Navy since 1815: A New Short History*, Palgrave Macmillan, Basingstoke (2005), p. 140; Op. Cit., Kennedy, *The Rise and Fall of British Naval Mastery*, p. 288. David Hobbs declares that the 'pernicious impact of an air policy that concentrated on a continental bombing strategy ... cost the British Commonwealth dearly'. That the experiments with using aircraft reconnaissance to spot poachers was entirely new in 1928–29 and again in 1933 were entirely novel underlines his point that, 'The few aircraft the RAF did deploy on maritime reconnaissance had crews that were not trained to operate as part of a fleet.' See David Hobbs, *Taranto and Naval Air Warfare in the Mediterranean, 1940–1945*, Seaforth Publishing, Barnsley (2020), p. 20.
34. ADM116/2640 *Fishery Protection Duties, 1928–30*. MAF 'Report on Co-operation with RAF in Fishery protection during 1929'.
35. Ibid., ADM116/2640, MAF Report.
36. Ibid.
37. Ibid.
38. Op. Cit., ADM116/2966 *Fishery Protection and Minesweeping Flotilla, 1933–34*. Report by Lt Cdr Dallison, HMS *Doon*, to Captain Fishery Protection and Minesweeping Flotilla on combined operations between HMS *Doon* and No. 210 Flying Boat Squadron, June 1933.
39. Jon Wise, *The Role of the Royal Navy in South America, 1920–1970*, Bloomsbury Publishing, London (2014, p. 16.

40. Op. Cit., ADM/116/2966, Captain K D W Macpherson: Letter of Proceedings 15 May to 6 June 1933.
41. Ibid.
42. ADM, 116/3079, *Report of Proceedings of the Fishery Protection and Minesweeping Flotilla 1935–36*.
43. ADM 116/3336 *Fishery Protection Flotilla, 1937*. Letter: Captain FP & M to Admiralty.
44. Ibid.
45. Rob Hoole, editor, *Last of the Wooden Walls: An Illustrated History of the Ton Class Minesweepers and Minehunters*, Halsgrove Publishing, Wellington (2012), p. 101.
46. Ibid., p. 102.
47. Author's telephone conversation with Rear Admiral John Lippiett, Royal Navy, 8 November 2022.
48. Op. Cit., *Last of the Wooden Walls*, p. 105.
49. Op. Cit., Author's conversation with John Lippiett.
50. Report of Proceedings: Commanding Officer, HMS *Shavington*, 4 September 1976.
51. The shortage of information about Operation Grenada stemmed from a ministerial injunction taken out in 1972 preventing any press access to Grenada ships. It was felt that to permit that would be to risk revealing the tactics employed on patrol and also, potentially, to upset the fragile relations with the Irish Government. The matter was reviewed six years later but the policy remained unchanged on that occasion. See: DEFE 24/3000 *Northern Ireland: Operation Grenada 1974–76*. Memo: Operation Grenada – Publicity, 13 October 1978.
52. DEFE 24/520 *Northern Ireland: RN Coastal Patrol 1969–70*. Memo: Director of Naval Operations and Trade, 24 October 1969.
53. Ibid., DEFE 24/520 Message: SNONI (N) to MoD Navy, 18 November 1969.
54. Ibid., DEFE 24/520 Minute: MoD to Secretary of State Northern Ireland: Anti-Gun Running activities on the East Coast of Northern Ireland, 2 June 1970. In the early days of the Troubles it was thought that Protestants were responsible for gun running by sea, working with sympathisers ashore on mainland Britain; it was concluded that the Catholics were using the land route from the Irish Republic.
55. ADM 201/306, *Northern Ireland, Operation Awless, 1975; submarine patrols off Northern Ireland, 1975*.
56. DEFE 24/3395 *Fishery Protection: General Policy 1990–91*.
57. All the quotations in this section have been taken from the transcripts of the two Grimsby Fishing Heritage Centre Oral History Projects: 'The Women they Left Behind' and 'Distant Water Project', 2008–2011.

Chapter Eight
1. Uri Bar-Noi, 'The Cold War and Britain's Dispute with the USSR over territorial waters and fishery limits, 1953–1956', in *Journal for Maritime Research*, Vol. 17, No. 2, 2015, pp. 195–97.
2. Ibid., p. 199.
3. TNA, ADM1/28914 *Instructions relating to patrols in Northern Waters (1951–56): Russian Waters*. FP COs were encouraged to visit the Director of Naval Intelligence prior to sailing in order to receive up to date briefings and to 'demand' a camera and film. They were asked to photograph naval and, to a lesser extent, merchant vessels. The pennant numbers or names of Soviet warships were to be noted as well as details of armaments, electronic equipment and position, course and speed. Descriptions of any exercises under way were to be observed, together with details of formations of warships and the range, accuracy and estimated rate of fire if possible. The names and approximate tonnage of merchant vessels, indications as to their likely cargoes, details of gun positions and radar aerials were also to be noted. Finally, the types, distinguishing marks and courses of overflying aircraft were to be recorded.
4. Op. Cit., Jóhannesson, *Troubled Waters: Cod War and Britain's Fight for Freedom of the High Seas*, p. 50.
5. Op. Cit., Boyd, *British Naval Intelligence*, p. 569; Peter Hennessy & James Jinks, *The Silent Deep: The Royal Navy Submarine Service since 1945*, Allen Lane, London (2015), pp. 95–6.
6. Richard J Aldrich, *The Hidden Hand: Britain, America and Cold War Secret Intelligence*, The Overlook Press, New York (2001), p. 523. A naval officer, at this period, recalls being shown

7. an echo sounder trace by a trawler skipper revealing a hitherto undetected trench in which Soviet submarines could hide. Subsequently, naval intelligence showed much interest in this discovery.
7. Ibid., Aldrich, *The Hidden Hand*, p. 523. Britain was not alone in using trawlers for this purpose in the Barents Sea. The Norwegian Defence Intelligence Staff began experimenting with trawlers for the same purpose in the mid-1950s. Richard Aldrich states that at first they were used for photographic reconnaissance but later this extended to SigInt monitoring. They even commissioned a fake shipping company called *Egerfast* to run the operations and its first vessel, *Eger*, was in service in 1956. It used equipment provided by the US National Security Agency. See, Ibid., Aldrich, *The Hidden Hand*, p. 398.
8. GFHC, 1347/2, *Distant Water Project 2010–2011*, Tom Smith.
9. Op. Cit., Boyd, *Naval Intelligence*, pp. 595–96.
10. A former officer of one of the four-strong RN SSBN force recalls that the first challenge on a patrol was getting out of the Clyde without being detected by a specially converted Soviet fishing trawler. 'There was always one on station off Malin Head, and there were others about.' See, John Parker, *The Silent Service: The Inside Story of the Royal Navy's Submarine Service*, Headline Book Publishing, London (2001), p. 324.
11. Op. Cit., Hennessey & Jinks, *The Silent Deep*, p. 96.
12. Hansard, *House of Commons Debate*, British Trawler (Detention), Vol. 475, 5 & 8 May, 1950.
13. Ibid., *House of Commons Debate*, 8 May 1950.
14. Op. Cit., Jóhannesson, *Troubled Waters*, p. 51.
15. Op. Cit., ADM 1/28914, Conduct of Patrols in Northern Waters.
16. Raymond V B Blackburn, editor, *Jane's Fighting Ships 1950–51*, David & Charles Reprints, Newton Abbot, (1975), p. 59; Ibid., Jóhannesson, *Troubled Waters*, p. 52.
17. TNA FO 371/94879 *Incidents involving British ships, including trawlers and HMS Truelove sailing within twelve mile limit of Soviet waters* (1951).
18. Ibid., FO371/94879, Report of Meeting: 'Patrols by HM Fishery Protection Vessels off the Soviet Coast'.
19. Op. Cit., Grove, *From Vanguard to Trident*, pp. 39–40.
20. Op. Cit., *House of Commons Debate*, Mr Callaghan's Statement, Vol. 485, 12 March 1951.
21. Op. Cit., Bar-Noi, 'The Cold War and Britain's Dispute with the USSR', pp. 199–200.
22. Op. Cit., Jóhannesson, *Troubled Waters*, p. 104. Jóhannesson is quoting from a MAF internal minute, FO371/209/1216.
23. Op. Cit., Op. Cit., Bar-Noi, 'The Cold War and Britain's Dispute with the USSR', p. 202.
24. Op. Cit., Helin, 'Soviet Fishing in the Barents Sea and the North Atlantic', pp. 390–391.
25. Op. Cit., Bar-Noi, 'The Cold War and Britain's Dispute with the USSR', p. 202.
26. Ibid., pp. 203–204.
27. Op. Cit., Boyd, *British Naval Intelligence*, p. 579.
28. Whether or not the White Sea should be considered a 'closed sea' or a 'bay' was another matter for debate. The Russians had declared it a 'closed sea' in 1893; in 1956 the international naval law handbook called it a 'historic bay'. In 1960, a Soviet statute included the area within its state boundary, declaring it to have 'special economic/strategic significance'. See William E Butler, 'Soviet Territorial Waters', in *World Affairs*, Vol. 130, No. I (1967), pp. 19–20.
29. Op. Cit., Bar-Noi, 'The Cold War and Britain's Dispute with the USSR', p. 207.
30. Op. Cit., Thór, *British Trawlers and Iceland, 1919–1976*, p. 101.
31. TNA ADM 116/2767 *Fishery Protection Flotillas 1930–31*. Senior Officer Report: Appendix II, Deductions, Proposals and Conclusions.
32. Ibid., ADM 116/2767 Senior Officer Report: Conclusions.
33. TNA, ADM 116/2966 *Fishery Protection & Minesweeping Flotilla 1933*. Letter of Proceedings, June 1933.
34. Op. Cit., Thór, *British Trawlers and Iceland, 1919–1976*, p. 102.
35. Ibid., p. 103.

36. TNA, ADM116/3504 *Fishery Protection Flotilla:* Quarterly Reports, 1936–37. Iceland. The same report voices concern over the increasingly aggressive tactics adopted by the Icelandic fishery protection vessels.
37. Ibid.
38. NA, ADM1/9490 *Arrest of British Trawlers by Iceland 1937–38.* Report by CO HMS *Boyne.* The Icelandic naval force was established around 1930 and consisted entirely of fishery protection vessels. In the 1930s it comprised two armed trawlers, *Aegir,* 497 tons and *Thór,* 226 tons, together with *Sudin,* 811 tons and dating from 1895. Two further vessels were added to the force later in the decade: in 1938, MFV *Óðinn,* 72 tons and *Esja,* 1939, 1,347 tons. See, Op. Cit., Gardiner, editor, *Conway's All the World's Fighting Ships 1922–46,* p. 425.
39. Jeffrey A Hart, *The Anglo-Icelandic Cod War of 1972–73: A Case Study of a Fishery Dispute,* University of California (1976), pp. 41–42. GIUK – Greenland, Iceland, United Kingdom.
40. Op. Cit., Jóhannesson, *Troubled Waters,* pp. 29–30.
41. TNA, ADM1/19737, *Quarterly Fishery Report of Proceedings 1April 1946–30 June 1946.*
42. Op. Cit., Thór, *British Trawlers and Iceland, 1919–1976,* pp. 111–112.
43. Jóhannesson, *Troubled Waters,* pp. 62–68.
44. Richard Osborne, The Third 'Cod War' 11.75 to 6.76, *Warships Supplement No. 52,* World Ship Society, Kendal (1978), p. 10.
45. Jóhannesson, *Troubled Waters,* p. 78.
46. TNA ADM1/28914. *Fishery Protection: Instructions relating to patrols in Northern waters, 1952–56.* Fishery Protection Charge Document 1, 8 May 1952.
47. GuÐmundur J. Guðmundsson, 'The Cod and the Cold War', in *Scandinavian Journal of History,* Vol. 31, No. 2 (2006), p. 98.
48. Ibid., p. 99.
49. Op. Cit., ADM1/28914 'Fishery Protection Charge Document No. 1. Section IV: Territorial Waters.'
50. TNA, ADM1/26774 *Icelandic Fishing Limits, 1955–58.* Despite the fact that Britain was officially rebuilding its armed forces after the Second World War, the devil was in the detail, as was so often the case. For example, the 1952 Navy Estimates showed an increase in spending of £38 million in construction but over 80 per cent of it would go on ships already building. See, Op. Cit., Wettern, *The Decline of British Sea Power,* p. 62.
51. Op. Cit., Guðmundsson, 'The Cod and the Cold War', p. 99.
52. Op. Cit., Jóhannesson, *Troubled Waters,* p. 114.
53. Op. Cit., Karlsdóttir, *Fishing Rights in the Post-War Period,* p. 108.
54. Op. Cit., Welch, *The Royal Navy in the Cod Wars,* p. 35.
55. Ibid., p. 35.
56. Op. Cit., Thór, *British Trawlers and Iceland, 1919–1976,* pp. 185–86.
57. Op. Cit., Welch, *The Royal Navy in the Cod Wars,* p. 39.
58. The term 'cod war' has remained synonymous with the eighteen-year conflict ever since.
59. Op. Cit., Welch, *The Royal Navy in the Cod Wars,* p. 26.
60. Op. Cit., Jóhannesson, *Troubled Waters,* p. 169.

Chapter Nine

1. Captain Helgi Hallvardsson, a junior Icelandic officer at the time of the First Cod War, commented later, 'I have been inclined to call the first fishing dispute a war of nerves of sorts. We tried to make the British nervous and the warships tried the same against us.' See, Op. Cit., Welch, *The Royal Navy in the Cod Wars,* p. 37.
2. Andrew Welch notes, 'They looked upon naval protection as a right but did not acknowledge any linked responsibility to follow the Navy's advice or their owner's instructions. They were generous with their fish when the Navy was in favour and withdrew their cooperation when they felt let down.'; Ibid., Welch, p. 273.
3. Ibid., Welch, p. 71. The Type 14s HMS *Palliser, Russell, Duncan* and *Malcolm,* between them, undertook thirty-five patrols between 1958–1961 providing 572 days off Iceland.
4. Op. Cit., Jónsson, *Friends in Conflict,* pp. 95–96.
5. Paddy Johnston, 'The Cod Wars against Iceland: The Royal Navy as political Instrument', in *Cambridge Review of International Affairs,* Francis

and Taylor Publishers, Oxford, (1991), Vol. 5, No. 2, p. 10.
6. Peter Hennessy, *Having It So Good: Britain in the Fifties*, Penguin Books, London (2007), pp. 461 & 463–468. Hennessy writes, 'The White Paper went through thirteen "final" drafts – there was blood on every page.' See also, Op. Cit., Dockrill, *Britain's Retreat from East of Suez*, pp. 22–25.
7. Ibid., Dockrill, p. 25.
8. The problem of what to do with the Icelandic boarding party lasted for some time as *Eastbourne* was not able to land them on the mainland. In the end they were placed in the frigate's whaler near Keflavik and they rowed themselves ashore. *Eastbourne*, thus, had to sacrifice one of its ship's boats. See Op. Cit., Welch, *The Royal Navy in the Cod Wars*, p. 43.
9. Naval Staff History BR1736(57), HMSO, London (1990). *The Cod War: Naval Operations off Iceland in Support of the British Fishing Industry, 1958-1976*, Chapter 2; Ibid., Welch, pp. 41–42.
10. Op. Cit., Jóhannesson, *Troubled Waters*, pp. 173 & 174.
11. Op. Cit., HMSO, *The Cod War: Naval Operations off Iceland*, Chapter 2.
12. Op. Cit., Welch, *The Royal Navy in the Cod Wars*, p. 42. See also, Op. Cit., Jóhannesson, *Troubled Waters*, p. 174.
13. Op. Cit., Welch, *The Royal Navy in the Cod Wars*, p. 78.
14. Ibid., Welch, pp. 44–45; Op. Cit., HMSO, *The Cod War: Naval Operations off Iceland*, Chapter 2.
15. Op. Cit., Welch, p. 47.
16. ADM306/32 *Report of Proceedings: 4th Destroyer Squadron, January–February 1959*. Captain E Sinclair.
17. Ibid., ADM 306/32 *Report of Proceedings*. Captain Sinclair is pretty damning in his report about two RFA tankers in particular, *Wave Baron* and *Wave Ruler*. Commenting on *Wave Baron*, he wrote, 'There were too many occasions when she stopped pumping during the operation. Its deck crew were the worst I have ever seen and abysmally slow.' He wrote of *Wave Ruler*'s performance, 'When not fuelling she was loathe to steer a course across the sea because, I understand, of the vulnerability of her upper deck fittings ...'.
18. ADM 306/31 *Report of Proceedings: 4th Destroyer Squadron, May 1959*. Captain E Sinclair.
19. Op. Cit., Welch, *The Royal Navy in the Cod Wars*, pp. 51–52.
20. Ibid., p. 52.
21. Richard Wright claims that he was involved in all three Cod Wars. In a probable reference to the First, he recalls, 'It was great, well we used to have a bag of spuds and chuck spuds at 'em ... we took it as a joke 'cos they only had little wooden boats then.' See, Op. Cit., GFHC, *Oral History Interview Transcriptions*, 1347/2, Richard Wright.
22. Ibid., Welch, *The Royal Navy in the Cod Wars*, p. 56.
23. ADM 306/60 *Operation Whippet: Intelligence from Icelandic Sources, 1958–59*. Letter: Director of Naval Intelligence to Head of MII, 29 January 1959.
24. ADM 306/6 Operation Whippet – organisation, 1959–60. Captain FPS's OP-ORDER, 3 September 1959. The selection of HMS *Apollo* was quite possibly driven by expediency rather than choice. The ex-fast minelayer was very lightly built because of its exceptional 40-knot speed and had a standard displacement of 2,850 tons. It rode high in the water when not loaded with mines, which made it roll uncomfortably even in good weather.
25. Ibid., ADM 306/6 Captain FPS's OP-ORDER.
26. Ibid.
27. Ibid., ADM 306/6, Appendix H.
28. ADM 306/38 *Icelandic Fisheries: proposals for future running of Icelandic Patrol, 1959–62*. Summary by Head of M Branch, August 1959.
29. Ibid., ADM 306/38, Summary.
30. Ibid., ADM 306/38, Memorandum K Pritchard, M Branch, April 1960.
31. Hansard, Vol. 625, *Grimsby Trawler Officers' Guild (Complaint)*, Wednesday, 22 June 1960.
32. Op. Cit., Jóhannesson, *Troubled Waters*, p. 232.
33. John Roberts, *Safeguarding the Nation: The Story of the Modern Royal Navy*, Seaforth Publishing, Barnsley (2009), p. 23.
34. Op. Cit., Paddy Johnston, 'The Cod Wars against Iceland', p. 11.
35. GFHC, *Oral History Interview Transcriptions*, 1347/2, Jim Clark.

36. Author's telephone conversation with Charles Wylie, 28 December 2022.
37. Op. Cit., Guðmundsson, 'The Cod and the Cold War', pp. 101–102.
38. The GIUK gap, at the height of the Cold War, was heavily patrolled by NATO aircraft, submarines and surface ships as well as monitored by undersea sensors (SOSUS) because it would have been a major access point for the Soviet Navy to break out into the Atlantic and threaten the principal transatlantic supply routes to continental Europe.
39. Op. Cit., Butler, *The Soviet Union and the Law of the Sea*, p. 99.
40. ADM 306/44 *Icelandic complaints re: conduct of trawler Milwood, 1963–64*. Appendix I to Captain Fishery Protection Squadron's Letter, 13 May 1963.
41. Ibid., ADM 306/44, Appendix I, Paragraph 6.
42. Ibid., Paragraph 7–21.
43. Ibid., Paragraph 22–32.
44. Op. Cit., Welch, *The Royal Navy in the Cod Wars*, pp. 85–86. Lieutenant Commander Hunt's career did not suffer in the long run. He went on to become Commander-in-Chief Fleet in the 1980s.
45. The civil servant-manned M Branch served as intermediaries between Ministers and the Office of the First Sea Lord. The protection of trade and fisheries was within its remit. This branch is the secret and political office of the Admiralty and is entrusted with the conduct of confidential affairs.
46. The aggressive attitude shown by the HMDNS *Niels Ebbesen* seemed to be accepted policy in the Danish Navy. The Captain RN Fishery Protection, following a tour of a Danish FP vessel in 1964, was told by the CO that he, 'would not hesitate to fire on British trawlers should skippers refuse to submit to Danish jurisdiction'. See Op. Cit., ADM 306/44, *Captain Fishery Protection, Report of Proceedings*, 1964. The Foreign Office recommended that the new Faroese 12-mile fishery limit, due to come into force in March 1964, should be formally recognised by Britain despite the fact that the decision was expected to be very unpopular with the British fishing industry. Unquestionably, the accommodating approach by the British Government was due to the ongoing high strategic value to NATO of the Faroe Islands, which can be directly compared with the fears over Iceland siding with the Soviets. See, DEFE, 6/84, Section 28, *The Importance of the Faroe Islands to NATO, 1963*.
47. Ibid., ADM 306/44, Head of Military Branch Memorandum, Paragraphs 3–6, 7 January 1964.
48. Ibid., ADM 306/44, Flag Officer, Scotland and Northern Ireland, Report: The Milwood Incident, 20 May 1963.
49. Ibid., ADM 306/44, Memorandum: First Lord of the Admiralty to Assistant Chief of Naval Staff, Civil Lord of the Admiralty, Head of MII, May 1963.
50. Op. Cit., Welch, *The Royal Navy in the Cod Wars*, pp. 88–89.
51. Britain signed the agreement in October 1964, with other countries following suit over a period of several years.
52. Hansard, House of Commons Debate, Vol. 696, *Fishery Limits Bill, Second Reading*, 15 June, 1964.

Chapter Ten
1. The term 'patrimonial sea', used in the documentation, arose from the 1972 'Santo Domingo Declaration on the Law of the Sea', which was signed by ten Central American states. This asserted 'sovereign rights over the renewable and non-renewable natural resources, which are found in the waters, in the seabed and in the sub-soil of an area adjacent to the sea is called the patrimonial sea'. See, Op. Cit., *Friends in Conflict*, pp. 117–118.
2. Op. Cit., Thór, *British Trawlers and Iceland*, pp. 200–201.
3. Op. Cit., Guðmundsson, 'The Cod and the Cod War', p. 103.
4. Ibid., p. 104.
5. Op. Cit., Hart, *The Anglo-Icelandic Cod War of 1972–7*, p. 11.
6. Op. Cit., Welch, *The Royal Navy in the Cod Wars*, p. 95.
7. Op. Cit., Thór, *British Trawlers and Iceland 1919–1976*, p. 204.
8. Op. Cit., Hart, *The Anglo-Icelandic Cod War*, p. 27, and Op. Cit. Welch, *The Royal Navy in the Cod Wars*, pp. 96–97.
9. Ibid., Welch, *The Royal Navy in the Cod Wars*, p. 101; Op. Cit., Jónsson, *Friends in Conflict*, p. 135.
10. Welch states that ICGV *Ægir* might have attempted an experimental trawl cutting run during the 1959–61 conflict.

See, Ibid., Welch, *The Royal Navy in the Cod Wars*, p. 99. According to Thór, the statistics for warp cutting come from three sources. See, Thór, *British Trawlers and Iceland 1919–1976*, pp. 204–205. Welch also notes that between March and April 1973 there were four incidents where guns were fired in the direction of the trawlers.
11. Op. Cit., Hart, *The Anglo-Icelandic Cod War of 1972–73*, pp. 28–31.
12. Ibid., pp. 32–33.
13. Op. Cit., Welch, *The Royal Navy in the Cod Wars*, p. 107; TNA, DEFE 25/710, *Contingency Plans and Operations, 20 February–1 April, 1973*. Minute: Iceland – Provision of Tugs, 30 March 1973.
14. Op. Cit., Guðmundsson, 'The Cod and the Cod War', p. 104; Op. Cit., Thór, *British Trawlers and Iceland 1919–1976*, p. 206. Thór remarks, 'the tugs were bigger and stronger than the trawlers, made better speed and were well suited for ramming the coastguard vessels'; Ibid., DEFE 25/710, MAFF Report: 'Iceland, Use of Tugs – assessment by Fisheries Department', 14 March 1973.
15. Ibid., DEFE 25/710. Hannes Jónsson dismisses the tactic as 'ineffective' and counter-productive as it reduced the potential catch by at least 50 per cent. Moreover, the ICGV commanders had little difficulty in outwitting this tactic. See, Op. Cit., Jónsson, *Friends in Conflict*, p. 137. Ægir had a maximum speed of 19 knots; Óðinn, 18 knots.
16. Ibid., DEFE 25/710, 'Behind the Cod War'. Royal Navy Board Bulletin (draft), 16 March 1973.
17. Op. Cit., Welch, *The Royal Navy in the Cod Wars*, pp. 113–115.
18. The notion that the various governmental departments always worked harmoniously and without interdepartmental rivalry at all times is misleading. A minute by a naval civil servant noted, 'We are using commercial vessels under commercial management (i.e. tugs, support ships) so we can't expect naval standards of maintenance.' Another minute, three days later, commenting on the liaison between MAFF, FOSNI and the Department of Transport, observed that the MoD was, 'trying not to make radical changes in the command of the tugs, which is jealously guarded by MAFF'. See, Op. Cit., DEFE 25/710, Minutes, 16 & 19 March 1973.
19. Ibid., Welch, *The Royal Navy in the Cod Wars*, pp. 117–118.
20. Op. Cit., Jónsson, *Friends in Conflict*, p. 139; Op. Cit., Thór, *British Trawlers and Iceland 1919–1976*, p. 206.
21. Op. Cit., Welch, *The Royal Navy in the Cod Wars*, p. 133.
22. DEFE 24/637, *Iceland Fish Patrol – Report of Proceedings, 1973*. FOSNI Report of Proceedings, Operation Dewey, 31 January 1974.
23. Ibid., The Icelanders viewed the Nimrod sorties as ineffective, at least prior to the arrival of the RN in May 1973.
24. DEFE 24/712, *Contingency Plans and Operations, 1973*. Letter: British Embassy, Bonn to Foreign and Commonwealth Office, 31 August 1973.
25. Op. Cit., Welch, *The Royal Navy in the Cod Wars*, p. 120.
26. DEFE 24/711, *Contingency Plans and Operations, April–May 1973*. MAFF Report on *Árvakur* Incident, 23 April 1973.
27. Ibid., DEFE 24/711, MAFF Report on *Árvakur* Incident, 23 April 1973. Commenting on the *Irishman* incident, Jónsson writes, 'The radar plots shows the first of five rammings made on this occasion, with the apparent purpose of sinking the *Árvakur*.' See, Op. Cit., Jónsson, *Friends in Conflict*, p. 143.
28. Op. Cit., DEFE 24/712, Memorandum: Director of Naval Operations and Trade – 'Leopard/Aegir Incident on 2 July', 5 July 1973.
29. Ibid.
30. Ibid., DEFE 24/712, Icelandic Coastguard Service Report to the Chief Criminal Judge, Reykjavik: Illegal fishing Lord St Vincent H-261, 14 July 1973. A copy of *Ægir*'s commander's evidence to the court is included among the various reports of proceedings in the MoD records.
31. Op. Cit., Welch, *The Royal Navy in the Cod Wars*, p. 138. Welch, perhaps generously, gives the benefit of the doubt to the trawler's skipper suggesting that he might have made a navigational error. The radar plots aboard both *Sirius* and *Englishman* showed that the *Lord St Vincent* was fishing at least a mile and a half inside the 12-mile limit.

32. Ibid., Welch, *The Royal Navy in the Cod Wars*, p. 139.
33. Ibid., p. 140.
34. TNA, DEFE 24/944, *Reports of Incidents off Iceland involving Royal Navy vessels*. Signal: HMS *Jaguar* to C-in-C Fleet, 4 October 1973.
35. Op. Cit., Thór, *British Trawlers and Iceland 1919–1976*, p. 211.
36. Op. Cit., DEFE24/944, *Reports of Incidents off Iceland*. Unclassified Signal HMS *Lincoln* to MoD, 23 September 1973.
37. Ibid., DEFE24/944, Unclassified Signal HMS *Lincoln* to MoD.
38. Ibid.
39. Op. Cit., Guðmundsson, 'The Cod and the Cod War', p. 105. The Icelandic Embassy in London employed staff to co-ordinate press coverage in order that their country's position on the issue of the day could be publicised quickly and efficiently. A British journalist, Llewellyn Chanter, was hired to present the Icelandic cause.
40. James Goldick, *Grey Zone Operations and the Maritime Domain*, Australian Strategic Policy Institute, Barton (2018), p. 9.
41. DEFE24/713 *Contingency Plans and Operations, 1973*. Letter: Foreign and Colonial Office to Secretary of State for Defence, 'Publicity for Incidents off Iceland', 21 September 1973.
42. Ibid., DEFE24/713 Note of Meeting: 'The Icelandic Dispute – Publicity', 25 September 1973.
43. Ibid., DEFE24/Minute: 'Iceland Publicity – Lincoln/Aegir', 1 October 1973.
44. Improvements were made by the time of the Third Cod War and certainly the PR 'machine' was fully engaged during the Falklands War of 1982, with TV cameras and journalists embarked as the Task Force sailed south. It is salient to note that the first book-length account of the Cod Wars, by Hannes Jónsson, distinctly slanted towards the Icelandic cause, was published in 1982. The first book written from the British point of view, by Captain Andrew Welch RN, did not appear in print until 2006.
45. Some idea of the intensity and the sheer numbers of the engagements that took place during the last Cod War can be gained by comparing the chart with statistics from the Second Cod War in which there were nine collisions between ICGVs and RN frigates (three with tugs) and six attempted arrests. Fourteen warps were cut. See, Op. Cit., Welch, *The Royal Navy in the Cod Wars*, p. 161.
46. TNA, ADM 330/101, *HMS Yarmouth and Thor, 24 February, 1976*. Commander M Jones: Report of Proceedings, 24 February, 1976.
47. Ibid., ADM 330/101, Report of Proceedings. 'Back and fill' refers to frequent and large variations in speed, much easier to execute with a diesel-engined ship than a steam-turbine frigate equipped with controllable-pitch propellers. Commander Jones's report is accompanied by a remarkable sequence of photographs that show the two vessels in the moments before and then at the point of impact. Clearly, this was a good 'spectator sport' for the crews who can be seen gathered aft watching the action. In one photograph, one of *Thór*'s crew members is watching while seemingly idly leaning on a stanchion.
48. Op. Cit., Welch, *The Royal Navy in the Cod Wars*, p. 194.
49. Chris Handley, 'Icelandic Patrol 18 February–2 March 1976' in *South West Maritime History Society Journal*, Issue 56 (2003), pp. 2 & 7. In the event Rosyth Dockyard did not repair *Yarmouth*, so it proceeded to Chatham and the frigate, 'was turned round in nine weeks, compared with the estimate of 16 weeks at Rosyth' reported a delighted *Periscope*, the in-house Chatham Royal Dockyard newspaper. Repairs to HMS *Yarmouth* required the fitting of almost a complete new bow section, which was complicated by the shape of the replacement part. See, *Periscope, Chatham Dockyard Newspaper*, June 1976.
50. Estimates of the number of attempts made to engineer collisions vary between twenty and thirty. Be that as it may, it has been made clear since the Cod War that personal ill-feeling had developed between HMS *Diomede*'s CO Captain McQueen and ICGV *Baldur*'s Captain Skarphéðinsson.
51. ADM 330/108, *HMS Diomede and Baldur 27 March 1976, 4 incidents*. Captain R McQueen: Report of Proceedings, 29 March 1976.
52. DEFE 13/1033, *Secretary of State's papers in the Cod War with*

Iceland, January – March, 1976. Memorandum: First Sea Lord to Secretary of State for Defence, 29 March, 1976. 'Iceland – Review of Rules of Engagement consequent upon Icelandic Coastguard Vessels' Ramming Tactics'.
53. An earlier brief for the Secretary of State on counter-ramming using CDVs notes, 'What is envisaged here is that Ministers might agree now, that if Baldur were to indulge in any further ramming attack on a frigate, CTG 600.1 should be free to contrive a situation in which one of the CDVs might ram Baldur in such a way as to cause a substantial amount of damage (though stop well short of sinking her). The aim would be that morale on board Baldur should thereby be undermined and that, even if she remained and was operational … it would serve as a deterrent.' See, Ibid., DEFE 13/1033, Note: Brief for secretary of State: Iceland – Rules of Engagement, 2 April 1976.
Only *Lloydsman* had the speed to match the four major ICGV vessels. The other option was to use the three civilian-manned RMAS tugs but their slow speeds and structural unsuitability ruled them out.
54. Ibid., DEFE 13/1033, Memo: Minister of Trade to Secretary of Defence, 12 April 1976.
55. Ibid: DEFE 13/1033, 'Iceland – Review of Rules of Engagement consequent upon Icelandic Coastguard Vessels', 29 March 1976.
56. TNA, ADM 330/110, *HMS Salisbury and Tyr, 5 incidents, 1 April 1976*. Commander H.M. White: Report of Proceedings, 9 April 1976. HMS *Salisbury*, a Type 61 frigate, had first commissioned in February 1957 and was thus the oldest ship involved in the Third Cod War. Its Admiralty Standard Range 1 diesels made it unique among the other RN frigates employed off Iceland. *Salisbury* had a modest top speed of 24 knots, which proved to be too slow for prolonged fleet work. On the other hand, its exceptionally long range of 7,500 miles was adequate for convoy operations. See, Captain John E Moore RN, *Warships of the Royal Navy*. Macdonald and Jane's, London (1979), p. 48.
57. Ibid.

58. For instance, Chatham Dockyard considered that the work required to repair HMS *Juno*, which sustained damage to its bow and port quarter on 12 March following a clash with *Tyr*, was the biggest job they faced, requiring some seventy men working continuously in two shifts until midnight each day. See, Op. Cit., *Periscope*, 'Cod War Frigates Repaired', April 1976, p. 2.
59. The 'Tribal' class were designed to serve as self-contained units in the Persian Gulf. Although the combination steam and gas propulsion system provided swift acceleration, manoeuvrability was inhibited by having a single screw – an unfortunate cost-cutting measure. See, Op. Cit., Moore, *Warships of the Royal Navy*, p. 43.
60. ADM 330/113, *HMS Gurkha and Odinn, 6 & 7 May 1976*. Commander T R Lee: Report of Proceedings, 12 May 1976.
61. Ibid.
62. ADM 330/114, *HMS Falmouth and Tyr, May–July 1976*. Letter: FOSNI to C-in-C Fleet, 21 May 1976.
63. Ibid., ADM 330/114, Commander G A Plumer, Report of Proceedings, 11 May 1976.
64. Ibid., ADM 330/114, Icelandic Press Report, 7 May 1976.
65. Ibid.
66. DEFE 69/675: *Fishery Protection off Iceland during the Cod War 1976*. Summary of Incidents.
67. The description given is by the *Sunday Independent* journalist Jim Dalrymple, who was on board HMS *Naiad* during the last days of the war.
68. Op. Cit., Welch, *The Royal Navy in the Cod Wars*, pp. 251 & 258.
69. Op. Cit., Thór, *British Trawlers and Iceland 1919–1976*, p. 224.
70. Op. Cit., Welch, *The Royal Navy in the Cod Wars*, p. 263.
71. DEFE 13/1034, *Secretary of State's papers on the Cod War with Iceland, March–June 1976*. Letter from Grimsby/Humberside Town Council to Leader of Council, 9 June 1976.
72. Ibid., DEFE 13/1304, MAFF Interim Policy for the Fishing Industry, 26 May 1976; Letter: MAFF to Department of Prices and Consumer Protection, 'Aid for Restructuring of Fishing Industry', 8 June 1976.

73. Ibid., DEFE 13/1304, Memorandum: Foreign Secretary to Prime Minister, 7 June 1976.
74. See Sir Lawrence Freedman, *Command: The Politics of Military Operations from Korea to Ukraine*, Penguin Books, London (2022).
75. Op. Cit., Welch, *The Royal Navy in the Cod Wars*, p. 224.
76. Op. Cit., email from Charles Wylie, 9 January 2023.
77. Op. Cit., Thriplow et al, *Distant Water*, p. 140.
78. GFHC, 1347/2, *Distant Water Project, 2010–2011*, Oral History Interviews, various.

Chapter Eleven

1. TNA CAB 164/1820 *Future of Fishery Protection Arrangements, 1985–86*. Report: Future Fishery Protection Arrangements, Appendix A, 1985.
2. Op. Cit., Welch, *The Royal Navy in the Cod Wars*, p. 265.
3. Ibid., Grove, *Vanguard to Trident*, p. 292.
4. Jórge Boveda, *All for One, One for All: Argentine Navy Operations during the Falklands/Malvinas War*, Helion & Co. Ltd, Warwick (2021), p. 19.
5. In common with many officers who served in this capacity, Michael Livesay later attained flag rank. He was appointed Assistant Chief of the Naval Staff in 1986 and Flag Officer Scotland and Northern Ireland in 1989. His final posting was as Second Sea Lord and Chief of Naval Personnel.
6. Op. Cit., DEFE 13/1350, *Fishery Protection*: Examination of Witnesses.
7. Ibid., DEFE 13/1350, Examination of Witnesses. A separate comment with regard to the 'Island' class also makes reference to the recent conflict off Iceland. It was felt that there was no need to further strengthen the new ships because it was thought, 'that a Cod War situation is most unlikely to develop'. See, DEFE 69/675, *Fishery Protection off Iceland during the Cod War, 1976*.
8. DEFE 48/971 *Shipborne helicopters in fishery protection operations, 1977*. Report.
9. Op. Cit DEFE 13/1350, Examination of Witnesses.
10. Ibid.
11. The unsuitability of HMS Tenacity is discussed in detail in DEFE 69/657, *Resources for Off-Shore Tasks, 1976–77*, 'HMS Tenacity – Future', Report for VCNS by Director of Naval Operations, 4 January 1977.
12. Ibid., DEFE 69/657, 'Study of the possibility of future off-shore tasks being carried out by ships with a high level wartime capability', February 1977. It is interesting to note the comment made in the report that, 'fitting "for but not with" introduces more problems than it solves'. Clearly opinion has changed radically on that matter during the past forty-five years.
13. Op. Cit., DEFE 13/1350, Examination of Witnesses.
14. DEFE 24/952 *Fishery Protection future regime, common fishery policy; contingency planning, 1977*. Letter, MoD to FCO, 1.2.77.
15. Ibid., DEFE 24/952 Letter MoD to FCO.
16. Certainly, suggestions that an aggressive approach should be adopted were not shared by everyone within the Navy. The Director of Plans, in the course of a wide-ranging assessment of the requirements for meeting the new Offshore Tapestry tasks, wrote that policing the extended fishing zone 'would not be enforced by confrontation methods such as those employed in the 3rd Cod War'. See, Op. Cit., DEFE 69/657, *Resources for Off-Shore Tapestry – a look to the future*.
17. DEFE 68/359 *Fishery Protection within UK limits, 1976–77*. Memo: 'The Daniel Roger Incident'. A few years later, a quick-thinking Lieutenant Kingwell managed to avoid being 'kidnapped' to Denmark aboard the fishing vessel *Ulla Moller*. As Fishery Officer aboard the FP minesweeper HMS *Sheraton*, he had discovered an illegal hoard of mackerel hidden in the hold. When the *Ulla Moller* headed off at top speed for Copenhagen, Kingwell told the skipper, 'the maximum fine for illegal fishing of mackerel was some £5,000 but the penalty for kidnapping a EU Fishery Officer was far more severe – it was his call. That evening we were alongside in Falmouth.' See: Rear Admiral John Kingwell, *Maritime Strike: The Untold Story of the Royal Navy Task Group off Libya in 2011*, Casemate Publishers, Oxford (2022), pp. 9–10.

18. Ibid., DEFE 68/359 Memo: Extension of Fishery Limits. October 1976.
19. The MoD had indeed anticipated the high level of public interest caused by the extension of the EEZ to 200 miles and the exploitation of North Sea oil and gas resources. See, Op. Cit., DEFE 69/657, *Resources for Off-Shore Tasks, 1976–77*.
20. *Daily Telegraph* & *Sunday Telegraph Magazine* articles: 3 October 1976 and 27 July 1977; DEFE 24/802 *Fishery Protection: foreign (including Soviet) fishing activity around the UK 1974–77*. Minute: Captain FPS 26 July 1976 & Letter: FOST to C-in-C Fleet, 27.11.75.
21. Hansard, House of Commons Debates, 'Exclusive Economic Zone', Vol. 373, 12 May 1976 and 'Royal Navy', Vol. 911, 12 May 1975.
22. Robert Gardiner, editor, *Conway's All the World's Fighting Ships, 1947–1995*, Conway Maritime Press, London (1995), p. 537. *Conway's* describes the design as 'so successful' in operation that it led to the ordering of two more vessels in October 1977, this time fitted with stabilisers. Eric Grove is less effusive, describing the 'Island' class as 'more successful sea boats (although not as good as hoped for) …'. See, Op. Cit., Grove, *Vanguard to Trident*, p. 333. The award of the shipbuilding contract exclusively to Hall Russell courted controversy at a time. Competition for orders was acute, particularly for naval work, as a result of the decision to nationalise British Shipbuilding. Hall Russell acknowledged the fact that they had based the design of the prototype *Jura* on its experience with building *Switha* (1948), a successful mainstay of the Scottish FP force for some years. See Op. Cit., Somner, *Scottish Fishery Protection*, pp. 18 & 39.
23. Grove, *Vanguard to Trident*, p. 333. Despite their credited sea-worthiness, the 'Island' class later needed to be fitted with stabilisers.
24. Of the 'pool' of eight 'Ton'-class vessels assigned to the FP task around 1975, the youngest was launched in 1957, the oldest in 1952.
25. DEFE 69/279, *Command Organisation of Mine Countermeasures and Fishery Protection Flotillas 1975–77*. Minute: Command Organisation for Mine Countermeasures/Fishery Protection, 21 March 1975.
26. MAF 452/9 *Fishery Protection: replacement of Royal Navy Ton Class minesweepers, 1977–81*. Memo: Conduct of Operations (The One/Two Tier System) 1977.
27. Interestingly, in a sign of the times, the welfare of personnel was regarded as an important factor. One of the advantages of the one-tier system was the opportunity it allowed for a mix of tasks. The more distant OPV role was described as arduous and tedious in comparison with the more attractive coastal tasks. It was felt that this would lead to more job satisfaction, general alertness and be beneficial to morale.
28. Utilising his extensive knowledge and experience, David Brown later became widely known for his books and articles on Royal Navy ship design. He wrote about the 'Castle'-class design in Op. Cit., Brown & Moore, *Rebuilding the Royal Navy*, pp. 135–37, and David K Brown, 'The Design of the "Castle" Class: a personal view' in John Jordan, editor, *Warship 2006*, Conway Maritime Press, London, 2006, pp. 78–85. Brown admits that he and his team were very inexperienced, 'it was eighteen years since I had been directly involved in design work and we all needed to learn'.
29. Ibid.. Brown & Moore, pp. 136–37.
30. Op. Cit., Brown, 'The Design of the "Castle" Class', pp. 78–9 & 82.
31. T475/52 *Fisheries Protection: cost sharing of Castle Class vessel, 1981*.
32. Hansard, *House of Commons Debate*, Vol. 80, Defence Estimates 1985, 13 June 1985.
33. The fact that 'cost' would be the key factor in any decision on the 'Ton'-class replacement was recognised a decade earlier, 'The future patrol vessel will of necessity have to be obtained at the lowest reasonable capital cost and its operating costs should also be kept as low as possible. With the precedent set that Defence Votes are not to be used for the provision of the ISLANDS at the expense of the Critical Level Fleet, and the running costs and future capital costs are to be shared by Civil Departments, too much emphasis on a war role may have to be avoided.' See, Op. Cit., DEFE 69/657, *Resources for Off-Shore Tasks*.

34. Op. Cit., MAF 452/9 Report: Coastal Fishery Protection – Replacement of Tons, submission to Minister of Agriculture and Fisheries, 1979.
35. According to Jorge Boveda, there was similar surprise and lack of preparation on the part of the Argentine armed services. The plan to invade the Falklands was only known by a very small number of the ruling Junta. See, Op. Cit., Boveda, *All for One, One for All*, p. 15.
36. Op. Cit., Dunn, *British Naval Trawlers and Drifters in Two World Wars*, p. 137.
37. Admiral Sandy Woodward, with Patrick Robinson, *One Hundred Days: The Memoirs of the Falklands Battle Group Commander*, HarperCollins, London (1992), p. 278.
38. Captain Roger Villar, *Merchant Ships at War: The Falklands Experience*, Conway Maritime Press & Lloyd's of London Press, London (1984), pp. 106–7; David Brown, *The Royal Navy and the Falklands War*, Guild Publishing, London (1987), p. 73.
39. Op. Cit., Dunn, *British Naval Trawlers and Drifters*, p. 138; Ibid., Villar, *Merchant Ships at War*, p. 107.
40. Lawrence Freedman, *The Official History of the Falklands Campaign: Vol. II: War and Diplomacy*, Routledge, London (2007), p. 622.
41. The Treasury report notes that the coastal aerial surveillance task covered 'some of the most sensitive fishing areas'. One can only conjecture whether this implied this included the approaches to the Clyde submarine base used by the SSBNs. See, T476/223, *Review of Fishery Protection Services 1981–83*.
42. Op. Cit., CAB 164/1820, Report: Future Fishery Protection Arrangements: The Offshore Protection Force & High Security Fencing, 21 July 1985. The protection of the North Sea oil platforms was of primary concern in the mid-1970s, being not only of economic importance but also as symbols of British power. They were deemed to be at risk of attack by various terrorist groups including the IRA and PLO. As part of OILSAFE, 5 SBS was permanently stationed at Commachio Company's base at Royal Marines Condor near Arbroath, Scotland, while 1 SBS was tasked with the protection of ports and shipping. The provision of high-security fencing for the installations was also under active consideration at the time.
43. Ibid., CAB 164/1820, Report: Future Fishery Protection Arrangements, 21 July 1985.
44. Ibid., CAB 164/1820, Press Statement, September 1985.
45. PREM 19/1493, *Fishing Industry, EEC CFP fishing limits etc*, 1981–85.
46. DEFE 69/1718/2 *Fishery Protection: General Policy, 1989–92*. Most likely the misgivings by the MoD centred around the sensitivity surrounding the security of the Clyde submarine base and the regular presence of Soviet trawlers in the approaches to the Irish Sea, which were thought to be trying to track the movements of the RN's ballistic submarine fleet.
47. Op. Cit., Roberts, *Safeguarding the Nation*, p. 202.
48. Op. Cit., DEFE 69/1718/1 Paper by ACNS: Minor War Vessels, 4 December 1989. The plan referred to in Admiral White's submission was called 'LTC90 Navy Grouping Submission, Saving Measure RN 27065'.
49. The 1690 'ship days' comprised 1330 allocated to MAFF and 360 to DAFS.
50. The second 'Castle' class had been seconded to act as the Falklands Guardship since shortly after the conflict ended. The 'River'-class MSF was adapted from an oil-rig support vessel design by Richards (Shipbuilders Ltd) to combat the threat posed to submarines by Soviet deep-water buoyant moored mines.
51. This was evident at the time with the ability shown to deploy 'Hunt'-class minehunters to the Gulf during the first Gulf War, 1991.
52. Op. Cit., DEFE 69/1718/1, Paper by ACNS.
53. Ibid., DEFE 69/1718/1, Paper by ACNS.
54. DEFE 24/3395, *Fishery Protection: General Policy 1991*. Note by ACNS, 18 September 1991.
55. Lieutenant Commander B G Wainwright RN, 'Whither or Wither Fishery Protection?' in *The Naval Review*, Vol. 80, No. 3 (1992), pp. 222–223.
56. Ibid., Wainwright, 'Whither or Wither Fishery Protection?', pp. 222–223.

57. MAF 641/2 *Fisheries Protection: provision of surface surveillance, 1992–98*. Letter: MAFF to MoD, 25 January 1998.
58. Op. Cit., Kingwell, *Maritime Strike*, pp. 13–14.
59. Ibid., Kingwell, *Maritime Strike*, p. 15.
60. Op. Cit., MAF 641/2 MAFF Internal Memo, 3 January 1995. The Spanish alleged that some British boats had been using driftnets longer than the permitted 2.5km, whereas the Spaniards used lines and hooks in the Bay of Biscay.
61. Ibid., MAF 641/2, MAFF Internal Memo, 3 January 1995.
62. Ibid., MAF 641/2, Draft Submission to the Parliamentary Secretary (Commons). Fisheries Enforcement: Surface Surveillance, January 1998.
63. A good example of the latter would be the newly completed 'Castle'-class OPVs, which were almost immediately withdrawn from their tasks in the EFZ to serve in the Falklands War.

Chapter Twelve
1. The Government documents for the period after 2000 have yet to be released. Therefore, this claim may be inaccurate.
2. As noted in the Introduction, the non-gender specific term 'fishers' will be used in this chapter in recognition of the fact that fishing vessels are no longer crewed only by men.
3. House of Commons Library, *UK Fishing Statistics, 11 October 2022*.
4. After Scotland, the next most productive regions were the South-West, Northern Ireland, the South-East and York/Humber in that order.
5. MoD, *Statistical Series 5 – Activities Bulletin 5.01 – Military Aid to the Civil Authorities, June 2014*. https://assets.publishing.service.gov.uk
6. Ibid., *Military Aid to Civil Authorities, June 2014*.
7. MoD, *Military Aid to Civil Authorities, June 2017*. https://assets.publishing.service.gov.uk
   This was the last year in which the MoD published this information in this format.
8. Thereafter, very brief information has been obtainable in the *Ministry of Defence Annual Report and Accounts*. https://assets.publishing.service.uk. The 2018–19 report mentioned that the FPS (in the last full year of its existence) achieved over the requested 2,000 Marine Enforcement patrol hours in the first eleven months of the financial year 2018–19. The FPS boarded 178 fishing vessels and issued thirty-one verbal re-briefs, six official written warnings, two financial penalties and forwarded written statements regarding an additional six fishing vessels to the MMO for further investigation and subsequent enforcement action. The equivalent 2021–22 report carried no specific mention of fishery protection.
9. See *2015 to 2020 Government Policy: Military Aid to the Civil Authorities for activities in the UK*. www.gov.uk and House of Commons Library Briefing Paper, 'Coronavirus: Deploying the Armed Forces in the UK' by Louisa Brooke-Holland, March 2020.http://researchbriefings.files.parliament.uk
10. Commodore Stephen Saunders RN, editor, *Jane's Fighting Ships 2002–2003*, Jane's Information Group Ltd, Coulsdon (2002), p. 784. Conrad Waters, 'British-Built Offshore Patrol Vessels: Balancing Cost and Capability', in Conrad Waters, editor, *Seaforth World Naval Review 2012*, Seaforth Publishing, Barnsley (2011), p. 109.
11. Ibid., Waters, 'British-Built Offshore Patrol Vessels', p. 109. The so-called 'decline of the Royal Navy' has often been associated with a reduction in numbers, exemplified in this case by three 'Rivers' replacing five 'Islands'. The counter-argument, promulgated among others by the current Chief of the Defence Staff, Admiral Radakin, is that by increasing availability in terms of 'sea time' backed up by imaginative manning schedules, it allows a navy to cope with reductions in numbers.
12. Ibid., Waters, 'British-Built Offshore Patrol Vessels', p. 110.
13. Ibid., Waters, pp. 110–112; Robert Gardiner, editor, *Conway's All the World's Fighting Ships, 1947–1995*, Conway Maritime Press, London (1983), p. 537.
14. Ibid., Waters, 'British-Built Offshore Patrol Vessels', p. 111.
15. Op. Cit., Kingwell, *Maritime Strike*, p. 161; Navy News, 'Navy ends decade-long loan by buying fishery ships outright', 13 September 2013.

16. BAE Systems acquired the Vosper Thornycroft shareholding in October 2009 to create BAE Systems Maritime and thus gain access to the OPV design. The five Batch 2 'River' class, constructed, built and delivered in a seven-year time frame between 2014 and 2021, are named HMS *Forth*, *Medway*, *Trent*, *Tamar* and *Spey*. The announcement of the decision to build the first three of the Batch 2 ships was made in the House of Commons in November 2013. See, Hansard, Vol. 570, 'Aircraft Carriers and UK Shipbuilding', *House of Commons Debate*, 6 November, 2013.
17. HMS *Severn* was also decommissioned in October 2017. Six months later it was announced that it too would be recommissioned following a refit at the A&P Appledore shipyard at Falmouth. The reinstatement of the three OPVs was paid for, at least in part, from a £12.7 million Treasury fund to Government departments intended 'to realise the opportunities from EU exit'. See, Louise Brooke-Holland, 'The Royal Navy, Brexit and UK Fisheries', *House of Commons Library*, 2 February 2019. www.commonslibrary. parliament.uk/the-royal-navy-brexit-and-uk-fisheries
18. 'Defence Secretary secures ships to protect home waters', *Royal Navy Website*, 23 November 2018. www.royalnavy.mod.uk
19. These machinations are explained succinctly in Conrad Waters, 'River Class Batch 2 OPVs: The Royal Navy's New "Colonial Gunboats"', in Conrad Waters, editor, *Seaforth World Naval Review 2022*, Seaforth Publishing, Barnsley (2021), pp. 136–149. HMS *Forth*'s entry into service was further delayed after it had been accepted off contract in January 2018. By April of that year it had become apparent that defects in the ship had made it unsafe to operate. Fortunately, these lamentable shortcomings in quality control were rectified at BAE's expense. See, Christopher Cope, 'Parliamentary Report, *Warship World*, Bol. 16, No. 10 (2020), pp. 16–17.
20. HMS *Mersey*'s 48,000-mile 2016 deployment included a key role in the seizure of cocaine off the coast of Nicaragua with a street value of over £12 million. What was intended to be a seven-month deployment lasted thirteen months after *Mersey* was later diverted to the eastern Mediterranean to assist other NATO ships in dealing with the latest migrant crisis. A measure of the 'over-stretch' experienced by the RN at the time is illustrated by the fact that the survey ship HMS *Echo* had to be tasked to take over HMS *Mersey*'s FP duties while RFA *Wave Knight* replaced the 'River'-class ship in the Caribbean. See, Steve Bush, 'First Report', *Warship World*, Vol. 14, No. 8 (2015), pp. 4–5.
21. MoD Guidance Paper, 'Integrated Operating Concept', September 2020, www.gov.uk/government/publications/the-integrated-operating-concept-2025. The paper heralded the new concept as, 'the most significant change in UK military thought in several generations'.
22. Chris Cope, 'Viewpoint', *Warship World*, Vol. 17:1, MCI Media, July/August 2021, p. 5.
23. John Perriam, 'At Sea with the Fishery Protection Squadron', in *Fishing News*, 1 November 2019. www.fishingnews.co.uk/features/at-sea-with-the-fishery-protection-squadron. This observation by Captain Ken Houlberg, then Captain Minewarfare, Fishery Protection, Diving and Patrol, was based on over thirty years' experience of the squadron. The Marine Management Organisation issues licenses and regulates marine activities in the seas around England and Wales in order that they are carried out in a sustainable way. Its activities in relation to the work it carries out directly in relation to the Royal Navy include managing and monitoring fishing sizes and quotas for catches; ensuring compliance with fisheries regulations such as fishing vessel licences, time at sea and quotas for fish and seafood; dealing with marine pollution emergencies including oil spills; and helping to prevent illegal, unregulated and unreported fishing worldwide.
24. John Perriam, 'On Patrol with the Royal Navy's Fisheries Protection Squadron', in *Fishing News*, 1 September 2017. www.fishingnews.co.uk/features/at-sea-with-the-royal-navys-fishery-patrol-squadron

25. Ibid.
26. Albacore, 'Fishery Protection', The Naval Review, Vol. XLI, No. 4, November 1953, p. 426.
    Op. Cit., Perriam, 'At Sea with the Fishery Protection Squadron'.
27. Hansard, *House of Commons Debate*, 'Scallop Fishing: Bay of Seine', Vol. 646, 13 September 2018. Statement by George Eustice, Minister for Agriculture, Fisheries and Food. Eustice's statement was understandably guarded as talks were under way at the time to try to resolve the dispute.
28. Ibid., Hansard, Vol. 646. Minister's Statement.
29. Tim Oliver, 'French Attack Scallopers – French 'Piratical' Attack on British Scallopers', in *Fishing News*, 3 September 2018. www.fishingnews.co.uk/french-attack-scallopers-french-piratical
    The *Fishing News* account did not refer to the *Honeybourne III* counter-attack, nor to the damage inflicted on the French fishing boats.
30. Op. Cit., Stephens, Britain Alone pp. 416–7.
31. The remark was made by the ex-Chairman of the MMO, Rear Admiral Parry. See, 'Four navy ships to help protect fishing waters in case of no-deal Brexit', *The Guardian*, 11 December, 2020.
32. Greg Heffer, 'Why is there a row over fishing in Jersey – and how might it escalate?', *Sky News*, 6 May 2021. www.news.sky.com/story/why-is-there-a-row-over-fishing-in-jersey; Tim Oliver, Navy Patrol Boats off Jersey as French Threaten Blockade, in *Fishing News*, 7 May 2021. www.fishingnews.co.uk/news/navy-patrol-boats-off-jersey
33. See, Christopher Cope, 'Viewpoint', *Warship World*, Vol. 17, No. 6 (2021), pp. 4–5.
34. William Shakespeare, *The Most Excellent and Lamentable Tragedy of Romeo and Juliet*, Act 2 Scene 1.

Bibliography

Primary sources

Hansard House of Commons
Debates
Volume 31 1, 1836; *303*, 1886; *318*, 1887; *283*, 1933; *465*, 1949; *475*, 1950; *485*, 1951; *625*, 1960; *696*, 1964; *911*, 1975; *373*, 1976; *570*, 2013; *646*, 2018.
Oral answers
Volume 2 1892; *52*, 1922, 80, 1985.

The National Archives (TNA), Kew
Admiralty (ADM)
ADM1/9490, 1/10039, 1/10042, 1/10045, 1/10511, 1/12092, 1/14947, 1/16398, 1/16994, 1/17785, 1/19339, 1/19737, 1/26774, 1/27623, 1/28914, 1/8553/74, 1/8742/102, 1/8700/128, 1/8760/226, 1/8576/339.
116/100, 116/866A, 116/2178, 116/2179, 116/2640, 116/2649, 116/2767, 116/2966, 116/3070, 116/3079, 116/3336, 116/3361, 116/3504, 116/3805, 116/3930.
131/70; 201/306; 204/16; 306/6, 306/31, 306/32, 306/38, 306/44, 306/60; 330/101, 330/108, 330/11, 330/113, 330/114.
The Cabinet (CAB)
CAB 24/196/35; 164/1820.
Ministry of Defence (DEFE)
DEFE 6/84; 13/1033, 13/1304, 13/1350; 24/520, 24/637, 24/711, 24/712, 24/713, 24/802, 24/944, 24/3000, 24/3395; 25/710; 42/952; 48/971; 68/359; 69/279; 69/657, 69/675, 69/1718/2.
Foreign Office
FO 83/714, 83/715, 371/209/1216, 371/94879.
Ministry of Agriculture sand Food (MAF, later MAFF)
MAF 12/4, 12/8, 12/10; 41/705; 209/76, 209/78; 452/9; 641/2
Prime Minister and Minister of Defence (PREM)
PREM 19/1493
The Treasury (T)
T1/11012; 475/52; 476/223; 161/204/16.

The National Maritime Museum, Greenwich (NMM)
ADL/Q/76; JoD/95/3; MDY/103; MSS/70/027; SOT/5.

Secondary Sources

Books

The place of publication is London unless otherwise stated.

Aldrich, Richard J, *The Hidden Hand: Britain, America and Cold War Intelligence* (The Overlook Press, New York, 2001).

Barback, Ronald, *The Political Economy of Fisheries: From Nationalism to Internationalism* (University of Hull Press, Hull, 1966).

Blackburn, Raymond V B, editor, *Jane's Fighting Ships 1950–51* (David & Charles Reprints, Newton Abbott, 1975).

Boveda, Jórge, *All for One, One for All: Argentine Navy Operations during the Falklands War* (Helion & Co. Ltd, Warwick, 2021).

Boyd, Andrew, *Naval Intelligence through the Twentieth Century* (Seaforth Publishing, Barnsley, 2020).

Breyer, Siegfried, *Soviet Warship Development: Vol. I, 1917–1937* (Conway Maritime Press, 1992).

Brown, D K & Moore, George, *Re-building the Royal Navy: Warship Design since 1945* (Chatham Publishing, 2003).

Butler, William E, *The Soviet Union and The Law of the Sea*, The John Hopkins University Press, London & Baltimore, 1971).

Cable, James, *Diplomacy at Sea* (The Macmillan Press, London and Basingstoke, 1985).

—— *Gunboat Diplomacy: Political Applications of Limited Naval Force* (Chatto & Windus, 1971).

Central Office of Information, 'Royal Navy Fishery Protection' leaflet prepared for Directorate of Public Relations (Royal Navy) (1975) and printed for HMSO by Cowells Ltd Dd. Pro.4438099266.

Chesneau, Roger, editor, *Conway's All the World's Fighting Ships, 1922–1946* (Conway Maritime Press, 1980).

D'Enno, Douglas, *Fishermen Against the Kaiser: Shockwaves of War 1914–1925* (Pen & Sword Publishing, Barnsley, 2010).

Dockrill, Saki, *Britain's Retreat from East of Suez: The Choice Between Europe and the World?* (Palgrave Macmillan, Basingstoke, 2002).

Dunn, Steve R, *Battle in the Baltic: The Royal Navy and the Fight to Save Estonia and Latvia 1918–20* (Pen & Sword, Barnsley, 2020).

—— *British Trawlers and Drifters in Two World Wars: From the John Lambert Collection* (Seaforth Publishing, Barnsley, 2021).

—— *The Power and the Glory: The Royal Navy Fleet Reviews from earliest times to 2005* (Barnsley, Seaforth Publishing, 2021)

—— *Southern Thunder: The Royal Navy and the Scandinavian Trade in World War One* (Seaforth Publishing, Barnsley, 2019).

Ellis, Stephen C, *The Russian Baltic Fleet: In Time of War and Revolution 1914–1918: The Recollections of Admiral S.N. Timerev* (Seaforth Publishing, Barnsley, 2020).

Freedman, Lawrence, *Command: The Politics of Military Operations from Korea to Ukraine* (Penguin Books, 2022).

—— *The Official History of the Falklands Campaign Vol. II: War and Diplomacy* (Routledge, 2007).

Friedman, Norman, *British Submarines in the Cold War Era* (Seaforth Publishing, Barnsley, 2021).

Friel, Ian, *Henry V's Navy: The Sea Road to Agincourt and Conquest, 1413–1422* (The History Press, Stroud, 2015).

Gardiner, Robert, editor, *Conway's All the World's Fighting Ships, 1860–1905* (Conway Maritime Press, 1979).

—— *Conway's All the World's Fighting Ships, 1947–1995* (Conway Maritime Press, 1995).

Goldrick, James, *Grey Zone Operations and the Maritime Domain* (Australian Strategic Policy Institute, Barton, 2018).

Gordon, Andrew, *The Rules of the Game: Jutland and British Naval Command* (John Murray, 1996).
Grainger, John D, *The British Navy in Eastern Waters: The Indian and Pacific Oceans* (The Boydell Press, Woodbridge, 2022).
Gray, Randal, editor, *Conway's All the World's Fighting Ships 1906–1921* (Conway Maritime Press, 1985).
Grove, Eric J, *The Royal Navy Since 1815: A New Short History* (Palgrave Macmillan, Basingstoke, 2005).
—— *Vanguard to Trident: Britain's Naval Policy since World War II* (The Bodley Head, 1987).
Gwyn, Julian, editor, *The Royal Navy and North America: The Warren Papers 1736–1752* (The Navy Records Society, 1973).
Hamilton, Sir R Vesey, *Naval Administration: The Constitution, Character, and Functions of the Board of Admiralty, and of the Civil Departments it Directs* (Forgotten Books, 2018).
Hansard: *British Parliamentary Papers.* Vol. XIV, 1883, Select Committee Report.
Harr, Gierr, *The Battle for Norway: April–June 1940* (Seaforth Publishing, Barnsley, 2009).
—— *The Invasion of Norway: April 1940* (Seaforth Publishing, Barnsley, 2010).
Hart, Jeffrey A, *The Anglo-Icelandic Cod War of 1972–73: A Case Study of a Fishery Dispute*, University of California Press, Oakland, 1976).
Hattendorff, John B, Knight R J B, Pearsall, A W H, Rodger, N A M, Till, Geoffrey, editors, *British Naval Documents 1204–1960* (Scolar Press, Aldershot, 1993).
Hennessy, Peter, *Having it so Good: Britain in the Fifties* (Penguin Books, 2007).
—— & Jinks, James, *Silent Deep: The Royal Navy Submarine Service since 1945* (Allen Lane, 2015).
Her Majesty's Stationary Office, *The Fundamentals of British Maritime Doctrine BR18067* (HMSO, 1995).
Hobbs, David, *Taranto and Naval Air Warfare in the Mediterranean, 1940–1945* (Seaforth Publishing, Barnsley, 2020).
Hoole, Rob, editor, *Last of the Wooden Walls: An Illustrated History of the 'Ton'-class Minesweepers and Minehunters* (Halsgrove Publishing, Wellington, 2012).
Jenkins, Alan C, *The Silver Haul: Trawling and Deep-Sea Fishing*, (Methuen & Co. Ltd, 1967).
Johnson-Allen, John, *'Rosy' Wemyss, Admiral of the Fleet: The Man who Created Armistice Day* (Whittles Publishing, Dunbeath, 2021).
Jónsson, Hannes, *Friends in Conflict: Anglo Icelandic Cod Wars and the Law of the Sea* (C. Hurst and Co., 1982).
Kennedy, Paul, *The Rise and Fall of British Naval Mastery* (Penguin Books, 2001).
Kingwell, Rear Admiral John, Royal Navy, *Maritime Strike: The Untold Story of the Royal Navy Task Group off Libya in 2011* (Casemate Publishers, Oxford, 2022).
Knight, Roger, *The Pursuit of Victory: The Life and Achievement of Horatio Nelson* (Allen Lane, 2005).
——, *Convoys: The British Struggle against Napoleonic Europe and America*, (Yale University Press, New Haven & London, 2022).
Lambert, Andrew, *The Challenge: America, Britain and the War of 1812* (Faber & Faber 2012).
Lavery, Brian, *The Island Nation: A History of Britain and the Sea* (Conway Maritime Press & The National Maritime Museum, 2005).
Lund, Paul & Ludlam, Harry, *Trawlers go to War* (W Foulsham & Co. Ltd, Harrow, 1971).
Luttwak, Edward, *The Political Uses of Sea Power*, The John Hopkins University Press, 1974).
Moore, Captain J E, Royal Navy, *Warships of the Royal Navy* (Macdonald and Jane's, 1979).
Naval Staff History BR1736(57), HMSO, London (1990). *The Cod War: Naval Operations off Iceland in Support of the British Fishing Industry, 1958–1976.*

Nudd, Derek, *Castaways in Question: A Story of British Naval Interrogators from WWI to Denazification* (Grove Cottage Editions, 2020).
Osborne, Richard, *The Third 'Cod War' 11.75–6.76* (World Ship Society Supplement, Kendal, 1978).
Parker, John, *The Silent Service: The Inside Story of the Royal Navy's Submarine Service* (Headline Book Publishing, 2001).
Parkes, O & McMurtie, F, editors, *Jane's Fighting Ships 1924* (David & Charles Reprints, Newton Abbott, 1973).
Roberts, John, *Safeguarding the Nation: The Story of the Modern Royal Navy* (Seaforth Publishing, Barnsley, 2009).
Robinson, Robb, *Fishermen, The Fishing Industry and the Great War at Sea: A Forgotten History?* (University of Liverpool Press, Liverpool, 2019).
—— & Hart, Ian, *Viola: The Life and Times of a Hull Steam Trawler* (Lodestar Books, 2014).
Rodger N A M, *Command of the Ocean: A Naval History of Britain, 1649–1815* (Penguin Books, 2004).
——, *Safeguard of the Seas: A Naval History of Britain, 660–1649* (Penguin Books, 2004).
Roskill, Stephen, *Naval Policy Between the Wars I: The Period of Anglo-American Antagonism 1919–1929* (William Collins, 1968).
——, *Naval Policy Between the Wars II: The Period of Reluctant Rearmament 1930–1939* (William Collins, 1976).
Rüger, Jan, *The Great Naval Game: Britain and Germany in the Age of Empire* (Cambridge: Cambridge University Press, 2007).
Saunders, Commodore Stephen, Royal Navy, editor, *Jane's Fighting Ships 2002–2003* (Jane's Information Group Ltd, Coulsdon, 2002).
Somner, Graeme, *Scottish Fishery Protection* (World Ship Society Monograph No. 7, Kendal, 1983).
Stephens, Philip, *Britain Alone: The Path from Suez to Brexit* (Faber & Faber, 2021).
Thor, Jon Th, *British Trawlers and Iceland 1919–1976* (University of Goteborg Press, Ebsjerg, 1995).
Thriplow, Nick, Bramhill, Tina & James, Sophie, *Distant Water: Stories from Grimsby's Fishing Fleet* (North Wall Publishing, Grimsby, 2011).
Toghill, Gerald, *Royal Navy Trawlers Part 2: Requisitioned Trawlers* (Maritime Books, Liskeard, 2004).
Villar, Roger, *Merchant Ships at War: The Falklands Experience* (Conway Maritime Press & Lloyd's of London Press, 1984).
Welch, Captain Andrew, Royal Navy, *The Royal Navy in the Cod Wars: Britain and Iceland in Conflict* (Maritime Books, Liskeard, 2006).
Wettern, Desmond, The Decline of British Sea Power (Jane's Publishing Group, 1982).
Wilson, Charles, *Profit and Power: A Study of England and the Dutch Wars* (Martinus Nijhoff, The Hague, 1978).
Wise, Jon, *The Role of the Royal Navy in South America, 1920–1970* (Bloomsbury Publishing, 2014).
Wolter, John A, Ranzan David A, & McDonagh, John J, editors, *With Commodore Perry to Japan: The Journal of William Speiden J., 1852–1855* (Naval Institute Press, Annapolis, 2013).
Woodward, Sandy, with Robinson, Patrick, *One Hundred Days: The Memoirs of the Falklands Battle Group Commander* (Harper Collins, 1992).

Essays in Books and Journals

'Albacore', 'Fishery Protection' in *The Naval Review*, Vol. XLI (1953).
Ashcroft, Neil, 'The Diminishing Commons: Politics, War and Territorial Waters', in Starkey, David J, Reid, Chris & Ashcroft, Neil, editors, *England's Sea Fisheries: the Commercial Sea Fisheries of England and Wales since 1300* (Chatham Publishing, 2000).

Bar-Noi, Uri, 'The Cold War and Britain's Dispute with the USSR over Territorial Waters and Fishing Limits 1953–56', in *Journal of Maritime Research*, Vol. 17, No. 2, 2015.

Brown, David K, 'The Design of the "Castle" Class: A Personal View', in Jordan, John, editor, *Warship 2006* (Conway Maritime Press, 2006).

Brugge, Jeroen, 'Fish Promotion in the Netherlands, *c.*1690–1983, in Starkey et al, *England's Sea Fisheries*.

Butler, William E, 'Soviet Territorial Waters', in *World Affairs*, Vol. 130, No. 1, 1967.

Childs, Wendy R, 'Fish Production, Trade and Consumption *c.*1300–1530: Control, Conflict and International Trade', in Starkey et al, *England's Sea Fisheries*.

Day, E E D, 'The British Fishing Industry', in *Geography*, Vol. 54, No. 2, 1969.

Graham, Gerald S, 'Fisheries and Sea Power', in *The Canadian Historical Association*, Vol. 20, No. 1, 1941.

Greenacre, John, 'The Admiralty's Interwar Planning with the British Fishing Industry 1925–1940', in *Journal for Maritime Research*, Vol. 22, Nos 1 & 2, 2020.

Guðmundsson, Guðmundur J, 'The Cod and the Cold War', in *Scandinavian Journal of History*, Vol. 31, No. 2, 2006.

Handley, Chris, 'Icelandic Patrol 18 February–2 March, 1976, in *South West Maritime History Journal*, Issue 56, 2003.

Heidbrink, Ingo, 'Fisheries', in Rodger, N A M & Buchet, Christian, *The Sea in History – the Modern World* (Boydell Press, Woodbridge, 2017).

Helin, Donald A, 'Soviet Fishing in the Barents Sea and the North Atlantic', in *Geographical Review*, Vol. 54, No. 3, 1964.

Janzen, Olaf, 'The French Raid upon the Newfoundland Fishery in 1762: A Study in the Nature and Limits of Sea Power', in Janzen, Olaf, *War and Trade in Eighteenth Century Newfoundland* (Liverpool University Press, Liverpool, 2013).

—— 'The Royal Navy and the Defence of Newfoundland during the American Revolution', in *Acadiensis: Journal of the History of the Atlantic Region*, University of New Brunswick, New Brunswick, 1984.

Johnston, Paddy, 'The Cod Wars Against Iceland: The Royal Navy as a Political Instrument', in *Cambridge Review of International Affairs*, Taylor & Francis Publishers, Oxford, 1991.

Josephson, Paul R, 'When Stalin Learned to Fish: Natural Resources, Technology and Industry under Socialism', in Diefendorf, Jeffrey M & Dorset, Kurk, editors, *City, Country, Empire* (University of Pittsburgh Press, Pittsburgh, 2005).

Karlsdóttir, Hrefna, 'Fishing Rights in the Post-War Period: The Case of the North Sea Herring', in Boyce, Gordon & Gorki, Richard, *Resources and Infrastructure in the Maritime Economy* (Liverpool University Press, Liverpool, 2002).

Knight, Roger, 'British North Atlantic convoys, 1812–14, and the subsequent rejection of the convoy system' in Paul Kennedy & Evan Wilson, editors, *Navies in Multipolar Worlds: from the age of sail to the Present* (Routledge, Abingdon, 2021).

Luzin, Grennady P, Pretes, Michael, Vasilev, Vladimir V, 'The Kola Peninsula', in *Geographical Review*, Vol. 47, No. 1, 1948.

Offerdal, Kristine, 'The 1920 Svalbard Treaty', in *Center for Strategic and International Studies (CSIS)*, 2016.

Osler, Adrian G & Porteous, Katrina, '"Benelfysch and Iseland Fish": Continuity in the Pre-industrial Sea Fishery of North Northumberland, 1300–1950' in *Mariner's Mirror*, Vol. 96, No. 1, 2010.

Pope, Peter E, 'The Scale of the Early Modern Newfoundland Cod Fishery', in Starkey, David J and Candow, James E, editors, *North Atlantic Fisheries: Supply, Marketing and Consumption, 1560–1990* (University of Hill Press, Hull, 2006).

Prince, E E, Territorial Waters and a Suggested Extension of the Three Mile Limit', in *Transactions of the American Fisheries Society*, Vol. 146, No. 6, 2017.

Robinson, Robb, 'The Common North Atlantic Pool', in Starkey et al, *England's Sea Fisheries*.

Rodger, N A M, 'The Naval Service of the Cinque Ports', in N A M Rodger, *Essays in Naval History, From Medieval to Modern* (Routledge, Abingdon, 2018).

—— 'Mobilizing Sea Power in the Eighteenth Century', in Rodger, N A M, *Essays in Naval History*.
Salmon, Patrick, 'Foreign Policy and National Identity: The Norwegian Integrity Treaty 1907–42', in *Forrvarsstudies*, No. 1, 1993.
Starkey, David J 'The Newfoundland Trade', in Starkey et al, *England's Sea Fisheries*.
Wainwright, Lieutenant Commander B G, Royal Navy, 'Whither or Wither Fishery Protection?', in *The Naval Review*, Vol. 80, No. 3, 1992.
Waters, Conrad, 'British-Built Offshore Patrol Vessels: Balancing Cost and Capability', in Waters, Conrad, *Seaforth World Naval Review 2012* (Seaforth Publishing, Barnsley, 2011).
——, 'River Class Batch 2 OPVs: The Royal Navy's New "Colonial Gunboats"', in Waters, Conrad, *Seaforth World Naval Review 2022* (Seaforth Publishing, Barnsley, 2021).
Webster, C J, 'The Economic Development of the Soviet Arctic and Sub-Arctic', in *The Slavonic and Eastern European Review*, Vol. 29, No. 72, 1950.
Wilcox, Martin, 'Concentration or Disintegration? Vessel Ownership, Fish Wholesaling and Processing in the British Trawl Industry 1850–1939', in Starkey, David J & Candow, James E, editors, *The North Atlantic Fisheries Supply, Marketing and Consumption 1560–1990* (University of Hull Press, Hull, 2006).

Newspapers & Magazines

Bush, Steve, 'First Report', in *Warship World*, Vol. 14, No. 8, 2015.
Cope, Christopher, 'Viewpoint', in *Warship World*, Vol. 16, No. 10, 2020; Vol. 17, Nos. 1 & 6, 2021.
Matthews, Simon, 'HMS Challenger', in Warship World Magazine, Vol. 17, No. 2, 2021.
—— 'Royal Navy Anti-Submarine Trawlers and Whalers in World War Two' Warship World Magazine, Vol. 17, No. 7, 2021.
Daily Telegraph, Fishing News, The Guardian, Navy International, Navy News, Sunday Telegraph.

Online Resources

Buck, Danny, Blog, 'Great Yarmouth Battle Against Piracy during the English Civil War', September 2019, Norfolk Record Office. www.norfolkrecordoffice.blog.org
Johannessón, Gudni, 'Troubled Waters: Cod War and Britain's Fight for Freedom of the High Seas, 1948–1964'. www.academia.edu./255064/Troubled_Waters_Cod_War_Fishing_Disputes_Britains_Fight_For_Freedom
Government Policy: *Military Aid to the Civil Authorities for Activities in the UK: 2015–2020*. www.gov.uk
Grimsby Fishing Heritage Centre. *Oral History Projects*: 'Distant Water Project' and 'The Women they Left Behind', 2008–2011. www.fishingheritage.com
House of Commons Library Briefing Papers: Brooke-Holland, Louisa, 'The Royal Navy, Brexit and UK Fisheries', February 2019; 'Coronavirus: Deploying the Armed Forces in the UK', March 2020.
Hullwebs History of Hull. www.hullebs.co.uk/content/1-20c/industry/fishing/cod-war/cod-war.1893
Marine Scotland Vessel List 1882 to Present Date. www.gov.scot/publications
Ministry of Defence (MoD), *Guidance Paper*, 'Integrated Operating Concept', September 2020; *Statistical Series 5*: Activities Bulletin 5.01; *Annual Report & Accounts*, June 2014. www.assets.publishing.service.gov.uk
Royal Navy Website. www.royalnavy.mod.uk/what-we-do/providing-security-at-sea
Watson, Graham, 'From Tsar to Commissar: Russian Organisation and Warships, 1914–1922'. www.naval-history.net/xGW-RussianNavy1914-1918

Index

Aberdeen 55, 96, 142, 143, 149, 150, 156, 206, 207, 208, 209, 210, 253, 258, 289
Abyssinia Crisis 89
Acadia, Nova Scotia 19
Achill Head, Ireland 80
Admiralty (British) 17, 20, 21, 22, 31, 32, 33, 34, 37, 42, 47, 49, 56, 57, 58, 60, 61, 63, 65, 66, 72, 73, 77, 79, 80, 81, 82, 85, 86, 87, 89, 90, 91, 94, 96, 97, 105, 106, 107, 109, 111, 117, 118, 119, 120, 132, 133, 136, 137, 138, 145, 148, 151, 152, 167, 170, 171, 172, 180, 181, 183, 187, 189, 193, 200, 201, 202, 204, 207, 208, 209, 210, 211, 261, 296
'Admiralty Responsibility for Protection of Fisheries' report 60
Agent X 110-13, 116, 124
Akureyri, Iceland 190
'Albacore' 55
Albania 83
Aldrich, Richard 167-8
Alexander, A.V., First Lord of the Admiralty 95
Alliance, lugger 38
Allin, Thomas 10
Althing, Icelandic Parliament 50, 175, 178, 181, 230
American Civil War (1861-5) 43
American Revolutionary War/War of Independence (1775-83) 18, 19, 20, 24, 25, 28
Amery, Leo, First Lord of the Admiralty 106
Amsterdam, Netherlands 155-7
Andanaer area 187
Andanaer Patrol 65
Anderson, Captain (later Commodore) Barry, RN 184-6, 189, 191-3
Annapolis Royal, New England 21
Anglo-American War (1812-15) 26, 42
Anglo-Danish Agreement (1901) 178

Anglo-Dutch War (1652-4) 15, 27
Anglo-French Convention (1867) 34
Anglo-French Wars xiv, 18-26
Anglo-Icelandic Exchange of Notes (1961) 215
Anglo-Norwegian Fisheries Convention 131
Anglo-Soviet Agreement (1956) 174-5
Anglo-Soviet Temporary Fisheries Agreement (1930) 121, 165-6, 170-2
Anson, Admiral George, RN 22
Antrim, County 161
Antwerp, Belgium 157
Anzac Bay, Turkey 83
Archangel, Russia 51, 100, 101, 113, 114
Archer, Captain E.R., RN 157-8
Arctic Convoys 95
Arctic Fleet 114
Arctic Ocean xvii, 30, 71, 73, 114
'Arctic Patrol' 71
Argentina 251, 262, 263
Argentine Navy Ship: *Cabo San Antonio* 262
Ascension Island, South Atlantic 261
Asdic 88
Ásgeirsson, Ásgeir, Icelandic President 187
Ashmore, Sir Edward, Admiral, RN 237-8, 240
Atkinson, George, British Minister of Agriculture and Fisheries 153
Atlantic Fleet 59
Atlantic Pact 134, 136
Atlantic Patrol Tasking (North, South) 281
Australia 168
Auxiliary Flotillas 58
Auxiliary Patrols 57-8, 64, 81, 82, 83, 84, 97, 105, 114, 118, 119, 274
Axis 134
Aylmer, Captain H.E.F., RN 105-8
Azores, The 179

335

Baas Fjord, Norway 135
BAE systems 279-80
Bailey, Captain Eric, RN 187
Balingers (by name):
   Adventure 10-11, *Elizabeth* 6, *Gabriel* 5, *Paul* 5, *Peter* 5
Baltic Fleet 114, 118
Baltic Sea 265
Bangladesh 277
Barbary pirates 9
Barback, Ronald 14
Barents Sea 51, 61, 70, 100, 101, 103, 105, 112, 114, 118, 123, 165-7, 171, 174, 181, 182, 187, 206, 256, 265
Barneville- Carteret, France 270
Barra Light 146
Battle of the Atlantic 83
Battle of Waterloo (1815) 29
Bay of Biscay 271
Bay of Seine 274, 283, 284
Bear Island 30, 69-70, 167
Beckett, Sir Eric, Legal Adviser, Foreign Office 136
Beira Patrol 160
Belfast 161
Belgium 36, 38, 40, 62, 80, 152, 153, 157, 181, 276
Belloram, Newfoundland 45
Benediktsson, Bjarni, Icelandic Foreign Minister 180
Beresford, Admiral Charles, RN 76
Bergen, Norway 7
Berkeley Sound, Falkland Islands 263
Berlin Blockade (1948) 134
Berwick-upon-Tweed 141
Beukelesz, Willem 12
Bevin, Ernest, General Secretary, Transport and General Workers' Union 89
Bilateral Temporary Commercial Agreement (1930) 166
Birkbeck, Sir Edward, MP 33, 41
Bjornsson, Commander, Norwegian Coastguard 199
Black Sea 114
Blake, Admiral Robert, RN 15-16
Blue Line (Norway) 135, 136
Board of Agriculture and Fisheries 57
Board of Trade 36-8, 41-3, 47, 61
Boeing hydrofoils 254
Bofors gun 187, 258
Bohun, John 5
Bolshevik Party 101, 105, 115, 123
Bolshoi Oleni Island, Russia 112
Bonar Law, Andrew, British Prime Minister 104

Bonn, Germany 214, 222
Boothby, Ambassador Basil 208
Boston, USA 20, 25
Botney Gat 42
Boulogne, France 17, 33, 37, 256
Boveda, Jórge 251
Bracken, Captain Hugo, RN 201
Brastrup, Captain 50
Breidifjord, Iceland 190
Bremen, Germany 222
Brest, France 23
Brexit xii, xiii, 273, 274, 281, 286
Breyer, Siegfried 118
Bridgeman, William, First Lord of the Admiralty 117
Bridlington 55
Brimelow, Thomas, British diplomat 193
Bristol Channel 154, 276
Britain xii, 2, 9, 17, 19, 28, 29, 3031, 35, 36, 42, 44, 47, 52, 53, 66, 67, 75, 100, 102, 103, 104, 105, 117, 121, 122, 125, 126, 127, 129, 130, 134, 135, 136, 137, 138, 141, 142, 143, 152, 165, 166, 170, 172, 174, 175, 176, 178, 179, 181, 183, 184, 187, 190, 191, 192, 200, 202, 203, 205, 206, 209, 212, 213, 214, 215, 216, 218, 223, 224, 228, 230, 231, 233, 243, 249, 250, 251, 255, 265, 274, 275, 283, 284, 285, 286
British Expeditionary Force (BEF) 92
British Trawlers' Federation (BTF) 88, 185, 191, 196, 202, 216-7, 219, 223, 227, 230, 244
British United Trawlers 262
British White Herring Fishery 141
Brixham 55, 284
Brodrick, Sir John, British Under Secretary of State for Foreign Affairs 49
Brookes, Commander John, RN 169
Brown, David K., RCNC xvii, 260
Buckie, Scotland 55
Budzbon, Przemyslaw 114
Bulganin, Nikolai, Soviet Defence Minister 169
Bulgaria 159, 257
Bundesmarine, Germany 220
Busses 12, 13, 15, 16
Butterscotch trawler haven 185-6, 189
Buzzard, Rear Admiral Anthony 167-8
Bynkershoek, cannon shot rule 102

Cable, James 123
Cabot, John 8
Calais, France 5, 33

Callaghan, James, Parliamentary and Financial Secretary to the Admiralty 172
Canada 16, 21, 42, 44, 52, 201, 249
Canso, Nova Scotia 20, 21
Cape Breton Island, Canada 19, 20-21
Cape Cod, USA 26
Cape Farewell, Greenland 30
Cape Kanin Nos, Russia 30, 103-4, 175
Cape Nymetski, Russia 122
Cape Ray, Nova Scotia 43
Cape Sviatoi Nos, Russia 103-4
Cape Teriberski, Russia 110
Cape Wrath 159
Cara Sea 102
Cardiff 91, 290
Caribbean Sea 281
Carrington, Peter, First Lord of the Admiralty 211
Carver, Nathaniel, US fishing schooner master 25-6
Catalina flying-boat 186
Catholic Church 3
Celtic Sea 276
Central Reserve, Royal Navy 58
Channel Islands 10, 67, 270, 285-6
Charlton, Rear Admiral, RN 77
Chatham 67
Cherbourg, France 270
Cherbourg Incident 270
Choiseul, duc de, French Minister of Marine, of War and of Foreign Affairs 22, 23
Churchill, Winston, First Lord of the Admiralty and later, British Prime Minister xiii, 81, 89-90, 91, 96-7
Cinque Ports 4, 9
Cirolana, MAFF research vessel 215
City of London 16
Civilian Defence Vessels (CVS), (by name): *Englishman* 217, 226, *Euroman* 236-7, *Irishman* 224, *Lloydsman* 224, 233, 236-7, *Statesman* 217, 224, 226, 237, *Welshman* 229
Clapp, Commodore Mike, RN 263
Clark, Jim 204
Clere, Sir John 7
Clyde, River 161, 280
Coast Guard Agency Act (1856) 31
Coastguard, H.M. xv, 31-2
Coastguard Force 286
Code of Prize Law, Russian (1869) 102
Cod Wars xv, 71, 72, 74, 138, 163, 165, 186, 200, 213-47, 248, 255, 268

Cold War 66, 134, 166, 167, 169, 172, 175, 179-80, 184, 190, 198, 206, 213, 255, 272
Collier, J. 17
Collisions Regulations Act (1965) 238
Combershall, William 6
Commodore Clipper cargo ship 285
Communist Party, Iceland 180
Communist Party, Norway 129
Confederacy, USA 43
Conference of Trawler Owners, Hull 114
Congress of Vienna (1814-15) 30
Conservative Party 104, 265, 281
Contractor Logistic Support (CLS) 277-9
Convoy Act (1803) 26
Cook Welton and Gemmell Ltd 150.
Copenhagen, Denmark 51
Corbett, Julian 21, 75
Cork, Ireland 25
Corn Laws 44
Cornwall 10
Corporation of the Royal Fishery 16
Corson, Lt. Cdr., RN 195
Coward, Cdr., RN 226-7
Crimean War (1853-6) 32
Crosland, Antony, British Foreign Secretary 243-4
Cross, Captain, RN 49-50
Crutchley, Captain V.A.C., RN 86, 150-1
Curry, Lt. Cdr., RN 110-17, 124
Curzon, Lord, British Foreign Secretary 104, 111
Customs and Excise, H.M. 31-2, 34, 61
Customs Code, Russian (1892) 102
Czechoslovakia 134

Daily Telegraph xiii
Dalison, Lt. Cdr., RN 146-7, 157
Danish-Icelandic Act of Union (1918) 175
Danish Navy Ships (by name): *Heimdal* 50, *Islands Falk* 151, *Niels Ebbesen* 210
Dardenelles, Turkey 83, 84
Dare, Commander, RN 50
Davies, Ernest, British Under-Secretary of State for Foreign Affairs 170
Day, E.E.D. xvi
Dean, Patrick, Chairman of the Joint Intelligence Staff 168
Defence Committee of the Cabinet 172
'Defence: Outline of Future Policy' White Paper (1957) 72, 191
Defence White Paper (1981) 261
Defence White Paper (1991) 265
Denmark xvi, 7, 27, 36, 46-51, 53, 118, 156, 175, 178, 179, 210

d'Enno, Douglas 81, 84
Department of Agriculture and Fisheries for Scotland (DAFS) 252, 253, 263, 266
Department for Environment, Food and Rural Affairs (DEFRA) 274
Department of Energy (DEn) 263, 266
Designated Fishing Area (DFA) 219, 220, 222, 233-5, 243
Devolution, Scottish 275
Devonport xiii
Dickens, Captain G.C., RN xvii, 64-5, 73
Dieppe, France 17, 33
Directorate of Naval Resources and Plans (DNRP) 279
Dobson, A., Ministry of Agriculture and Fisheries 96
Dogger Bank 40, 42
Dover 79, 256
Down, County 161
Drake, Francis 8, 182
Dugmore, Captain, RN 60-1
Duke of Newcastle, Secretary of State for the Southern Department of the Admiralty 17
Duke of Northumberland 15
Duke of York 16
Dunkirk, France xiii, 17, 92
Durham Priory 3
Dutch East Indies 15, 16
Dutch Republic 11-12, 13, 14-16, 27

Eastern Bloc 249, 255, 257
East India Company 11
East Indies 13, 15
East Looe 10
Edinburgh 148
Egede-Nissen, Adam, leader of the Norwegian Communist Party 129
Eden, Anthony, British Prime Minister 170, 191
Egypt 184
Elgin-Macey Treaty (1854) 44
Ellis, Lieutenant T., RN 112-3
Ellison, Commodore, RN 61-2
Emden Herring Fisheries 40
England 5, 6, 7, 8, 9, 10, 11, 12, 13, 27, 34, 57, 84, 96, 121, 140, 165, 273, 274
England's Treasure by Forraign Trade 13
English Channel 9, 33, 34, 59, 65, 66, 70, 80, 139, 152, 158, 159, 257, 276
English Civil War 10-11
Esbjerg, Denmark 156
Escort Groups 83
Etherington-Smith, Gordon, British Foreign Office official 171-2

European Common Fisheries Policy (CFP) 216, 263-5, 271, 272, 284, 285
European Economic Community (EEC) 216, 243-4, 249, 256-7, 265
European Fisheries Conference (1964) 211-2, 244, 249
European Union (EU) xii, xiii, 270, 274, 275, 283, 285, 286
Exclusive Economic Zone (EEZ) 144, 249, 255, 258, 265
Extended Fisheries Zone (EFZ) xvi, 249, 259, 272, 284
Extra Deep Armed Team Sweep (EDATS) 262-3
Eyemouth 160

Fair Isle Channel 151
Falkland Islands 260, 266, 281
Falklands Sound 262
Falklands Task Force 261
Falklands War (1982) 186, 251, 261-2, 268
Far East 16, 114, 281
Faroe Islands 46, 47, 48-50, 69-70, 92, 125, 145, 178, 206, 210, 216, 226, 256
Faxa Bay, Iceland 182
Faxa Flói, Iceland 182, 190
Felixstowe 152
Finland 100, 130, 134
Finnmark Coast, Norway 100, 110, 129
First Cod War (1958-61) 72, 187, 189, 191, 197, 203, 204-5, 211, 215, 221, 247
First Gulf War (1990-91) 265
Firth of Forth 73, 143, 212
Fish Agreement (1916) 127
Fisheries Administration Penalty (FAP) 276
'Fisheries Enforcement: Surface Surveillance' (1998) 271
Fisher, Lord, Admiral Sir John, RN 81
Fishery Associations 39
Fishery Board for Scotland 56, 57, 141-3, 145
Fishery Committees 87
Fishery Limits Act (1976) 256
Fishery Manual (1914) 58
Fishery Protection and Minesweeping Flotilla (FP&MF) 59, 65, 131-3
Fishery Protection and Minesweeping Squadron (FP&MS) 69, 70, 86, 143, 155, 254
Fishery Protection Flotilla (FPF) 54, 123, 132, 152, 177
Fishery Protection Squadron (FPS) vii-viii, xii, xvi, 1, 54, 72-3, 133, 136, 139-42,

149, 161-2, 171, 184, 187, 190, 198, 201, 204, 206-7, 210-12, 233, 256, 259, 261-2, 264-8, 271-3, 275-6, 281, 283, 284
Fishery Reserve Force 87
Fish, William, fishing vessel skipper 40
Fishing News 284
Fitzmaurice, Rear Admiral Maurice, RN 115-6
Flag Officer Scotland and Northern Ireland (FOSNI) 208, 209, 210, 219, 221, 225, 228, 241, 245, 259
Flannan Islands 80
Fleetwood 30, 55, 63, 96, 146, 147
Flint, James 37
Focker Friendship aircraft 228-9, 252
Foreign and Commonwealth Office (FCO) 231-2, 254-5
Foreign Office 36, 47, 49, 51, 106, 109, 118, 123, 126, 129, 135, 136, 166, 167, 170-3, 181, 201, 209, 210, 211
Forrest, Leading Seaman 146-7
Fortune Bay, Newfoundland 45
France 2, 5, 6, 8, 9, 16, 17, 18, 19, 23, 24, 33, 34, 35, 36, 44, 45, 47, 56, 74, 80, 92, 101, 134, 152, 153, 181, 256, 270, 274, 276, 283-6
Freedman, Sir Lawrence 245
Freetown, Sierra Leone 262
French naval coastguard vessels (by name):
Athos 286, *Esteron* 284
Friel, Ian 4
Future Offshore Patrol Vessel (FOPV) 277

Gdansk, Poland 144
Geddes Axe 108
General Assembly, Massachusetts 20
Geneva, Switzerland 184, 200, 201, 206
German Democratic Republic (GDR) 256
German Merchant Marine Ships (by name):
Frithof 224-5, *Königen Luise* 76
German Navy Ships (by name):
Kolberg 78, *U9* 78, *U34* 80, 82, *U35* 80
German Trawler Owners' Federation 222
Germany 36, 40, 41, 44, 76, 78-82, 84, 86, 92, 93, 98, 101, 104, 116, 117, 118, 119, 120, 126, 127, 129, 134, 156-7, 176, 178
Germany, West 206, 213-7, 222-5
Gibraltar 281
GIUK gap (Greenland, Iceland, UK) 179-80, 206
Glasnost 265

Global positioning system (GPS) 269
Glyndŵr, Owain 4
Goering, Hermann, German politician and military leader 86
Goldrick, Rear Admiral James, RAN 231
Goldsmith, Captain M.E., RN 120-1, 123, 150, 176
Gordon, Andrew 116
Gordon, Cdr., RN 197
Governance of England, The 6
Government Interdepartmental Conference (1907) 60
Grainger, John 8
Grand Banks, Newfoundland 17, 25, 30
Grand Fleet 75, 78
'Grandmother telegrams' 177
Grant, Sir Richard 43
Great Britain 2, 36, 67
Great Depression 87, 165
Great Famine, USSR (1932-3) 173-4
'Great Fishery, The' 12
Great Yarmouth 1, 3, 4, 9, 10-11, 14, 16, 40, 41
Greaves, Samuel 114-5
Greenland 30, 46, 73, 145, 178
Greenwich xii, 174
Grimsby 35, 37, 41, 47, 48, 55, 59, 65, 76, 78, 79, 90, 91, 96, 97, 99, 107, 131, 136, 141, 162-4, 168, 177, 178, 182, 191, 193, 202, 204, 206, 216, 246, 292, 294
Grimsby Daily Mail 78
Grimsby Heritage Centre 141
Grimsby Oral History Project 162-4
Grimsby Trawler Officers' Guild 202
Grimsey Island, Iceland 190
Grotius, Hugo xvii, 13
Grove, Eric 250-1, 258
Guernsey 270
Gueterbock, Captain, RN 240, 245
Guinness, Walter, British Minister of Agriculture and Fisheries 117
Gulf of Bothnia 134
Gulf of Guinea 281
Gulf of St. Lawrence 19, 21, 22, 25
Gulf Stream 100
Gwynn, Julian 22

Hall, Admiral Reginald 'Blinker', RN 116
Hallgrimsson, Geir, Icelandic Prime Minister 243
Hall, Russell and Co. Ltd., Aberdeen 143-4, 253, 258, 260
Hall's Bay, Newfoundland 45
Hamburg, Germany 157

Hamilton, Admiral R. Vesey, RN 29, 32
Hammerfest, Norway 110, 118
Hammond, Philip, British Defence Secretary 279
Handley, Chris 235
Hankey, Robin, Head of the Northern Department, British Foreign Office 136, 167
Harr, Geirr 134
Hartlepool 55
Harwich 285
Hastings 17, 285
Hawke, Admiral Edward, RN 22
Hawker Siddeley 748 252
Hearn, Engineer Lieutenant 115
Heath, Edward, British Prime Minister xii, 223i
Hebrides 70
Helin, Robert 173
Hennessy, Peter 191
Hepworth, Captain, RN 232
Herring Fisheries Act of Scotland (1899) 146
'Herring Industry: post-war condition': memo 94
Hewett, Messrs 41
Hewson, Alf 163
Hezlet, Vice Admiral, RN 209-11
Hitler, Adolf, German Chancellor 156
H.M. Coastguard Vessels (by name): *Argon* 57, *Julia* 57, *Squirrel* 57, *Thrush* 57, *Watchful* 57
Hohler, Henry, British Foreign Office Northern Department 173
'Home Division' 158
Home Fleet 58, 193
Home Office 272
Honningsvaag, Norway 108, 111, 113
Hoole, Lt. Cdr. Rob, RN 158
Horn (North Cape), Iceland 190
House of Commons 4, 33, 34, 41, 48, 49, 106, 126, 137, 169, 172, 202, 212, 243, 244, 261
House of Lords 34
Howard, Commander, RN 228-9
Hull 35, 47, 48, 51, 55, 90, 91, 95, 96, 97, 106, 108, 120, 121, 131, 140, 149, 150, 169, 177, 182, 191, 215, 262
Hull Fishing Vessel Owners' Association 152
Hull Maritime Museum 245
Humber, River 30, 66, 205
Hundred Years' War 5
Hunt, Lt. Cdr. N., RN 207-11
Hvalfjörour, Iceland 95, 187

Iberian Peninsula 6
Iceland xv, 6, 7, 8, 10, 30, 36, 46, 47-51, 53, 65, 66, 69, 70, 72, 92, 95, 116, 117, 121, 125, 143, 144, 145, 165, 175-88, 189-212, 213-47, 249, 256
Icelandic Coastguard 175, 177, 185-7, 189-212, 213-47
Icelandic Coastguard Vessels (by name): *Ægir* 186, 194, 197, 200, 216, 218, 220, 223, 224-7, 228-9, 231-2, 243, 247, 290, *Albert* 186, 199, 202, 220, 227, 290, *Árvakur* 220, 223, 224, 290, *Baldur* 234-8, 240, 243, 290, *Hermodur* 290, *Maria Júlia* 192, 193-4, 290, *Odinn* 180, 186, 196, 197, 199, 202, 207-9, 211, 216, 218, 220, 224, 239-240, 245, 290, *Suborn* 290, *Thør* 175, 186, 192, 195-7, 199, 200, 202, 220, 223-5, 234, 290, *Týr* 220, 238-9, 240-2, 290, *Ver* 240, 243, 290
Icelandic Ministry for Foreign Affairs 230
Indian Ocean 8, 160
Ingøy, Norway 112
'Integrated Operating Concept' paper (2020) 281
International Court of Justice (ICJ) 69, 125, 134-8, 181, 203, 205, 214, 230
International Law of the Sea 226
International Mine Clearance Committee 84
Invergordon 150
Ireland 6, 11, 33, 78, 80, 276
Irish Channel 80
Irish Sea 65, 139, 276
Isle of Man 67, 159
Italy 98

Jane's Fighting Ships 105, 261
Jan Mayen island, Norway 167
Japan 97, 102, 104
Jellicoe, Admiral Sir John, RN 82
Jersey 274, 285, 287
Jinks, skipper Bert 65, 145-9, 157
Johannessón, Gudni, Icelandic President 123, 125, 203
Johnson, Boris, British Prime Minister xii, 285
Johnson, trawler skipper 48-9
Johnston, Paddy 204
Jones, Commander Mike, RN 234-5
Jonnsen, Commander, Norwegian Coastguard 200
Jónsson, Hannes 74, 224
Jopling, Michael, British Minister for Agriculture, Fisheries and Food 264

Josefsen, Alison 163
Jósepsson, Lúdvík, Icelandic Minister for Fisheries 186
Judd, Frank, British Under-Secretary of State for Defence (Navy) 258
Judiciary Appeal Court 149

Kalmar Union 7
Kara Sea, Russia
Karlsdóttir, Hrefna 184
Keflavík, Iceland 179-80, 184, 190, 202, 205, 215, 230, 246
Kennedy, Captain, RN 45
Kent 33
Kharlov Light, Russia 112
Khrushchev, Nikita, Soviet leader 174
King Charles I 13, 14
King Charles III xiv
King Edward III 1, 3
'King George's War' (1744-8) 19, 22
King Henry II 6
King Henry IV 4
King Henry V 4
King Henry VII 8
King Henry VIII 7-8
King James I 8-9, 14
King John 1
King Richard III 5, 6
'King's Chambers' 9
Kingston Steam Trawling Co. Ltd.150
Kingwell, Lt., later Rear Admiral, RN 270, 279
Kinneard Head 150, 151
Kinuna-Gällivare district, Sweden 134
Kirkenes, Norway 100, 102, 113, 118, 122, 128
Kirk, Simon 37
Kirkwall, Orkney 93
Kissinger, Henry, US historian, US Secretary of State and National Security Advisor 135
Kjærnested, Captain, Icelandic Coastguard 239, 242
Knipovich, N.M. 103
Knot End Buoy 148
Kola Bay, Russia 101
Kola Inlet, Russia 113, 171
Kola Peninsula, Russia 51, 100, 112, 125, 175
Kolbeinsey, Iceland 190
Kolguev Island, Russia 175
Korean War 158
Kristófferson, Captain Eiríkur, Icelandic Coastguard 192, 197, 199
Kuznetsov, Vasili, Soviet First Deputy 173-4

Labour Party 104, 105, 231, 250, 265
Labrador, Canada 17, 25, 45
Lake Onega, Russia 101
Lambert, Andrew 42
Landhelgisstríoin 165
Land's End 159
Lapland 134
Law of the Sea Conference 184, 200
League of Nations Codification Conference (1930) 74
Lee, Commander, RN 240
Leeward Islands 21
Leith 55, 151
Lenin, V.I., Soviet leader 103
Lerwick, Shetland 127, 131
Lewis, Hebrides 11
Liberal Party 104
Ligue Maritime 157
Lippiett, Rear Admiral John, RN 158, 159
Liverpool 280
Liverpool and Manchester Railway 35
Livesay, Captain M.H., RN 252-3
Lloyd George, David, British Prime Minister 104
Lloyd, Selwyn, British Foreign Secretary 200
Lloyd's List 47
Lødingen, Norway 149, 150
Lofoten Islands, Norway 30, 100, 149-150
London 3, 20, 47, 120, 128, 129, 136, 182, 207, 208, 214
Londonderry 161
London Gazette 40
Lorraine, France 134
Lough Swilly, Ireland 78
Louisbourg, Cape Breton Island 19, 20-21
Low Countries 6
Lowestoft 10, 37, 38, 41, 55, 59, 65, 66, 67, 153
Ludlam, Harry 91-2, 95, 98
Luleå, Sweden 134
Lund, Paul 91-2, 95, 98
Lundy Island 80
Lune Deep 147
Luns, Dr. Joseph, NATO General Secretary 223
Lynas Point 159
Lyness, Orkney 209

Mackay, Captain, RN 67
Mackenzie Committee 143, 145
Macmillan, Harold, British Prime Minister 188

Macpherson, Captain K. 59, 155-6
Malta 86
Manchester, Corporation of 156
Manchester, Sheffield and Lincolnshire Railway 35
MAN diesels 278
Manoeuvre Warfare 23
Mare Clausum 13, 16, 27, 53
Mare Clausum Seu Maris 14
Mare Liberum 13, 14, 27, 71, 213
Marine and Fisheries Agency (MFA) 273
Marine Management Organisation (MMO) xvi, 273-7, 282-4
Marine Scotland 139
Marr, J. and Son Ltd.262
Mason, Roy, British Defence Secretary 238
Masterman, Captain John, RN 45
Mayhew, Christopher, Under-Secretary of State, British Foreign Office 137
McMullen, Angela 163
McQueen, Captain, RN 236
Mediterranean Sea 8, 9, 26, 83, 281
Mercantilism 11, 18
Merchant vessel SS *Gitra* 79
Merlin helicopter 260
Metropolitan Police 64
Middlesbrough 150
Milford Haven 55, 59, 81, 96
Military Aid to the Civil Authorities (MACA) 276
Milwood Incident 190, 206-11
Minerva, US privateer 25
Mingan Islands, Canada 43
Ministry of Agriculture and Fisheries (MAF/MAFF) 85, 86, 87, 90, 96, 97, 106-9, 116, 123, 129, 132, 152, 153, 160, 165, 168, 170, 171, 180, 202, 212, 215, 217, 219, 232, 243-4, 252, 263-4, 266-9, 271, 272, 277
Ministry of Defence (MoD) 219, 225, 226-7, 230, 231-2, 234, 236-7, 245, 253-5, 258, 260, 261, 264, 265, 267, 268, 272, 276-9, 281
Ministry of Food 90, 95
Ministry of Labour 90
Miranda, Civilian Support Vessel 215
Molotov, Yvacheslav, Soviet Foreign Minister 173
Monroe Doctrine 42
Montagu, Vice Admiral, RN 25
Morecambe Bay 159
Moscow 104, 109, 173, 174
Mozambique 160
MSA (Auxiliary Minesweeper) 263
Mull of Galloway 147

Mull of Kintyre 147
Mun, Thomas 11, 12, 13
Murman Coast 65, 66, 99-124, 128, 149, 152
Murmansk, Russia 51, 99, 100, 101, 103, 104, 110, 113, 114, 115

Napoleon Bonaparte 29
Narvik, Norway 100, 134
Nasser, Gamal, Egyptian President 175
National Audit Office (NAO) 280
National Federation of Fish Fryers 244
National Joint Industrial Council 182
National Socialist Workers Party (Nazi) 85
Naval Air Arm 63
Naval Construction Programme, Soviet (1926-31) 117
Naval Defence Act (1889) 52
Naval Review, The 54, 55, 268, 283
Naval Staff History (1958) 193
Naval Staff Target (NST) 258
Naval Wasp helicopters 222, 235
Navigation Act (1651) 15
Navigation Acts 29
Navy Board 7
Navy Vote 60, 87, 109
Nelson, Captain Horatio, RN 25, 28, 182
Netherlands, The 7, 8, 9, 11, 15, 17, 34, 36, 37, 38, 40-1, 42, 78, 157, 181
Newcastle 280, 282
New Economic Policy, USSR (1923-8) 101
Newfoundland, Canada 8, 9, 16, 17, 18, 19, 20, 21, 22, 23, 25, 26, 30, 42-3, 45
Newhaven 89
Newlyn 55
Nordland, Norway 100, 130
North America 8, 9, 18-9, 21, 30, 42, 43, 44
North Atlantic xvii, 23, 31, 47, 93, 165, 179, 183, 205, 245, 251
North Atlantic Drift 100
North Atlantic Treaty Organisation (NATO) 69, 70, 134, 137, 138, 158, 166, 178, 180, 182, 183, 184, 187, 190, 200, 202, 203, 205, 213, 215, 223, 225, 230, 237, 243, 245, 251
North Cape, Norway 121
North East Atlantic Fishery Commission (NEAFC) 142, 159, 248
Northern Ireland xii, xiii, 67, 140, 147, 159, 160-2, 259, 274
Northern Patrol 92-3
North Pole 127

North Sea xvi, 2, 5, 6, 7, 9, 10, 12, 27, 30, 33, 36, 38, 39, 40, 41, 42, 46, 47, 52, 55, 56, 57, 60, 63, 65, 66, 67, 68, 69, 70, 76, 78, 80, 91, 92, 125, 126, 131, 139, 213, 214, 244, 248, 251, 254, 257, 258, 276
North Sea Fishery Protection Flotilla 55, 56, 57
North Sea Fisheries Act (1883) 33
North Sea Fisheries Convention (1882) xv, 30, 37-42, 46, 47, 52, 60, 63, 126, 131
North Shields 55
Norton, skipper 122
Norway xv, xvi, 7, 30, 39, 46, 51, 52, 69, 70, 79, 80, 92, 95, 99-105, 108, 110, 111, 118, 121, 122, 124, 125-138, 149, 167, 181, 182, 206, 233, 249, 250, 256
Norwegian Banks 129, 130, 131, 132
Norwegian Fishery Protection Service 129
Norwegian Naval Vessels (by name):
Heimdal 126, *Michael Sars* 131
Norwegian Royal Decree (1935) 130-1, 133, 165
Nott axe (1981) 261
Novaia Zemla, Russia 104
Nova Scotia, Canada 8, 9, 16, 17, 19, 20-21, 43

October Revolution, Russia (1917) 100, 101, 118
Offences Against the Person Act 148
Office for National Statistics 274
'Off-Shore Patrol Vessels' 248
Offshore Tapestry xvi, 248-72
Oliver, Chief of War Staff 81
Operation Bailiff 202
Operation Corporate 260-1
Operation Dewey 219, 225, 230, 236
Operation Granby 265
Operation Grenada 140-1, 160-2, 164
Operation Hornbeam 169
Operation Island Chief 281
Operation Mint 203
Operation Relentless 160
Operation Weserübung 134
Operation Whippet 184, 190, 192, 198, 199-200
'Option Charlie' 219
'Options for Change' study 162, 265-6
Orfordness, Suffolk 152
Organisation for European Economic Co-operation (OEEC) 183
Orkney 7, 93

Orr-Ewing, Ian, Civil Lord of the Admiralty 202
Oslo, Norway 128, 131, 134, 243
Ostend, Belgium 10, 38, 41, 62, 153, 155
Otranto, Straits of - Italy 83
Outer Hebrides 11, 146
Overfishery Convention (1954) 69
Overseas Patrol Squadron 273-4, 281

Pacific Ocean 8, 214, 281
Palestine Patrol 160
Parliament 1, 10, 11, 15, 141, 257-8
Parliamentary Select Committee Report (1883) 33-4
Parrott, Cecil, British *chargé d'affaires*, Moscow 174
Partridge fishing haven 202
Patreksfjord, Iceland 194
Patriot, Guernsey fishery protection launch
Patrol, Minesweeping and Fishery Protection Squadron 57
Pax Britannica 29
Peace Dividend 266, 272
Pechell, Captain, MP 34
Pembroke 80, 152, 154-5
Pennington, Vice Admiral, RN 14
Pentland Firth 72
People's Alliance, Iceland 183, 214
Pepys, Samuel 16
Permanent Court of International Arbitration, The Hague 132
Permanent Cruiser Service 57
Peterhead 82
Petrozavodsk, Russia 101
Pheasant fishing haven 202
Pipe, Commander J.H., RN 150
Pitreavie Castle 208, 259
Pizey, Captain Mark, RN 65
Plumer, Commander Gerald, RN 241-2
Plymouth 10
Point of Ayr 159
Poland 69, 235, 256
Port Edgar 72, 73, 143, 158, 206-8, 210
Portland, HM Naval Base 66, 76, 89, 151, 257
Port Said, Egypt 184
Portsmouth xiii, 142, 153, 280
Port Stanley, Falklands 261-3
Portugal 8, 13, 17, 179, 271
Poyntz, Captain 16
Prague Coup (1948)
Press Association 231
Preston, Captain L.G., RN 57-8
Prince Charles, Denmark 53
Progressive Party, Iceland 183

Quebec, Canada 25, 43
Queen Anne 17
Queen Elizabeth I 14, 18
Queen Elizabeth II xiv
Queenstown, Ireland 81
Queen Victoria 29

RAF Nimrod 221-2, 231, 233-5, 252, 263-5
Ramsey Bay 147
Rathlin Island 147
'Reception Trials parties' 166
Reciprocity Treaty 44
Red Crusader incident (1961)
Red Line (Norway) 125, 130, 131, 132, 133, 135, 136
Regulations for the Prevention of Collisions at Sea 146
Report of Proceedings (1872) 47
Report of Proceedings (1928) 119
Report of Proceedings (1959) 195
Report of Proceedings (1976) 159, 241
Reserve Forces Act 268
Reykjanes Peninsula, Iceland 179
Reykjavik, Iceland 48, 177, 184, 190, 193, 203, 207, 208, 256
Reykjavik Maritime Museum 245
Rhodesia, Southern 160
Ribachi Peninsula, Russia 122
Rimmer, David 163, 246
Roberts, John 203-4
Robinson, Robb 84
Rockall 142
Romania 257
Romanov-on-Murman, Russia 99
Rooke, Lt. Cdr., RN 55-6, 57
Room 40 80-1
Roskill, Stephen 85
Rosyth 107, 142, 151, 159, 198, 233, 236, 262, 263
Royal Air Force (RAF) 63, 85, 152-3, 154-5
Royal Corps of Naval Constructors (RCNC) xvii, 260
Royal Fleet Auxiliary (RFA) 185, 193, 196, 201, 209, 219, 230
Royal Fleet Auxiliary (RFA) Ships (by name):
    Black Ranger 186, Olwen 224, Tidepool 203, 233, Wave Chief 219, Wave Ruler 201
Royal Fleet Review xiii
Royalists 10
Royal Maritime Auxiliary Service (RMAS) 268

Royal Maritime Auxiliary Service (RMAS) Vessels (by name):
    Rolliker 217, 236, *Roysterer* 217
Royal Naval Air Service (RNAS) 152
Royal Naval Museum, Portsmouth 245
Royal Naval Reserve Patrol Service (RNPS) 85, 97, 268
Royal Naval Reserve (Trawler Section) (RNR(T)) 76, 77, 84
Royal Navy xii, xiv, xv, xvii, 1, 2, 4, 10, 16, 18, 19, 20, 21, 23, 24, 26, 28, 29, 30, 33, 37, 43, 47, 50, 51, 52, 54, 60, 71, 73, 74, 75, 76, 77, 78, 84, 85, 89, 92, 102, 104, 105, 116, 123, 135, 138, 141, 142, 144, 160, 169, 171, 182, 183, 184, 186, 188, 189, 190, 191, 192, 194, 195, 198, 200, 205, 207, 211, 212, 218, 219, 220, 221, 227, 233, 235, 246, 247, 248, 251, 260, 261, 264, 265, 266, 267, 268, 269, 271, 272, 273, 275, 276, 277, 278, 279, 281, 283, 285, 286, 287, 288,
Royal Navy Equipment Exhibition (1979) 260
Royal Navy Overseas Patrol Squadron xiv
Royal Navy Sea Devons 263
Royal Navy Ships (by class):
    Aberdare (minesweeper) 153
    Alarm (torpedo boat) 56
    Algerine (ocean minesweeper) 65, 66, 67, 144, 158, 171, 184, 186, 194, 258
    Anchusa (convoy sloop) 57, 105
    Arabis (fleet sweeping sloop) 57, 105, 119, 149
    Axe (trawler) 107, 110
    Battle (destroyer) 194, 195, 198
    Bird (patrol boat, large) 254, 259
    Blackwood (frigate) 72, 258
    Bridgewater (sloop) 85
    'C' (destroyer) 195
    'D' (destroyer) 204
    Caroline (cruiser) 118
    Castle (corvette) xvii, 65, 72, 258, 260, 266, 268, 271, 272, 280
    Daring (destroyer) 194
    Dryad (torpedo gunboat) 56
    Flower (convoy sloop) 61, 72, 107, 176
    Grimsby (sloop) 65
    Halcyon (torpedo gunboat) 85
    Hunt (mine countermeasures) 254, 262-3, 266-7, 269, 270, 286
    Improved Battle (destroyer) 195

INDEX

Island (offshore patrol vessel) 143, 252-4, 258, 259, 261, 263, 266, 269, 271, 272, 277, 278, 280
Kingfisher (patrol boat, large) 152, 254
King George V (battleship) 78
Leander (frigate) 236
Ley (inshore sweeper) 72
Mersey (trawler) 59, 77, 119, 146, 149
Modified Black Swan (frigate) 135
Queen Elizabeth (aircraft carrier) 279, 281
Redbreast (composite gunboat) 56
River (destroyer) 56
River (fleet minesweeper) 266, 268-9, 273, 277-81
Sandown (mine countermeasures) 286
Sandown (Single Role Minehunter) 266-8
Sharpshooter (torpedo gunboat) 56
Ton/Coniston (coastal minesweeper) 71, 72, 141, 158, 160, 212, 254, 258, 259, 261, 262, 266, 267, 272
Type 12 Whitby (frigate) 186, 198, 234
Type 14 (frigate) 72, 73, 186, 190, 193, 194, 195, 198, 212, 258
Type 21 (frigate) 159
Type 22 (frigate) 159, 254
Type 23 (frigate) 159
Type 26 (frigate) 281
Type 31 (frigate) 281
Type 61 Salisbury (frigate) 198
Type 81 Tribal (frigate) 239
'W' (destroyer) 147
Weapon (frigate) 194, 195
Royal Navy Ships (by name):
Aboukir 78, Adventure 10, Agincourt 195, 197, Albemarle 25-26, Alcide 167, Allington Castle 65, 180, 288, Andrew 167, Andromeda 226, 236, Anglesey 271, Apollo 198, 227, Armada 198, Audacious 78, Bamborough Castle 65, Battleaxe 201, Belton 72, 158-9, Blazer 270, Blonde 50-1, Boyne 122, 133, 149-151, 178, Bramble 184, Brighton 233, Brinton 256, Broadsword 195, 247, Bullfrog 45, Burley 72, Cachalot 162, Carysfort 195, Champion 42-3, Chaplet 195-7, Charybdis 225, Cherwell 133, 149-150, 157, Cleopatra 219, Colne 119-120, 131, Comus 118-9, 123, 187, Cordella 262-3, Corunna 197, Coyne 133, Cressy 78, Crossbow 202, Cygnet 135, Dart 133, Delight 201, Diana 194, Diomede 236-7, Doon 119, 120, 133, 146-8, 154-5, Druid 45, Dumbarton Castle 260, 280, Duncan 72, 198, 202, Dundas 198, Eastbourne 186, 192, 243, Falmouth 233, 240-2, Fantome 45, Farnella 262, Fleetwood 65, Forth 280-1, Foyle 133, Galatea 49-50, 237, 240, 242, 288, Godetia 99, 105, 107-111, 113, 118, 119, 120, 123, 176, 288, Gossamer 133, Gurkha 239-240, Halcyon 56, 60, Harebell 105-6, 107, 109-113, 114, 115, 118, 119, 120, 122, 123, 128, 133, 150, 151, 155-6, Hastings 133, 157-8, 288, Hawke 78, Hearty 42, Hermes 79, Hogue 78, Hound 186-7, 194, 288, Jaguar 227-8, Jersey 252, Junella 262-3, Jupiter 219, 223, Kingfisher 133, 150-2, Launceston 20, Leander 243, Leda 56, 60, Leeds Castle 260, 280, 289, Leopard 224-6, 233, Lincoln 219, 228-9, 231-2, Llandaff 198, Loch Fyne 198, Lochinvar 212, Lupin 58, 107, 131, 133, 177-8, Malcolm 72, 195, 198, 203, Mariner 171, Medway 281, Mermaid 240, Mersey 277, 279, 281, 282, 284, Newark 105, Northella 262, Osprey 89, Paladin 198, Palliser 72, 186, 198, 201, 207-11, 289, Phoebe 230, Pict 262-3, Plymouth 219, 226, Pursuer 270, Rhyl 203, Ringdove 56, Romney 24, Rosemary 119, 149, Russell 72, 186, 194, 195, 198, 204, Salisbury 238-9, 240, Selkirk 153-4, Severn 277, 279, 281, 285, Shavington 158-9, Sheldrake 133, 152, Sherborne 105, Sirius 226-7, Skipjack 56, 60, 288, Soberton 72, 158, Spanker 56, 60, 62-4, Spartan 261, Spey 144, 149, 281, Squirrel 20, 72, Stork 65-9, Surprize 24, Tamar 281, 285, 289, Tartar 243, Tenacity 254, Tenby 197, Torquay 198, Trent 281, Truelove 171, Tyne 277, 279, 280, 289, Undine 198, Valorous 47, Viceroy 147, Victory 254, Wasperton 72, 158, Watchful 72, Wave 67, 187, Wear 56, Welcome 144-5, Whitby 229, Windflower 57, Wotton 72, 158, 289, Yarmouth 234-6
Royal Navy radar system: Type 271 (surface search) 93

Royal Navy Shore Establishments
(by name):
Lochinvar (Port Edgar) 212, *Osprey*
(Portland) 89
Royal Ulster Constabulary (RUC) 161
Rüger, Jan xiii
Rules on Prize Law, Russian (1869) 51
Russell, Commander, RN 42
Russia 30, 46, 51-2, 53, 56, 80, 84, 95, 99-124, 125, 166-75, 249, 253, 257
Russian *Atlantic Class* trawlers 253
Russian Maritime Province 102
Russian (Soviet) Navy Ships (by name):
Setteles 115, *T-23* 110, *Yaroslavna* 109, 113, 115
Russo-Japanese War (1904-5) 76
Ruston diesels 278

St. Ann's Head 80
St. George's Banks 26
St. Helier xii, 274, 285
St. John's, Newfoundland 23- 24, 25
St. Nazaire, France 92
St. Peter Port, Guernsey 270
St. Petersburg, Russia 99, 101
Sámi, Scandinavia 51
Sanders, Sir Robert, British Minister for Agriculture and Fisheries 108-9
Sandys, Duncan, British Minister of Defence 191
Scallop Wars 274, 283-6
Scandinavia 6, 39, 125, 126, 134
Scarborough 1, 55, 78
Scheldt, River 157
Scientific Preservation of the Continental Shelf law (1948) 181
Scilly Isles 81
Scotia, DAFS research vessel 215
Scotland xv, xvi, 7, 9, 11, 12, 15, 27, 33, 58, 66, 68, 80, 84, 86, 96, 139, 140, 141-9, 150, 160, 209, 210, 254, 275, 284
Scottish Executive Environment and Rural Affairs Department 142
Scottish Fishery Protection Agency (SFPA) 63, 142, 275
Scottish Fishery Protection Ships
(by name):
Brenda 142-3, *Fidra* 143, *Freya* 143, *Freya (2)* 145, *Garland* 142, *Hirta* 144, *Jura* 143-4, 253, 258, *Norna (2)* 143, *Spey*, *Sulisker* 144, *Switha* 143, *Vigilant* 63, 142, *Vigilant (2)* 142, 144, *Vigilant (3)* 143, *Violet* 142, *Westra* 258
Scottish Home Department 90, 143, 145

Scottish Office 63, 145
Sea Fisheries Act (1868) 34-5
Sea Fisheries Act (1964) 212
Sea Fisheries Manual 39, 64, 139
Sea Fisheries Protection Agency 49, 57
Sea Fisheries Statistical Tables 165
Sea Fishery Act (1883) 148, 212
Seath, Lt. Cdr. Ted, RN 158-9
Second Cod War (1972-3) 215-232, 245
'Second Leftist Government' (Iceland) 214
Selden, John 14
Sem Island, Barents Sea 99, 109, 112, 113, 169
Serbia 83
Seven Years' War (1756-63) 20, 22, 24, 28
Seydisfjord, Iceland 190, 197
Shakespeare, Geoffrey, British Parliamentary and Financial Secretary to the Admiralty 90
Sheerness 89, 107, 153
Shetland 61, 70, 127, 149, 151, 152, 158
Shetland Patrol 152
Ship Money 14, 27
Shirley, William, Governor of Massachusetts 21
Short Blue Fleet 41
Signal derived intelligence (SIGINT) 80, 169
Sigtryggsson, Captain, Icelandic Coastguard 226, 228-9
Sigurdsson, Pétur, Head of the Icelandic Coastguard 186
Silver Pits 40, 42
Sinclair, Captain E., RN 195-6
Singapore 86
Sizewell Bank 153
Skarphéöinsson, Captain Höskulder, Icelandic Coastguard 235
Smith Dock, Middlesbrough 150
Smith, skipper 207-9, 211
Smith, Tom 168
Soames, Christopher, British Minister for Agriculture, Fisheries and Food 212
Social Democrats, Iceland 180, 183
Socialist Unity Party, Iceland 180, 183
Solent xiii, 277
Solway Firth 141
South Atlantic 260-2
Southern Patrol Force Operation Orders 81, 82
South Georgia 263
Southwold, Suffolk 62
Spain xvi, 8, 17, 24, 271
Spearmint trawler haven 185-6, 189, 192

INDEX 347

Speiden, William 43
Spitzbergen Archipelago 30, 127
Spitzbergen, Norway 100, 101
Spooner, Joseph, smack skipper 37
Stalin, Joseph, Soviet leader 134
Statutes on Maritime Prizes, Russian (1898, 1914) 51-2
Stephens, Philip 285
Stephenson, George 35
Stone, Andrew, Under Secretary of State for the Southern Department of the Admiralty 17
Stornaway 146, 148, 149
Storting, Norwegian Parliament 118, 128, 135, 137
Storton, Lt. Cdr. George, RN 282
Strategic Defence and Security Review (2010) 273
Supreme Court of Norway 126, 130
Suez, Egypt 175, 184, 191, 250
Sunday Telegraph Magazine 257
Sussex 33
Suvla Bay, Turkey 83
Svalbard, Norway 101
Sweden 39, 52, 100, 126, 134, 229

Taylor, Vice Admiral Ernest, MP 137
Tenth Party Congress, USSR (1921) 114
Ternay, chevalier de, French naval commander 23
Thacker, Gorad 37
Thames, River xiv, 77
The Hague Judgement (1951) 69, 137-8
The Hague, Netherlands 74, 134
The Whaleback, Iceland 190
Third Cod War (1975-6) 216, 220, 233-47
Thomas, Edward 198
Thór, Jón 243
Thornborough, Admiral, RN 26
Thornhill, Sir James xii
Thors, Ólafur, Icelandic Prime Minister 183
Thorsteinssen, Captain, Norwegian Coastguard 199-200
Thrupp, Captain, RN 47
Toffeeapple trawler haven 185-6, 189
Tor Point 147
Tórshavn, Faroe Islands 48-9, 210
Tower Bridge xiv
Traener, Nordland, Norway 130
Trafalgar, Battle of 26
Transport and General Workers Union (TGWU) 89, 90
Trawlers (by name):
  Belgium: *O.100* 62, *Delta B* 80

  Britain: *Afghan* 41, *Aldershot* 216, *Algoma* 76, *Amethyst* 140, 150-1, *Andes* 76, *Arctic Galliard* 169, *Brilliant* 40, *Burfell* 194, *Cambri* 121, *Cape Palliser* 136, *Cape Spartel* 120, *Carella* 197, *Caspian* 48-9, 50, *Cevic* 180, *Corvos* 48, *Crestfallen*, *Crestflower* 129, *Etruria* 169-170, *Etrurl* 136, *Everton* 223, *Fulmar* 50, *Girard* 119, *Girl Macey* 285, *Golden Promise* 284-5, *Grampian* 131, *Grimsby Town* 202, *Guy Thorne* 110, 115, *Gwenlillian* 146, *Hackness* 195, *Henry and Lydia* 37, *Hirose* 80, *Honeybourne III* 284, *Invincible* 169, *Iolanthe* 48, *James Johnson* 104, *Jeria* 99, *Jessamine* 37, *Joanna C* 284, *Juniper* 208-9, 211, *Kingston Emerald* 226, *Lady Godiva* 41, *Lancer* 167, *Lifeguard* 194, *Loch Eribol* 234, *Loch Torridon* 129, *Lord Astor* 110, 114, 115, *Lord Ernle* 112, *Lord Halifax* 111-13, *Lord Montgomery* 197, *Lord Nelson* 169, *Lord Nuffield* 137, *Lord Reading* 106, *Lord Roberts* 126, *Lord St. Vincent* 226-7, *Lucida* 65, 140, 144, 146-9, *Macbeth* 224,, *Magneta* 104, 108, 112, *Marconi* 106, *Mary Gowland* 41, *Milwood* 206-11, *Monravia* 131, *Nab Wyke* 180, *Nellis* 136, *Northern Foam* 192, *Northern Queen* 202, *Onward Ho* 52, 102-3, *Paynter* 194, *Portia* 223, *Preston North End* 131, *Primella* 243, *Red Crusader* 210, *Ross Ramilles* 230, *Rudyard Kipling* 110,115, *St. Alcuin* 227, *St. Hubert* 104, 108, *St. Just* 130, *St. Leger* 223-4, *St. Loman* 93, *St. Louis* 140, 149 150, *SSAFA* 223, *Surfflower* 122, *Swanella* 197, *Teutonia* 225, *Thuringia* 202, *Tranquil* 146, *Valafell* 196-7, *Vambrey* 178, *Victoria* 80, 81-2, *Vivaria* 247, *Welbeck* 136, *Wellard* 168-9
France: *Alsace Lorraine* 37, *Daniel Roger* 256, *DG.901* 153, *DG.916* 153, *Impatiens* 270, *La Calypso* 270
Netherlands: *Anna Mararetha* 37
US fishing schooner: *Harmony* 25-26
Trawler Owners' Federation 120, 156-7
Treasury, H.M. 60, 62, 63, 108, 142, 244, 263, 272
Treaty of Alliance (1778) 25
Treaty of Kiel (1814) 46

Treaty of Paris (1783) 19
Treaty of Rapallo (1922) 117
Treaty of Spitzbergen (1920) 127
Treaty of Utrecht (1713) 19
Treaty of Versailles (1919) 108, 127
Treaty of Westminster (1654) 16
Trevose Head 159
Trincomalee, Ceylon (Sri Lanka) 86
Triple Alliance 127
Tromp, Admiral Maarten 15-16
Tromsø, Norway 100, 114
Troup, Vice Admiral, RN 241, 245
Trowbridge, Captain R.J., RN 207-10
Truman Declarations (1945) 74, 181
Turkey 101
Turner, Robert, trawler skipper 226-7
Twiss, Captain F.R., RN 144-5
'Two power standard' 52
Tynes, Oli 242
Type 271 (surface search radar) 93
Type 123 (asdic sets) 88

U-boats 79-82
Ullapool 55
United Kingdom xii, xv, xvi, 30, 54, 95, 125, 135, 139, 141, 149, 158, 179, 183, 201, 205, 212, 213, 231, 234, 256, 263-5, 267, 271-6, 279, 281-5
United Nations Conference on the Law of the Sea (UNCLOS), (1958) 184, 187, 200-1, 202, 206, 214, 230
United Towing Company of Hull 217
Upper Canada 44
Uruguay 74
USA 16, 19, 32, 42, 43, 44, 172, 174, 178-9, 181, 184, 187, 193, 201, 205, 246, 249, 268
'Use of Force by Fishery Protection Vessels' paper (1925) 64
US navy vessel: USS *Mississippi* 43
USSR (Soviet Union) xv, 69, 70, 99-124, 127, 129, 134, 135, 159, 165-75, 183, 184, 187, 205, 206, 225, 250, 256, 265
US Strategic Air Command 189

Vadsø, Norway 100, 166
van Dorp, Admiral Philips 15
Varanger Fjord, Norway 126, 128, 129, 166
Vardø, Norway 111-12, 135, 137
Vosper Thornycroft (VP) 277, 279

Wainwright, Lt. Cdr. B.G., RN 268-9
Wales 10, 34, 57, 84, 96, 165, 273, 275
Walker, Captain F.J., RN 65
War of the Austrian Succession (1740-48) 19

War of the Spanish Succession (1701-15) 19
Warren, Captain, later Admiral Peter, RN xvii, 20-22
Warsaw Pact (1955) 137, 178, 265
Warwick, Lieutenant Colin, RN 93
Washington D.C., USA 193
Waterloo, Battle of 29
Waters, Conrad 278
Weatherall, Commander James, RN 245
Weir, Captain, RN 226
Welch, Captain Andrew, RN 197, 215, 227, 245
Welsh Department (WOAD) 263
Wessex 3 helicopters 222
Western Approaches 25, 80, 81, 276
Western Charter (1634) 18
Western Waters Regime 283
West Indies 27
Westmann Islands, Iceland 180, 190, 206
Whitby 55
White, Commander, later Rear Admiral Hugo, RN 238-9, 266-8
Whitehaven 55
White Russians 101
White Sea 30, 84, 100, 102, 103, 166, 169, 175
Williamson, Gavin, British Defence Secretary 280
Willox, Mr., trawler company manager 207
Wilson, Admiral, RN 81
Wilson, Charles 15
Wilson, Harold, British Labour Party leader, later Prime Minister 231
'Winter of Discontent' (1978-9) 250
Winterton, Lincolnshire 153
Wood, Mr., trawler owner 207-9
Woodcock fishing haven 202
Woodward, Admiral Sir John 'Sandy', RN 261-3
World War One xiii, 30, 33, 56, 57, 58, 59, 62, 65, 75, 76-84, 85, 87, 89, 92, 94, 97, 98, 101, 116, 118, 119, 126, 132, 216, 274
World War Two xvi, 65, 66, 72, 74, 75, 86, 89-98, 143, 152, 162, 165, 168, 178, 180, 183, 212, 222, 250, 262
Wright, Richard 246
Wylie, Commander Charles, RN 72, 204, 245, 292-3

Yellow Line (Norway) 136-7

Zimbabwe 160